VISIONS FROM PIERS PLOWMAN

NEVILL COGHILL

Langland, William

VISIONS FROM PIERS PLOWMAN

TAKEN FROM THE POEM OF

William Langland

AND TRANSLATED INTO MODERN ENGLISH BY

Nevill Coghill

NEW YORK
OXFORD UNIVERSITY PRESS

FOR

Claude Chavasse

Hallam Fordham

Michael Tippett

First published in Great Britain in 1949
First published in U.S.A. 1970

RULE OF CONDUCT   First point: Necessity for a rule.

2nd. Morals consist in establishing a hierarchy among things and in using the lesser to obtain the greater. This is an ideal strategy.

3rd. Never lose sight of the end. Never prefer the means.

4th. Regard oneself as a means; thus never prefer oneself to the chosen end, to the work . . .

CONTENTS

ILLUSTRATIONS

TRANSLATOR'S PREFACE

Piers Plowman, like *Pilgrim's Progress*, is an imagination which, save for the immediate difficulties of language, is open to everyone. Few explanations are necessary. I have tried, in this version, to remove the difficulties of language, and for those who wish to know more about the circumstances in which the poem came originally to be written and what sort of a poem, technically speaking, it is, I have added an Appendix. As will be seen from this, almost everything we know, or think we know, about *Piers Plowman* and its author is a guess or an inference. Here, very briefly, are stated the main conclusions reached about it, but not the arguments by which they were reached.

The poem was being written and re-written almost continuously between about 1360 and 1400. The author, William Langland, was a Malvern peasant, born, probably out of wedlock, towards 1332. He was educated, chiefly at his father's expense, at Malvern Priory (?), took (minor?) Holy Orders, and went later to London. There he lived in Cornhill in a cottage, with a wife and daughter, in great poverty, and earned a meagre living by saying prayers for people richer than himself. Where or when he died is not known. There are no contemporary records of him whatever, and but for his poem we should not have known he existed.

The manuscripts show it to have been cast by him in three main forms, known as the A, B, and C Texts. The B Text is a revision and expansion of the A, and the C of the B. Their respective dates seem to be approximately A—1362 and onwards, B—1376 and onwards, C—1392-98 (?). In short, the author was writing it nearly all his life. In this version I have mainly followed the B Text, which seems to me the most poetical.

The form of the poem is a series of allegorical visions of the Kingdom of England and the Kingdom of Heaven, and how to reach the one from the other. This includes a splendid vision of the Incarnation, Passion, Descent into Hell, the Founding of the Church, and the Attack on It by Anti-Christ. The hero, Piers Plowman, is a symbol of the good life as it should be lived, first by the laity, then by the priesthood, and lastly by the episcopate. Although a symbol, he appears in the poem first as a solid, lovable, common-sensical, humorous and irascible farmer. Later, as a priest, he is identified with Christ, type of perfect priesthood. Lastly, as a bishop, with Saint Peter and his successors.

The poem is written in alliterative verse, imitated in this rendering, which will be found easy to read aloud if the natural emphasis dictated by the sense and reinforced by alliteration is conversationally followed. A kind of recurrent rhythm will then spring into being of itself. Attempts at exact scansion, however, will be defeated.

The original poem is exceedingly long, and what is here presented is heavily cut. I hope, however, it will be found to contain what is most important and beautiful in it, the true substance of the original. As cuts are very frequent and vary in length from a line to long passages I have not always marked where they occur, for fear of disfiguring the text with notes. The longer cuts, however, are indicated by a two-line break. What I have omitted is for the most part theological disquisition, as, for instance, whether the soul of the Emperor Trajan was saved by his good works or by the prayers of Gregory the Great, and other topics no longer of burning interest.

Having allowed myself some freedom in the matters of metre and of cutting, I have attempted a greater strictness in conveying the meaning; but this version is not minutely literal, nor is it meant to be. It is meant to convey feeling and quality as well as meaning, and to do this I have taken liberties with a phrase here and there. I hope it will be found faithful in substance, gist for gist, if not always phrase for phrase.

The poem is peppered with Latin tags and quotations, mostly from the Bible, some of which I have included. The less familiar of these will be found in translation at the bottom of the page on which it occurs.

If William Blake had known the poem I cannot but think he would have been moved to illustrate it as magnificently as he did the Book of Job or the Divine Comedy. Since, unfortunately, he did not (for the poem seems to have been completely unknown from the late sixteenth to the early nineteenth century), I have chosen some drawings by Blake, and his pupil and disciple Samuel Palmer, both of whom seem to me to share the kind of vision that Langland had, and to be of a like quality, whether or not they represent the actual episodes and persons mentioned where they occur in the poem. They are therefore to be considered not so much as illustrations of *Piers Plowman* itself as of the similarity in vision of three men of very strange genius, separated by four centuries and more.

PART I

PROLOGUE

THE VISION OF THE FIELD OF FOLK

Langland In a summer season, when soft was the sunlight,
I shook on some shreds of shepherd clothing,
And habited like a hermit, but not a holy one,
Went wide in this world, watching for wonders.
But on a May morning, on a Malvern hill-top,
A marvel befell me, as might a fairy-tale.
I was weary and far-wandered and went to rest myself
On a broadish bank, by a running brook,
And as I lay leaning and looking in the water,
I slipped into a slumber, it slid away so merrily.

   Then I began to move into a marvellous dream
That I wandered in a wilderness, would I could say where;
As I beheld into the East, high in the sunlight,
I saw a tower on a hill-top, of true workmanship,
A deepening dale beneath, and a dungeon within it,
With deep ditches and dark, and dreadful to see.

   A fair field full of folk. found I there between them,
Of all manner of men, the meaner and the richer,
Working and wandering, as the world asks of them.
Some were putting out to plough, had little play-time,
In setting seed and sowing, sweated at their labour,
Winning wealth that the worthless wasted in gluttony.
Some pranked themselves in pride, preciously apparelled,
Coming under colour of costly clothing.
To prayer and to penance many put themselves,
All for the love of our Lord living austerely,
In hope they might have their happiness in heaven,
Such as anchorites and hermits who hold to their cells,
And do not covet to go off gadding round the country
For bodily liking of a lecherous livelihood.

   And some chose business, with better achievement,
For it seems to our sight that such are successful.
Beggars and blackguards went busily about
With their bellies and their bags all brimming with bread,
Feigning sick for food, and fighting in the ale-house;
In gluttony, God knows, they go off bedwards,

And rise up with ribaldry, the knavish robbers,
Sleep and sorry sloth in hot pursuit of them.
 Pilgrims and palmers plighted themselves together
To seek shrines in Spain and sanctities in Rome.
They went on their way with many wise stories
And had leave to lie about it all their lives after.
I saw some that said they had been seeking saints;
In every tale they told their tongue was tempered to lie
Rather than to tell truth, it seemed from their talk.
 Hermits in a heap with hook-headed sticks
Went off to Walsingham, and their wenches with them,
Long lousy lubbers that were loth to labour.
I found the friars there, all the Four Orders,
Preaching the people for their private profit,
Gabbling about the gospel as seemed good to them,
Their money and their merchandize on the march together;
For since charity has been a cheap-jack in charge of confession,
Many a fine thing has befallen in a few short years.
 There preached a pardoner, as if he were a priest,
Dragging out documents with bishops' affidavits
And saying he himself could absolve them all
For having failed to fast, or being false to their vows.
Illiterates believed him and liked what he said,
Came up and crossed themselves, kissing his charters;
He bounced them with his brevets and bleared their eyesight
And they gave up their gold to gorge the glutton
For they trust these tricksters that trot after lechery.
Were the bishop awake, or worth his two ears,
His seal would never sanction this deceit of the people.
But it's not by the bishop that the bold boy preaches,
For the parish priest and the pardoner pocket the silver
Which the poor of the parish should have but for them.
 Parsons and parish priests complain to the bishop
That their parishes are poor since the pestilence time
Asking leave and license to live in London
And sing there for simony, for silver is sweet.
Bishops and bachelors and doctors of divinity,
Curates under Christ with the tonsure for token,
(Showing that they should be shriving their parishioners,
Preaching and praying for them and feeding the poor),

Lodge lazily in London all the long year.
Some serve the king, counting his silver,
In exchequer and chancery, challenging his debtors,
And some are in service to lords and ladies,
In the status of steward to step up their stipends;
Their masses and matins and many other services
Are undevoutly done, and I dread that at last
Christ at His coming may curse the whole lot of them.
I was conscious of the power in Saint Peter's keeping
To bind and to unbind, as the Bible tells us,
How he left it with love, as our Lord commanded,
Among the four virtues, best of all virtues,
That are called cardinal, closing the gateways
Where Christ is in kingdom, closing and shutting,
And opening to offer the happiness of heaven.
But of the cardinals at court, that catch at the name,
(Presumed to have power in appointing popes),
That they have Peter's power I do not impugn,
But in love and learning the election should lie.
So I can, yet I cannot, criticize that court.
　　Then there came a king, accompanied by knighthood;
The might of the community made him their ruler.
Then came Common-sense, making men of learning,
To counsel the king and to save the community.
And common men managed, by manual craft,
And for the profit of all people, to ordain plowmen
To till and to toil, as a true life asks.
　　Then there looked up a lunatic, a lean sort of fellow,
And kneeling to the king, he knowingly cried,

Lunatic 'Christ keep you, Sir King, and all your kingdom,
And let you lead your land so that loyalty loves you,
And for your righteous rule be rewarded in heaven!'

Langland　And then in air on high an angel of heaven
Launched into Latin—lest the illiterate
Should jabber and judge and justify themselves,
When they should suffer and serve—he therefore said,

Angel　　'*Sum Rex, sum Princeps, neutrum fortasse deinceps;*
O qui iura regis Christi specialia regis,
Hoc quod agas melius, iustus es, esto pius!
Nudum ius a te vestiri vult pietate;

Qualia vis metere, talia grana sere.
Si ius nudatur, nudo de iure metatur.
Si seritur pietas, de pietate metas!'[1]

Langland   Then there glowered a grumbler, a glutton for phrases,
         And to the angel on high instantly answered,

The Glutton   '*Dum rex a regere dicatur nomen habere,*
for phrases   *Nomen habet sine re, nisi studet iura tenere.'*[2]

Langland   And the common people caught it, countering in Latin,
The Common   '*Precepta regis sunt nobis vincula legis.*[3]
People

Langland   With that there ran a rout of ragged rats together
         And little mice among them, more than a thousand,
         And came to hold council for their common profit;
         For a cat of the court, who killed for pleasure,
         Leapt lightly over them and laid them low
         Playing with them perilously and pushing them about.

Rats and 'In doubt of his divers doings we dare but look at him;
Mice   And if we grumble at his games, he will grieve us all,
         Catching us and clawing us, holding us in his clutches,
         And life is loathsome till he lets us go.
         If we did not want wit to withstand his will
         We'd be the lords of life, and live at our pleasure.'

Langland   A rat of some renown, very ready with his tongue,
         Said in suggestion of a sovereign remedy,

Rat 'I have seen several,' said he, 'in the City of London,
         Who bear bright bangles round about their necks;
         Were there a bell on the bangle, by Jesu, it strikes me,
         One would know when they were near, and nip away out of it!
         So I reckon,' said this rat, 'that reason would lead one

---

[1] (Thou mayest say) 'I'm a King, I'm a Prince!'
But thou mayest perhaps be neither hereafter;
O thou that dost administer the special laws of king Christ,
That thou mayest do this the better, be merciful as thou art just.
Naked justice needs to be clothed by thee in mercy.
Such harvest as thou wouldest reap, such the seeds thou shouldest sow.
If thou strip justice naked, mayest thou meet with naked justice;
If thou hast sown mercy, mayest thou reap mercy!

[2] Since a king may be said to take his name from the act of ruling,
He has the name without the reality, unless he studies to keep the laws.

[3] The king's commandments are the chains of law to us.

[18]

To buy a bell of brass, or of brightest silver,
And clamp it on his collar for our common profit,
Noose it on the cat's neck, that we might hear and know
If he was roaming round or resting, or running out to play.'

Langland And all this rout of ratlings ratified his reasons,
And then the bell was bought, and buckled on a collar;
But there was no ratling in all the rout ready to risk it
Or dared to bind the bell about the cat's bosom,
Or thread it round his throat, for the throne of England!
　A mouse of some moment, as it seemed to me,
Struck out sternly and stood before them all,
And to the rout of ratlings rolled out his reasons:

The Mouse 'Were we to kill the cat, yet there would come another,
To claw us and all our clan, though we crept under benches;
Therefore I counsel the community to let the cat be;
Better not be so bold as to show him the bell;
For I heard my sire say, seven years ago,
That where the cat is a kitten, the court is in trouble.
Holy Writ reckons (for those who can read it),
　　Vae terrae ubi puer rex est, &c.
Better a little loss than a long sorrow,
And the murder of a mouse than a general massacre.
Many a man has malt that we mice destroy,
And you, you rabble of rats, would rend a man's clothing,
Were there no cat at the court to catch and control you;
For if you rats had your way you could not rule yourselves.
And I say for myself,' said the mouse, 'seeing so far ahead,
Vex neither cat nor kitten, I can advise you.
No more babble about bells that are not worth buying;
Though it had cost me cash, I shouldn't care to touch it,
But would suffer the decisions of the cat in silence;
Collared or uncollared, let him catch what he can,
So I warn every wise one "Look well to his own".'

Langland There may be a moral to this, my merry men;
Guess it if you can, for by God I give it up!
　A hundred men were hovering like hawks, in silken hoods,
Serjeants-at-law, they seemed, in service at the bar,
And pleading at law for pounds and for pennies;
Never once for the love of our Lord did they loosen their lips.
You might better measure the mist on Malvern hill-tops

[19]

Than get a mumble from their mouths, unless money were
shown them.
Barons and burgesses and bondsmen too
I saw in this assembly, as you shall see later,
Bakers and brewers and butchers galore,
Weavers of wool and weavers of linen,
Tailors and tinkers and tax-collectors,
Masons and miners and many other craftsmen,
All kinds of labourers alive, leaping out together,
Such as diggers and ditchers, doing an ill day's work,
Dallying through the long day with a 'Darling, how goes it?'
Cooks and their kitchen-boys calling 'Hot pies!
Good geese and gammon! Get a good dinner!'
Advertizing taverners told the same tale
With a 'White Alsatian wine! Red wine of Gascony!
Rhenish and claret give relish to a roast!'
All this I saw sleeping, and seven times more.

THE VISION OF THE HOLY CHURCH

Langland The meaning of this mountain, and of the murky dale,
And the field full of folk I shall fairly show you.
A lady of great loveliness, in a linen garment,
Came down from the castle and called me by name,
Saying,

Holy Church 'Son, are you asleep, and do you see this people
And how busily they are bustling about these mazes?
The greater part of this people that pass their way on earth
Have their honour in this world and wish for nothing better,
Of other heaven than here holding no opinion.'

Langland I was afraid of her face, though fair it was,
And said, 'Madam, I thank you; but what is the meaning?'

Holy Church 'The tower at the top,' said she, 'is where Truth is living,
Who wishes you to work, as his Word teaches.
For He is Father of Faith; formed every one of you,
Both in face and feature, and gave you five senses
To worship him with for the while you are here.
He built the world and bade it to offer you its bounty,
Woollens and linens and livelihood at need,
In measure and moderation to make you at ease,
And commanded, of his courtesy, three things commonly;
None but they are necessary, so I think to name them.
One of them is clothing, to cover you from cold,
Then, meat at meal-time, to amend hunger,
And drink when you are dry, but draw it in reason,
Lest you wake the worse for it when you should be working.
So dread the delight of drinking, and you will do better;
Moderation is your medicine, much as you may hanker.
Not all things are good for your soul that your guts clamour for,
Nor is that bound to please your body that benefits your soul.
Never trust your body; it's taught by a liar,
I mean this wretched world, that works to wreck you;
For the fiend and the flesh will fall on you together,
And each is seeking your soul, if you see into your heart.
And so I bid you beware, and warn you for the best.'

Langland 'Madam,' said I, 'I thank you; I think your words are wise;
But the money that is made, that men are so mad after,

Tell me, Madam, truly, whose is that treasure?'

Holy Church 'Go to the gospel,' said she, 'and see what God answered
When the people posed him with a penny in the temple,
Whether they were right in rendering it to Caesar,
God said in answer, "Whose is the superscription?
Whose image stands there, stamped upon it?"
"Caesar's," they said, "we can see it for ourselves."
"*Reddite Caesari*," said God, "what belongs to Caesar,
Et que sunt dei, deo, or else you do ill."
For right and reason should rule every one of you,
With Common-sense controller and keeper of your wealth,
Tutor to your treasure, to take it when you need it,
For thrift and Common-sense thrive on each other.'

Langland 'That dungeon in the dale, so dreadful to look at,
What may be its meaning, Madam, I beseech you?'

Holy Church 'That is the Castle of Care, and he who comes within it
May bewail that he was born to body or to soul.
There is a wretch that rules it; Wrong is his name,
The father of Falsehood; he founded it himself.
Adam and Eve he egged on to evil
And he counselled Cain that he should kill his brother,
He jockeyed Judas, by Jewish silver,
And hanged him later aloft on an alder.
He lies in wait for love, a liar to all,
And those who trust his treasure are soonest betrayed.'

Langland I fell into a wonder who this woman was
And hailed her by the High Name, ere she went hence,
To tell me her title, having so fairly taught me.

Holy Church 'I am Holy Church,' said she, 'You may chance to know me,
I was the first to feed you, and taught you the Faith;
You brought me surety to obey my bidding
And to love me loyally while your life lasted.'

Langland Then on my naked knees I knelt for her grace
Praying her pitifully to pray for me, a sinner,
And also teach me tenderly to trust in Christ,
And do what He meant me to, in making me a man.
'Teach me no treasure,' I said, 'but tell me truly
How I may save my soul, O you, that are held sacred!'

Holy Church 'When all treasures are tried,' said she, 'Truth is the best;
I base it on *Deus Caritas*, to tell the truth.

[22]

It is as great a jewel as Jesus Himself.
He who is true of his tongue, telling no other,
In word and in work willing no man evil,
Is a God, says the gospel, on this ground as in heaven,
And like to our Lord, so Saint Luke tells us.
Christ, King of Kings, created ten His knights,
Cherubim and seraphim, and seven such, and one;
Gave them mastery and mirth in the might of His majesty,
And over his main multitudes made them archangels,
Teaching them by the Trinity to know the Truth,
And obey His bidding; nothing else he bade them.
   Lucifer and his legions learnt it in heaven,
Loveliest to look at, after our Lord,
Until he broke obedience and was beggared of bliss
And fell from that fellowship in a fiend's likeness;
Out of heaven into hell they hobbled in haste
Into a deep, dark hell, to dwell there for ever,
And more thousands with him than man could number
Leapt out with Lucifer in their loathsome shapes
Falling with fiends' faces nine days together,
Till God in His goodness, staying and stablishing,
Stilled heaven that it stayed firm and stood in quiet.
When these wicked ones went, wondrously falling,
Some to air and some to earth, some to uttermost hell,
Lucifer lay there, lowest of them all;
And all that work wickedness shall wend their way thither
At the day of death, dwelling there for ever.
But those that work aright, as Holy Writ teaches,
May be certain that their souls shall ascend to heaven
Where Truth is in Trinity to enthrone them all.
So I say as I said before, if you search the scriptures,
When all treasures are tried, Truth is the best.'
Langland 'But I have no inborn knowledge,' said I, 'You must instruct
                                          me better;
Where, in what part of my body, does it begin?'
Holy Church 'You blunted blockhead,' said she, 'blind in your wits!
Too little the Latin learnt in your youth;
      Heu, michi! Quod sterilem duxi vitam iuvenilem![1]

---

[1] Alas! What an unfruitful life I led as a boy!

[23]

It is a knowledge instinctive, stirring you at heart
To love our Lord better than you love yourself,
And do no deadly sin, though you should die for it.
This, I trust, is Truth. Whoso can teach you better,
Look that you listen to him, and learn it after.
 For Truth tells that Love is the treacle of heaven,
No sin may be seen on him that savours of that spice.
On all that the Lord laboured He lavished His love.
Love is the plant of peace, most precious of virtues;
All heaven could not hold it, so heavy in itself,
It fell in fulness forth on the field of earth
And of the folds of that field took flesh and blood;
No leaf thereafter on a linden-tree was ever lighter,
No needle-point so piercing or nimbler to handle,
No armour can withhold it or high wall hinder.
 Therefore is Love leader of the Lord's folk in heaven,
And, to know its nature, it is nurtured in power,
And in the heart is its home and fountain-head.
Instinctively at heart a strength is stirring
Flowing to the Father that formed us all,
Looked on us with love, and let his Son die,
Meekly, for our misdoings, to amend us all.
Yet appointed He no punishment for the pain they put Him to,
But meekly with His mouth besought mercy for them,
And pity for the people that were putting Him to death.
See it an example, only seen in Him,
That He was mighty and yet meek, and had mercy to grant
To those that hung Him on high and thrust Him through the
                                                          heart.
So I recommend you rich ones to have pity on the poor,
For the measure that you mete out, amiss or fairly,
Shall be used to weigh you with, when you wander hence.
    Eadem mensura qua mensi fueritis, remecietur vobis.[1]
For though you be true of your tongue and true in your
                                                    winnings,
And as chaste as a child that's whimpering in church,
Unless you live loyally, showing love to the poor,
Giving them in fair portion such goods as God sends you,

---

[1] 'The measure that ye mete with it shall be meted unto you again.'

You have no more merit at mass or at matins
Than Molly of her maidenhead that no man desires.
For James the gentle judged in his writings
That faith without works is in no way worthy,
As dead as a door-post, unless the deed follows:
    Fides sine operibus mortua est, &c. Faith without works is dead
And so chastity without charity will be chained in hell,
It is as lazy as a lamp that has no light in it.
Many a chaplain is chaste but has no charity,
And none are greedier when advanced to greatness,
Careless of their kin and unkind to all Christians,
They chew up their charity and chase after more;
And that is no Truth of the Trinity, but the treachery of hell.
It is for this it was written, if you read the gospel,
give & it comes back *Date et dabitur vobis,* for I deal evenly;
That is the lock of love that lets forth my grace,
To comfort the care-stricken, the sin-encumbered.
Love, the most pleasant thing that our Lord pleads of us,
Is also the ready roadway, running into heaven.
So I say, as I said before, if you search the scriptures,
When all treasures have been tried, Truth is the best of them.
Now I have told you what Truth is; no treasure is better.
I may linger no longer with you; may our Lord look to you!'

THE VISION OF LADY MEED

Langland Still curbed upon my knees, I made call on her graciousness,
And said, 'Have mercy, Madam, for Mary of Heaven's love,
Who bore the blessed babe that bought us on the cross,
Give me power, I pray you, to perceive the false!'

Holy Church 'Look towards your left; lo, there she stands
With Falsity and Flattery and all her fine fellows!'

Langland And I looked leftwards, as the lady bade me,
And was aware of a woman wonderfully clothed,
All fringed with fur, the finest upon earth,
And crowned with a coronet. The king has none better.
Fancifully her fingers were fretted with gold wire,
And on it red rubies, ruddy as live embers,
Diamonds of dearest price and double-dainty sapphires,
Beryls and pearls, potent against poisoning.
Her robe was very rich, red-scarlet, grained with gold,
With ribbons of red gold and with rarest jewels.
Her array ravished me, I never saw such richness
And I wondered what she was and whose wife she were.
'What is this woman?' said I, 'so wealthily attired?'

Holy Church 'That is Meed, the maiden,' said she, 'a mischief to me often;
She makes light of my lover, who is called Loyalty.
She lies about him in law-courts, putting justice in jeopardy;
In the pope's palace she is as privy as myself.
Truth will not bear with her, for she is bastard-born.
Sir False was her father, that has a fickle tongue;
Meed gets her manners from him, as might be expected.
 My birth is above hers, I came of a Better One.
My Father is the great God, and ground of all graces,
One God without beginning, and I his goodly daughter.
He has made of mercy my marriage portion;
Whatever man is merciful and loyally loves me
Shall be my lord and I his lover in the height of heaven.
But the man that marries Meed, I make bold to say,
Her love will cheat him of a lap-ful of charity.
The comment of David the King on those that are covetous
And on those that may be trusted to maintain the truth

You can see for yourself, as the psalter bears witness,
   Domine, quis habitabit in tabernaculo tuo, &c.
And now Meed is to be married to a cursed malefactor,
To one False Fickletongue, fiend-begotten;
Flattery by fair speaking, has put a spell on people,
And it is Liar who has led them to this love-banquet.
To-morrow they are making this maiden's bridal;
There you may watch, if you will, what a world is with her,
And who her guests and gallants, the greater and the less.
Cast an eye if you can, and keep your mouth shut;
Do not judge them; let them be, till Loyalty is Judge
And has power to punish them. Then show your proof!
  Now I commend you to Christ,' said she, 'and to His
                                 clean Mother,
And may Conscience not accuse you of coveting Meed.'

Langland   Thus that lady left me as I lay sleeping
And I moved into a dream of the marriage of Meed.
All the rich retinue that rules with Falsehood,
Both family factions, were bidden to the bridal,
All manner of men, meaner and richer,
A multitude massed for the marriage of this maiden.
Knights and noblemen, commoners and clerics,
Assize-men and summoners, sheriffs and their clerks,
Beadles and bailiffs, brokers and businessmen,
Chafferers and grocers and chancery lawyers . . .
I cannot reckon the rout that ran about Meed.
  Then out leapt a liar, saying,

Liar   'Look! A list,
A galaxy of gifts that Guile has given them!
Be witnesses and warranty, you worldly-wise ones,
That Meed is being married more for her money
Than for any fair virtue or frankness of nature.
Falseness is fond of her, reckoning her riches,
And Devilry endows her with the Deadly Sins;
They shall be princes in *Pride* and despise poverty,
To backbite and boast and to bear false witness,
To scorn and to scold and to utter scandal,
Bold in disobedience to break the commandments.
The earldom of *Envy* and the acres of *Anger*,
The treasure-chest of champing and chattering out of reason,

And the county of *Covetousness* and all the coasts about it.
Usury and avarice are all arranged for
In bargaining and brokery, and all the borough of Theft.
And all the lordship of *Lechery* in length and breadth
In word and in work, in watchings and winkings,
In wish and in will and in wearing wily garments,
Ogling and angling and idling their time.
Gluttony shall be given them to blossom in blasphemy
And all-day drinking in divers taverns,
Jabbering and japing and judging their fellow-Christians,
And then sitting and supping until sleep assails them
When bedded in beastliness, they shall breed like parish pigs,
Till' their sides are sleek with sleep and *Sloth*.
They shall waken wanly, willing no amendment,
Believing they are lost at the latter end,
To have and to hold, and their heirs after them,
A dwelling with the devil and be damned for ever
With all the appurtenances of purgatory and the pains of hell,
Yielding, for these favours, at the years' end,
Their souls to Satan to share in his sufferings
And dwell with him in darkness while God is in heaven.
Written and witnessed and registered by Wrong
And Peter the Pardoner, the Pauline Doctor,
Bertie the Beadle of Buckinghamshire,
Reginald the Reve of the County of Rutland,
And Mumps the Miller and many another.
In the date of the devil the deed was sealed
In presence of Sir Simony by Sir Civil Law.'

Langland Theology was thoughtful, when this was announced,
And said to Sir Civil,

Theology   'Sorrow upon you,
Working for a wedding that wars against Truth!
Meed is a maiden whose mother, Fair Pay,
Would grant her to Truth, were she given in marriage;
You have given her to Guile, God give you sorrow!
 So set your wits to work, and your wisdom too,
And lead her off to London, where the law can be known,
If the law will allow them to lie with each other.'

Langland Sir Civil assented, but Sir Simony not,
Till he had silver for his services; so too the notaries.

	Then Fawner fetched forth a handful of florins
	And ordered Guile to give the gold about
	With a fee to False Witness, more than sufficient.
Fawner	'For he can master Meed, and make her obey me!'
Langland	When this gold was given, great was the gratitude
	To Fawner and False for all their fair gifts;
	'Meed,' they said, 'is mastered by our merry mood
	And is game to get ready to go up to London.'

Fawner and False were glad of the frolic
And raked up the riff-raff from all the region round
Bidding them get busy, beggars and all,
To wend their way to Westminster to witness the wedding.
They took care to get a cart-horse, to carry them thither
And shoved Meed on a sheriff recently shod.
Sir False on an assize-man, softly trotting,
And Fawner on a flatterer, foppishly attired.
But there was nothing for the notaries, who were much annoyed
That Simony and Civil Law must slop along on foot.

Then Sir Simony swore, and so did Sir Civil,
That summoners should be saddled to serve for them both,
And billeting officers bridled as beasts of burden.

Simony and 'Sir Simony himself shall sit upon their backs;
Civil Law Deans and you sub-deans, draw in together,
Archdeacons and officials and all you registrars!
Have them saddled with silver to settle for our sins,
Like adultery and divorce and double-faced usury.
And cart-saddle the commissioners to lead our carriages
And fry the fornicators till they fetch us victuals.
And turn Liar into a lorry, to lead the lot of us!'

Langland Now False and Fawner went forward together
With Meed in the middle and her men in rear of her.
I have no time to tell of the tail behind them
Of all manner of men, as many as live.

But Honesty saw them, and saying but little,
Pricked on his palfrey and passed on before them;
He came to the king's court and Conscience was told,
And Conscience as quickly acquainted the king.

The King 'Now, by Christ!' said the king, 'could I but catch them,
False or Fawner or any of his fellows,
I'd reckon with those wretches for ruining the land,

And have them hanged by the neck and all that uphold them!'

Langland And he ordered an officer, ready at hand,

The King 'Tether those tyrants, whatever it costs you,
Put False in fetters and refuse his favours,
And to counteract Guile, cut through his gullet!
Lay hold on Liar, let him not escape you,
And put him in the pillory, whatever he pleads;
And bring Meed to me, for all her merry men!'

Langland At the door stood Dread and heard the decision,
And went like the wind to give warning to False
And bade him fly for fear, and his fellows with him.
Sir False was frightened and fled to the friars,
And Guile made haste to go, he was aghast of death;
But merchants met with him and made him easy,
And shut him in their shop to show off their goods,
Apparelled as an apprentice to wait upon people.

Liar, the light of foot, leapt away quickly,
Lurking through lanes and lugged hither and thither.
He was nowhere welcome for his nasty tales,
But howled at and hooted and told to get out,
Till the pardoners had pity and pulled him inside.
They washed him and wiped him and wound him in relics
And sent him all sealed on a Sunday to church
To get pennies for pardon, pounds at a time;
Doctors deliberated and delivered letters
Asking his assistance in assessing urine.

But all fled for fear and went crouching in corners;
Except Meed the maiden, they fled to a man.
And she, to tell truly, trembled for terror
She wept and wrung her hands, wailing when arrested.

LADY MEED AT WESTMINSTER

Langland Now was Meed the maiden, and not another more,
    Brought before the king by beadles and bailiffs.
    The king called a cleric, (I can't say his name),
    To take maiden Meed and make her at home.
The King 'I shall sound her myself and question her sincerely
    Whom she would have for her husband in marriage.
    If she does what I tell her and takes my advice
    Her guilt shall be forgiven, so help me, God!'
Langland Courteously the cleric, as the king commanded,
    Took Meed by the waist and went into a chamber
    Where there was mirth and minstrelsy, to make her merry.
    Not one in all Westminster but offered her worship
    Gently and with joy. Some of the justices
    Brisked into the bower where the bride awaited,
    To give her kind comfort by the leave of clergy,
    And said,
Justices   'Never mind! Don't moan nor lament;
    For we'll advise the king and work out a way for you
    To wed whom you will, whatever your wishes,
    For all the contrivance and cunning of Conscience!'
Langland Meed then mildly murmured her thanks
    For all their great goodness, and gave, to each of them,
    Cups of clean gold and goblets of silver,
    Rings set with rubies, rarest and richest.
    Up came a confessor, coped like a friar,
    And faltered in a fluting confessional whisper,
The Friar 'Though you have lain with both learned and illiterate
    And Falsehood has followed you all these fifty winters
    I'll absolve you myself, for a seed of wheat.'
Langland Then Meed, for her misdoings, knelt to the man
    And was shriven for her short-comings, shamelessly, I thin
    She told him a tale and tossed him a coin
    And he soon absolved her, saying as he did so,
The Friar 'We're working at a window; we'll have to pay a packet.
    If you would glaze the gable, with your name engraved,
    Your soul could be certain in its hope of heaven.'
Meed 'Were I sure of that,' said she, 'I shouldn't shrink;

I'll befriend you, friar, and never fail you
As long as you love a lord that lurks after lechery
And have no lack of ladies that love the same thing.
It's a frailty of the flesh, (as the books affirm),
Only a knack of nature, as everyone knows.
If you escape the scandal, your skin is safe,
For of the Seven Sins it is the soonest pardoned.
Be merciful,' said Meed, 'to the men that haunt after it,
And I'll champion your church and clap up a cloister,
Wash the walls white and put glass in your windows,
Paint it with portraits and pay for the building!'

Langland But God to all good folk forbids such engraving
Where windows are the witness of your worthy deeds.
Maybe pride is painted there, the pomps of the world;
For Christ knows your conscience and the calls of your nature
The cost and the covetousness and who owns the capital.
     Nesciat sinistra quid faciat dextra.
Mayors and mace-bearers, that act as a mean
Between king and commons in keeping the law,
Are to punish in pillories and on stools of penitence
The brewers, the bakers, the butchers and cooks;
For these are the men that do the most mischief
To the poorer people that pay by the parcel,
They poison the people, privily and often,
Getting rich by retail, and buying up rents
With what the poor people should put in their bellies.
  The king from council came, and called out for Meed,
Summoning her swiftly by a troop of serjeants,
Who brought her to his bower in bliss and delight.
Courteously the king then started to question her:

The King 'Woman, how foolish, how frequent are your faults!
But you never did worse than in this wicked wedding.
I forgive the guilt, and grant you my grace;
Henceforth, until death, do so no more!
I have a knight called Conscience, lately come home;
If he wishes you for wife, will you accept him?'

Meed 'Yes, my Liege,' said that lady, 'Lord forbid I shouldn't!
I am wholly in your hand; hang me if I'm not!'

Langland And then Conscience was called to come into presence
Before the king and his council, clerics and others.

[32]

He went down on his knees in duty to the king
And enquired his will, and what he should do.
The King 'Will you wed this woman,' said the king, 'if I should wish it?
For she is keen for your comradeship, liking your company.'
Conscience Said Conscience to the king, 'Christ forbid it me!
Ere I wed such a wife, may woe overtake me!
For she is frail in her faith, fickle in her speech,
A mistress in mischiefs, many a score of them.
Trust in her treasure has tried out too many.
To wives and to widows she teaches wantonness,
Luring into lechery those that love her gifts.
There is no better bawd, by Him that gave me breath,
Between heaven and hell, though you hunted the earth!
She is tickle of her tail and treacherous of tongue,
As common as a cart-way to every customer.
By Jesus, with her jewels she corrupts your judges;
Your barons and burgesses she brings to sorrow.
Clergy and covetousness she couples together.
This is the life of that lady, the Lord give her grief!'

(*Here follows a long and somewhat obscure debate between* MEED
and CONSCIENCE *in which mutual recrimination is freely exchanged
and* CONSCIENCE *attempts to explain the difference between a fair
price for honest work and a heavy bribe for corrupt service. The time
will come, he says, when money shall no longer be the master, and
when truth and love shall lead into a Millennium*):

Conscience 'No more shall Meed, as she is now, be mistress,
But love and loyalty and humbleness of heart;
These shall be sovereigns on earth, for the saving of Truth.
And he who trespasses against Truth, or takes what's not his,
Shall be laid by Loyalty under the law.
But loving-kindness shall come yet, and Conscience too,
And make of law their labourer; such love shall arise,
And such a peace among the people, so perfect a truth,
That Jews shall imagine, with joy and amazement,
That Moses or Messiah are among us on earth.
All that carry cutlasses, broad-sword or lances,
Axes or hatchets or any other weapon
Shall be condemned to death unless they dull them

[33]

Into scythe or sickle, ploughshare or coulter;
> *Conflabunt gladios suos in vomeres, &c.*[1]

Every man to play with his plough, his pick-axe or spade
Spin or spread dung, or spill himself in sloth.
Priests and parsons will go hunting with *placebo*
Dinning the psalms of David, every day till evening.
As for hawking and hunting, any that hankers for it
Shall be soon beggared of his boast of a benefice.
Neither king nor knight, constable nor mayor
Shall coerce the community or summon men to court.
True-of-tongue shall be a tidy man, for he never attacked me.
There shall be no more battles, nor bearers of weapons,
And any smith that smithies one shall be smitten with it.
> *Non levabit gens contra gentem gladium, &c,*[2]

But ere this fortune be found, the worst will befall, . . .'

(*The dispute between* MEED *and* CONSCIENCE *then continues until the* KING *tries to put a stop to it, trying to reconcile them by sending for* REASON, *who arrives, accompanied by his sinister counterparts* WIT *and* WORLDLY WISDOM. *The debate goes on, only to be interrupted by the arrival of* PEACE *who complains of the behaviour of* WRONG. *This refers to the unscrupulous way in which great lords and their retinues, in making cross-country journeys, would billet themselves upon chance villages, with all the disorders attributed to* LEAR'S *'Hundred Knights', and depart without more payment than a promise.*)

Langland And then came Peace into parliament and put forth a plea
How Wrong against his will had ravished his wife
And how he had raped Rose, Reginald's sweetheart,
And had Margaret's maidenhood, much as she struggled.
Peace 'My pigs and my poultry are pinched by his gadabouts,
And I dare not, for fear of him, scold or show fight.
He borrowed the brown mare, but never brought her back;
And never a farthing for her! Aye, he outfaced me,
Maintaining his men to murder my servants;
Forestalled me at the fair, fought me in bargaining,
Broke down my barn-door and bore off my wheat,

[1] They shall beat their swords into ploughshares.
[2] Nation shall not lift up the sword against nation.

[34]

Tendering me a tally for ten quarters of oats!
And on top of that he beat me and lay with my maid;
But I haven't the hardihood to look at him, hardly.'

(WRONG, *aided and abetted by* WIT *and* WORLDLY-WISDOM, *attempt to get help from* MEED. *The matter is thus about to be adjusted but* REASON *intervenes and says there will never be a case for mercy until lords and ladies love truth and hate harlotry, till clerics are less covetous and kinder to the poor, and the* KING'S *council is for the common profit. Then, at last,* LOVE *shall lead his land. The episode of* MEED *ends as follows with the conversion of the* KING *to* CONSCIENCE *and* REASON.)

Langland The king called to Conscience and after to Reason
        And recorded that Reason had read the case rightly,
        Looking moodily at Meed in the might of his majesty:
The King 'I will have loyalty in my laws; let be this disputing!'
Reason 'By Him that was racked on the Rood,' said Reason to the king,
        'Unless I rule your realm, rend out my guts!'
The King 'I assent,' said the king, 'by Saint Mary, my Lady,
        As long as I live you shall never leave me!'
Reason 'I am ready,' said Reason, 'to remain with you ever
        If Conscience counsel us; that's all that I care for!'

THE VISION OF THE DEADLY SINS

Langland   The king and his chosen ones went off to church
To hear matins and mass, and then on to their meal.
I awoke out of sleep, and felt very sorry
I hadn't slept sounder and seen a lot more.
But a furlong farther, a faintness befell me
And I couldn't fare a foot, for default of sleep;
I sat down softly and said my creed,
And so, babbling at my beads, they brought me to slumber.
  Much more then I saw than I had yet imagined,
For I saw the field of folk, of which have spoken,
And how Reason robed himself to preach to the realm,
With a cross before the king, and thus he commented:
He proved that these pestilences were for pure sin,
And the south-west wind on a Saturday at evening
Was patently for pure pride, and for no other purpose.
Pear-trees and plum-trees were puffed to the earth
As a sign that you sinners should all do better.
Beeches and broad oaks were blown to the ground
And turned tail-upwards to betoken the dread
That deadly sin at Doomsday may undo you all.
  I might well mumble on this matter long,
But I shall say as I saw, (so help me God!)
How pertinently Reason preached to the people.
  He bade Waster go work as well as he could
And win back what he had wasted in some way or other.
And he prayed Peronella to put away her frippery
And keep it in her coffer, in case she need money.
He taught Tom Stowe to take a pair of sticks
And fetch home Felicity from the house of correction.[1]
He gave warning to Walter his wife was to blame
That her hat cost five pounds, and his a few pence.
And his bidding to Betty was to cut a bough or two
And give Biddy a beating unless she worked better.
To chasten their children was his charge to merchants
Not to pamper them with plenty when appetite was young.

[1] Where Felicity was undergoing punishment for being a scold.

And Solomon said the same, fountain of sapience,
    Qui parcit virge, odit filum.
The English for this Latin, if you'd like to know,
Is 'He who spares spanking will spoil his children.'
    And then he prayed the prelates and the priesthood also,
Reason 'Preach to the people, but practice it yourselves;
If you live your lessons we shall love you the better;
And you that seek saints, in Spain or in Rome,
Seek rather Saint Truth, for He can save you all,
Qui cum patre et filio; fair fortune befall
All that follow my sermon.' And Reason had finished.
Langland Then Repentance ran to repeat his message,
And I, William, was left, weeping water from my eyes.
    Peronella Proud-heart fell flattened to earth,
And lay a long time ere she looked up, crying 'Lord have
                      mercy!'
And meekened herself to Him that made every one of us.
She would unsew her silks, and set a hair-shirt there
To disfavour her flesh that was so fierce to sin.
Peronella 'Never shall high heart harden me, for I will keep humble,
(Pride) And be silent under slander, that never so have been;
But now I will be meek, and beseech mercy.
All this have I long while hated in my heart.
I have laughed aloud, so that light-headed people
Should wonder at my wit, think me wiser than others;
I have scorned and scolded those that showed any skill,
Using many a method to make my name known,
Boasting and bragging and bold in blasphemy,
Vaunting in my vain-glory, even when reviled for it,
Setting up for singularity in the sight of men
None such as myself, not one so pope-holy,
Now in one class of men, now in another!'
Reason 'Now God of His goodness, give you grace for amendment.'
Thus said Reason; and then arose Lechery.
    Lechery said 'Alas!' and cried to our Lady,
Lechery 'Lady, to thy loving Son, lift up my prayer,
That He pity my putrefaction, in his pure mercy!
I, guilty to the soul, ask succour of God
For the liking of lechery in my sinful limbs,
In my words and what I wear, and in my waiting eyes.

[37]

Every maid I meet with, I make a sign to her,
A signal to sin, and I sometimes taste
The movement of her mouth, and begin groping
Till our will is at one, and to work we go,
Making love in Lent, or out of Lent, all times alike
—Work of such kind is seldom out of season—
Till we can do no more; then we dally the moments
With a smile well-smeared, in smut and in small-talk,
Hugging and handling and back again to kissing
Each exciting the other to our old sin.
I have lain with the loveliest, yet never loved them after.
Now, Lord, in thy loyalty, be merciful to lechers!'

Langland Envy, with a heavy heart, asked to be shriven;
He was as pale as a pebble; he seemed in a palsy.
And like a leek that had lain a long time in the sun,
So he looked, lean of cheek, and louring foully.
His body bulged with anger, and he bit his lips,
And wrung his fist for wrath, to revenge himself.
Every word he uttered was adder-tongued,
Scolding and scoffing and scandal were his livelihood,
Bile and back-biting, and bearing false witness.
That was all his courtesy, wherever he came.

Envy 'I would be shriven,' said this shrew, 'If I durst, for shame.
By God, I am gladder, if Gilbert is unlucky
Than though I had won, this week, a weight of Essex cheese!
I have a next-door neighbour, and have often annoyed him,
Making his friends his foes, by my false-speaking.
When I meet at market my most-hated man
I hail him as happily as my firmest friend;
But when I come to church, and creep to the cross
I cry as I crouch there ''Christ give him sorrow!''
Away from the altar as I turn my eyes
I notice that Nancy has a new coat
And I wish it were my own, in envy of the weaving;
I laugh at men's losses, they lick about my heart,
And I weep at their winnings, and bewail hard times.
And thus I live, loveless, like a lying dog,
And all my body boils, for bitterness of gall.
May no sugar sweeten or assuage the swelling,
No drug or *diapendion* drive it from my heart,

No shame or shrift, unless you scrape my belly?'

Repentance 'Yes, indeed,' said Repentance, reaching out help,
'Sorrow for sin is the salvation of souls.'

Envy 'Sorry I am,' he said, 'and very seldom other.
What makes me look so meagre is missing my revenges.
I will amend if I may, through the might of God Almighty!'

Langland And now Wrath rouses, with his restless eyes,
Snivelling at the nose, and his neck hanging,

Wrath 'I am Wrath,' said he, 'a wrangler, ready for a blow
With a stick or a stone; to steal upon my enemy
Is all my study, to slay him by sleight.
If I sat for seven years, I should still be assessing
The harm I have contrived by hand or tongue.
Among all manner of men I have made my dwelling,
Learned and illiterate, if they like hearing
Mischief of other men, before or after.
I have an aunt, a nun (not to say an abbess);
I've been the cook in her kitchen, serving the convent,
And made broth of the breath that Dame Joan was a bastard,
And Dame Clarice a knight's daughter, but her father was
cuckolded.

Peronella, a priest's child, would never be prioress,
For she had a child at cherry-time, as all the chapter knew.
So I cooked the cabbage of their cross-temper
Till "Liar!" and "Liar!" leapt out at once,
And each hit the other hard on her cheek-bone;
Christ! If they'd had carving-knives, they'd have killed each
other!

Among the monks I might be, but I mostly shun them,
For prior and sub-prior perceive my pranks,
And if I tell any tales, they talk it over
And make me fast on Fridays, on bread and water,
Chide me in the chapter-house, as if I were a child,
And birch me on my bare bottom, with no breeches between.
So I have little liking to live among them.'

Repentance 'Be penitent,' said Repentance, 'and never repeat
Any confidences you come by, by countenance or word,
And don't drink too delicately, nor too deep either,
Lest the taste of it turn the temper of your will.
Weep for your wickedness and work at your amendment.'

Langland   Then came Covetousness; I can't describe him,
He looked as hungrily and hollowly as old Sir Harvey;
He was beetle-browed, and blubber-lipped also,
With two bleary eyes, like a blinded hag;
And like a leather purse his cheeks were lolling
Lower than his chin, and chittering with age;
His beard, like a bumpkin's, bedraggled with bacon,
A hood upon his head, with a lousy hat above it.
He wore a tawny tunic, twelve winters old,
All tattered and filthy, and full of lice, creeping,
And unless a louse could have leapt a little
She could never have walked on so threadbare a weave.

Covetousness 'I have been covetous,' said this caitiff, 'I do confess it,
I was put as an apprentice to make profit for my master;
First I learnt to lie, little by little,
And to falsify weight, my very first lessons.
But for the grace of guile in the grading of my goods
They had been unsold these seven years, so help me, God!
I was drawn into drapery, and by devious tricks
Learnt to lay out linen so that it look longer,
Till ten or twelve yards had told out thirteen.
  My wife, at Westminster, made woollen cloth
And spoke to the spinners to spin it out softly.
I bought her barley-malt; she brewed it for sale
Pouring in penny-ale to impoverish the potion.
Retail-Rosy was her right name.'

Repentance 'Did you never repent, or pay in restitution?'

Covetousness 'Yes, once, in a hostel, with a heap of hucksters,
I arose while they were resting and rifled their luggage.'

Repentance 'That was no restitution, but a robber's theft!
You deserve hanging better for that bit of business
Than for all the felonies you have yet confessed to!'

Covetousness 'I thought "restitution" meant "rifling"; I never learnt
                                  my letters;
Faith, I'm no good at French; I'm from the far end of
                                  Norfolk.'

Repentance 'Had you pity on poor men that were put to borrowing?'

Covetousness 'I have as much pity on poor men as a pedlar has on cats,
Who would kill them if he could catch them, coveting their
                                  skins.'

Repentance 'Are you manly-mild among your neighbours, giving them
                                             meat and drink?'
Covetousness 'I am held to be as hospitable as a hound in a kitchen.'
Repentance 'You are an unkind creature, I cannot absolve you
              Till you make restitution, and pay your reckoning.
              And unless Reason has enrolled it in the register of Heaven
              That you have made all good, I may not absolve you.
                 Non dimittitur peccatum donec restituatur ablatum, &c.[1]
              Shall never workman in this world do well on such winnings!'
Langland Then hope died within him; he would have hanged himself,
           But quickly Repentance called him to comfort:
Repentance 'Have mercy in mind, and with your mouth beseech it.
              God's mercy is more than all else that He made:
                 Misericordia eius super omnia opera eius, &c.
              All the wickedness in this world that man may work or think
              Is no more to the mercy of God than an ember in ocean.'
Langland Now began Glutton to shamble off to shrift,
           Footing it church-wards to confess his faults.
           But Betty the brewer's girl bade him good-morrow,
           Asking as she did so where he was off to?
Glutton 'To Holy Church,' said he, 'so as to hear mass
           And secondly to be shriven, and sin no more.'
Betty 'I have good ale, gossip; will you try it, Glutton?'
Glutton 'Can you spare spices for it, specially hot ones?'
Betty 'I have pepper and peony-seed,' said she, 'and a pound of
                                                      garlic,
         And a farthing's worth of fennel-seed, fit for fasting days.'
Langland Then in goes Glutton and Great-Oaths with him;
           Cissy the sempstress sat on a bench,
           Robin the rabbit-catcher, and his wife with him,
           Tim the tinker and two of his apprentices,
           Hickey the hackney-man and Hodge the huckster,
           Clarice of Cock's Lane and the clerk of the parish,
           Parson Peter Proudie and his Peronella,
           Davy the ditcher and a dozen others,
           A fiddler, a rat-catcher, a Cheapside crossing-sweeper,
           A rope-maker, a road-man, and Rosy the dishwasher,
           Godfrey of Garlick-hithe, and Griffin the Welshman,

---

[1] Never the sin wiped out unless the thing taken be restored.

And several salesmen of second-hand furniture.
All greeted Glutton with a glass of good ale.
  Clement the cobbler cast off his cloak
Which he set up for auction and asked for a price.
Hickey the hackney-man offered his hood,
Bidding Betty the butcher's girl be on his side.
Chafferers were chosen to chase up the bidding.
Whichever won the hood had to forfeit the cloak.
  Two rose up rapidly, growling together,
Pricing these pennyworths apart by themselves,
But could not in conscience accord with each other
Till Robin the rope-maker rose by request
Being named as an umpire to nip the debate,
Hickey the hackney-man collared the cloak,
On condition that Clement should fill up the cup,
And the hood should be his if he held this was payment;
And if either poor beggar repented the bargain,
He should give Glutton a gallon of ale.
  There was laughing and leering and 'Let go the cup!'
And so they sat till evensong, singing at times,
Till Glutton had englobed a gallon and a gill.
His guts began to grumble like two greedy sows
And before you could say your *pater-noster* he had pissed a
                                                    panful,
And blown the round trumpet in rear of his rump.
And all who heard that horn were holding their noses
And wishing it were wiped with a wisp of gorse.
  He could neither step nor stand till he had his staff
And he blundered about like a blind man's bitch
From side to side, and sometimes backwards.
When he drew towards the door there was a dimming in his eyes
He tottered on the threshold and was thrown with a thump.
Clement the cobbler caught him by the middle,
Lifted him aloft and laid him on his knees;
But Glutton was a great grim fellow to grab
And he coughed up a caudle over Clement's clothing.
There is no hound so hungry in all Hertfordshire
As to lap up his leavings, they smelt so unlovely.
  With all the worry in the world, his wife and his wench
Bore him home to his bed and bolstered him into it.

After these excesses he slumped into a sloth
And slept Saturday and Sunday, till the sun was sinking.
Then he woke up winking and wiping his eyes
And his very first word was '*Where is the can?*'
His wife began to warn him, about his wicked life,
And right so Repentance added a rebuke.
Ashamed to be screwed, Glutton scraped his ears;
Groaning and grieving for his guilty life,
Glutton 'O God,' said Glutton, 'I am guilty again!
But here let me vow, whether hungry or thirsty,
To fast till Aunt Abstinence asks me to eat;
And yet I have hated her all my life long!'
Langland Then came Sloth, all beslobbered, with two slimy eyes;
Sloth 'I shall have to sit,' said Sloth, 'or I shall fall asleep.
I can't stand or stoop, with no stool to kneel on.
Were I borne to bed, nothing, bar my bowels,
Certainly not bell-ringing, would rouse me out of it,
Until I was ready, and ripe for my dinner.'
He began *benedicite* with a belch, and beat his breast,
Gave a groaning yawn, and grunted off to sleep.
Repentance 'What! Wake up, you wretch!' said Repentance, 'Rouse and
confess yourself!'
Sloth 'Though I should die to-day, I daren't look up.
I am not perfect in my *pater-noster*, as the priest sings it,
I know rhymes of Robin Hood and Randolph, Earl of Chester,
But of our Lord and our Lady, not the least ever written.
I have made forty vows, but they vanished by morning,
I performed no penance, as the priest enjoined me,
And have never sincerely sorrowed for my sins.
What I tell with my tongue is two miles from my heart.
God's pain and passion I seldom ponder.
I have visited no feeble folk, fettered in prison;
I'd rather hear harlotry, or a lie to laugh at,
Than all that Mark ever made, Matthew, John, or Luke.
And I lie about in Lent, with Lizzie in my arms.
I have been priest and parson, thirty winters past,
But can neither sol-fa, nor sing, nor read Saints' lives,
But I can find a hare in a field or furrow,
Better than in *beatus vir* or in *beati omnes*[1]

[1] Psalms i and cxxviii.

[43]

I can construe a clause to a class of parishioners.
If any man does me a benefit, or helps me at need,
I am unkind towards his courtesy, and cannot understand it,
For I have, and long have had, something of a hawk's way,
I am not lured with love, unless there's a bribe.'

Repentance 'Did you never repent?' Sloth fell in a swoon
Till the virgin Vigilance lifted her voice,
And he wept as she spoke saying,

Vigilance   'Never despond.
But say to yourself "I am sorry for my sins."
Beat upon your breast and beg of His grace,
For no guilt is so great, but His goodness is greater."

Langland Then Sloth sat up, and made the sign of the cross,
Confessing to God for his filthy sloth:

Sloth 'Christ, that on Calvary died upon the cross,
Dismas, my brother, the thief that begged mercy,
Was given Thy grace, that we might remember;
So have pity on this penitent, that cannot repay Thee!
In Thy might and mercy, make mitigation,
Damn me not at Doomsday, that I did so ill!'

Langland What befell of this felon I cannot fairly say;
Well I know he wept; there was water in his eyes,
For he had lain with *Latro*, Lucifer's aunt.

    Then Repentance had pity and put them to their knees,

Repentance 'For all sinful souls I shall beseech our Saviour
To amend our misdeeds, and do mercy to us all.
O God, that of Thy goodness began to make the world,
And madest all from naught, and man most like Thyself,
And hast since suffered us to sin, a sickness to us all,
And all for the best, as I believe whatever the Book says,
    O felix culpa! O necessarium peccatum Adae![1]
For through that sin, Thy Son was sent into the world
And became man of a maiden, to save mankind,
Making Thyself and Thy Son like to us sinners;
And since in Thy Self-Son, wearing our suit of flesh,
Thou didst upon Good Friday, in the fulness of day-time,
Feed with Thy fresh blood our forefathers in darkness,
    Populus qui ambulabat in tenebris, vidit lucem magnam;[2]

[1] O fortunate guilt! O necessary sin of Adam!
[2] The people that walked in darkness have seen a great light.

And through the light that leapt out of Thee, Lucifer was
blinded.
And all Thy blessed ones were blown into the bliss of paradise;
And the third day following, in our suit of flesh,
A sinful Mary saw Thee, ere Saint Mary, Thy Mother,
And all to solace the sinful thou sufferedest it should be so.
All that Mark has made, Matthew, John, and Luke,
Say that Thy doughtiest deeds were done in our armour,
Verbum caro factum est, et habitabit in nobis.[1]
And by so much, it seems to me, the more certainly
We may pray and implore Thee, if it be Thy will,
Thou that art our Father and our Brother, be merciful to us,
Have ruth on these ribald ones that repent so sorely
That ever they withstood thee in this world, in word,
thought, or deed!'

Langland   Then Hope took up a horn and blew it for the blessed,
So that all saints in heaven sang forth as one.
Thousands of men then thronged forth together,
Crying upwards to Christ and to His clean Mother
That grace might go with them to seek Saint Truth. God
grant they may do so!

[1] The Word was made flesh and dwelt among us.

THE VISION OF THE COMING OF PIERS PLOWMAN

Langland These folk all rode off, or went walking on foot,
To seek out that saint in little-known lands.
But yet not one of them was wise as to the way there;
They blustered forth like beasts over banks and hillocks
Until a long time later, they met a lad at last
All got up like a gollywog in pilgrim's gear.
His staff was stuck about with stuffs and ribbons
Wound all about it like wisps of bind-weed.
A bag and a begging-bowl he bore at his side,
And he had twenty trinkets tucked in his head-gear,
Mementos from Mount Sinai, cockleshells from Compostella,
And many a cross on his cloak and the keys of Rome,
And right in front a picture of Saint Veronica
As a sign for all to see what saints he had sought.
Everyone asked him where he had come from.

The Palmer 'From Sinai,' he said, 'and from our Lord's sepulchre;
From Bethlehem and Babylon—I have been in both—
Armenia, Alexandria, and many other places.
You can see by the signs that are set upon my hat
That I have wandered widely, whether wet or dry,
And sought the good saints for my soul's welfare.'

The Folk 'Can you tell us of a saint that men call Truth?
What road should we follow to find the fellow?'

The Palmer 'Not a notion, so help me!' the palmer replied,
'Never heard of a pilgrim with pike-staff or scrip
Even mention the name till now at this moment.'

Piers 'By Peter!' said a plowman, and put forth his head,
Plowman 'I know him as naturally as a scholar knows books.
Conscience and Common-sense acquainted me with him
And made me swear for certain to serve him for ever,
Setting seed and sowing in the sweat of my brow.
I have been his follower these fifty winters
Sowing his seed, and seeing to his cattle,
Day in and day out delivering his dues.
Digging and ditching, I do as Truth tells me,
Times I'm at sowing and times I'll be thrashing,
Tailoring and tinkering, whatever Truth tells me to,

Winding wool and weaving it, the way Truth wants it.
For though I say so myself, I give satisfaction,
He pays me good wages, and often adds a present,
He's the punctuallest payer that a poor man knows.
His men get their money when the morning's done.
He's as lowly as a lamb and loving in his speech,
And if you want to know the way, and are willing to walk it,
I'll put you on the path to his place, with pleasure.'

The Folk 'Good for Piers!' said the pilgrims, and proffered him money
To take them along to the dwelling of Truth.

Piers 'No, on peril of my soul!' said Piers, starting to swear,
Plowman 'I won't touch a farthing, for the shrine of Saint Thomas!
Truth would love me the less for it a long time after!
   But if you want to walk wisely, this is the way:
You must go through Meekness, both men and women,
Till you come into consciousness that Christ knows the truth
And that you love our Lord God liefest of all things;
And then your neighbours next, in no way to injure them,
Doing as you would they should do to yourself.
   So you shall come to a court as clear as the sunshine;
The moat is of mercy, rounding that mansion,
And the walls are of wisdom against wicked will,
And crenellated with Christendom, to save mankind,
Buttressed with ''Believe, if you would see salvation.''
The bridge is built of prayer, the better to prosper you,
On pillars of penitence and prayer to the saints;
The gates hang high on the hinges of charity;
But the tower that Truth is in is set above the sun;
He may do with the day-star as he deems best.
Death dare not do what He disallows.
Grace guards the gateway. He's a good fellow!
His man is Amend-yourself; many men know him;
And this is the pass-word: ''Truth knows all.
I have performed the penance that the priest enjoined;
I am sorry for my sins, and ever shall be so.''
   And if Grace should grant your going within,
You shall yourself see Truth, sitting in your heart,
In a chain of charity, as if you were a child.
   And there are seven sisters that serve Truth for ever
And are porters at the postern belonging to that place.

One is Abstinence; Humility another,
Charity and Chastity are his chief maidens,
Patience and Peace, that help many people,
And Bounty another, that has bettered many.
She has pulled a thousand out of the Devil's pinfold.
If you have no sister in some of these seven
By my head it will be hard,' said Piers, 'for any to enter
Or go beyond the gateway, if Grace is not greater!'

Cut-purse 'Now, by Christ!' said a cut-purse, 'I have no kin there!'
Ape-leader 'Nor I!' said an ape-leader, 'far as I know.'
Baker 'God knows,' said a baker, 'if this news were certain,
I shouldn't stir a step to follow the friars!'
Piers 'Yes,' said Piers Plowman, plucking at their goodness,
Plowman 'Mercy is a maiden there, mighty above them all,
Sister to all sinful men, and her Son also;
If those two help you, you may hope for certain
That grace will be given you, if you go betimes.'
A Pardoner 'By Saint Paul,' said a pardoner, 'Perhaps I'm not known
there;
I'll go fetch my box of brevets and my letters from the bishop.'
A Common 'By Christ!' said a common woman, 'I'll join the company;
Woman Say I'm your sister; what has become of them?'

THE VISION OF THE WORLD AT WORK

The Folk 'This were a wicked way to go without a guide
To follow with us on foot!' So the folk said.
Piers But Peterkin Plowman said, 'Now, by Saint Peter,
Plowman I've a half-acre to harrow, here, on the highway;
Had I but harrowed it, and sown it after,
I'd gladly go with you, and guide you in the way.'
A Lady 'That were a long delay,' said a lady with a scarf,
'What should we women be working at the while?'
Piers 'Some shall sew the sack,' said Piers, 'for the shedding of
Plowman wheat,
And you, lovely ladies, with your long fingers,
That have silks and satin to sew at your leisure,
Make chasubles for chaplains, in honour of the churches.
Wives and widows, spin wool and flax,
Clap it into cloth, and counsel so your daughters;
The needy and the naked, take note of how they lie,
And cast clothes upon them, for so commands Truth.
For I shall lend them livelihood, unless the land fail,
Both in bread and in meat, to rich and to poor,
As long as I live, for the Lord of Heaven's love.
And all manner of men, that live by meat and drink,
Help in the weight of work that wins you your food.
A Knight 'By Christ,' said a knight, 'he knows what we need;
It's teaching on a text that I never was taught.
But show me a shovel and I'll have a shot at it!'
Piers 'By Saint Paul,' said Peterkin, 'you proffer so fairly
Plowman That I will sweat and see to it, and sow for us both,
And labour for your love, all my life-time,
If you charge yourself to cherish Holy Church and myself
And chase off the wicked that lay the world waste.
And be a hardy hunter of hares and of foxes
Of boars and of badgers that break down my hedges;
Go and fly falcons to fall upon wild-fowl
That come into my croft and crop up my wheat.'
The Knight 'To the best of my power, I promise you, Piers,
To fulfil this fairly, though I should fight for it;
As long as I live I will look to maintain you.'

Piers
Plowman

'Aye, but there's point yet, still to be promised;
See you torment no tenant but as Truth allows you;
If you must amerce them, let Mercy fix the taxes,
And Meekness be your master, in spite of Lady Meed.
And though the poor proffer you presents and gifties,
Touch or take nothing; you may not deserve it;
For you shall have to yield it at the end of the year
In a perilous place that is called purgatory.
Never bully your bondmen; it will be the better for you;
Though he be your underling here, happen in heaven
He'll have a better seat, above you in bliss,
Unless you amend your manner of life.
   Amice, ascende superius.
For in the charnel churchyard a churl is hard to know,
Or a knight from a knave there; know this in your heart.
  And I shall apparel myself,' said Peter, 'like a pilgrim,
And cast on my clothes, the clouted and the clean,
My clogs and my cuffs for the cold in my nails,
And hang a hopper at my neck, rather than a scrip,
Bringing a bushel of breadcorn within it,
For I will sow it myself and set me on my way
Of pilgrimage, as palmers do, hoping for pardon.
  For every kind of craftsman, capable of Truth,
I shall find their food, if they live faithfully,
Save Jack the juggler, and Janet of the stews,
Daniel the dice-player and Denis the bawd,
And Friar Fickle-tongue and folk of that feather,
And ribald Robin, the rhymer, for his rusty words.
Truth told me once, and bade me tell again
Deleantur de libro viventium, I shall not deal with them.
They've lost the great adventure, alas, God help them.'

Langland

Dame Work-when-there's-time-for-it was wife to Piers,
His daughter was Do-right-so-or-your-dame-will-beat-you,
His son was called Suffer-your-superiors-to-have-their-way-
Judge-them-not-for-if-you-do-you-shall-pay-dearly.

Piers
Plowman

'God shall be with us; for so his Word teaches.
Now that I am old and hoary, and have of my own,
To penance and to pilgrimage, I will pass with these others
But first, before quitting, I make my bequests.
  In dei nomine, amen. I make it myself.

He shall have my soul that best has served it,
And defended it from the fiend (for such is my faith),
Till I come to give account, as my *credo* tells me;
The kirk shall have my carrion and the keeping of my bones;
My wife shall have of that I won with honesty, no more,
To deal among my daughters and my dear children.
For though I die to-day I am quit of my debts
And bear home what I borrowed ere I went to bed.
And with the residue and the remnant, by the rood of Jesus,
I will try to worship Truth by my way of life,
And be His pilgrim at the plough for poor men's sake!'

Langland Now are Peterkin and his pilgrims pitted to the plough;
Many were helping to harrow his half-acre
Diggers and ditchers dug up the furrows,
Peterkin approving and quick to praise them.
Others worked willingly, as well as they could,
Every man in some manner made himself useful,
And some, to please Peterkin, plucked up the weeds.
 At high prime of day, Piers let the plough stand,
So as to see for himself who served him best,
And hire them later when harvest-time came.
 Now there were some sitting, and singing at their ale,
Helping him to harrow with a 'Hey trolly-lolly!'

Piers 'Now by the Prince of Paradise,' said Piers in anger,
Plowman 'If you don't rise rapidly and reach for work
Not a grain that grows shall gladden your needs;
Though you die in distress, the devil can deal with you!'

Langland Then those lead-swingers were alarmed and let on to be blind,
Some laid their legs crooked as if they were cripples,
And made a moan to Piers, praying for his pity.

Wasters 'We have no limbs for labour, Lord 'a mercy on us!
But we're praying for you, Piers, and for your plough as well.
God in His grace multiply your grain!
We can't go sweating and sowing, we're far too sickly.'

Piers 'If what you tell me is true,' said Piers, 'I can soon test it;
Plowman You are wasters, well I know it, and Truth knows it too.
You eat up what's earned in travail and trouble;
But Truth shall teach you how to drive his team!
But he who is blind, or broken-legged, or bolted with irons,
Shall eat wheaten bread, and drink like myself,

Till God in His goodness gives him back health.
But Robert Runabout shall nothing have of mine.'

Langland Then one of these wasters worked up to a fight
And put up his fists in the face of Piers Plowman;
A brute and a braggart, he boasted at Piers
And bade him go piss with his plow, the pitiful knave.
Then Piers the Plowman complained to the knight
To guard him, as agreed, from wretches and rogues,
And the wolves and wasters that worry the world.
Then, nobly, the Knight, as his nature taught him,
Warned these wasters to work a bit better,
And threatened them with law and his own authority.

A Waster 'I'm not wont to work,' said Waster, 'and won't begin now!'
Langland He thought little of the law and less of the Knight,
And put Piers and his plough at the price of a pea,
Menacing him and his men when they met.

Piers 'Now by the peril of my soul,' said Piers, 'I'll punish you all!'
Langland And he hopped off for Hunger, who heard him at once.
Piers 'Avenge me on these villains that make the earth void!'
Langland Hunger, in haste, hooked Waster by the maw,
And groped in his guts till his eyes gushed water;
He buffeted Boaster all about the jaw-bone,
That he looked like a lantern all his life after.
He gave him such a beating, his belly near burst,
Till Piers with a pease-loaf prayed Hunger to stop.
And had he not done so, he would have been in danger,
As good as dead and buried, not a doubt about it.
Lead-swingers took alarm and leapt off to labour
And flapped with their flails from morning to night,
Digging and delving to drive away Hunger;
What was destined for Dobbin was dealt to the hungry,
And beans made beggars obedient to work;
The poor felt paid with peas for their wages,
And Piers in compassion prayed Hunger to go:

Piers 'I'm avenged of these vagrants, by virtue of your power
Plowman Yet I beg you to tell me, before you take leave,
With beggars and boasters, what's best to be done?
For well I know, with you away, they'll work very badly;
Misery has made them meek for the moment,
And in default of food these folk are at my will.

Yet the fear of famine is no final love;
They are my blood-brethren, for God bought us all;
Truth told me once to love them, every one,
And help them in everything, aye, as they need it.
And now I would know of you what would be best,
How may I master them, and make them work?'

Hunger 'Hear me,' said Hunger, 'and hold it for wisdom;
Bold beggars, the big ones, that can put their backs to it,
Hold up their hearts with hounds' bread and horse-bread,
Assuage the swelling of their bellies with beans,
And if they grumble or grouse, bid them go and work,
And they shall sup the sweeter when they have sweated for it.
And if you find any fellow that fortune has impaired,
Comfort and care for him, for Christ's love in Heaven,
Love and lay all before him, as is the law of nature;

    Alter alterius onera portate.[1]

And all manner of men that you may meet with,
That are needy and have nothing, help them with your goods,
Love them, belittle them not. Leave judgment to the Lord,
Though they do evil, leave all to God.
And if you would seem gracious to God, follow the gospel,
And the love of the lowly shall lift you into grace.'

Piers 'I would not grieve God,' said Piers, 'for all the gold on
Plowman   earth.

May I serve them as you say, and be held sinless?'

Hunger 'You may build on it, believe me, or the Bible is a liar.
Go to Genesis, the giant, engenderer of us all,
"In the sweat of thy brow shalt thou eat thy bread."
Matthew had a man's brow, and in his mouth these words,
(And what he has said, Holy Church has heard),
"He that hath, shall have, and help if he need it,
And he that hath not, shall have nothing. I will take it from
                                    him." '

Piers 'By Saint Paul,' said Piers, 'these are profitable words!
Plowman Leave us, now, Hunger, when you like, and good luck to you!'

Hunger 'I assure you,' said Hunger, 'I sha'n't go away
Till I've done my dinner, and my drink, too.'

Piers 'I haven't a penny,' said Piers, 'to pay for a pullet,
Plowman Nor for pork or for goose, but two green cheeses,

---

[1] Bear ye one another's burdens.

[53]

A few curds and some cream and an oatmeal cake,
And two loaves of bean and bran, baking for my children.
By my soul I say, I have no salt bacon,
Nor, by Christ, a kitchen-boy for cooking a stew;
But I have onions and parsley, cole-wort and cabbage,
A cow and a calf, and an old cart-mare
To draw my dung afield, while the drought lasts us.
That's the livelihood we live by, until Lammas-time,
And by then I hope to have a harvest in my croft,
Then I could do you a dinner, as I'd dearly like to.'

Langland   All the poor people fetched out their pease-cods,
Beans and baking-apples they brought him in their laps
Chervils and shallots and many a ripe cherry,
Proffering Piers these presents, to appease Hunger.

And Hunger ate all in haste, and hankered after more.
Then the poor folk, out of fear, fed Hunger eagerly
With green leeks and peas, thinking to poison Hunger.
By then harvest was nighing, new corn came to market,
And folk were fain of it and fed Hunger with the best,
With good ale, as Glutton told them; and Hunger was got

to sleep.

Then Waster refused work, and wandered about;
No beggar would eat bread, if beans were in the baking,
Only if it were morning-white, of the cleanest wheat;
And ha'penny ale they would not touch or taste,
But the best and brownest that the brewers sell.
Labourers with no land but their hands to live on
Did not deign to dine off day-old cabbage,
Penny-ale wouldn't pay them, nor a piece of bacon,
Nothing but fresh meat or fish, fried or from the oven.
But while Hunger was their master, not one of them murmured,
Or strove against his statute, so sternly he looked at them.

But I warn all you workmen to work while you can
For Hunger is hurrying; he'll be here soon.
Before five years are fulfilled, such a famine shall arise
Through floods and foul weather, that fruit shall fail us;
And so says Saturn, who is sent to warn you.

THE VISION OF THE PARDON SENT BY TRUTH

Truth heard tell of this and sent Piers word
To take out his team and till the whole earth,
And He purchased him a pardon, *a pena et a culpa,*
For him and his heirs for evermore after.
All that helped him to harrow, or to set his seed,
Or try any trade that was trusty and useful,
Were put beside Piers in the pardon of Truth.
Kings and their council that keep the Church safe
And are righteous in their realm to the people they rule
Have a pardon that will pass them lightly through purgatory
To the fellowship in paradise of patriarchs and prophets.
Bishops that are blessed in being as they should be,
Legislators of two laws, 'Love God', 'Love your neighbour',
And, inasmuch as they may, amending the sinful,
Are peers with the apostles, so the pardon showed,
And shall sit on the dais in the Day of Doom.
Some merchants, in the margin, were remitted many years,
But Truth sent them a letter, under secret seal,
That they should buy boldly and what they liked best
And sell it again, saving their winnings
For the help of hospitals, and those in poor health,
And for mending rough roads, a danger to many,
And building up bridges that were broken down;
They should find food for poor people in prison,
And send scholars to school or skilled occupation,
Truth 'And I shall send you myself Saint Michael my Archangel,
That no devil shall dare to dismay you at death,
But send your soul in safety to my saints in joy.'
Langland Then the merchants were merry and wept for delight
And praised Piers the Plowman that purchased this pardon.
Lawyers had but little, they litigate for money;
The psalter does not save them, such as take reward
Against the innocent especially, that have spared to do evil;
The business of barristers should be to benefit,
And princes and prelates should pay for their work.
But he who spends his speech in speaking for the poor
(If needy and innocent, and has injured none),

[55]

Is showing the law for the love of our Lord
And no devil at death shall dismay him a jot.
 All living labourers that live by their hands
And take a just wage, having done a just work,
Living in love and by law, with lowliness of heart,
Have the same absolution as was sent to Piers.
But there were no beggars in the bull of pardon,
Save those who were driven, with reason, to do it;
For he who badgers you with begging when he needs it not
Is as false as the fiend, and defrauds the needy;
Beguiling the giver against his will;
For if he knew they were not needy, he would give it to
                                                              another,
Needier than they, and the neediest would be helped.
He that begs borrows, bringing himself in debt,
Borrowing on the security of God Almighty.
 The most needy are our neighbours, if we note it well,
As prisoners in pits, and poor folk in hovels,
Charged with their children and charged by their landlords.
What they can spare from their spinning, they spend on the
                                                              rent,
And in milk and meal, to make a mess of porridge
For the comfort of their kiddies, crying out for food.
Also they themselves suffer much in hunger,
Wasting away in winter, and waking up of nights
Rising to rock an unruly cradle,
Combing and carding wool, patching old clouts,
Rubbing and reeling yarn, and peeling their rush-lights,
That pity it is to read of it, or put it into rhyme,
The woe of these women that work in such hovels
And of many another man, ground down in grief.
Thin with thirst and hunger, yet they turn the fair side
                                                              outward,
And are abashed to beg, lest it be acknowledged
What they need from their neighbours, at noon and at even.
 Of all this I am well aware, for the world has taught me
How men are made to suffer that have many children,
With not a penny but their pittances to clothe and keep them
And many a mouth to fill, and few the pennies.
A loaf and a little ale, less than a pittance,

Cold fish or flesh, in place of roast venison,
And on Fridays and fasting-days, a farthing's-worth of
mussels
Were a feast for such folk, or a few cockles.
This would be a charity, to help them, overcharged,
And comfort such cottagers, the crippled and the blind.
But for beggars with their bags, whose churches are breweries,
If they be not blind or broken, or bowed with illness,
Never care a rap, you rich ones, if such rascals perish.
And yet are there other beggars, apparently in health,
But wanting in their wits, both men and women,
Those that are lunatic, lolling and leaping,
Or sit about as mad as the moon, more or less.
They care not for the cold, nor take account of heat,
But move according to the moon; moneyless they wander,
With a good will, but witless, over many wide countries,
Just as Peter did and Paul, save that they preach not
And do no miracles; but many times it happens
That they utter prophecy, all as if in play;
God suffers such to go; and it seems to my judgment
They are his apostles, such people, or his privy disciples;
For he sent them forth, silverless, in a summer garment,
Barefoot and breadless, and they beg of none.
And though they were to meet the mayor in the middle of
the street,
They do not reverence him, rather than another;
Neminem salutaveritis per viam.
Men of this manner, Matthew teaches us,
We should have into our houses and help them when they come,
For they are merry-mouthed men, minstrels of heaven,
God's boys, the Bible says, jesters of Jesus,
Under his secret seal their sins are covered.
But old men, hoary, helplessly feeble,
And women with child that may work no longer,
The blind and the bed-ridden and the broken-limbed
That being maimed are meek in all their maladies,
Have as plain a pardon as the Plowman himself;
For the love of their lowly hearts, our Lord has granted them
Their penance and their purgatory here on this earth.
A Priest 'Piers,' said a priest then, 'I'll have to read your pardon,

[57]

	For I will construe each clause into clear English.'
Langland	And Piers, at his prayer, unfolded the pardon.
	Now I was behind them both and beheld this bull.
	All in two lines it lay, not a leaf more,
	Written and ratified by the hand of Truth:

> *Et qui bona egerunt, ibunt in vitam eternam,*
> *Qui vero mala, in ignem eternum.*[1]

The Priest	'Peter!' said the priest then, 'I can find no pardon,
	But "Do well and have well, and God shall have your soul,
	And do evil and have evil, and hope for nothing better
	Than that after your death-day the devil shall have your
	soul!" '

Langland	And Piers in despair pulled the pardon in pieces,
Piers	And said, '*Si ambulavero in medio umbre mortis,*
Plowman	*Non timebo mala; quoniam tu mecum es.*[2]
	I shall cease my sowing,' said Piers, 'and sweat no longer,
	And be no more busy about my belly-joys!
	Of prayer and penance my plow shall be hereafter
	And weep when I should sleep, though wheaten-bread fail me.
	Who loves God loyally, his livelihood is easy,
	Unless Luke was a liar, who learnt from the birds.
	We should not be too busy about the world's bliss,
	"*Ne solliciti sitis,*" he says in the Gospel,
	Showing us by a parable how to shape ourselves.
	The fowls of the field—who finds them meat in winter?
	They have no garner to go to, but God finds for them all.'

The Priest	'What!' said the priest to Peterkin, 'By Saint Peter, it seems
	You have a little learning, aren't quite illiterate?'
Piers	'Abstinence, the abbess, taught me my A B C,
Plowman	And Conscience came later and taught me much more.'
The Priest	'Were you a priest, Piers,' said he, 'you might preach a sermon
	As a doctor of divinity, taking for your text
	Dixit insipiens.'
Piers	'You're a lewd lout,' said Piers, 'little you know the Bible!
Plowman	Seldom have you seen the sayings of Solomon.'
Langland	The priest and Peterkin opposed each other

[1] And those who do good shall go into eternal life,
But those who do evil into eternal fire.
[2] Though I walk in the valley of the shadow of death, I will fear no evil, for
Thou art with me.

[58]

And with their words I awoke and waited about,
And saw the sun shining in a summer sky,
Meatless and moneyless in the Malvern Hills.
Marvelling at my vision, I moved into the valley;
  Many a time its meaning has moved me to study
All that I saw sleeping, and if it might be so.
Also for Piers the Plowman am I pensive at heart;
And what a pardon Piers had to comfort his people,
And how the priest impugned it with a couple of pert words.
And all this makes me meditate my vision,
And how the priest proved that Do Well gets no pardon;
Yet I deem that Do Well passes all indulgences;
Do Well at the Day of Doom shall be dealt with honour,
Passing all the pardon of Saint Peter's Church.
  Now the Pope has power to pardon his people;
This is our creed, and this the credential:
    Quodcunque ligaveris super terram, erit ligatum in
                                        coelis, &c;[1]

And so I believe loyally, Lord forbid otherwise!
Pardon and penance and prayer can save
Souls that seven times have done deadly sin.
But to trust in pardons truly appears to me
Less certain for the soul, surely, than Do Well.
  At the dreadful day when the dead shall arise
And all come before Christ to render their account,
How you led your life here, looking to His Law,
And how, day by day, you did, will then be dealt with;
A pocket-full of pardon there, and patents from the pope,
And indulgences redoubled . . . unless Do Well helps you,
I set your patents and your pardons at the price of an old
                                        pie-crust!
  So I counsel all Christians to cry God mercy.
May Mary, His Mother, be our mediator,
That God give us grace here, ere going hence,
That after the day of our death, at the Day of Judgment,
Do Well may declare we did as he commanded.

  Thus, in a robe of russet, I roamed my way about
All a summer season, seeking for Do Well,

_____
[1] Whatever thou shalt bind on earth shall be bound in Heaven.

Frequently questioning the folk I met with
If any could inform me where Do Well might be found. . . .
 So I went widely, walking all alone,
Through a wild wilderness by a woodland side;
A bliss of birdsong in the blaze of summer
Led me to lean a little, under a linden,
To listen to the lay of these lovely fowl.
The mirth of their mouths then moved me into dream,
And I was visited by visions under the veil of sleep
More marvellous than any that ever man has dreamed.

NOTE. *As has been explained in the Preface heavy cuts have been made in translation, indicated by a break in the text. The largest and most frequent occur in Part II, which I have here arranged as a sort of anthology of the more important themes and the finer passages of this part of the original. In the B Text this part of the poem, called the 'Vita de Dowel', extends from Passus VIII to XV inclusive, covering many hundreds of lines. The main subject of discourse is an enquiry into the moral virtues of the three ways of life, Do Well, Do Better, and Do Best, and it is threaded on to a sort of phantom-biography of the poet, pictured through Beings that represent stages in his instruction, such as Thought, Wit, Study, Clergy, Scripture, Imaginative, and the like. Occasionally (with some help from the C Text) there are autobiographical fragments less allegorical in manner that come down to the solid facts of his existence in London.*

As the moral enquiry into the nature of the good life is fraught with many adjacent theological problems, Langland often turned aside (as we would think) from his main theme to consider them. To him, no doubt, they lay directly in the path of his poem as a whole, however digressive they may seem to us.

FRAGMENTS OF THE POET'S AUTOBIOGRAPHY

Langland Then Scripture scorned me and spoke scathingly,
Belittling me in Latin, and set a light beside me,
  And said, '*Multi multa sapiunt, et seipsos nesciunt,*'[1]
Then I wept wildly, angry at her words,
And in a twinkling I was taken into a tangled dream,
Ravished right away; for Fortune fetched me
Into the land of longing. Alone she brought me,
And in a mirror, called the Middle World, she made me look,
Saying to me,

Fortune   'See! Here is a world of wonders,
Could you but know what you covet, you might come to it.'

Langland Fortune had, following her, two of the fairest girls;
Concupiscentia-carnis they called the elder,
And Covetous-eyes was the younger's name.
Pride-of-perfect-living pursued them both,
And calling me from continence, bade me account it little.
Concupiscentia-carnis comforted me thus,

Concupi- 'You are brisk and young,
scentia-   and there are years enough
Carnis For a long life of ladies to love;
Look and reckon in this mirror many a merry romp
Leading to what you like, all your life-time.'

Covetous- And the second girl said, 'I shall flatter your fancies
eyes Be sure I shan't leave you, till you're a lord at least,
Following you in fellowship, if it please Fortune.'

Fortune 'He shall find me his friend,' said Fortune then,
'Him that it pleases me to help has no mishap.'

Langland Then there was one called Eld, ancient and weary,
Eld 'Man,' said Eld, 'if I meet you, by Mary of Heaven,
You shall find Fortune fail you at your need,
And Concupiscentia-carnis clean forsake you!
Then you shall bitterly bewail, both day and night,
Her kiss of acquaintance, and Covetous-eyes.
And Pride-of-perfect-living shall bring you into peril.'

Recklessness 'Never reckon on that,' said Recklessness, rushing up in rags,

---

[1] Many there are who know much, but do not know themselves.

[63]

'Follow forth as Fortune wills; Eld is far off;
Time enough to stoop when your brows are bald.
Go to hell or go to heaven, you'll hardly go alone!
If Scripture can be trusted for a scrap of truth,
There's never a lord or lady living on earth
That shall sit in God's seat, or see God in His bliss!'

Eld and   'Alas!' said Eld, and Holiness also,
Holiness 'Your wits will go to waste if your will turns to pleasure!'
Langland But Covetous-eyes comforted me after,
And followed me for forty years, and a fifth longer;
Do Well and Do Better did not seem a delicacy;
I had no liking, believe me, even to look at them,
Till I forgot my youth, and yielded to Eld.
And then Fortune was my foe, for all her fair promise,
And poverty pursued me and put me down. . . .

Thus I awoke, Lord knows, living in Cornhill,
Kitty and I in a cottage, lolling through life,
But little to the liking, as you may believe,
Of those London lollers, the illiterate hermits;
For I made rhymes about them, as Reason taught me.
Then, as I came along, Conscience and Reason
Met me in the heat of harvest, when I had my health,
And limbs to labour with, and liked good living,
And had nothing to do but drink and sleep.
Roaming my memory, Reason berated me:
Reason   'Can you serve a mass,' he said, 'or sing in church?
Or cock up my Haycocks and pitch them in the cart?
Can you handle a scythe or make a heap of sheaves?
Or keep my corn in my croft from pickers and stealers?
Can you shape a shoe, cut clothes, or take care of cattle?
Can you hedge or harrow, or herd the hogs or geese?
Or any kind of craft the community needs
To find food quickly for the feeble and bed-ridden?'
Langland 'Certainly,' I said, 'but so help me God,
I am too weak to work with a sickle or a scythe.
And too long in the body, believe me, to bend
And labour like a workman for any length of time.'

[64]

'Then I began to move into a marvellous dream'

'He proved that these pestilences were for pure sin'

Reason   'Then you have land to live by, or a rich lineage
         Who find your food for you, for you seem idle?'
         Or are you broken in body, or maybe in your members,
         Maimed by misadventure? That might excuse you.'
Langland 'When I was young,' said I, 'many years ago,
         My father and my friends found the fees for my schooling
         Till I was reasonably happy in Holy Writ,
         And what is best for the body, as the Book tells us,
         And most certain for the soul; and so I will continue.
         Yet, faith! I never found, since my friends died,
         A life to my liking, other than lolling.
         Yet if I must live by labour and earn a livelihood,
         This is the labour I learnt best and hope to live by:
           I live in London, and on London too,
         And the limbs I labour with to earn a living
         Are my *pater-noster* and my prayer-book, with *placebo* and
                                                                    dirige,
         And my psalter sometimes, and my seven psalms;
         And I sing for the souls of such as help me,
         And those that find me my food seem friendly enough
         And are willing to welcome me, once or twice a month.
         Now with him, now with her, that's how I beg
         Without bag or bottle but my bare belly.
         Therefore, rebuke me not, Reason, I beg you.
         For I know in my conscience what Christ would have me do.
         The prayers of a perfect man and a pure penance
         Are a labour of love that delights our Lord.
Conscience 'By Christ!' said Conscience, 'I can't see the catch in it,
         But it seems hardly perfect to beg through a city!'
Langland 'That's certain,' I said, 'and so I acknowledge,
         I have spilt my time in much mis-spending;
         And yet I have a hope, as he who in business
         Has lost and lost again, and at last has happened
         To buy so good a bargain, he was ever the better;
         And so of Him Almighty, still I hope to have
         A gobbet of His grace, and begin on a time
         When all the times of my time shall turn to a profit.'
Reason   'I counsel you,' said Reason, 'to reach out quickly
         For a life allowable and loyal to your soul.'
Conscience 'Yes, and continue,' said Conscience; and I went to church.

Langland On to the church, going to honour God,
       Kneeling on my knees before the cross, I knocked my breast,
       Sighing for my sins, saying my *pater-noster*,
       Weeping and wailing, and went into sleep.

SOME DEFINITIONS OF DO WELL, DO BETTER, AND DO BEST

Thought 'Do Well, and Do Better, and Do Best,' said Thought,
'Are three fair virtues, not far to find.
He who is true of tongue, and true of his handiwork,
And by labour, or as a landlord, earns his living,
Trustworthy in his accounts, taking but his own,
And neither drunken nor disdainful, is the man for Do Well.
   Do Better does all this, but he does much more.
He is as lowly as a lamb, and loving-kind of speech,
And has run into religion and taught the Testament
And preaches to the people in Saint Paul's words
   Libenter suffertis insipientes, cum sitis ipsi sapientes.
Suffer fools gladly; so God commands you.
Do Best is above both, with a bishop's crozier,
Hooked at one end to hale you from hell;
There's a spike on that spear, that will not spare the wicked.'

Wit 'The dwelling of Sir Do Well is not a day hence,
In a castle that Kind made, of four kinds of substance;
Of earth and of air it is made, mingled together,
Of wind and of water, wonderfully joined.
There Kind nourishes, craftily enclosed,
A lady that He loves, made in His image;
Anima her name, and Envy attacks her,
Sir *Princeps hujus mundi*, a proud one, a prancer,
Who would win her away with his wiles if he could.
   But Nature knows this well, and for perfect protection
Has dowered her with Do Well, the duke of these marches
Do Better is her damsel, Sir Do Well's daughter,
To serve this lady loyally, early and late.
Do Best is above both, equal to a bishop,
What he bids must be done; he rules over them all.
But the constable of that castle, who keeps the watch,
Is a knight of wise counsel whose name is Conscience.
He had five fair sons, by his first wife,
Sir See-well, Sir Say-well and happy Sir Hear-well,
Sir Work-with-your-hand-well, a strong sort of warrior,
And Sir Godfrey Go-well; a gallant crew.

These five have been set, to save Lady Anima,
Until Kind shall come or send, to save her for ever.

Langland 'What sort of thing is Kind?' said I, 'Can you inform me?'
Wit 'Kind,' said Wit, is a Creator of all kinds of things,
Father and Former of all that was ever fashioned,
Great God Himself, that never had beginning,
Lord of life and of light, of joy and of pain.
Angels and all things are ever at His will,
But man is most like to Him in mark and make.
He gave him a ghost out of heaven's Godhead,
And this castle that Kind made, *Caro* it is called,
Is as much as to mean, a man with his soul.

Wit 'Do Well is to dread God, Do Better is to suffer,
And Do Best springs from both, to abash the arrogant,
The wicked will, that is at war with work,
And drives Do Well away, through the deadly sins.'
Dame Study 'They go carping about Christ, these clerics and laymen,
At meat, and in their mirth, when their minstrels are still,
Then of the Trinity they tell a tale or two,
And bring forth a bald reason, with Saint Bernard as witness,
Putting forward a presumption to prove a truth.
Thus they drivel on their daïses, defining the Deity,
And gnaw God in their gorges, when their guts are full.
And the cry of the care-stricken calls at their gate
The hungry and the thirsty, that quake for cold,
With none to take them in, or tend their suffering,
For they harry them like hounds and hunt them away.
God is much in the gorge of these grand gentlemen,
But among meaner men are his works of mercy.
Clerics, and other kinds of men, carp a lot of God,
And have Him much in their mouths, but meaner men at heart.
I have heard high ones holding forth at table,
And laying fault upon the Father that formed us, each one:
High Ones 'Why did our Saviour suffer a serpent in His bliss
So to entangle the woman, and the man too,
That for his wiles and words they went their way to hell,
And all their seed, for their sin, suffered the same?
Why should we, that are here now, for the work of Adam,
Be rent and rot away? Reason forbids it.'

Langland Such are the motions they move, these masters in their glory,
And make men misbelieve that muse much on their words.
Never wish to know why it was God's will
To suffer Satan to beguile his seed,
But believe loyally in the lore of Holy Church,
And pray Him for pardon, and penance in your life,
And for the multitude of His mercy to amend you here.
For he that wishes to show wisdom on the ways of God
                                      Almighty,
I wish his eye were in his arse, and his finger after it.
All was as thou wouldest, Lord, worshipped be Thou!
And all will be as thou wilt, however we argue.
  And those who use these sophistries to blind men's wits ,
May they be deaf to the difference of Do Well from Do Better!
Unless they live the life belonging to Do Well
I dare be their surety they'll never Do Better,
Though Do Best were to draw them on, day after day. . . .
  Theology is thankless, a thousand times!
The more I muse in it, the mistier it seems,
And the deeper I divine, the darker I find it.
It's no science, I say, to subtle about in,
But a lazy word-game, were it not for Love.
But if Love be its lesson, I like it the better,
Love is a thing of liking, loth to give pain.
Learn then to love, if you like to Do Well,
For Do Better and Do Best are of Love's kinship.

Conscience 'Now, Clergy,' said Conscience, 'account for Do Well.'
Clergy 'I have seven sons,'[1] he said, 'who serve in a castle,
Where the Lord of Life lives, to learn about Do Well.
Till I see those seven,' said he, 'and agree myself,
I won't be so hardy as to hold forth about it.
For one Piers the Plowman has impugned us all,
And set all sciences at a sop, save only Love.
And he takes no text to maintain his opinion
But *Dilige Deum* and *Domine, quis habitabit, &c.*
And he says that Do Well and Do Better are two infinities,
Which infinities, by faith, will find out Do Best,
Which shall save man's soul. Thus says Piers Plowman.'

[1] The seven sciences of the Medieval University curriculum: Grammar,
Rhetoric, Dialectic, Music, Arithmetic, Geometry and Astronomy.

PARADOXES OF SALVATION

Langland 'This is a long lesson,' said I, 'and I'm little the wiser;
Where Do Well is, or Do Better, you darkly show,
Throwing out theories taught by Theology.
That I was made man, and my name was written
In the legend of life, long before I was,
Or else unwritten for some wrong, as Holy Writ witnesses,
I well believe it,' said I, 'by our Lord, no lesson better.
As for Solomon the sage, who taught us sapience,
God gave him the grace of wit, and of worldly goods also,
And he used them well and wisely, as the Bible witnesses.
Aristotle and he, who has taught us better?
Masters of God's mercy that they teach and preach,
Waking us with their words, the wisest of their time,
And yet Holy Church holds them both damned!
And were I to work by their wisdom, to win my way to Heaven,
When they, for their works and wisdom, wallow in torment,
I should work unwisely, whatever you preach. . . .
 But I imagine that many, in the time of Noah,
When he gave shape to his ship, planking and shafting it,
Many a man, I say, helped him to make it,
Yet never one was saved, for all that service,
But birds and beasts, and the blessed Noah,
And his wife and his sons, and their wives with them.
God grant it fare not so with folk that have taught the Faith
Of Holy Church, that is a harbour, God's house of salvation,
And have shielded us from shame in it, as Noah's ship the
                                                        beasts,
And the men that made it, drowned amid the floods.
 The conclusion of this clause is that the curators
That are carpenters under Christ, should cherish the Church
For laity folk, the fowls of God, and his free-born beasts;
At Doomsday there will be deluge, death, and fire together,
So I counsel you clerics, use your chisels on the Church
And build it by the Book, lest you be abandoned.
 I find that on Good Friday there was a felon saved
That had lived all his life in lying and theft,
But because he knew Christ on the cross, and made confession,

He was sooner saved than Saint John the Baptist,
Adam, Isaiah, or any of the prophets.
  A robber was ransomed rather than any of them,
Without the penance of purgatory, to perpetual bliss.
Mary of Magdala, what woman did worse?
Or who did worse than David in the death of Uriah?
Or Paul the Apostle, that had little pity,
Persecuting Christians, consenting in their killing?
Yet these are now as sovereigns among the saints of heaven.
  There are wise ones, living well, but their works are hidden
In the hands of God Almighty; He knows the truth,
Whether for his love, a man is allowed there, and his loyal work,
Or else for his evil and envy of heart.
God lets him live so that we may learn of evil,
White will look white when all else is black.
He that may all amend, have mercy on us all!
  The doughtiest doctor, diviner of the Trinity,
Was Augustine of old, that ever we have heard of;
Thus he said in a sermon, (I once saw it written),
> *Ecce ipsi idioti rapiunt celum, ubi nos sapientes in inferno*
> *mergimur,*[1]

And to Englishmen this means, neither more nor less:
'None are more readily ravished from the right belief
Than are these cunning clerics, that con so many books,
And none sooner saved, nor of sincerer faith,
Than ploughmen and pasturers and poor common people.
Shoemakers and shepherds, such simple jots as these,
Pierce with a *pater-noster* the palace of heaven,
And pass purgatory penanceless at their hence-parting
Into the bliss of paradise for their pure belief,
Imperfectly here as they knew, and even lived.'

---

[1] Behold, the very fools assault Heaven, where we wise ones are overwhelmed in Hell.

RICH AND POOR

Dame Study Wisdom and wit now are not worth a curse,
They card their covetousness, like clothiers combing wool.
Whoever can contrive deceits or conspire trickery,
Having a cunning craft, is called in to counsel;
They lead their lordships to lie against truth.
Read the writings of Job the gentle,
That the wicked are the wielders of wealth in this world.
The lords, in every land, live beyond the law.
The psalter says the same, of such as do evil.
Those with most capital are the unkindest.
Harlots for their harlotry may have of their goods,
Jokers and janglers and juggling minstrels.
For mirth and minstrelsy among us in these days
Is all lechery and laudation and lewdness of tongue.

Langland I lay down long in this thought, and at last I slept,
And, as Christ willed it, there came Conscience, to comfort
                      me that time,
And bade me come to his court, to dine with Learning.
And there I saw a master, (what man he was I knew not),
But Conscience knew him well, and gave him fair welcome.
They washed and wiped themselves and went in to dinner.
But Patience stood in the palace, in pilgrim's clothing,
Begging meat in pity for a poor hermit.
Conscience called him in and courteously said
Conscience 'Welcome! Go and wash, and you shall soon be seated.'
Langland This master was made to sit, as if more than worthy,
And then Learning and Conscience and Patience came after;
Patience and I were put as companions
And sat by ourselves, at a side-table.
Conscience called for food, and Scripture came
And soon had served them many and sundry foods.
But this master and his man would eat no manner of flesh
For they ate costlier stuff, rich stews and soups.
Conscience most courteously commanded Scripture
To bring some bread, for Patience and myself.
Patience was proud of so proper a service,

And was merry at his meat; but I lamented
For this doctor on his dais drank his wine so fast
And ate of so many dishes, and delicate puddings,
Tripe and wild boar-flesh, and eggs fried in butter,
I said to myself, so that Patience could hear,
'It isn't four days since this fellow, before the Dean of
St. Paul's,
Preached about the penances the apostles suffered,
In fame & frigore, and the flapping of scourges.
But they hop one passage, every time they preach,
Where Saint Paul in his Epistle gave warning to people
Periculum est in falsis fratribus.
Now this God's glutton,' said I, 'with his great cheeks,
Has no pity on us poor; it's an evil performance,
He doesn't practise what he preaches,' I said to Patience,
Wishing wildly, and with eager will,
That the dishes and dainties before this doctor
Were molten lead in his maw, and Mahomet in the midst!
'I shall chaff this chamber-pot, with his heavy-charged belly
To tell me what penance he preached of so piously.'
Patience perceived what I thought, and gave me a wink to
be silent,
Saying,
Patience   'Soon you shall see, when he can manage no more,
He'll feel his penance in his paunch, and puff at every word,
And then his guts will grumble, and he'll give a yawn,
For now he has drunk so deep, he'll soon be divining
And proving by the apocalypse and the passion of the saints
That neither bacon nor brawn, blancmange or beef-stew
Is either fish or flesh, but food for a penitent!'

Patience Alas! That riches should rive and rob a man's soul
From the love of our Lord at the latter end!
Servants paid in advance are always the poorest,
Seldom he dies out of debt that dines before dinner is due,
And before he has done his duty, his day's journey.
And so I say about you rich ones, it seems you shall not
Have your heaven here, and your heaven hereafter.
For there is much mirth among the rich, in their meat and
clothing,

And much mirth in May among the wild beasts,
And so as long as lasts a summer, their solace endures.
But beggars, about midsummer, breadless they sup,
And yet the winter is worse for them, for they go wet-shod,
Thirsty and famished and foully rebuked,
And so berated by the rich, that one rages to hear it.
Now, Lord, send them summer, some manner of joy,
Heaven after hence-going, that here have such default!
And have pity on the rich that relieve no prisoners
From the good things thou hast given, the ungrateful many;
But, God, in Thy goodness, give them grace to amend.
 But poor people, Thy prisoners Lord, in the pit of mischief,
Comfort those creatures that suffer many cares,
Through dearth or drought, all their days here,
Woe in winter-time, for want of clothing,
And in summer-time seldom have a full supper;
Comfort Thy care-stricken, Christ in Thy Kingdom,
For how Thou comfortest all creatures, the wise have borne
                                                    witness,

Convertimini ad me, & salvi eritis.

CHARITY AND PATIENCE

Langland   For Saint John said it, and his word is certain,
   'Qui non diligit, manet in morte,'
   'Who loves not, believe me, lives a dying death.'
   Not to give is not to love, God knows the truth,
   Who commanded every creature to conform to love,
   For we are all Christ's creatures, rich from His coffers,
   And brethren, as of one blood, beggars and earls.
   For on Calvary, from Christ's blood, Christendom sprang;
   Blood-brethren we became there, bought of one body,
   Not a beggar-boy among us, but for our sins.
   Let us be brothers and love, laughingly together,
   And every man help another, for we must all go hence.
   Alter alterius onera portate.

Langland   'What is Charity?' I said,
 Anima   'A child-like thing,
   " Nisi efficiamini sicut parvuli, non intrabitis in regnum
             celorum,"[1]
   Yet not infantile or foolish; a free and liberal will.'
Langland   'Where should one find such a friend, so free of heart?
   I have lived on the *land*, and my name is *Long Will*,[2]
   But I found no charity, before or after!
   Clerics have told me that Christ is in all places,
   Yet I never saw Him for certain, save as myself in a mirror.'
 Anima   'Charity,' said Anima, 'does no chaffering, challenging, or
               craving,
   As proud of a penny as of a pound of gold,
   And as glad of a garment of russet grey
   As of a silken tunic of scarlet tint.
   He rejoices with the joyful, and is generous to the wicked,
   Loving and believing in all that our Lord made.
   He curses no creature, but contains his anger,
   And has no liking for lies, or laughing men to scorn.
   What men will say of him he lets be said, taking it in solace;

---

[1] Except ye become as little children ye shall in no wise enter the Kingdom of Heaven.
[2] Believed to be a pun on the author's name.

[75]

All manner of mischiefs he mildly suffers,
Coveting no earthly good, but the joy of heaven.
Fiat voluntas tua will always find him.
He tends, at other times, to take a pilgrimage
To seek pardon of the poor, and of those in prison.
Though he bring them no bread, he bears them sweeter life,
Loving them as our Lord has bidden, looking how they are.'

Langland 'By Christ, I wish I knew him,' said I, 'no creature more!'
Anima 'Without the help of Piers the Plowman, you can never
know him.'
Langland 'Do the Clergy know him, the keepers of the Church?'
Anima 'Clergy have no knowledge, save by your word and deed;
But Piers the Plowman perceives more deeply,
Et vidit deus cogitationes eorum.
For there are proud-hearted men, pacient of tongue,
Obedient in their bearing to burgesses and barons,
That with poorer people have pepper in their noses;
Even so beggars with their blessings, or telling their beads,
Looking like lambs, seem of holy life,
But it's more to have their meat in such an easy manner
Than for penance and perfection in their choice of poverty.
Therefore by his look, or your learning, you never shall
know him,
Nor by his words, nor by his works; only by his Will,
And that no cleric knows, nor earthly creature,
Except Piers the Plowman, *Petrus, id est, Christus.*

For Charity is God's champion, a cheerful child,
The merriest of mouth where he sits at meat.
The love that lies in his heart has made him light of speech,
Comforting and companionable, as Christ Himself bade.
I have seen him in silk, and in coarsest cloth,
Grey or gaudy, or in gilt harness,
And as gladly he gave it to good fellows needing it;
I have seen Charity singing and reading,
Riding, or running round in ragged clothes,
But more readily in richest robes.
And in a friar's frock he was found once,
But it was far away, in Saint Francis' time.'

Hawkin   'Where does Charity live?' said Hawkin, 'All my life I never
(a London   knew
bread-seller) Any that spoke with him, wide as I have wandered!'
Patience 'Where there is perfect truth and poverty of heart and patience
                                  of tongue,
        There is Charity, the chief chamberlain of God Himself!'
Hawkin   'Is patient poverty,' said Hawkin, 'more pleasant to our Lord
        Than riches rightfully won, and reasonably spent?'
Patience 'Though men run after riches, right to the world's end,
        Yet I never knew one that was wealthy, when it came to the
                                  .reckoning,
        Nor, as it drew to the day of death, one that did not dread it;
        Or whose reckoning was not in arrears, rather than out of debt.
        As the poor dare plead and prove in pure reason
        To have allowance from his lord, as the law sanctions,
        He, that never had joy, asks joy of a rightful judge,
        Saying, "Look! Birds and beasts, that no bliss blesses,
        And wild snakes in the woods, that grieve in winter,
        Thou hast made them well-nigh meek, mild in their default,
        But after, thou sendest them summer; that is their sovereign joy,
        Bliss to all that have being, both wild and tame.
        Then may beggars, like beasts, look for a benefit,
        That have lived all their lives in languor and default."
        But God some time will send them some manner of joy,
        Either here or otherwhere, it were pity else.
        Angels, that are now in hell, had, at one time, their joy,
        And Dives lived daintily, and in a *douce vie*;
        And right so Reason will prove it of the rich
        Who lived with their mates in a life of merriment.
        But God's will is wonderful, as common wit can see,
        And gives many a man His mercy long ere he deserves it.'

Langland And all the wise that ever were, for all I can see,
        Praise poverty for the best life, if Patience follow it,
        As both better and more blessed by many times, than riches.
        For though it be sour to suffer, there comes a sweetness after,
        As with a walnut, that has a bitter bark,
        But after the bitter bark, (if it be shelled),
        There is a kernel of comfort and kindly food;

So, after poverty and penance, patiently taken,
That makes a man to have God in mind,
Though he have a will to weep, there waxes a mercy
Of which Christ is the kernel, to comfort the soul.

Langland Then Hawkin laughed a little, and swore lightly,
Hawkin 'By our Lord, believing you leads to no blessings!'
Patience 'No?' said Patience, patiently, and plucked from his pocket
Victuals of great virtue for all kinds of creature,
Saying, 'Look, here's livelihood enough, if our belief is true!
For never was life lent but where there was a livelihood,
Whereof, or wherefore, or whereby to live.
Take the wild blind-worm, under the wet earth,
Fish that live in the flood, and by the fire the cricket,
The curlew and her kind in the air, cleanest of birdflesh,
And beasts by grasses and grain, and green-headed roots,
As a meaning for all men that they also might
Live in their loyal belief, and love as God witnesses:
Non in solo pane vivit homo, sed in omni verbo quod
procedit de ore dei.
Langland And when I looked what livelihood it was that Patience so
praised,
I saw it was a piece of *pater-noster, fiat voluntas tua.*
Patience 'Have of it, Hawkin!' said Patience, 'and eat this when hungry,
Or when you feel cut with the cold, or your clothes cling in heat.
No gyves shall take away your joy, nor any injustice,
Prison or pain shall prevail, for *pacientes vincunt.*
If men were to live in moderation, there would be full measure
Among Christian creatures, if Christ's words are true.
But unkindness makes a dearth in the duty of Christians
And over-plenty makes for pride among poor and rich.
Let us measure ourselves, and make our faith our shelter,
Which drives away deadly sin, or diminishes to venial,
And though a man could not speak, he were spared for
contrition,
For contrition, faith and conscience are the form of Do Well,
And surgeons to deadly sin, when speech fails in confession.'

THE ORDER OF NATURE

Langland   All this I saw in sleep, and suddenly Nature
              Came herself and called me that I might take account
              Of the wonders of the world, to bear them witness;
              And I moved upon the mountain of this Middle-Earth
              As she fetched me forth, to fathom by the example
              Of every kind and creature, how to love my Creator.
              I saw the sun and the sea, and the sand along it,
              And where the birds and beasts made towards their mating,
              The wild-wood creatures and wonderful wild-fowl,
              With their flecked feathers, fancifully coloured.
              Man and his help-meet I beheld also,
              Poverty and plenty, peace and war,
              Bliss and blight, I saw both together,
              And how men took money and refused mercy.
              I saw that really Reason ruled over animals,
              In their eating and drinking and engendering their kind;
              After the course of conception they connected not,
              As when they had ridden in rutting-time; but right at once
              Males withdrew themselves to males, together at morning,
              And at even also they followed not their females.
              No cow, no kind of cattle that had conceived,
              Bellowed for her bull, nor boar for his sow;
              No hound or horse, or other beast either,
              Meddled with their mates that were found in foal.
              I beheld the birds, that built in the bushes;
              Never had human hand the knack to make such nests.
              I was lost in amazement where the magpie learnt
              How to twist and twine the twigs for her breeding;
              I suppose no carpenter, not if he were paid,
              Could make such a nest, no mason mould it.
               And yet I marvelled more how many other birds
              Hid and held away their eggs from harm or hurt
              In secret moors and marshes, lest men should meddle;
              Their eggs lay hidden when they had to leave them,
              In fear of other fowl, or of fiercer beast.
               Some trod their mates and built upon trees,
              And brought forth their birdlings well above ground;

Some birds through billing seemed to conceive,
And some by copulation. I took account of peacocks,
And much I marvelled what mastery they had
And who taught them so to timber among the tall branches,
That neither boy nor beast could reach their brood.
  And out to sea I stared, and so up to the stars,
And saw many a marvel, more than I can mention;
I saw the flowers in the forest, and their fair colours,
And how among the green grass grew so many shades,
Some sour and some sweet; it seemed a mystery,
Too long to count all their kinds and colours.
  But what most moved me, and altered my mood,
Was that Reason rewarded and ruled all animals
Save man and his mate; many a time and often
No reason reached them, and I fell to rebuking
Reason herself, and thus I said to her,
'It's a wonder,' said I, 'that you, who are held witty,
Never pursue man and his mate to save them from mischance?'

Reason And Reason rated me, and said, 'Don't rack your brains
What I suffer or not. You have yourself to think of;
Amend yourself if you may, and let me wait my time.
In sufferance there is sovereign virtue, and a swift vengeance.
Who suffers more than God? Not one, as I suppose!
He might amend in a minute all mischief whatever,
But suffers, an example that we should suffer also.
So I reckon,' said Reason, 'that you should rule your tongue
And ere you find fault with me, think of your failings.
There's no creature under Christ that can create himself;
And if Christian creatures were able to create
Not a person but would be perfect, I dare prophesy!
You will find very few that are fain to listen
When their filthy faults are rehearsed before them.'

Imaginative 'Why one thief on the cross yielded himself to Christ
Rather than the other thief, think as you will,
But all the clerics in Christendom cannot account for it;
And so I say to you, who seek so many whys
And have berated Reason, as if rebuking her,
Questioning the fair colours of the forest flowers,

'The day for dread withdrew, and dark became the sun'

'I will become a pilgrim . . .'

And where they caught those colourings, so bright and clear,
Asking about birds and beasts in the mystery of breeding,
Why some were below, and some aloft, as you liked to learn,
And of the stones and the stars that you stood studying,
Neither learning nor the light of nature can enlighten you,
But Christ Creator knows the causes, no creature else.
He is the magpie's patron, and puts it in his ear
Where the thorn is thickest for building and breeding;
He taught the peacock the treading of his mate.
  But of the birds and beasts, men in bygone times
Have taken parables, as these poets will tell you,
That the fairest fowl is the foulest in engendering
And the feeblest in flight, of all that swim or fly;
And that is the peacock and the peahen, betokening the proud;
By the trailing of his tail he is soon overtaken,
And his flesh is foul flesh, and so are his feet,
And he has a vicious voice, that is vile to hear.
Just as the peacock's plumage imperils his flight,
So possessions are a pain, from a penny to a pound,
To all that possess them, until their tails are plucked;
Thus the poets prove that the peacock is praised for his feathers,
Just as the rich are reverenced by reason of their goods.
  The lark is a little fowl, lovelier in song,
And well away on the wing swifter than the peacock;
To men who live in lowly heart the lark is likened.
Aristotle, the teacher, told such a tale.'

ANECDOTE ABOUT MAHOMET

Langland 'Can Saracens,' I said, 'have a sense of Charity?'
Anima 'It may be that Saracens have such a sense,
Loving the Lord Almighty by the light of nature.
It's a natural thing for a creature to honour his Creator.
For no man that has a mind, but will be meek and pray
To the Lord that lent him life and sends him a livelihood.
But there are many kinds of men, such as Saracens and Jews,
That do not love God rightly, by the Golden Legend,
Believing not our Lord, but a man, their mediator.
A man called Mahomet they hold for Messiah,
And live by what they learnt of him, and the law of nature.
  There is mention that Mahomet was a Christian man,
And a cardinal at court, cunningly learned,
Who purposed to be pope and prince of Holy Church.
So he set off for Syria, giving subtle thought
How to master men, and did it in this manner.
He took a dove and tamed it, and taught it to take food,
Having secretly slipped, into either ear,
Such corn as the dove should peck from his shoulder.
Whatever place he preached in, teaching the people,
There the dove would come, to this cleric's ear,
And make for her meat. Thus Mahomet amazed them;
When the dove came to nestle, they all knelt in duty,
For Mahomet maintained it was a messenger from Heaven,
And that dear God Himself, in likeness of a dove,
Told him and taught him how to teach the people.
  So man, by Mahomet, was brought to misbelief,
And in his lore they still live, learned and illiterate.
Our Saviour suffered him to deceive the Saracens,
This Christian cleric of accursed soul;
And for the dread of death, I dare not tell the truth
How English divines have a dove called Avarice
And take their manners from the tricks of Mahomet.'

PART III

The Return of Piers
The Incarnation
Abraham (Faith) and Moses (Hope)
The Good Samaritan (Charity)
Palm Sunday to Easter Morning
The Harrowing of Hell

THE RETURN OF PIERS

Langland 'Now all good luck to you,' said I, 'for your fine lecture;
But I'm still in a maze about the meaning of Charity.'
Imaginative 'It's a fine and trusty tree,' said he, 'to tell you the truth,
Mercy is its root, the main trunk is Pity.
The leaves are loyal words, the law of Holy Church,
And the blossom obedient speech and benignity of look.
The tree itself is called Patience, and simple heart's poverty,
And so, through God, and through good men, grows the
fruit of Charity.'
Langland 'To see such a tree I would travel two thousand miles,
And to have my fill of that fruit, forsake all other food.
Sir, is there any that can say where I should seek it?'
Imaginative 'It grows in a garden that God made Himself,
In the midst of man's body; stemming from that stock.
Heart is the arbour and the earth about it,
And Freedom of Will is the farmer there,
To prune and weed it, under Piers the Plowman.'
Langland 'Piers the Plowman!' said I then, and all for pure joy
To hear him name the name, I suddenly swooned,
And lay long in a lone dream, till at the last
It seemed that Piers the Plowman was showing me the place,
Bidding me take in that tree, from top to root.
Three piles underpinned it, as I perceived.
'Piers,' I said, 'pray, why have they put these piles?'
Piers 'Lest the winds weaken it, if you want to know;
Plowman And they bite in blossom-time, but for these balks.
The world is a wicked wind for those who want Truth;
Covetousness comes with it, creeping among the leaves.
Then with the first balk, I beat him down ,that is, *Potencia*
Dei Patris.

The flesh is a fell wind, and in time of flower,
Through longing and lusting, begins to blow loud,
With all its wicked works and the worms of sin,
Biting down the blossom to the bare leaves.
Then I set the second balk, *Sapiencia Dei Patris,*
That is the passion and the power of our Prince Jesu.
Next, the fiend would find out my fruit to destroy it,

[85]

With all the wiles he can reckon he rages at the root,
And encourages the unkind to crop my fruit,
Back-biters and bullies, brawlers and scolders,
And lays a ladder to it, whose rungs are lies;
He filches away my flowers sometimes, before my very eyes.
But Freedom of Will forbids him often,
My lieutenant looking to it, under my leave.
  But when the fiend and the flesh, fellowed by the world,
Menacing behind me, fain would fetch my fruit,
Then Freedom of Will fastens on the third balk,
And drives the demon down, by the divine grace
And help of the Holy Ghost; and thus I have the mastery.'
I prayed Piers to pull down an apple if he would,
And suffer me to see what savour it had.
  Yet even as they dropped the Devil was ready,
And gathered them all together, both great and small,
Adam, and Abraham, and the prophet Isaiah,
Samson and Samuel and Saint John the Baptist;
He bore them away boldly, nobody hindered him,
And made of holy men his hoard, in *Limbo Inferni*,
Where there is darkness and dread, and the Devil is master.
  And Piers, in pure anger, seized on one pile
And hit hard after him, happen how it might;
It was *Filius*, by the Father's Will and the Holy Spirit,
To go rob that rascal and wrest away the fruit.

THE INCARNATION

Langland And then spake *Spiritus Sanctus*, in Gabriel's mouth,
To a maiden named Mary, a meek thing she was,
That one Jesus, a judge's son, should in her chamber gently
Rest Himself and feed there, till the fulness of time,
When Piers' fruit should flower and fall to ripeness.
And then should Jesus joust, by the judgment of arms,
For which of them should feast on the fruit, the fiend or
Himself.

Mildly then the maiden assented to the Messenger,
Saying from her heart,
Mary   'Lo, here His hand-maiden,
Willing to do His will, without spot of sin.'
Langland In the womb of that woman forty weeks He lay,
And was made man of her flesh, of stature to fight
With the fiend and his fellows in fulness of time.
He sought out the sick, and the sinful too,
Salving sick and sinful, the blind and the crooked;
Common women He converted, turning them to good,
The lepers and the mute, those with a flux of blood,
Healing all such and holding it no marvel.
Some, who saw that sight, said at the time
That He was the leech of life and Lord of high heaven.
The Jews joined against Him, and judging by their law,
Said he worked by witchcraft and the Devil's power.
Jesus 'Then you are churls,' said Jesus, 'and your children too,
And Satan is your saviour, as you say yourselves.
For I have saved you, and your sons also,
Your bodies and your beasts, and have helped the blind,
And have fed you with fishes and with five loaves. . . .'
Langland And He withstood them manfully, menaced them with beating,
And scourged them with a cord, casting down the stalls
Of those that chaffered in church, or exchanged money,
Saying in the sight of all, so that all heard it,
Jesus 'I shall overturn this temple, and throw it down,
And in three days after, build it anew,
And make it as mighty, or more, in every manner,
As ever it was, and as wide; and so I warn you

That this place be called a place of prayer and of penance:
Domus mea domus oracionis vocabitur.'

Langland   Envy and evil-will entered the Jews,
They cast and contrived to kill him when they could,
Day after day they bided their time,
Till there fell a Friday, a little before Easter.
On the Thursday before, He made His mandate,
Saying these words, as He sat at supper—

Jesus   'I am sold by one of you, who shall sorrow for the day
That ever he sold his Saviour, for silver or gold.'

Langland Judas joined in against this, but Jesus told him
It was he himself, saying, 'Thou hast said.'
Then went forth that wicked man and met with the Jews,
And told them a token by which to take Jesus,
Which token to this day is too much in use,
That is, kissing with a fair countenance and unkind will;
And so it was with Judas then, who betrayed Jesus.
'Hail Rabbi!' said that ribald wretch, went right up to Him,
And kissed Him that he might be caught, and killed by the
Jews.

Then to the Jews and Judas, Jesus said,

Jesus 'I find falseness in your fair speech,
And guile in your glad face, and gall in your laughter.
You shall be a mirror to many a man for deceit.'

Langland   On a Thursday, in the thick of night, He was thus taken
By Judas and the Jews. Jesus was His name,
Who on the Friday following, for mankind's sake,
Jousted in Jerusalem, a joy to us all.
On a cross upon Calvary Christ took the battle
Against death and the devil, and destroyed their might;
He died, undoing death, and making day of night.

ABRAHAM (FAITH) AND MOSES (HOPE)

And I awoke at that, and, wiping my eyes,
Peering and prying, I looked for Piers Plowman,
Eastward and westward I went wildly walking
Asking like an idiot, everywhere I went,
For Piers the Plowman. Many a place I sought,
Until I met with a man, in the middle of Lent,
Hoary-white as hawthorne, and Abraham his name.
I asked him where he came from and whither he was going.

Abraham 'I am Faith,' the fellow said, 'and that's no falsehood,
Of the House of Abraham, a herald of arms.
I am looking for a lad that once long ago
I saw, one summer, as I sat in my porch.
I rose and did Him reverence with a ready welcome,
Washed His feet and wiped them, and waited upon Him.
My affiance and my faith are firm in His belief,
For He uttered a promise to me and my issue
Of land and lordship and life without end,
And mercy for our misdeeds, as many times as we asked it.
    Quam olim Abrahe promisisti, & semini eius.
And since He has sent word saying I should do sacrifice
And worship Him in bread, and in wine as well.
He called me the foot of His faith, defender of His folk,
A fence against the fiend, if they follow my belief.
Thus I have been His herald, both here and in hell,
Comforting the care-stricken that watch for His coming.
And thus I seek Him, for I heard lately say
That a boy had baptized Him; John Baptist was his name
Who, to patriarchs and to prophets, and to people in darkness,
Said that he saw here One that should save us all.
    Ecce Agnus Dei, &c.

Langland I wondered at his words and at his wide clothes,
For he bore a thing in his bosom, blessing it with his hands.
And I looked into his lap. A leper lay in it,
Amongst patriarchs and prophets, playing there together.

Abraham 'What are you wondering at?' he said, 'What do you want?'
Langland 'I would like to learn,' said I, 'what is in your lap?'
Abraham 'Look!' said he, letting me see.

Langland   'Lord!' I said, 'Mercy!
That's a present of some price! What prince is to have it?'
Abraham 'It is a precious present,' said he, 'but the powers of Satan
Have bound us down; no bail may redeem us
Out of the Devil's pinfold, no deliverer,
Till He shall come of whom I spoke. Christ is His name.
He will deliver us some day, out of the Devil's power,
Paying a better bail than our business deserves,
That is, a life for a life; else they will lie for ever
Lolling in my lap, till such a Lord fetch us.'
Langland 'Alas!' I said, 'that sin should so long hinder
The might of God's mercy, that might amend us all!'
I wept at his words; and as I watched, another
Came rapidly running, right in our direction.
I asked him at once where he had come from,
What might be his name, and whither he was going.
Hope 'I am *Spes*,' said he, 'a spy, and my special mission
Is to seek my Master, who on Mount Sinai
Gave me a Rule for all realms. I have it written here.'
Langland 'Is it sealed?' I said, 'or may we see the writing?'
Hope 'No,' he said, 'I'm seeking Him, who has the seal in keeping,
That is, the cross and Christendom, and Christ hanging there,
And when it is so sealed, I know for certain
That Lucifer's lordship shall last no longer.'
Langland 'Let me see your letters,' said I, 'that we may know the Law.'
He plucked forth his patent, a piece of hard rock,
Two were the words written on it; the text went thus:
            Dilige Deum et proximum tuum, &c.
With a gloss, written gloriously, with a golden pen:
            In hiis duobus mandatis tota lex pendet & prophetia.
'Are these all the Laws of your Lord?' said I.
Hope   'Believe me,' said he,
'Whoever is ruled by this writing, I am ready to assure you,
Shall be daunted by no devil, nor shall death grieve him.
For though I say it myself, I have saved by this charm
Many score thousands of men and of women.'
Abraham 'That's the truth,' said the herald, 'I have often tried it.
Look in my lap; here are those who believed in it,
Joshua and Judith and Judas Maccabaeus,
Yes, and sixty thousand more souls than I can say.'

[90]

Langland 'These are wonderful words,' said I, 'but which of you is
the weightier,
The truer to trust in for my life and soul?
If I take for truth what Abraham has taught me,
He has defended, for their Faith, those sorry for their sins,
So many that he cannot count them, lying in his lap.
What then was the need of a newer Law
Since Faith was first, and sufficient for salvation?
Yet now comes *Spes* and speaks of spying out
A Law that tells nothing of trust in the Trinity
But bids me believe and love One Lord Almighty,
And then to love others as I love myself.
He who stalks with one stick seems to be sturdier
Than he who trusts in two, as anyone can tell.
It's hard enough for any man to hold the faith of Abraham
And even less easy to love your enemies!
So go your way,' I said to *Spes*, 'for God so help me,
Those that learn your Law will use it but little!'

THE GOOD SAMARITAN (CHARITY)

And as we went thus by the way, wording it together,
We saw a Samaritan, sitting on a mule,
Riding rapidly in the same direction,
And coming from a country that they call Jericho,
To a jousting in Jerusalem, journeying swiftly.
He, and the herald, and Hope, happened to meet
Where a man lay wounded where thieves had left him.
He could neither step nor stand, nor stir a foot,
Nor help himself, hardly. Half alive he seemed,
And as naked as a needle, with no help about.

Faith had first sight of him, but he fled aside;
He wouldn't go near him, not by nine furlongs.
Hope came hopping after, with his high boasting
Of help to so many through Moses' commandments;
But at the sight of that sufferer, he sidled off,
As a duck would dodge the dive of a falcon.

But as soon as the Samaritan had sight of the fellow,
He alighted from his horse and led it by the hand,
And to the fellow went, to watch over his wounds.
He perceived by his pulse he was in peril of death,
With wine and with oil he washed his wounds,
Poured balm on him, bound up his head, and laid him in
                                                his lap,
And led him forth on horse-back to *Lex Christi*, an inn,
Harbouring him at that hostelry; and he called the host

The Good And said, 'Just see to this man gently, till I come back from
Samaritan   the jousting;
Look, here's some silver, to salve his wounds with;
Anything more he spends, expect me to make good

Langland Later; I cannot linger just now,' and he left,
And rapidly to Jerusalem, he rode at once away.
Faith followed after him fast, fain to keep up with him,
And *Spes* spurred on in a sprightly way, with what speed
                                                he might,
To overtake and talk to him, ere they came to town.
And when I saw this, I did not stay, but started to run,
And followed that Samaritan, so full of pity,

And he granted that I might be his groom, and gratefully,
Saying, 'You'll find me your friend and fellow if you need me.'
I thanked him then, and asked what he thought
When Faith had fled away and *Spes* had faltered
At sight of the sorrowful man that fell among thieves.

The Good 'Have them excused' said he, 'little their help avails him;
Samaritan There may no medicine in the world help him to his health
But the blood of a babe, born of a virgin.
If he be bathed in that blood, baptized as it were,
And take penance for a plaster, and the passion of that baby,
He could stand and step forward; and yet be stalwart never,
Till he has fed upon his flesh, and made fare of his blood.
For never went one in this world, wilderness as it is,
But was robbed and rifled, ride where he might,
Save Faith, and *Spes* his fellow, and I myself,
And yourself now, and such as seek to work with us.
An outlaw is about the woods, and waiting under banks;
He saw me, a Samaritan, following Faith and his fellow
On a cart-horse called *Caro*, (I took it from mankind),
But the hound lacked hardihood, and hid *in inferno*.
Yet, ere three days are done, I dare well undertake
The felon will be fettered and fastened in chains,
Never again to rifle those who ride my road.
    O mors, ero mors tua, &c.
Then Faith shall keep the forest and the firth shall be free,
Taking care of the common man who doesn't know the country,
And Hope shall be host at the inn, where the man lies healing,
And all that are feeble and faint whom Faith cannot teach,
Shall be led in love by Hope, as his letters said,
He their hostel and health, through faith in Holy Church,
Till I have a salve for the sick; and then I shall return
And come again to this country, comforting all
That crave or covet comfort, or cry out for it.
For the babe was born in Bethlehem, whose blood is salvation
To all that live in Faith and follow his fellow's teaching.'

(LANGLAND *here asks the* GOOD SAMARITAN *whether he is to believe
in the Trinity, as* FAITH *and* HOPE *had directed, and there follows a
long exposition, given by the* GOOD SAMARITAN, *on the nature of the
Trinity, how that it is like a hand; fist, palm and fingers, all working*

*in unity and yet separable in thought; or like a torch, where the wax
and wick are twined together and a flame proceeds from them that
is of both. Each of these images is moralized, at some length, and
then the* GOOD SAMARITAN *gallops away with these final words:*)

The Good   'Covetousness and unkindness can quench God's mercy,
Samaritan For unkindness is contrary to every kind of reason;
For there is none so sick or sorry, none so much a wretch,
But he may like and love, and lend out of his heart
Good will and good word, wishing and willing,
To all manner of men, mercy and forgiveness.
And love them like himself, and amend his life.
I've no more time to spare.' And he spurred his horse
And went away like the wind, and thereupon I woke.

PALM SUNDAY TO EASTER MORNING

Langland Woollen-clad and wet-foot I went forth after,
            Like any empty-head, heedless of grief,
            And loitered lazily all my life-time
            Till I grew weary of the world, and, wanting to sleep,
            I lolled about till Lent; and I slept a long while.
            Of Christ's passion and penance, reached out to the people,
            (As I lay, sunk in slumber, till Palm Sunday).
            And of children giving glory to God, greatly I dreamed,
            And of organ-toned hosannas of the older folk.
             One similar to the Samaritan, and somewhat to Piers Plowman,
            Barefoot, on an ass's back, rode forth un-booted,
            Without spear or spur, but splendid he looked,
            As is the nature of a knight when nearing a battle
            To win his golden spurs and gorgeous gear.
            Then Faith, watching from a window, cried,
                                       'Ah! Son of David!'
            As should a herald of arms at the entry of a jouster.
            And Jews of old in Jerusalem, sang for their joy,
               Benedictus qui venit in nomine domini.
            I frowned up at Faith, questioning this affair
            And who was to joust in Jerusalem.
Faith   'Jesus,' he said,
            'And fetch what the Fiend claims, the fruit of Piers Plowman.'
Langland 'Is Piers in this place?' said I, and he gazed at me keenly,
Faith   'This Jesus of gentle breed will joust in Piers' armour,
            In his helmet and his hauberk, *humana natura.*
            That Christ be not comprehended as *Consummatus Deus*
            In the Plowman's appearance He rides forth proudly,
            For no dint shall daunt Him *in Deitate Patris.*'
Langland 'Who shall joust against Jesus?' said I, 'Jews or Scribes?'
Faith   'Neither,' said he, 'The foul Fiend, and falsehood and death,
            Death says he will undo and bring Him down
            With all that lives or lurks on land or in water.
            Life says Death's a liar, and lays his life in pawn
            That, for all that Death can do, within three days
            He will fetch from the Fiend the fruit of Piers Plowman
            And lay it where Love would have it, and bind Lucifer,

And beat away and bring down bitterness and Death for ever:
O mors, ero mors tual
Then came Pilate forth, with many people, to the place of
judgment,
To see how doughtily Death would do, and deal with both
in judgment.
The Jews and their justices were all against Jesus
And all their court cried out upon him, 'Crucify Him,
crucify Him!'
Then a perjurer put forth before Pilate, saying
A Perjurer 'This Jesus has made jests at our Jewish temple,
Deeming he could dash it down, and in three days after
Establish it anew, (there he stands who said it),
And make it as mighty, or more so, in every kind of manner
Not only as long and as large, but as lofty also.'
Langland '*Crucifige!*' cried a Corporal, 'I warrant he's a wizard!'
'*Tolle, tolle!*' said another, and took some keen thorns,
And began of keen thorn to make him a garland,
And set it sorely on his head, saying in envy,
'*Ave, Rabbi!*' cried the ribald, and threw reeds at Him,
Nailed Him with three nails, naked on the rood,
And poison on a pole they put up to His lips,
And bade Him drink His death-evil, His days were done.
'And since you are so subtle, save yourself now,
If you are Christ and a king's son, come down from the cross;
Then we will believe that Life loves you, and will not let you
die!'
Langland '*Consummatum est,*' said Christ, and began to swoon,
Piteously pale, as a prisoner, dying;
The Lord of life and of light laid his eye-lids together.
The day for dread withdrew, and dark became the sun,
The walls wagged and were cleft, and the whole world quivered.
At the din the dead came from their deep graves,
To tell why that tempest endured so long a time.
The Dead 'For a bitter battle,' the dead body said:
'Life and death in this darkness are destroying each other;
No man can verily know which shall have the victory
Till sunrise on Sunday.' And sank so to earth.
Langland Some said that He was Son of God that in such beauty died,
Vere Filius Dei erat iste,

[96]

And some said He was a wizard,

Voices   'It were well to try
Whether he be dead or not, before he's taken down.'

Langland Two thieves also suffered death that day
Upon a cross beside Christ. So was the common law.
Then came a corporal and cracked both their legs,
And their arms after, for either thief.
But no boy was so bold as to touch God's body
For He was noble and a King's Son; Nature saw to it
That no henchman was so hardy as to lay hand upon Him.
 But yet there came a captain, with a keen-edged spear,
Named Longinus, as the legend says, who had been long blind.
He was one of Pilate's people, placed there on duty,
And, in the teeth of his intention, was made to take his spear,
His hand-javelin, to joust against Jesus;
For all the rest who rode there, or stood, were unready
To touch Him or to taste of Him, or take Him from the cross.
But this blind officer thrust through His heart;
The blood sprang out upon the spear, sprinkling his eyes,
And he received suddenly the sense of sight.
Then fell this knight upon his knees, gasping

Longinus   'Forgive me!
It was against my will, O Lord, to wound you so sorely!'
And with a sigh he said, 'O sorrow of my heart!
For the deed that I have done I yield to your mercy;
Pure Jesus, have pity on me!' and he wept for pardon.

Langland Then, in a fell voice, Faith gave judgment on those Jews,
Calling them cowards and accursed for ever,

Faith 'It was never an act of knighthood, on a bound body
To strike such a blow with any bright weapon,
Or dishonour the dead by day or night.
Yet when this darkness is done, His death will be avenged;
You, lords of the world, have lost; for life shall have mastery;
You that were free shall fall into thraldom,
Churls as you are, and your children, you shall achieve nothing.
Your great days now are done, as Daniel prophesied,
When Christ shall come, the crown of your kingdom shall cease.

[97]

THE HARROWING OF HELL

Langland Then I withdrew in that darkness, and descended into hell.
And there I saw, coming, according to the Scripture,
A young woman, walking, out of a western region,
And as she went her way, her eyes were watching hell.
Mercy was that maiden's name, a meek thing she was,
Benign as a bride, obedient in her speech.
  Her sister also, as it seemed, came softly
Out of the east, walking, with the west in her eyes.
She was a comely creature. They call her Truth.
When these maidens met, Mercy and Truth,
Either asked other in awe and wonder
Of the din and darkness, and if day were dawning,
And what light it was that lay on the lids of hell.

Truth 'I am amazed at these doings, indeed,' said Truth,
'And waiting to witness what this wonder can mean.'

Mercy 'Never wonder a jot,' said Mercy, 'for it means joy.
A maiden called Mary has become a mother,
Though a very virgin, by the visitation
And grace of the Holy Ghost; grew great with child,
And without blot or blemish, into this world she brought Him,
And that my tale is true, I take God to witness.
This Babe was born, thirty winters back;
To-day He died, suffering death at noon.
That is the cause of this eclipse that now has closed the sun,
Its meaning is that man shall mount out of the murk,
And the beam of His light shall be the blinding of Lucifer.
For patriarchs and prophets have often preached of it,
That man shall save man, by a maiden's help.
All that a Tree betrayed, a Tree shall win again,
And that which death brought down, another death shall
                                    ransom.'

Truth 'What you're telling me,' said Truth, 'is a trumped-up tale;
For Adam and Eve, with Abraham and other
Patriarchs and prophets, in pain are lying,
Never believe that yonder light can lift them aloft,
Or hale them out of hell! Hold your tongue, Mercy!
It's but a trifle you're telling me. I am Truth and I know.'

For he that is once in hell never comes out of it.
You can judge by Job that what you say is jargon:
Quia in inferno nulla est redemptio.'
Langland Then, mildly, Mercy lent her mouth to this:
Mercy 'I have a sign,' she said, 'and hope they may be saved.
Poison drives out poison, and that I prove by reason.
So shall this death undo (I dare my life upon it!)
All that death first undid, through the Devil's enticement;
And just as through a guile mankind was gulled,
So Grace shall take the trick, turning the tables.
Ars ut artem falleret.'
Truth 'Silence a moment, sister; do you not see someone
Out of the nip of the north, not very far from us;
Is it not Righteousness, racing towards us?
He will know more than we do, being our elder brother.'
Mercy 'So he may,' said Mercy, 'but see, to the south!
Where Peace comes pleasantly, clothed in patience,
By Love long coveted, I well believe,
She has a letter, surely, about this light
That hovers over hell. He will have told her.'
Langland When Peace, clothed in patience, approached them nearer,
Righteousness reverenced her for her rich apparel,
Praying Peace to tell them whither she purposed
In such a gay garment, in greeting for whom?
Peace 'I am making my way,' said she, 'to welcome all those
I have not seen these many days, through the murk of sin,
Adam and Eve, and others now in hell,
Moses and many more, that shall have mercy
And I shall dance to see it; dance with me, sister!
For Jesus jousted well. Joy begins to dawn;
Ad vesperum demorabitur fletus, & ad matutinum laetitia.[1]
Love, who is my lover, has sent a letter, saying
That Mercy my sister, and I, have the saving of man,
And that God has forgiven, granting me and Mercy
To be man's maintainers, now and for ever more.'
Righteous- 'What, are you raving?' said Righteousness, 'Are you sober,
ness   sister?
Do you believe a light can unlock hell yonder,

[1] Heaviness may endure for a night, but joy cometh in the morning.

And save the soul of man? Sister, never think it!
At the beginning God gave judgment Himself
That Adam and Eve and all that came after them
Should downright die and dwell in their torment
If they touched that Tree, and tasted the fruit.
Yet Adam, afterward, has overstepped it.
And fingered the fruit, forsaking, as it were,
The love of our Lord and his loyal obedience,
Following what the Fiend taught, and his female's will,
Against all reason; and I, Righteousness, make record
That their pain be perpetual, and no prayer help them.
So let them chew as they chose; why should we challenge it?
It's a bottomless bitterness, that bite they took!'

Peace 'But I shall prove to you,' said Peace, 'their punishment
                                   shall end,
And out of their woe shall awake their well-being.
If there were no night, how should the day dawn?'

Langland Then came forward a fellow with two fine eyes,
Book was his name, and he was bold of speech.
Book 'By God's body,' said Book, 'I will bear witness
That when this Boy was being born, there was blazing a star,
And all the wise ones of the world were well agreed
That such a boy born in Bethlehem City
Should save the soul of man and destroy sin.
All the elements entered their testimony.
The welkin first witnessed that He was God Almighty,
And those that steer the stars, started forth a comet
And tended it as a torch, in reverence of His birth;
Light followed the Lord into this lowly earth.
The waters witnessed that He was God, for He walked upon
                                   them;
And see how the sun has locked her fire within herself,
When she saw Him suffer, Who sun and sea has made.
And earth in agony to see His anguish
Quaked like a quickening thing, quashing the rock-rows.
Look! Hell could not hold, but opened her Gates
At sight of God's suffering, to see Him hang.
Now Lucifer must believe it, little though he like it,

And I, Book, shall be burnt, but Jesus rise to live
In all the might of man, and to gladden His Mother,
Comfort all His kindred, and bring them out of care!'

Truth 'Hush!' said Truth, 'for I hear and see
How a spirit, speaking to hell, bids unspar the gates,
Attollite portas, &c.'

Langland A voice, loud in that light, to Lucifer crying,
A Voice 'Princes of this place, Open! Undo the doors,
For here comes crowned He that is King of glory.'

Langland Then Satan sighed, and said to them all,
Satan 'Such was the light that against our leave fetched Lazarus forth;
Care and calamity are come upon us all.
If this King come in, he will capture mankind
And lead it whither he likes, and lodge us in bondage.
Patriarchs and prophets long have promised
That such a Lord and a light should lead them all hence.'

Lucifer 'Listen,' said Lucifer, 'I know this Lord,
Both the Lord and the light; long ago I knew them.
No death can dash Him down, no dodge of the devil.
Where there's His will, there's His way; yet let Him beware—
If he robs me of my rights, it's robbery by violence,
For by right and by reason, the wretches that are here
Body and soul are mine, the better and the worse;
For He Himself said, that is the Sire of heaven,
If Adam ate of the apple, all were to die,
And dwell with us devils; this was His threat,
And since He that is Truth has said these words,
And such a law was made by the Lord of light,
This law, as I believe, will not allow Him the least of them.'

Satan 'That is so,' said Satan, 'yet I sorely dread it,
For you got them by guile, and broke into His garden,
And in semblance of a serpent, sat on the apple-tree,
Egging them on to eat, first Eve, by herself,
Telling her a tale, and treason were the words;
That's how you had them out, and haled them hither,
There's little good in gain, when guile is at the root.'

Goblin 'God won't be beguiled,' said Goblin, 'no, nor tricked;
We have no true title to them, damned through our treason.'

The Devil 'I dread it,' said the Devil, 'Truth will fetch them.
As you beguiled God's image, going like an adder,

[101]

So has God beguiled us, going like a man.'

Goblin 'For God has been going about,' said Goblin, 'with a man's
                                                            gait,
These thirty winters, as it proves, preaching.
I have assailed Him with sin, and have sometimes asked Him
Whether He were God, or God's Son. He gave me short
                                                    answer.
And thus He has trawled round these two-and-thirty winters;
And when I saw it was so, I went, and as she slept,
Warned Pilate's wife what sort of person was Jesus.
I would have lengthened His life, believing if He died
That His soul would suffer no sin in His sight;
For His body, while it went on bone, was ever about
To save men from sin, if they wished for salvation.
  And now I see where a soul comes hitherwards, sailing
With glory and with great light, God it is, I well know.
Quick, take to flight,' said he, 'fast away with you,
For it were better not to have been than to abide His presence.
Your lying, Lucifer, has lost us all our prey.
By you we first fell from the height of Heaven
We believed all your lying and leapt away out with you,
And now, for your latest lie, Adam is lost to us,
And all our lordship, I believe, on land and on water.
      Nunc princeps huius mundi eicietur foras.'

Langland Then the Light bade unlock, and Lucifer answered,
Lucifer 'What Lord art Thou?' said Lucifer, '*Quis est iste?*'
Christ '*Rex Gloriae,*' the Light soon answered,
    'And Lord of might and of main and all manner of virtues,
        Dominus virtutum.
    Dukes of this dim place, at once undo your gates
    That Christ may come in, Son of the King of heaven!'
Langland And with that breath, hell brake, and the bars of Belial,
    For all the watch and the ward, wide went the gates.
    Patriarchs and prophets, *populus in tenebris,*
    Sang the song of Saint John, '*Ecce, Agnus Dei.*'
    Lucifer dared not look, being by Light blinded,
    And those that Our Lord loved, He lifted into light,
    Saying thus to Satan,
Christ   'Lo, here my soul in amends
    For every sinful soul, to save those that are worthy.

Mine they are, and of me. I may claim them the better,
Though right and reasoning record it of me
That if they ate of the apple, all should die,
I did not doom them to hell for ever.
For the deed they did was of your double dealing,
By guile you got them against all reason;
For out of paradise, my palace, in person of an adder,
Falsely you fetched hither what I well loved.
Thus like a lizard, featured like a woman,
Thievishly you robbed me; the Old Law reckons
That guile shall be beguiled, and that is good reasoning,
     Dentem pro dente, et oculum pro oculo;
Ergo, soul shall pay for soul, and sin to sin shall turn,
And all that man has misdone, I, a man, shall amend.
Member for member, by the Old Law, made amendment,
And life for life also; and by that Law I claim it,
That Adam and all his issue be at my will hereafter.
What death in them fordid, my death shall ransom,
Quickening and requiting what was quenched by their sins.
That Grace should destroy guile good faith demands;
Believe it never, Lucifer, I fetch them against Law,
But by right and reason ransoming here my liegemen;
     Non veni solvere legem, sed adimplere.[1]
So that which you got by guile, by Grace is recovered.
You, Lucifer, in the likeness of a loathsome adder,
Got by your guile those that God loved;
And I, in likeness of a leader, that am Lord of heaven,
By Grace have beguiled you, go guile against guile!
And as Adam and all through a Tree took their death
Adam and all, through a Tree, shall turn again to life,
And guile is beguiled and fallen in a gully,
     Et cecidit in foveam quam fecit.[2]
Now your guile begins going against you,
And my Grace to grow ever greater and wider.
The bitterness that you have brewed, break your fast upon it!
You, that are doctor of death, drink your prescription!
  For I, that am Lord of life, Love is my drink,
And for that drink, to-day, I died upon earth.

[1] I came not to destroy the Law but to fulfil it.
[2] And he fell into the ditch that he himself had made.

I fought so, I thirst still, for the sake of man's soul;
No drink may moisten or slake my thirst
Until the day of vintage in the vale of Jeosaphat.
That which I drink must ripen aright, *resurrectio mortuorum*,
And then I shall come as a King, crowned with angels,
And hale out of hell the souls of all men.
Fiends and phantoms shall stand before me
And be at my bidding, wherever I please.
 And to show mercy to man is the main of my being,
For we are brethren of one blood, though not all of one
baptism.
For if a king of some kingdom should come at such a time
As when a felon is fetched out for death or punishment,
The law allows him life if the king looks upon him.
And I, that am King of Kings, shall come at such a time,
As when the doom of death damns all the wicked;
And if the Law wills that I look upon them, it lies in my grace
Whether they die or die not for having done ill.
 But my right and righteousness shall rule over hell
And my mercy over mankind before me in heaven.
I were an unkind King, did I not help my country.
Thus, by the Law,' said our Lord, 'I will lead hence
Those that have loved me and looked for my coming;
And for your lying, Lucifer, that laid a snare for Eve,
You shall bitterly abide it.'

Langland
          And He bound him in chains,
Ashtaroth and all rout of them, crouched into corners,
The deadliest dared not look on our Lord,
But let Him lead forth whom He loved, and left Him to his
liking.

Many hundreds of angels were harping and singing:
 Culpat caro, purgat caro; regnat Deus Dei caro.[1]
And then Peace piped a note of poesy,
Peace '*Clarior est solito post maxima nebula phebus*
  Post inimicitias clarior est et amor.[2]
After sharp showers,' said Peace, 'how shining the sun!
There's no weather warmer, than after watery clouds.

[1] The flesh sins, the flesh redeems from sin: the flesh reigns as God of God.
[2] Brightest is the sun after the darkest clouds, brightest is love after estrangement.

Nor any love that has more delight, nor friendship fonder,
Than after war and woe, when Love and Peace are the masters.
Never was war in this world, nor wickedness so cruel,
But that Love, if he liked, could bring all to laughing,
And Peace, through patience, put stop to all perils.'

Truth 'Truce!' said Truth, 'You tell truly, by Jesus!
Close with me in covenant, and let each kiss the other!'

Peace 'And let no people,' said Peace, 'perceive that we wrangled!
For nothing is impossible to God Almighty.'

Righteous- 'You are right,' said Righteousness, and kissed her reverently,
ness Peace, and Peace here, *per saecula saeculorum.*

    Misericordia et veritas obviaverunt sibi; iustitia et pax
                             osculatae sunt.[1]

Then Truth trumpeted, and sang '*Te Deum laudamus*',
And Love on a lute loudly struck her string
    Ecce quam bonum et quam iocundum, &c.[2]

Langland Till the day dawned these damsels were dancing,
So that men rang out the Resurrection; and right with that
                                  I woke,
And called Kitty my wife and Calotte my daughter,
'Arise and reverence God's Resurrection,
And creep to the cross on your knees; kiss it for a jewel!
For God's blessed body it bore for our bettering,
And it puts the Fiend to fear, for such is its might
There may no grisly ghost glide where it shadows us!'

[1] Mercy and Truth are met together, Righteousness and Peace have kissed
each other.
[2] O how good and how joyful a thing it is, brethren, to dwell together in
Unity. (N.B. '*Unity*' is the name given later to the Barn that Piers builds, 'Holy
Church in English.')

PART IV

THE FOUNDING OF HOLY. CHURCH

Langland Thus I arose and wrote, right as I had dreamed,
And in my Sunday best, bundled off to church,
To hear the whole of mass and to make my communion.
In the middle of mass, as men made their offering,
I fell suddenly asleep and I saw, as soon, a vision,
Of Piers the Plowman, painted all in blood,
And coming with a cross before the common people;
Right like he was in every limb to our Lord Jesu;
And then I called to Conscience to tell me the truth.
'Is this Jesus, the Jouster?' said I, 'that the Jews did to death?
Or is it Piers the Plowman? Who painted him so red?'

Conscience Said Conscience, kneeling, 'These are the arms of Piers,
His colour in heraldry, his coat. But He who comes in them,
Covered in blood, is Christ with His cross, conqueror of
Christendom.'

Langland 'Why do you call Him Christ?' said I, 'since the Jews called
Him Jesus?
Patriarchs and prophets prophesied before
That all kinds of creature should kneel and acknowledge
At the naming of the Name of God Who is Jesus.
Ergo there's no name to match the name Jesus,
And none so needful, by night or by day.
For all the dark devils are in dread of hearing it,
And the sinful are solaced, and by that Name are saved.
And yet you call Him Christ; what causes you to do so?
Is "Christ" a mightier name, or of more honour
Than Jesus or Jesu, of which comes all our joy?'

Conscience 'You know well enough,' said Conscience, 'being nursed in
reason,
That knight, king, and conqueror may be one person.
To be called a knight is fair, for men shall kneel to him;
To be called a king is fairer, for he may create knights.
But to be called conqueror comes of a special grace,
A hardiness of heart, joined with gentleness.
He makes lords of the lads when he wins his lands,
And enthralls the free that follow not his laws.
Those Jews of gentle birth that despised Jesus,

His learning, and His Law, are now the lowest churls.
And those that became Christian, by the counsel of the Baptist,
Are franked and free, for they came to the font
Of gentle birth, like Jesus, for Jesus was baptised,
And upon Calvary, on a cross, crowned King of the Jews.
But as He conquered on that cross, in a noble conquest,
No death undoing Him, or bringing Him down,
(Rather He arose and reigned, ravishing hell),
He was then called "Conqueror of the Quick and Dead".
And He has given largely to His loyal liegemen
Their places in paradise at hence-parting.
Well may He be called "Conqueror"; that is what "Christ"
          means.
But the cause of His coming with the cross of His passion
Is to teach us by that token that when we are tempted,
We may fight and defend ourselves from falling into sin,
And see by His sorrow that he who longs for joy
Must put himself in patience to poverty and penance,
Willing well to suffer in a world of much sorrow.
  But to speak more of Christ, and how He came by that name,
To tell you justly, His first name was Jesus.
When He was born in Bethlehem, as the Book tells us,
And came incarnate; kings and angels
Reverenced Him fairly with the riches of the earth.
Angels out of heaven came kneeling and singing
    Gloria in excelsis Deo, &c.
Kings came afterwards, kneeling and offering
Myrrh and much gold, not asking mercy
Or any reward, but recognizing Him Sovereign
Of sand, sun, and sea; and they departed since,
To their kin and kingdoms, by the counsel of angels.
For all the angels of heaven were kneeling at His birth
And all the wisdom of the world was in those three kings.
  It becomes a conqueror to have care and cunning,
Wisdom and wiliness if he wills to be a leader;
And so, in His days, did Jesus, had I time to tell it,
Sometimes in suffering, sometimes in hiding,
Sometimes in fiercer fight, and other times fleeing.
Good he sometimes gave, and granted healing
In life and in limb, even as He liked.

In youth this Jesus, at a feast of the Jews,
Turned water into wine, as Holy Writ tells us,
And there began God of His grace to Do Well.
Before His Mother Mary that miracle He made,
That she, first and foremost, might firmly believe
That He was begotten by Grace, and by no other.
And when He became a man, in the absence of His Mother,
He made the lame to leap, and gave light to the blind,
And fed with two fishes, and with five loaves,
More than five thousand of His famished folk.
Thus, comforting the care-stricken, He caught a greater name,
And that was Do Better, wherever He went.
The deaf, through His doings, heard, and the dumb spoke,
And all were healed and helped that asked for His grace.
Then, in that country, He was called, by the common people
For all the deeds He did, Jesus, Son of David!
Therefore Caiaphas in envy, and other of the Jews
By day and by night sought to do Him to death,
And had Him killed, crosswise, on Calvary, on a Friday,
And buried His body; and, at their bidding,
Soldiers were sent, to keep it from night-comers,
Lest a fiend fetch Him; for prophets had foretold
That that blessed body should arise from burial
And go into Galilee to gladden His apostles.
Angels and archangels, ere the day sprang,
Came kneeling to His corpse and sang "*Christus resurgens*"
And Mary of Magdala met Him by the way,
Going towards Galilee in Godhead and manhood,
In man's living likeness, and she cried aloud
To the company, where she came, "*Christus resurgens!*"
And as all these wise ones, huddled together,
Were shut inside a house, and the door shackled,
Christ came in, (and all was closed, both door and gateway),
And to Peter and His apostles He said, "*Pax vobis!*"
And took Thomas by the hand, teaching him to grope
And feel with his fingers for His fleshly heart.
Thomas touched it, and said with his tongue,
    "*Deus meus et dominus meus.*"
And when this deed was done, He taught Do Best,
And gave Piers Plowman power and pardon,

For all manner of men, mercy and forgiveness,
Authority to absolve all sinners from their sins
If they came in covenant, confessing the account,
And pay for Piers' pardon; *Redde quod debes.*
  Thus has Piers the power, be his pardon paid for,
To bind and to unbind, both here and elsewhere,
And absolve every sin, save the sin of debt.
And He went thereafter high into Heaven;
There He lives, the Lord who will come at last
To give a right reward to *Reddit quod debet,*
To him who pays perfectly, as pure Truth would.'

Langland   Thus Conscience gave account of Christ and His cross,
And counselled me to kneel to it; and then I thought there came
One *Spiritus Paraclitus* to Piers and his fellows;
In the likeness of lightning He lit on them all.
I feared and faltered at the flame of fire
When the Holy Spirit overspread them all.
But Conscience, kneeling, cried,

Conscience   'This is Christ's messenger
Coming from great God, and His name is Grace.
Kneel we now,' said Conscience, 'and if you can sing,
Welcome Him and worship Him with "*Veni Creator Spiritus*".
  Then I sang that song, and so did many hundreds,
And cried out with Conscience, "Help us, God of Grace!"
And then began Grace to go with Piers Plowman
And counselled him and Conscience to call the common people,

Grace 'For I will deal out to-day, and divide my Grace
Among all kinds of creature that are capable of sense
A treasure to live by until their lives end,
And a weapon to fight with that will never fail.
For Anti-Christ and all his men shall menace the world
And encumber you, Conscience, unless Christ help you.
Therefore, ere I go, I will give you a treasure,
And a weapon to ward you when Anti-Christ attacks you.'

Langland   And He gave each man a grace to guide himself by,
          Divisiones graciarum sunt, &c.
And to some he gave the wit to handle words,
Wisdom to win a livelihood, as the world demands,
Such as preachers and priests and apprentices at law.
And some He taught a craft, or a capable foresight

In selling and buying to win themselves bread.
Some learnt to labour, a loyal life and true,
Some were taught tilling, ditching, and thatching,
And some learnt to live in longing to be hence
In poverty and penance to pray for all Christians.

Grace 'For I make Piers the Plowman my vicar and deputy
And registrar to receive *Redde quod debes.*
My plowman and provider Piers shall be on earth,
And that he may till the truth, he shall have a team!'

Langland Grace gave Piers a team, of four great oxen;
One was Luke, a large beast, lowly of heart;
One was Mark, one Matthew, mighty beasts both,
And joined one John to them, gentlest of all,
The pride of Piers' plow, surpassing all others.
    And Grace gave Piers four bullocks to bless him,
One was Augustine and Ambrose another,
Gregory the learned and Jerome the good.
These four, to teach the Faith, followed Piers' team,
Handily harrowing all Holy Scripture,
With two harrows they had, an old and a new one,
    Id est vetus testamentum et novum.
And Grace gave the grain, the cardinal virtues,
To sow in man's soul; these were the seeds.

(*Here follows a long account of* PRUDENCE, TEMPERANCE, FORTI-
TUDE, *and* JUSTICE, *the seeds in question.*)

Grace 'Against the time when your grain shall begin to ripen,
Build yourself a barn, Piers, to hold your harvest.'

Piers 'By God! Grace,' said Piers, 'you'll have to give me timber,
And base me my building before you depart.'

Langland And Grace gave him the cross, with the crown of thorns
That Christ had on Calvary for the sake of man;
And of His baptism and the blood that He bled from the cross,
He made a manner of mortar; and it was called Mercy.
And then Grace began to make a good foundation
And wattled it and walled it with His pain and passion,
And of all Holy Writ He made the roof afterwards
And called that house UNITY, Holy Church in English.
    And when this deed was done, Grace then ordained

A cart called Christendom, to carry Piers' sheaves,
And cart-horses He gave him, Contrition and Confession,
And Priesthood for a drover, and He Himself
Went as wide as the world is with Piers to till Truth.

THE ATTACK UPON IT

Langland   Now Piers is at the plough, and Pride espied it,
And gathered a great host together, to grieve him
And Conscience and all Christians and the cardinal virtues,
To blow them down and break them up and bite their roots
                          in two.

And he sent forth Sir Arrogant, his Serjeant-at-arms,
And his spy, Sir Spill-love, also called Speak-evil,
These two came to Conscience and all Christian people
And told them these tidings, that they would lose their toil,
And the seeds they had sown, the cardinal virtues;
And Piers' Barn would be broken;

Sir Spill-love   'And those that be in Unity
Should come out with Conscience and those two cart-horses,
Confession and Contrition; and the cart of the Creed
Should be coloured up quaintly and covered with sophistry,
So that Conscience couldn't tell Christians from heathen.'
  Said Conscience to all Christians,

Conscience   'My counsel is to come
Hastily into Unity, and hold ourselves there,
And pray there may be peace in the barn of Piers Plowman.'

Langland   Then Common-sense came with instructions to Conscience
And cried out commands to all Christian people
To dig a great ditch, deep about Unity.

Conscience   'I care not,' said Conscience, 'though Pride should come now,
The Lord of Lust shall gain little, all this Lent long.
Here is bread, blessed, and God's body thereunder,
For Grace, by God's word, has given Piers power
And might to make it, and man to eat it,
In help of their health, once in a month,
Or as often as they have need, that is, those who have paid
To the pardon of Piers their *Redde quod debes*.'

Community   'What!' said the Community, 'you advise us to pay
Any debt we may owe before taking communion?'

Conscierce   'That's my advice, and so say the virtues,
And sc says the *pater-noster*, that there may be pardon,
     Et dimitte nobis debita nostra, &c.
And thus be absolved, and so take communion.'

A Brewer 'Ya! Boo!' said a brewer, 'I won't be bound down
By Jesu! for all your juggling with *Spiritus Justitiae,*
Nor care much for Conscience, by Christ! if I can sell
The dregs and the draff, and draw the same bung
For thick ale and thin ale, for such is my nature,
Not hacking after holiness; hold your tongue, Conscience!'

THE COMING OF ANTI-CHRIST

Langland Then, as I went by the way, after I had awoken,
    Heavy in my spirit, and ailing at heart,
    I knew not where to eat or at what place.
    And it drew near to noon when I met with Need
    Who advanced viciously, and called me a vagabond.
 Need 'Can't you excuse yourself, as did King David,
    For filching a livelihood in food and clothing,
    According to the teaching of *Spiritus Temperantia*,
    That you took nothing but what Need dictated?
    Necessity knows no law, and never falls in debt.
    Three are the things he takes, if he wishes to thrive:
    Food, when men refuse him and he fails of money,
    (If he be caught in such a case, coming to it by theft,
    It is no serious sin, if so he win his food);
    So, when it comes to clothing, if he can claim no better,
    His immediate need will make his excuses.
    So if he longs for a lap of water to his lips
    He will be led by the law of nature
    To drink at any ditch ere he die of thirst.
    So at need, at greatest need, he may take his nourishment
    Without counsel from Conscience, or the cardinal virtues,
    Provided he pursues *Spiritus Temperantiae*;
    There's no virtue to touch *Spiritus Temperantiae*,
    Neither *Spiritus Fortitudinis*, nor *Spiritus Justitiae*,
    And *Spiritus Prudentiae* in many points will fail.
     Wise men have forsaken wealth, willing to be needy,
    Some went into the wilderness, abandoning their wealth.
    And God has gladly left His greatness of joy
    And came, taking manhood, and made Himself needy.
    So needy He was, says the Book, in sundry places,
    That He said in his sorrow, on the cross itself,
    "Both fox and fowl may fly to earth or nest,
    Fishes have fins that flicker them to safety,
    But Need has taken me where I must needs await
    And suffer my sour sorrows, that shall turn to joy."
    So never be abashed to beg, or to be needy,
    Since He that made the world was wilfully needy.

None was ever so needy, nor died so destitute.'
　As Need was pronouncing, I nodded off to sleep,
And imagined most marvellously that in man's form
Anti-Christ came; and all the crop of Truth
He turned upside-down and tore out by the roots,
Made wickedness to spring and spread and sponsor man's
　　　　　　　　　　　　　　　　　　　　　need;

In every country he came to, he cut away Truth,
And got Guile to grow there, as if he were a god.
Friars followed that fiend, for he gave them gifts,
The Religious reverenced him, and rung out their bells,
There came out of the convents a world of welcome,
These fellows, those fellows, all except fools;
And fools felt a longing for death, not for life,
Since they saw loyalty laid under rebuke.
And the false fiend Anti-Christ ruled over all folk.
Anti-Christ harboured hundreds at his banner,
Borne about boldly and brandished by Pride,
With a Lord, his lieutenant, who lived for his lusts.
　And then Conscience came, the keeper and guardian
Of all kind Christians and the cardinal virtues.

Conscience 'I counsel you,' said Conscience, 'come, Fools, in with me,
Into Unity, Holy Church; let us hold there,
And call to kind Nature to nurse and take care of us
Fools, from these limbs of the Fiend, for the love of Piers
　　　　　　　　　　　　　　　　　　　　　Plowman.

Let us cry to common people to come into Unity
And bide there for battle with the children of Belial.'

Langland　And Nature listened, and leapt to attack;
At the call of Conscience, he came out of the planets,
And sent forth his foragers, fevers and fluxions,
Coughings and cramps and cardiac troubles,
Colds, cancers, tooth-aches, terrible ulcers,
Scrofula, skin-disease, scabs and scurvy,
Boils and blisters and burning agues,
Frenzy and filthiness, the foragers of Nature,
Pricking and piercing and preying on the populace,
And a large legion of them lost their lives.

Populace 'Help!' they cried, 'Horror! Here comes Nature,
With Death the dreadful, to undo us all!'

Langland   The Lord that lived for his lusts then cried aloud
          Calling for Comfort, the knight of his banner,
  A Lord 'Arm yourselves! Arm yourselves! Each for himself!'
Langland   Old Age the hoary one hacked in the vanguard
          And bore the banner before Death, as befitted.
          And Nature came next with noxious diseases,
          Poxes and pestilence, pasting the peoples
          And rallying Corruption in ruin on the rout.
          Death came driving after, dashing all to dust,
          Kings and commanders, kaisers and popes;
          Learned and illiterate, none were left standing,
          Of those that he struck, none stirred again.
          Many a lovely lady and light-hearted lover
          Swooned and sickened in sorrow, at the dint of Death.
           Conscience compassionately called upon Nature
          To cease his assault and see who were ready
          To part with their pride and be perfect Christians;
          And Nature relented to mark their amendment.
           Then Fortune flattered the few left alive
          With the lure of long life, and sent Lechery forth
          Among all manner of men, married and single,
          And gathered a great host, to go against Conscience.
          Lechery laid it on with a laughing look,
          Whispering promises and painted words.
          Then came Covetousness, casting about
          How to overcome Conscience and the cardinal virtues,
          And armed with avarice, he hunted in hunger,
          All his weapons were wiles for winning and hoarding.
Conscience 'Alas!' cried Conscience, 'Would that Christ in mercy
          Could make a Christian of Covetousness, that is so keen a
                                                fighter!'

Langland   And then Life laughed, and flaunted his feathers,
          Hastily armed in a hauberk of harlotry,
          And held Holiness a joke and Humbleness a waster
          Loyalty a churl and Liar a champion.
          Conscience and counsel he accounted folly.
          Thus Life relied for a little on Fortune
          And pranced forth with Pride, approving no virtue,
          Not caring if Nature should come, as she will,
          And kill all earthly creatures, save only Conscience.

Life leapt aside and landed on a lover.

Life 'Health and I', said he, 'and highness of heart
Shall deliver you from dread, from Death and Old Age,
From sorrow and suffering and the thought of sin.'

Langland Life found her to his liking, his lover Dame Fortune,
And begot, in their glory, a son who was Sloth.
And Sloth grew up suddenly, and was soon of age,
And was wedded to Despair, a wench from the stews.
Then care-stricken Conscience cried to Old Age
And begged him to come and to combat Despair.
And Old Age took hope, and made shift in haste,
And spurning Despair, he launched against Life,
And Life fled for fear and foraged for physic,
Not doubting a Doctor could drive away Age,
And deliver him from Death with drugs and lotions.
And Old Age came after me, over my head,
And made me bald in front, and bare on my crown.
He hit me so hard it will mark me for ever.
'Ill-mannered Old Age!' said I, 'Evil attend you!
Since when was there right-of-way over my head?
If you were polite, you'd have asked my permission!'

Old Age 'Yes, indeed, dear my lord,' said he, laying upon me,

Langland And dotted me on the ear; I am almost deaf.
He buffeted me about the mouth, and beat out my teeth,
And gravelled me with gout, I can't get about.
Of the woe I endured, my wife had such pity
She whole-heartedly wished I would wake up in heaven.
The limb she loved me for, and was fain to feel
Especially at night, when we lay naked,
I was by no means able to nourish her with;
She and Old Age had beaten it down.
And as I sat in this sorrow, I saw how Nature passed
And Death drew nigh me, and I quaked for dread,
And I called out to Nature, to bring me out of care.
'Look! Old Age, the hoary one is hot on my tracks!
Help and avenge me! Would I were hence!'

Old Age 'If you hope for help, you must hasten into Unity;
Hold you there for ever, until I send for you;
And try to learn some trade there, before you travel thence.'

Langland 'O Nature, let me know,' said I, 'what trade is best to learn?'

Nature '*Learn to love,*' said Nature, '*and leave all other learning.*'

Langland 'How then shall I come,' said I, 'to food and clothing?'

Nature 'If you love loyally,' said Nature, 'you shall never lack
For food or for clothing, long as life may last.'

Langland And there, by the direction of Nature, I began to roam
Through Contrition and Confession, till I came to Unity,
Where Conscience is the constable to save Christians,
Savagely besieged by the seven great giants
That held with Anti-Christ, hard against Conscience.
Sloth with his sling pressed hard in his assault,
And Pride with the priesthood, more than a thousand,
Came against Conscience and allied with Covetousness.

An Irish 'By Mary!' said an unfrocked priest from the frontiers of
Priest   Ireland,
'I count no more for Conscience, if I can catch some silver,
Than I do when I'm drinking a draught of good ale!'

Langland And so said sixty, from the same country.

In Unity, in Holy Church, Conscience held firmly,
And made Peace porter, to padlock the gates
Against all tale-tellers and idle tittle-tattle.
Hypocrisy and they made powerful assault,
Wickedly they wounded many a wise teacher
In accord with Conscience and the cardinal virtues.
Conscience called Doctor Shrift to deal with them kindly.

Conscience 'Go and salve those that are sick, and by their sins wounded.'

Langland And Shrift, with a sharp salve, made them show penitence
And pay Piers the Plowman *Redde quod debes.*
Some disliked this doctor, and sent out letters
If there were any surgeon at the siege with a softer plaster.
Sir Love-to-lie-in-lechery lay there and groaned
And from his Friday fasting was afraid to die.

Sir Love-to- 'There's a surgeon at this siege that can handle softly,
lie-in-lechery And knows far more of physic, and has finer plasters,
One Friar Flatterer, surgeon and physician.'

Contrition Contrition said to Conscience, 'Let him come to Unity,
For here are many men, hurt by hypocrisy.'

Conscience 'No need,' (said Conscience) 'I know of none better
Than a parson or parish-priest when it comes to penance,

Except Piers the Plowman, who has power over all.
Yet, I am willing,' (said Conscience) 'if it is your wish,
To fetch Friar Flatterer, to physic the sick.'

Langland   The friar heard of this and hurried apace
And came where Conscience was, and clanged at the gate.
Peace unpinned it, the porter of Unity,
And quickly demanded what he could do for him.

Friar   'Faith,' said this friar, 'for the sake of health and profit,
I would catechize Contrition, that's why I came here.'

Peace   'He is sick,' said Peace, 'and so are many others,
Hypocrisy has hurt them; they can hardly recover.'

Friar   'I am a surgeon,' the friar said, 'and can make salves;
Conscience knows me well, and my work too.'

Peace   'Please let me know,' said Peace, 'before you pass,
What is your name? I should like to know it.'

Friar   'Certainly,' said this fellow, 'Sir *Penetrans Domos*.'

Peace   'Oh? Then be off with you, you and your physic;
If you can't do a job, there's no joining us here!
I knew one of your kind, eight winters ago,
Who looked after my lord, and my lady as well;
In the end this physician (my lord being absent)
Had so doctored our women that some were with child!'

Langland   Fair-speech then bade Peace to open the gates,

Fair-speech   'Let the friar come in; we'll find him a welcome.
It may happen so he will see and hear something
To teach Life a lesson and release him from Avarice,
And in the dread of death to withdraw him from Pride
And accord with Conscience; they shall kiss each other.'

Langland   So, thanks to Fair-speech, the friar came in,
And Conscience accosted him, with courteous greeting.

Conscience   'You are welcome,' said Conscience, 'Can you heal the sick?
Here is Contrition, my cousin, terribly wounded;
Comfort her,' said Conscience, 'take care of her sores.
The parson with his plasters and powders stings to the quick;
He lets them lie too long, and is loth to change them,
Lent after Lent he lets his plasters bite her.'

The Friar   'That's far too long,' said this friar, 'I think I can relieve her.'

Langland   And off he goes and gropes, and gives her a plaster
Of private payment;

The Friar   'And I shall pray for you,

[122]

And mention you, madam, in mass and at matins,
As a friar of our fraternity, for a little silver.'

Langland So on he went, and made his winnings, with wily absolution,
Till Contrition had clean forgotten her crying and weeping,
And lying wakeful for her wickedness, as she was wont.
Sloth saw this, and so did Pride,
And came keenly on to the conquest of Conscience.
Conscience cried out and bade Clergy to help him
And called on Contrition to keep the gate shut.

Peace 'He lies asleep, dreaming,' said Peace 'and so do many others;
This friar with his physic has bewitched the world,
His plasters are so easy, no one fears to sin.'

Conscience 'By Christ,' said Conscience then, 'I will become a pilgrim
And wander as wide as the world may last
To seek Piers the Plowman who can destroy Pride
That counter-pleads Consciencc. Now, Nature, avenge me,
And send me good hap and health till I have Piers the
Plowman!'

Langland He grasped after Grace, and I began to waken.

EXPLICIT

APPENDIX

The Author
The Texts A, B, and C
The Form and Meaning of the Poem
Medieval Allegory
The Metre
Some Forms of the Half-line
The Present Version

THE AUTHOR

Nothing is known for certain of the author of *Piers Plowman*, or, to give the poem its full title, *The Vision of William about Piers the Plowman and the Visions of the Same about Do-Well, Do-Better, and Do-Best*. Some scholars have doubted whether it was the work of one man, some have even thought it the work of five or six successively. No fourteenth-century record has yet been found that refers beyond doubt to its author. Although the poem had an immense popularity in that and the next century, nothing except his poem remains to prove that he existed. There is what seems to be an allusion to it in the famous letter of John Ball, the revolutionary of 1381, writing to incite the people of Essex:

'. . . greteth welle Johan Nameles, and Johan the Mullere, and Johan Cartere, and biddeth hem that thei ware of gyle in borugh, and stondeth togiddir in Goddis name, and biddeth *Peres Plou3man* go to his werke, and chastise welle Hobbe the robber, and taketh with 3ou Johan Trewman, and alle his felaws. . . . And *do welle and bettre*, and fleth synne, and seketh pees, and holde therynne. . . .'

But it is not impossible that these italicized phrases, like the other stock names in the quotation, come from a general idiom of oral tradition from which the author of *Piers Plowman* may also have taken them, and John Ball's use of them may be a natural coincidence.

The popularity of the poem, however, is proved by the fact that some three score manuscripts have come down to us from the fifteenth century. Among these is the Trinity College Dublin MS., which contains a marginal note asserting in Latin that one Stacy de Rokayle was the father of William de Langlond, that this Stacy was a gentleman and lived at Shipton-under-Wychwood in Oxfordshire, that he was a tenant of the Despensers, and that the aforesaid William made the book which is called *Piers Plowman*.

This information is partly confirmed by a note in the Huntingdon MS.: 'Robert or William langland made pers ploughman', and by the assertion of Robert Crowley, who was the first to print the poem (in 1550). He wrote: 'Beyinge desyerous to knowe the name of the Autoure of thys most worthy worke, (gentle reader) . . . I haue learned that the Autour was named Roberte langelande, a Shropshere man borne in Cleybirie, aboute viii. myles from Maluerne hilles.

Wherever the author refers to himself by name in the poem he calls himself Will (once 'Long Will'), which leads one to believe that 'Robert' is a blunder.

The discrepancies between these various accounts and topographical fact (Cleybirie, or Cleobury Mortimer, is not eight but twenty-three miles from the Malverns), have been much argued by scholars and variously fitted to the fragments of information about the author that are volunteered in the poem itself. Mr. A. H. Bright (in *New Light on Piers Plowman*) has plausibly conjectured that 'Cleybirie' is a mistake for 'Ledbury', and he has, further, found a field in that district, near the village of Colwall, that is still named *Longlands*. It lies to the south of Ledbury Hospital and to the east of the railway line running from Worcester through Malvern to Hereford. He has also discovered an entry showing that at the parish church of Bromyard, on 20 December, 1348, John de Trillek, Bishop of Hereford, ordained one *Willelmus de Colewell*, an acolyte. This may well be our William, for the date fits with the date of the poet's birth (1332), inferred from a passage in the poem. This passage occurs in the B Text (see below) that can be roughly dated 1376-7. In it the poet says he has been followed by 'Imaginative' (that is, roughly speaking, by his *memory*) for forty-five winters. By subtracting forty-five from 1377 we reach the date 1332, perhaps as near as we shall ever get to the date of Langland's birth.

To spare longer argument I offer a brief life of the poet which I believe to be substantially true, compiled from such sources as I have mentioned, from what the poem itself says of its author, and from the work of other scholars in the field, particularly the late Mr. A. H. Bright and the late Professor R. W. Chambers, whose chapters on *Piers Plowman* in his book, *Man's Unconquerable Mind*, put forward a masterly exposition of the poem.

Towards the year 1331, Stacy ('Eustace', as we should call him) de Rokayle went to visit the Despensers, his overlords, at Hanley Castle, near the Malvern Hills. While in the neighbourhood he met some now nameless bondwoman who probably lived in a cottage near the field called Longlands. Upon her he begot a boy who was then named William at the font and took his surname from the field where his mother lived. It is not known whether Stacy married this woman or not, but it is an inference (too easy perhaps) that he did not do so, from the fact that his son did not take the name Rokayle.

Stacy did not neglect him, however, but had him sent to school, probably at Malvern Priory, with a view to fitting him for a career in the church. He enjoyed his schooling and made enough progress to be ordained an acolyte at the age of sixteen or so. It is not impossible that he later became a deacon or even a priest (notwithstanding that he seems to have married), though there is no positive evidence that he did. All that we are told of this by the poet (and he is the only authority) is that he made a kind of living later on in London by saying prayers for men richer than himself.

He says he was a long-limbed, weak-backed boy, unfitted for farm-work. But he was evidently endowed with a strong common sense, a great aptitude for learning and an imagination ready to fill itself with living vision of the Christian universe. Nothing else made sense for him of a life lived in grinding poverty and a callous world in which fortune had failed him.

For in early manhood he set out to seek his fortune. He left the mists of Malvern, 'moneyless', he says, and looked to London for a livelihood. There he lived, perhaps for the rest of his life. At first, he tells us, he followed the desires of the flesh ('*Concupiscentia Carnis*', he calls them), and the pride of life ('*Pruyde-of-parfit-lyuynge*'), and suffered an all-unsatisfied hunger for possessions ('*Couetyse-of-eyen*').

Some time later he took a wife called Kitty and had a daughter by her, Calotte. All three lived in a hovel in Cornhill. He was regarded with distaste as an eccentric who lolled his way through life, and did nothing except say prayers for pittances, lazily accepting his poverty. He lived, he says, both in London and on London.

All this time he was writing and re-writing *Piers Plowman*. Gradually old age came upon him, baldness, toothlessness, and gout. His death is not recorded. A reasonable guess would place it towards 1400, the year also of Chaucer's death. Chaucer lies buried in Westminster Abbey, but where Langland lies is lost beyond conjecture.

THE TEXTS A, B, AND C

Apart from the manuscripts and Robert Crowley's first printed edition, already mentioned, of which there were three impressions, there was an edition by Owen Rogers in 1561, and then nothing until Whitaker's edition of 1813, which was followed by Wright's in 1842, revised and enlarged in 1856. Then, in 1886, the splendid and scholarly edition of W. W. Skeat appeared and is still the standard text. This is the one I have followed. It is true that in the light of more recent scholarship much revision of Skeat's edition will be required before a final and definitive text can appear. Professor Chambers, until his lamented death, was at work on one with Professor Grattan, but the immensity of the task undertaken at their level of scholarship did not permit its completion. Their work, which I understand has established the A Text, has not yet appeared, and so Skeat's edition remains standard for the present. It is a consolation to know that Professor Chambers held the highest opinion of it.

Just as there is doubt as to the author's life, so there is doubt as to what he wrote and how he wrote it. The manuscripts are incredibly divergent in detail as well as in the larger matter of the shape or disposition of the poem. Roughly speaking, they present the poem in three main forms to one or other of which each group of manuscripts mainly conforms. These are called the A, B, and C Texts.

The A Text is the earliest and can be roughly dated, by a fluke of internal evidence, to the year 1362, or a little later. This is the fluke: on *Saturday*, 15 January, 1362, there was a prolonged *south-westerly gale* that blew with great violence. It not only blew down trees and even belfries, but also blew its way into contemporary chronicles, such as Walsingham's *Historia Anglicana*, where it is recorded with amazement. This can be no other than the storm that Langland took to be God's judgment on English pride:

> He proved that these pestilences were for pure sin,
> And the *south-west wind on a Saturday*, at evening,
> Was patently for pure pride, and for no other point.

As this passage occurs early in the A Text, we cannot suppose much, if any at all, to have been written before 1362. It may well have been written later, but there are some corroborative hints, also in the A Text, that lead one to think that that year was very fresh in Langland's mind when he wrote.

The B Text (mainly followed in this translation) is about three times as long as the A Text and is a revision of it, including and expanding almost everything in it, and adding a great sequel (if that is the right expression). This sequel includes a long new meditation by the poet on his earlier visions and follows them with an intensely vivid account, arising from these meditations, of the Incarnation and Passion of Christ, the Descent into Hell, the founding of His Church, and the attack upon it by Anti-Christ.

The date of the B Text is also partly in doubt, but another fluke of allusion allows us to believe that revision was in progress between 1376 and 1377. The allusion comes in the fable of Belling the Cat (see page 19). There we are told about the old Cat (Edward III), and the poet remarks that where the Cat is a kitten the Court is in trouble. The kitten can only mean Richard, Edward's grandson, and seems to assume a situation in which Richard is to succeed him. That being so, Richard's father, the Black Prince, must have been dead at the time of writing, but Edward III still alive. Now the Black Prince died in 1376, and Edward III in the following year, and therefore this part at least of the B Text must belong to 1376-7.

The C Text is only a little longer than the B Text and differs from it mainly in arrangement, though there are innumerable changes of phrase, excisions, and interpolations. Save for a flash of the old fire here and there these changes seem to me changes for the worse. It is the B Text that is poetically the most tremendous of the three.

The C Text cannot be exactly dated. The consensus of scholarly opinion places it between 1392 and 1398, but this is guesswork. If this, too, is by Langland (and some scholars deny it to him) the poem as a whole must have been his lifework, a poetical and religious meditation lasting up-wards of thirty years. After the opening burst of vision the poem, I think, must have continued to flash and rumble round his mind for the rest of his days. It is not known that he ever wrote anything else.

THE FORM AND MEANING OF THE POEM

Here we are in deep water and in this brief Appendix only a very summary exposition can be attempted to deal with the most obvious and important things.

The poem falls into four great sections, each as it were a continent of meaning. The first is the vision of Piers Plowman proper and is given, with a few omissions, in Part I of this version. It is a picture of fourteenth-century England judged by the standards of Christianity. It begins with a picture of the human predicament, seen as a field full of folk intent on earning a living, both honestly and not. The field is flanked by the Tower of Truth (heaven) and a dark Dungeon (hell), the alternative but eternal destinies of this folk, who, for the most part, take no notice of either, being too busy at their various jobs and jobberies.

All this raises the question of the true purpose of life, which is answered by Holy Church. The end of life, she says, is Truth, which is Love, which are God. Man, made in His image, should live for Him in Truth (honesty) and Love (neighbourly loving-kindness), and she speaks of these things and of her authority over the dreaming poet.

There follows a vision of the opposite of Truth, Lady Meed, who embodies the notion, ancient and modern, that money is the root of all evil. She is seen about to be married to False Fickletongue, and is endowed at the wedding with the lordship of the Seven Deadly Sins. She is surrounded by all Officialdom and we gradually become aware that this is a satirical vision of England as she was administered in those days. The wedding of Lady Meed is challenged and she is brought before the king who attempts to persuade Conscience to marry her instead. After a long debate during which Reason is sent for to advise, the king declares he will in future rule by Conscience and Reason. What happened to Lady Meed we are not told; she had served the poet's purpose sufficiently in his exposition of the evils of government, bribery and simony. Another political evil, the oppression exercised by the nobility on chance villages through which they and their retinues might be riding, is complained of by Peace, who appears in the middle of the trial of Meed.

The dreamer then returns to the Field of Folk, where Reason preaches a sermon before the king and his people, and Repentance brings them to confession. The mouthpieces of England in this are the Seven Deadly Sins, Meed's marriage portion. What they have to confess is in Langland's liveliest style and pictures the evils at large in society, rather than those that beset government.

The penance imposed after confession is a pilgrimage to seek Saint Truth. But no one can tell where he lives until a simple farmer 'puts forth his head' from the crowd of penitents. This is the first entry of Piers Plowman into the poem. Here he stands for an honest and neighbourly way of Christian life, which if it were followed (and he gives the necessary instructions) would lead the folk to salvation. But the way seems too hard for them without a guide, so they ask Piers to lead them. He replies that he will do so if they will first help him to harrow his half-acre.

This is another symbol for the world itself, and is the means by which Langland turns to consider the economic evils of his day, famine and unemployment. In a lively picture of the work done and not done, we are shown that hard work will banish famine. As for the unemployed, those that are genuinely bedridden are promised equal sustenance with Piers himself. Those that will not work are to be supported by a dole, for even they are the blood-brothers of Piers in Christ, and 'fear of famine is no final love'. But if they want better fare, let them work for it.

England is now ready for her pardon, and Truth sends her one through Piers. It lay in two lines, taken from the Athanasian Creed:

> Et qui bona egerunt ibunt in vitam eternam
> Qui vero mala in ignem eternum.

This baleful promise ('Those who do well will go into eternal life, but those who do ill into eternal fire') is disputed by a priest in the company who says it is not a pardon at all, but a statement of merciless justice, an eye for an eye and a tooth for a tooth. An altercation arises between the priest and Piers. Piers loses heart and tears up his pardon, preferring to devote himself to prayer, contemplation and trust in God, rather than to be busy about his belly-joys. By this hint we see Piers changing from his character as an honest simple layman and taking on the function of a priest or religious contemplative. It is the change from Do Well to Do Better. The dreamer then awakes and Piers vanishes from the poem for a long time. When he returns to it, at the beginning of the third great section of the poem, he is no longer a simple farmer, but a teacher of the meaning of charity and of the nature of the Trinity. Meanwhile the dreamer, having awoken, wanders a long time, 'meatless and moneyless in the Malvern Hills', pondering what the pardon of Piers can have meant.

The second great section or continent of meaning gives us the results of his ponderings. In this version are offered a selection of them, those passages that seemed to me most typical and poetic; much, however, has been cut, for his subject leads Langland into many theological disquisitions no longer suited to modern taste. such as it is.

In the original Langland threads his meditations on a ghostly sort of narrative of his own mental development. He meets with various phantoms, each a stage in his education, such as Thought, Wit, Clergy, Scripture, Imaginative and others, and asks them the meaning of Do Well (*qui bona egerunt*) since salvation depends, according to the 'pardon', on knowing. By an easy grammatical jump, Do Well multiplies itself into Do Better and Do Best, and these three seem to represent respectively the active or lay life, the priestly or contemplative life, and the episcopal life of governing authority over Christendom, humanly speaking. It will be seen at once that Piers stands for each of these in turn, and so is in a sense omnipresent in the poem, though he so seldom appears in person.

In addition to the search for the moral nature of these three lives, this second section of the poem covers many other theological and social problems, notably the effectualness of Faith as opposed to Works (and vice-versa), the value of learning in the search for salvation, the beauty and hatefulness of poverty, the prevalence of sin and hypocrisy, the problem whether the heathen can be saved, predestination, the order of Nature, and the quality of Charity. It is the moral backbone of the poem as a whole.

In these tangles of theology and speculation Langland's more obvious kind of poetic force is at times diminished. The wonder to us (less addicted as we are to such meditations) is that it was not extinguished. He himself admits freely that theology has troubled him 'many score times'. But he struggled through and said what he had to say, often magnificently enough, as may be seen from the excerpts here rendered. They represent fairly, with some omissions, the general gist of this part of the poem.

The third great section begins with the re-entry of Piers into the poem. He appears in a vision to the dreamer and tells him of the Tree of Charity that grows in the arbour of the human heart, supported by the three great balks that are the Holy Trinity against the winds of the world, the flesh, and the fiend.

Then begin the first adumbrations of the great theme that is to swell into the crowning glory of the poem: the life and passion of Christ and the descent into hell. One of the skills of this poet, whether used with calculation, or manifesting a lovely but unselfconscious turn of mind I do not know, is to sound a theme or the fragment of a theme among the other music of his thoughts, and then, later, and after the reader has forgotten it in other interests, to return to it in strength. It can have the effect of that distant trumpet that startles the Leonora Overture of Beethoven, far off at first, and then, later, close and splendid. In a like way the story of the Incarnation as told in *Piers Plowman* begins to steal on the reader from the first notes sounded by Holy Church (page 24); then it swells in the words of Repentance, speaking in mercy after the confession of the Deadly Sins (page 44), and now returns once more in the mouth of the dreamer under the visitation of Piers (page 87). It will return again in final solemnity when we reach the first Palm Sunday of the world. But first Langland chooses to gather up those tortuous strands of argument he had struggled with in the antithesis of Faith and Works. Being a poet, he found them easier to express visually than logically. And so we meet with Abraham who stands for Faith, and Moses who is also called *Spes* (Hope) and who promises salvation to those who obey the commandments that have been entrusted to him. That is, he promises salvation to men by their *Works*.

But there is a third and more excellent virtue, Charity, of which he had said so much, that must also enter the picture. And this it does in the person of the Good Samaritan. The dreamer walked in his dream with Abraham and Moses, 'wording it', as he says, in their contention as to which could save more souls. And as they did so they were overtaken by the Good Samaritan, *riding upon a mule*, and all four came upon the man who had fallen among thieves. At the sight of him Faith and Hope (Abraham and Moses) fled away on one side, like the priest and Levite in the parable; but Charity alighted and tended him.

One might think that allegorical vision could go no further than this in drawing meaning, on a new plane, from our Lord's greatest parable. Yet there is more, for the Good Samaritan explains afterwards to the dreamer that the man who fell among thieves is mankind itself, fallen by a theft from Paradise, and there is no medicine in the world to heal him but the blood of a child born of a maid. Yet he says Faith and Hope are necessary, too, and he teaches the dreamer how the Trinity may be understood as a hand, fist, palm, and fingers, or as torch, wax, wick, and flame proceeding from them.

Then Langland falls into another dream; it is Lent and he finds himself in Jerusalem, and there comes one *riding upon an ass*, like to the Samaritan, and something like Piers Plowman; and it is Faith that tells him it is Jesus, wearing the armour of Piers, *humana natura*; our suit, as Repentance had called it so long before (page 44).

The story of the Crucifixion follows, and the Descent into Hell, the finest things in all *Piers Plowman*, and with the ringing of the bells of London on Easter morning Langland awakes and takes his wife and daughter to mass. So ends the third great section of the poem, called by Langland the Vision of Do Better. Do Better is the life of a priest, teaching, healing, and suffering, and its exemplar is Christ, seen as Piers.

The last section of the poem, called the Vision of Do Best, tells of the Authority over sin and death won by Christ, and how He delegated it to the Apostles. And then it is told how the Spirit of the Holy Ghost overspread them all, and how Piers Plowman was commissioned to build a great barn to be called *Unity*, Holy Church in English. Piers has thus become Do Best, Peter, the first bishop of the Church, and the successors of Peter. It is the life of Authority.

The barn is built and the seed of the cardinal virtues is sown. But Anti-Christ launches his attack, and there are found many traitors to join him. In sore need Conscience calls on Nature to help her and the simple (the 'fools'), who have taken refuge in Unity. Nature hears the call and pours out plagues upon humanity to put the fear of death in them and so the fear of God. It is a *memento mori* to prompt repentance.

The attack of Anti-Christ continues, and inside Holy Church there are many wounded, especially Contrition. A fellow-travelling Friar gains admission with a promise to cure her. He cures her so well that she no longer weeps for her sins. Seeing this, Pride from without renews the assault and Conscience calls out in an utterance that ends the poem:

> 'By Christ!' said Conscience then, 'I will become a pilgrim
> And wander as wide as the world may last
> To seek Piers the Plowman who can destroy Pride
> That counter-pleads Conscience. Now, Nature, avenge me,
> And send me good hap and health till I have Piers the Plowman!'
> He grasped after Grace, and I began to waken.

In this may be seen an allegory for all times when authority seems to have failed or disappeared and the individual soul is forced back on the pure strength of conscience, from which alone, humanly speaking, authority can be re-established. But perhaps Langland had in mind the specific predicament of his own age and the crisis in Christendom that followed the Great Schism. While he was re-writing his poem (in the B version) men were perishing in Europe, Englishmen among them, in the wars between pope and anti-pope. Authority was divided against itself.

MEDIEVAL ALLEGORY

A brief note on this highly philosophical and complex subject may here be offered. Medieval allegory at its best was not a writer's trick or a piece of excogitated ingenuity, but a whole way of looking at experience. It was based in the belief that the Universe was all of a piece, that the greater was reflected in the less, that one thing could be understood through another, that God could be known through His works. Man, as this poem repeatedly asserts, was made in His image. Thus what is true on one plane of meaning must reveal some truth on another. All experience, therefore, is packed with meanings at various levels, and one of the functions of a poet, the chief function according to Dante and Boccaccio, is allegorical, to interpret or present the unknown through the known. Shakespeare had a like view:

> And, as imagination bodies forth
> The forms of things unknown, the poet's pen
> Turns them to shapes . . .

I have been told by a friend that the late Eric Gill claimed never to have created a major work without having three simultaneous meanings for it in his head. The statue, for instance, of the sage and the child over the entrance to Broadcasting House (he said) represented (a) the Governors of the Corporation sending forth their messages to the world, (b) the Shakespearian vision of Prospero and Ariel and all that it may suggest, and (c) God the Father sending forth the Word. If this anecdote is true, as I believe, it indicates a trebly rich way of artistic creation very like the medieval ways of allegory. Allegory was then the life, not the death, of poetry.

There was a secular as well as a religious kind of allegory, but both were organized on like principles (for in the Middle Ages, when clarity and logic were so important and the Latin mind in dominance, there were logical schemes underlying the airiest fancies).

In England, Chaucer may stand for the greatest secular, and Langland for the greatest religious, allegorist. Briefly the principles of secular allegory were as follows: in every allegorical poem there tended to be at least three planes of meaning. First, the simple meaning of the story, considered as mere narrative. This was called *sensus litteralis*. Secondly, the transferred meaning, its parable-sense, from which the reader could infer his own situation, or as in the case of some of Chaucer's allegories and Langland's, too, a contemporary social or political event. This was called *sensus allegoricus*. Thirdly, the moral meaning, extracted by the poet and peppered through the poem, or put as a conclusion in aphoristic form. A large number of the *Canterbury Tales* are treated in this way by Chaucer, sometimes in earnest, sometimes with a laugh. This was called *sensus moralis*.

Religious allegory added a fourth plane of meaning, sometimes hinted at in secular allegory (for instance, in the *Parliament of Fowls*), which adumbrated the spiritual world of being. In its intensest form it was a transference of the meaning seen on the human plane to 'the life in eternal glory'. I think this way of interpretation arose from the Biblical studies of the early Fathers of the Church. To them the Bible was a repository of information, divinely revealed, (a) about the history of the creation and what followed from it, (b) about their own personal human predicaments, (c) about moral truth, and (d) about the life of God. This fourth was called *sensus anagogicus*.

Piers Plowman constantly exhibits all these four meanings, often simultaneously, sometimes one or more at a time. This should be borne in mind if the richest and deepest meanings are to be derived from reading it. As anagogical thinking no longer comes easily to us, an example or two from *Piers Plowman* may help. Man, says the poem, is made in God's image. Therefore what is true of man (but for his Fall) is in some transferred sense also true of God. For instance, there are three (no more) ways of Good Life, called in the poem Do Well, Do Better, and Do Best. Do Well is the Active, that *creates* that by which we live. Do Better is the Contemplative or Priestly that helps in our *redemption* by teaching, healing, and suffering. Do Best is the life of Authority that governs and *inspires* the Church by which, spiritually, we live. Thus the possible activities of man are a trinity, paralleled in Heaven by God-Creator, God-Redeemer, and God-Inspirer. The first section of the poem considers God mainly as Creator, the third mainly as Redeemer, and the fourth mainly as the inspiration of the Church. I have no doubt that this was part of Langland's conscious plan. Not that he excogitated it, but that when he looked at life, that was what he saw.

To give another example, I would again refer to the story of the Good Samaritan and the identification of him with Charity, with Piers and with Jesus. Here the *sensus litteralis* is the parable itself, considered as narrative; the *sensus allegoricus*, bound up with it, is the dreamer's personal situation present with Piers in the story, and the questions it prompts him to ask (and us, too); the *sensus moralis* is what it teaches us of Charity, and the *sensus anagogicus* is in the identity of Piers and the Good Samaritan with Christ, the priestly love of God.

It may be added that allegory is not meant to be *explained* but *perceived imaginatively*. Explanation, of its nature, is far too categoric, and the thing explained dwindles in proportion as it is merely intellectual, a thing of the brain rather than of the total perception of one's whole imaginative being. Explanation is a key, not an opening door; but if it fits it has its uses.

THE METRE

The metre of the original is unruly though descended from a style of some severity and stateliness, the measure of *Beowulf* and *Judith*, a courtly, complex manner of versification. But by Langland's time it had run wild, a metrical Perdita of royal origin in shepherd clothing. It ranged from Chester to the Severn, for the most part, driven west by the social after-effects of the Conquest, one supposes. Several other fine poems remain, coming from that time and region in their somewhat ragged Anglo-Saxon dress. But *Piers Plowman* is the greatest, and perhaps the last until modern times, that need be mentioned. Recently Mr. Auden's *Age of Anxiety* has finely revived something like it, and there are reminiscences of it in some poems by Mr. W. R. Rodgers.

Though it is a difficult metre to write in (at least for those brought up in a syllable-counting tradition), it is easy to read, for the natural sense follows the beat; it is like emphatic talk. For it was a rule in *Beowulf*, intuitively observed by Langland also, that the stresses must be filled by important words, such as nouns, adjectives, verbs, and occasionally adverbs. He seldom goes lower in the hierarchy to fill a stress. Between stresses, in the dip of the wave, there may be any convenient number of light, unimportant syllables, just as when we speak.

Fundamentally every line is divided, for metrical purposes, into two half-lines, and in the last analysis the half-line, not the line, is the unit of composition. Consequently every line has a pause in the middle that must be felt for when reading aloud. In conformity with the first rule, that pause marks a pause, great or small, in the sense. Very rarely does the sense overrun this caesura and it almost never overruns the end of the line.

The gap made by this pause is bridged by alliteration, and the alliteration, in theory, can only fall on stressed words. The normal Anglo-Saxon line had two such stresses in each half-line, and the rule was that in the first half of a line either or both of these stressed words could alliterate, but in the second half-line only the first stressed word could do so. Often this happens in *Piers Plowman*, for instance in the second line of the poem:

> I *sh*ope me in *sh*roudes / as I a *sh*épe were
> (I shook on some shreds / of shepherd clothing)

However, the original rules were far more elaborate than this, and traces of them remain everywhere in Langland's work. Some instances of the more important elaborations may be given.

SOME FORMS OF THE HALF-LINE

In *Beowulf* there were five permissible types of half-line, each capable of minor variation. Ignoring the variations, the five types may be represented thus, with examples of them added from *Piers Plowman*, as nearly as I have found them occurring.

TYPE	EXAMPLE	MEANING
A] ́ × ́ ×	Worchyng and Wandryng (B. Prol. 19)	Working and wandering
	Feynen hem Fantasies (B. Prol. 36)	Feigned fantasies for themselves
	Fayteden for here Fode (B. Prol. 42)	Shammed sick for their food
B × ́ × ́	As it Semeth to owre Sy3t (B. Prol. 32)	As it seems to our sight
	Thei Went forth in here way (B. Prol. 48)	They went forth on their way
	His seel shulde nou3t be sent (B. Prol. 79)	His seal should not be sent
C] × ́ ́ ×	Ac on a May Mornynge (B. Prol. 5)	But on a May morning
	In a Somer Seson (B. Prol. 1)	In a summer season
	And somme chosen chaffare (B. Prol. 31)	And some chose business
D] ́ / ́ × ́	Went / Wyde in this World (B. Prol. 4)	Went widely in this world
	Crist / Kepe the, sire Kyng (B. Prol. 125)	Christ keep thee, Sir King
	Beren / Bi3es ful Bri3te (B. Prol. 161)	Bear very bright collars
E] ́ ́ × / ́	Deuine 3e, for I ne Dar (B. Prol. 209)	You guess, for I dare not
	Gode Gris and / Gees (B. Prol. 226)	Good piglings and geese

Even over some of these examples the poet of *Beowulf* would have shaken his head, and a majority of Langland's lines cannot be made exactly to conform with the older rules. I do not think he knew or cared about metrical exactitude; rather he had the sound of some traditional movements in his mind, and fashioned his half-lines to his meaning while observing a rough metrical equivalence that pleasingly but inaccurately echoed the more ancient style, examples of which I do not suppose him ever to have seen. Nor would he have understood them if he had. No one, so far as I know, has published a treatise on his versification, and indeed it would be hardly possible to do so with fairness to him until a definitive text can be established. Even then, in view of the enormous number of variant readings and the doubts as to the precise value he would have given to certain syllables, it is probable that his metrical practice would prove irreducible to rule and as intuitive as his thought.

What I have said is to show that his style shows traces of a six-hundred-year tradition, much degenerated, an aristocratic mode of language on a peasant's tongue centuries later. It will be at once noticed that Langland often has three main stresses sometimes all alliterating in one half-line, and that occasionally a line is not alliterated at all. Sometimes he pursues the alliteration from one line to another. Sometimes there are different alliterating letters for each half-line. Here are some examples:

Four stresses

A Faire Felde ful of folke / fond I there bytwene
(B. Prol. 17)

(A fair field full of folk / found I there between (them))

Three Stresses

With Depe Dyches and Derke / and dredful of sight
(B. Prol. 16)

(With deep ditches and dark / and dreadful to see)

No alliteration

That one is vesture / from chele the to save
(B. Passus I. 23)

(The former is clothing, / to save thee from chill)

Pursued alliteration
and alliteration half-line by half-line

And alle his Werkes he Wrou3te / with Love as him Liste
And Lered it Moises for the Levest thing / and Most Like to hevene
(B. Passus I. 148-9)

(And all His works He wrought / with love, as it pleased Him,
And taught it to Moses as the loveliest thing / and likest to Heaven)

THE PRESENT VERSION

Metrically I have tried to follow the main movements in Langland's verse, not always line for line it is true, but attempting in every line of my own some measure I could parallel elsewhere in Langland. I do not claim always to have been successful in this and it may be that he would have rejected some of my lines as faulty to his ear.

Though this version is not a literal crib, I hope he would not complain that some freedoms I have taken have mangled his meaning, for that was always his first consideration. In all the revising he did to his poem, never once, so far as I can detect, did he alter a line for merely aesthetic considerations. He never polished as an artist for shapeliness, but only to clarify or add to his meaning. With this intention paramount in his mind he is as liable to spoil as to embellish a line in revision, aesthetically speaking, and did not much care which. So at least it seems to me.

I have made frequent cuts, not only in the second part of the poem, but throughout, without comment. What I have translated, however, is aimed to convey a line-for-line fidelity of tone and meaning, apart from cuts. I have tried above all to maintain the natural freshness, vigour, and speech-like spontaneity of the original in all its moods, whether Blake-like or Hogarthian.

The names of the speakers in dialogue have been supplied in the margin. I have often found it troublesome in the original during the longer speeches to remember who is speaking, particularly in the second section of the poem.

LE BONE FLORENCE OF ROME

OLD AND MIDDLE ENGLISH TEXTS

General Editor: G. L. BROOK

Le Bone Florence of Rome

Edited by

CAROL FALVO HEFFERNAN

MANCHESTER UNIVERSITY PRESS

BARNES & NOBLE BOOKS · NEW YORK

© MANCHESTER UNIVERSITY PRESS 1976

Published by Manchester University Press
Oxford Road, Manchester M13 9PL

UK ISBN 0 7190 0647 3

USA
HARPER & ROW PUBLISHERS INC
BARNES & NOBLE IMPORT DIVISION
US ISBN 0 06 492790 3

Library of Congress catalog card No. 76 7656

Printed in Great Britain by T. & A. Constable Ltd., Edinburgh

TO
MY PARENTS
and
BELOVED HUSBAND and SON

PREFACE

Seven manuscript versions of the story of Florence—one in English, five in French, and one in Spanish—as well as the many related tales of innocent, persecuted high-born women, both in eastern and western literature attest to the fascination the story held for the medieval imagination. Also, the tale's relationship to Chaucer's *Man of Law's Tale* makes it a useful touchstone against which to measure Chaucer's greatness.

Despite the scholarly attention given to the tale of Florence in the nineteenth and twentieth centuries,[1] there is no adequate, accessible edition of *Le Bone Florence of Rome*. Both nineteenth-century editions have long been out of print. The romance first appeared in a collection by Joseph Ritson[2] which provided readable texts of manuscripts most of which had not appeared in print before. Ritson did not produce consistently reliable scholarly texts, but he did provide a real service to readers of his generation interested in medieval romance.

While comparatively free of errors, a later nineteenth-century text, that of Wilhelm Vietor,[3] is not easily readable, nor is W. A. Knobbe's introduction[4] to it in all points reliable. In addition, the absence of a glossary and explanatory notes is a significant shortcoming.

In its original form this edition was approved as a dissertation for the Ph.D. degree at New York University in 1973 and I am pleased to acknowledge my great debt to Professor

[1] Lillian H. Hornstein, 'Le Bone Florence of Rome', *A Manual of the Writings in Middle English 1050–1400*, ed. J. Burke Severs (New Haven, 1968), Fasc. 1, i, 290–1.

[2] Joseph Ritson, ed. 'Le Bone Florence of Rome', *Ancient English Metrical Romances*, 3 vols. (London, 1802), iii, 1–92.

[3] Wilhelm Vietor, ed., *Le Bone Florence of Rome*, Diss. Marburg, 1893 (Marburg, 1899). I disagree with his readings in only eighteen instances and I introduce several emendations which challenge Vietor's interpretation of words or phrases.

[4] W. Albert Knobbe, 'Über die Mittelenglische Dichtung *Le Bone Florence of Rome*', Diss. Marburg 1899 (Marburg, 1899) (Introduction precedes Vietor's text).

Lillian Hornstein, who first kindled my interest in medieval romance literature, and whose guidance was constant and generous over the full period I was engaged in writing the dissertation. I would also like to thank my readers at that time, Professors Jess B. Bessinger, Jr. and Robert R. Raymo, for their valuable suggestions for the improvement of my work. Thanks are also due for the courtesies extended to me by Miss Jayne Ringrose and Miss Margaret Pamplin, Assistant Library Officers of University Library, Cambridge. The staff of the Adelphi University Computer Center was of invaluable assistance in helping me to compile a complete list of the words in the romance and the lines in which they occurred. I was, thereby, enabled to check every appearance of every word, so that accuracy in the glossary, I hope, has been more nearly achieved. My colleagues in the Department of Humanities of the U.S. Merchant Marine Academy, Kings Point are also to be thanked for their encouragement of this project.

I am grateful, finally, to my parents, who have always applauded my scholarly interests, and to my husband and son, who cheerfully endured the preparation of this book.

CONTENTS

ABBREVIATIONS

Archiv	*Archiv für das Studium der neuren Sprachen und Litteraturen*
EETS, OS, ES	Early English Text Society, Original Series, Early Series
ES	*Englische Studien*
JEGP	*Journal of English and Germanic Philology*
MÆ	*Medium Ævum*
MED	*Middle English Dictionary* (Michigan)
MLN	*Modern Language Notes*
MP	*Modern Philology*
MLR	*Modern Language Review*
OED	*Oxford English Dictionary*
PAPS	*Proceedings of the American Philosophical Society*
PQ	*Philological Quarterly*
SATF	*Société des Anciens Textes Français*
Spec.	*Speculum*

INTRODUCTION

THE MANUSCRIPT

MS Cambridge Ff. 2.38 is a folio, on paper, of 247 leaves, 11¾ in. × 8⅛ in. For the most part, the manuscript contains religious literature[1] and didactic romances, suggesting that it may have been a tale book copied in a monastery.

The manuscript was number 690 in the collection of John Moore (1646–1714), Bishop of Ely, whose library was purchased by King George I and presented to the Cambridge University Library in 1715. Nothing further is known about its provenance.

The foliation of the entire manuscript as assembled until June 1972 was originally numbered 1–247 throughout. However, Henry Bradshaw, who was Librarian from 1867 to 1886, realised that the first thirty-three leaves had been bound out of order and, moreover, that the original fol. 1, 2, 22–7, 141, 144 and fol. 157r–160r were lost. He accordingly renumbered the folia, leaving two sets of handwritten numbers in the upper right-hand corner of each leaf.

In June 1972 the old nineteenth-century brown calf binding was replaced by boards covered with marble paper and a red leather spine. Also, the disorder in the early leaves of the manuscript was rectified.

The *Catalogue of Manuscripts* describes the handwriting as 'uniform';[2] however, my study of a microfilm copy of the manuscript and, later, personal examination of the actual folio in Cambridge reveal that this is not the case. Although the hands are quite similar, there are certainly variations from page to page in the evenness of the hand and in the colour of

---

[1] Among the religious pieces there are twenty short poems—one of these a saint's life—and eight prose narratives, three of these also saints' lives. Of the sixteen long narrative poems in the manuscript nine are romances: *The Erle of Tolous, Syr Egyllamoure of Artas, Syr Tryamoure, A Tale of the Emperor Octavian, Sir Beves of Hampton, Dioclesian the Emperor . . ., Guy, Earl of Warwick, Le Bone Florence of Rome, Robert of Sicily, Sir Degaré.*

[2] H. R. Luard *et al., A Catalogue of the Manuscripts Preserved in the Library of the University of Cambridge* (Cambridge, 1857), II, 404.

the ink, a major change to blacker ink occurring on fol. 64r–67r and on 42r where the ink becomes darker, but reverts to the usual brown on the verso of the leaf. The marked change occurring at fol. 93r–156v does tempt one to conclude that there has been a change of scribes, as the handwriting becomes very heavy and widely spaced. The light hand which begins *Guy, Earl of Warwick* at fol. 161r is probably the same hand that wrote *Le Bone Florence of Rome* which follows. Besides the similarity in the graphs, both romances average thirty-six lines per column and contain marginal scribbles, written in the same hand as the text, which are boxed in the same way ('4 gat tyn haste', fol. 180v.; 'full grete othys', fol. 241v.).

The handwriting of *Le Bone Florence of Rome* is essentially a blend of two kinds of cursive script. The first has usually been referred to in England as 'court hand' or 'charter hand'. Parkes[3] names it 'Anglicana' book hand since the varieties of this hand are peculiar to English manuscripts of the fourteenth and fifteenth centuries. The second type of cursive script is secretary hand, a continental script which possessed letter forms and stylistic features which had no counterparts in traditional English hands. It was introduced into England during the third quarter of the fourteenth century.

Mixed hands are particularly difficult to date unless one is able to relate enough separate details to those in datable examples of the script. The results of my comparison of the individual ingredients of the hand in *Florence* to other dated scripts indicate that it is probably a late fifteenth-century copy.[4] However, the fullest reservations must be added as to the possible persistence of old forms. There was, in fact, some resemblance to early sixteenth-century hands.[5]

---

[3] Malcolm B. Parkes, *English Cursive Book Hands, 1250–1500* (Oxford, 1969), 21–4.

[4] Cf. especially the plate in Wright's *English Vernacular Hands: From the Twelfth to the Fifteenth Centuries* (Oxford, 1960) and the sketches based on dated manuscripts in Charles Johnson and Hilary Jenkinson, *English Court Hand A.D. 1066–1500* (1915; rpt. New York, 1967), I, 3–55.

[5] Cf. the sixteenth-century hands in G. E. Dawson and L. Kennedy-Skipton, *Elizabethan Handwriting, 1500–1600* (New York, 1968), pp. 29 (Plate 1B), 33, 35.

Among the late fifteenth-century features of the handwriting the most notable is, perhaps, the mixed hand itself. Another striking end-of-the-century feature is the habit the hooks of ascenders have of trailing into the body of letters. Also descenders tend to be longer than ascenders and frequently run into the letters in the line below.

Some of the shapes of individual letters are particularly characteristic of the late fifteenth century; for example, double *f* sometimes has the curious compass-like appearance in the downstroke which is noticeable toward the end of the century.

Finally, there are two special signs in *Florence* which can be fairly well dated; the Tironian sign for *and* (1478) and the final curl which stands for *-ys* (1488).[6]

There are no markings to indicate punctuation. We have only the capitals at the beginning of each line to mark the individual verses of the poem.

VERSIONS AND ORIGINS

Versions. 'The unfortunate, persecuted maiden! The subject is as old as the world . . .';[7] and there are hundreds of permutations of the tale in popular folk legend as well as in romance. The version to which Florence gives her name is distinguished from the other tales about persecuted women, such as Emaré, Constance and Griselda, by two characteristics: (i) exile is always caused by the accusations of a rejected brother-in-law, and (ii) after numerous persecutions and sufferings, the heroine's healing powers bring together her persecutors, who confess their crimes.

Wallensköld[8] bases a reconstruction of the outlines of a lost Sanskrit version of the Florence story on three extant Oriental texts: the *Touti-Nameh*, the *Thousand and One Nights*, and

---

[6] Johnson and Jenkinson, 62–3. These pages contain sketches of dated symbols.

[7] Mario Praz, *The Romantic Agony* (London, 1933), 97.

[8] A. Wallensköld, 'Le Conte de la Femme Chaste Convoitée par son Beau-frère', *Acta Societatis Scientiarum Fennicae*, 37 (Helsingfors, 1907), 9.

the *Thousand and One Days*. It is Wallensköld's belief that the
original may have been transmitted to Europe before the end
of the eleventh century. The earliest extant version, the
Persian *Touti-Nameh* (1330) of Nakhchabi, derives from a
portion of an earlier *Touti-Nameh* which was a twelfth-century
translation of a Sanskrit original, now represented by the
Soukasaptati. There is a Turkish version of the primitive
Touti-Nameh dating from the beginning of the fifteenth
century in which our tale is called the 'Tale of Merhuma'.[9] In
the Arabic *Thousand and One Nights*, the earliest manuscript
of which dates from 1400, there are three versions of the story
represented by the 'Adventures of the Cauzee, His Wife . . .',[10]
'The Jewish Cadi and His Pious Wife',[11] and 'The Pious
Woman Accused of Lewdness'.[12] The story of chaste Repsima[13]
occurs in the third branch of the Oriental versions, the
Thousand and One Days, which is probably a translation from
Persian; the earliest redaction is a fifteenth-century manuscript in Turkish.

Two features distinguish the Oriental stories from the two
hundred and sixty European versions. First, the husband in
the western tales is always a man of high rank: an emperor or
king,[14] and second, the heroine has her brother-in-law im-
prisoned after his attempted assault on her virtue.[15] The oldest
European version is the story of Crescentia, whose name is
frequently used to describe the general type of 'la femme
chaste convoitée par son beau-frère'. Crescentia first appears

[9] *Tuti-Nameh*, ed. George Rosen, 'Geschichte der Merhuma' (Leipzig,
1858), I, 89–108.

[10] *Arabian Nights Entertainments*, ed. Jonathan Scott, 'The Adventures of the Cauzee, His Wife . . .' (London, 1811), VI, 396–408.

[11] *The Book of the Thousand Nights and One*, ed. John Payne, 'The
Jewish Cadi and His Pious Wife' (London, 1883), V, 9–13.

[12] *Tales from the Arabic*, ed. John Payne, 'The Pious Woman Accused
of Lewdness' (London, 1884), III, 263–74.

[13] *Mille et un Jours*, trans. Petis de la Croix, 'Histoire de Repsima'
(Paris, 1840), V, 241–95.

[14] See *infra*, p. 13: I argue that the profession of the husband in the
Oriental versions—that of judge—seems to be a significant factor in
determining origins.

[15] Wallensköld, 23–4.

in the Old High German *Kaiserchronik*[16] (*c.* 1150). The tale also occurs as a derivative *chanson* in several fourteenth-century manuscripts.[17] According to Wallensköld, the story of Crescentia is probably a variant of a Miracle of the Virgin which appeared in a collection of quasi-historical tales about the Roman emperors. Other scholars, for example Stefanovic, consider the Miracle part of an independent group.

It was inevitable that a tale about the vindication of a falsely accused woman should become a Miracle of the Virgin; by the twelfth century Mary had become the Mother of Mercy whose privilege it was to intercede for justice from God.[18] The presentation of the Florence story as a miracle occurs at least as early as the second half of the twelfth century in a *mariale* of the Bibliothèque Nationale (MS 14463).[19] It is an anonymous prose account in Latin which appears as the forty-fifth tale. Wallensköld identifies four classes of this miracle—in Latin, French, Dutch, and Icelandic;[20] he seems to have overlooked the English rendering of the miracle.[21] Hilka also points to three additional Latin versions of the twelfth-century Miracle in fourteenth- and fifteenth-century texts.[22] The Miracle was evidently a popular tale. Since the heroine of the story is an empress of Rome and we know that she has Oriental ante-cedents, it seems likely that this Miracle may be an example of what Evelyn Wilson describes as the 'quickening interest of the twelfth century in the matter of ancient Rome' prompting 'the transformation of some highly pagan tales into Mary legends'.[23]

Vincent of Beauvais incorporates the Miracle into his

[16] *Die Kaiserchronik*, ed. Edward Schröder, 'Crescentia' (Hannover, 1892), 289–314.

[17] A. Wallensköld, *Florence de Rome: Chanson, D'Aventure du Premier Quart du 13e Siècle*, Société des Anciens Textes Françaises (1909; rpt. New York, 1968), I, 125.

[18] *The Stella Maris of John of Garland*, ed. Evelyn Faye Wilson (Cambridge, Mass., 1946), 4.

[19] Wallensköld, 'Le Conte de la Femme Chaste', 33.

[20] *Ibid.*, 36.

[21] This version is anthologised by Beverly Boyd in *The Middle English Miracles of the Virgin* (San Marino, 1964), 64–7.

[22] Alfons Hilka, 'Zum Crescientiastoff', *Archiv*, 133 (1915), 136.

[23] Wilson, 8.

Speculum Historiale (1244–7), and many subsequent anthologisers of exempla for sermons used it. Although it usually appears as an exemplary story under the heading *castitas*, it should be noted that the story has also been used to illustrate *pietas*—a point I shall return to.

Gautier de Coinci produced a famous French poetic version[24] of the Latin Miracle before 1222. A French miracle play[25] of the end of the fourteenth, or beginning of the fifteenth, century, is more or less based on an account in *Les Vies des Pères* which is an abbreviated version of the twelfth-century Miracle in which the empress is exposed on a rock in the middle of a river.[26]

Closer to the original Latin Miracle is a seventeenth-century Italian drama[27] based on Giovanni Briccio's poem, 'La Historia di Flavia Imperatrice'[28] (sixteenth century). Also in Italian is a prose narrative in which the heroine is named Guglielma[29] (fourteenth century), and a sacred play based on this narrative by Antonio Pulci[30] (end of the fifteenth century).

On the Iberian peninsula, a Galician translation of De Coinci's work probably served as a basis for one of Alfonso el Sabio's *Cantigas de Santa Maria*.[31] Balthasar Dias (sixteenth century) may also have based a Portuguese romance on the same translation.[32] According to Wallensköld, Juan Timoneda,

---

[24] 'De l'Emperirix qui Garda Sa Chastée par Moult Temptacions', *Nouveau Reueil de Fabliaux et Contes Inédits*, ed. Dominique Martín Méon (Paris, 1823), II, 1–128.

[25] Louis Monmerqué and F. Michel, eds., *Théâtre Français au Moyen Age*, 'Mystère de l'Empereris de Rome' (Paris, 1814), 365–416.

[26] This abbreviated version is told in prose as 'De La Bonne Imperatrice' in *Fabliaux ou Contes du XIIe et du XIIIe Siècle*, ed. P. J. B. Legrand, 3rd ed. (Paris, 1829), V, 125–9.

[27] Wallensköld, 'Le Conte de la Femme Chaste', 48.

[28] Giovanni Briccio, *La Historia di Flavia Imperatrice* (Venice, 1812).

[29] Wallensköld, *Florence de Rome*, I, 121.

[30] 'Santa Guglielma', *Sacre Rappresentazione*, ed. Alessandro d'Ancona (Firenze, 1872), III, 208–34.

[31] *Cantigas de Santa Maria*, ed. Walter Mettman (Coimbra, 1961), II, 7–12.

[32] 'Historia da Imperatriz Porcina' in *Floresta de Varios Romances*, ed. Theo. Braga (Portugal, 1869), 104–49.

a fifteenth-century writer of novellas from Valencia, based a tale in his *Patrañuelo*[33] directly on the Latin Miracle.[34]

A German poem[35] by the fifteenth-century poet Hans Rosenblut is also largely based on the Latin Miracle. It is notable, however, for naming the emperor Octavianus, the name of the emperor in the Continental *Gesta Romanorum*, which contains still another rendering of the Florence story.

The *Gesta Romanorum* was intended as a compendium of edifying stories for the use of preachers. Its nucleus may have been an actual series of stories derived from Roman history, though in its extant forms it is a mélange of folklore and pseudo-history. In the fourteenth century, an abridged version of the Florence story appeared in the *Gesta* and was included in the Continental and Anglo-Latin manuscripts. The *Gesta* version was given also in a metrical paraphrase by Thomas Hoccleve in 1421.[36]

Florence of Rome gives her name to seven manuscripts. In enumerating these, I will adopt the letters first assigned to them by Rudolph Wenzel.[37] There are two manuscripts which present the *chanson* of *Florence de Rome*[38] in its entirety: MS Nouv. acquis franc. 4192 of the Bibliothèque Nationale (P.), belonging to the end of the thirteenth or beginning of the fourteenth century, and a late thirteenth-century manuscript owned by the d'Arcy Hutton estate. There is also a badly mutilated fragment of the *chanson*, Lansdowne 362, ff. 75-6, 77 of the British Museum (L.).

Besides these three manuscripts, there are four other redactions of the story about Florence of Rome: an early

[33] 'Patraña Veintiuna' in *El Patrañuelo* (Madrid, 1958), 201–10.

[34] Wallensköld, 'Le Conte de la Femme Chaste', 55.

[35] 'Ein Liepleich History von Groszer Schone, Gedult und Kuscheit einer Edeln Keyseryn' in *Fastnachtspiele aus dem Funfzehnten Jahrhundert*, ed. Adelbert Keller (Stuttgart, 1853), III, 139–49.

[36] 'Fabula de Quadam Imperatrice Romana' in *Hoccleve's Works*, ed. F. J. Furnivall, EETS, ES, 61 (London, 1892), 140–73.

[37] *Die Fassungen der Sage von Florence de Rome*, Diss. Marburg, 1890, 5–6.

[38] The definitive edition has been published by Wallensköld, *Florence de Rome*, II. He collates the manuscripts.

fourteenth-century *Dit de Flourence de Rome* in quatrains of the Bibliothèque Nationale, Paris (Notre-Dame 198) (D.);[39] MS 24384 of the *fond français* of the Bibliothèque Nationale which contains a long fifteenth-century version of *Florence de Rome* in alexandrines (Q.);[40] a Spanish prose version (S.), based on a late fourteenth-century manuscript in the Biblioteca Escorial;[41] and the fifteenth-century unique Middle English version (R.).

A consideration of the relationship of the English version to the oldest extant French text follows later in this Introduction.

While all the other versions of the Florence story are patently about fictitious women, Hildegard, the heroine of a well-known sub-group,[42] was said to be Charlemagne's wife. According to one theory, represented by Wallensköld,[43] the story of Hildegard goes back to a Bavarian schoolmaster, Johannes Birck, who introduced it into his chronicle of the Abbey of Kempten in 1484 or 1485. He attributed the role of the heroine to the patroness of the abbey, Queen Hildegard. This theory has been strongly contested by Stefanovic,[44] who maintains that the Hildegard story is based on a popular tradition independent of, and earlier than, Birck's version.

Origins. Five scholars have advanced as many theories in an effort to establish the origin of the Florence story. The easiest to defend—though not solely with the arguments the author offers—seems to be that of Wallensköld.

Since all five suggestions hinge ultimately on the essential

---

[39] *Dit de Flourence de Rome* in *Nouveau Recueil de Contes, Dits, Fabliaux et Autres Pièces Inédits des XIIIe, XIVe, et XVe Siècles*, ed. Achille Jubinal (Paris, 1839–42), VI, 88–117.

[40] Wallensköld, *Florence de Rome*, I, 4.

[41] *Historia Critica de la Litteratura Española*, ed. Amador de los Ríos, 'Cuento Muy Famoso del Enperador Ottas de Roma' (Madrid, 1864), V, 391–468.

[42] The brothers Grimm include the tale in *Deutsche Sagen* (Leipzig, 1818), II, 83–5.

[43] Wallensköld, 'Le Conte de la Femme Chaste', 65 ff.

[44] S. Stefanovic, 'Die Crescentia–Florence Sage: eine Kritische Studie ueber ihren Ursprung und ihre Entwicklung', *Romanische Forschung*, 29 (1908), 461–557.

elements of the different versions, it may be useful here to enumerate the nine principal incidents: (i) the wooing of the heroine by her brother-in-law; (ii) the heroine's rejection of him and his accusation of adultery; (iii) her condemnation; (iv) her exile; (v) refuge in a household where she is accused of murdering the child of her protector by a rejected, revengeful, and murderous suitor; (vi) the second exile; (vii) a debtor, freed from the gallows by the heroine, sells her to a ship's captain; (viii) her escape after a storm wrecks the boat; (ix) her reputation as a healer draws all her afflicted persecutors together.

Grundtvig[45] rejected absolutely the hypothesis of an Oriental origin for the story. He regarded *le conte de la femme chaste convoitée par son beau-frère* as closely related to stories which actually fall within the more general cycle of tales about innocent persecuted women. As a result of his too unrestricted classification of the story, he concluded that the Danish ballad *Ravengaard og Memering* represented the oldest version of the Florence story. The Scandinavian ballad is actually related to the English *Sir Aldingar*.[46]

Stefanovic[47] also defended the idea of Germanic origins but, unlike Grundtvig, he addressed himself to the distinguishing elements of the various versions. According to Stefanovic, the core of the story, the episode of the brother-in-law's treachery, is of Germanic origin. He considered the prototype the Old English poem, *The Wife's Complaint*, and argued that the story, having long existed as a popular legend, gave birth to the legend of Hildegard, which was introduced late in the chronicles. By a combination of the story with others in which the heroine is accused of murdering an infant by a rejected suitor (notably the tale of the incestuous father), a new story was produced which has two persecutors. *Crescentia* represents the

---

[45] Svend Grundtvig, H. G. Nielsen, and A. Olrik, *Gamle Folkeviser*, I (Copenhagen, 1853), 195; III (Copenhagen, 1862), 782; IV (Copenhagen, 1883), 730.

[46] Francis J. Child, ed. *The English and Scottish Popular Ballads*, II (Boston, 1882–98), 33–48.

[47] Stefanovic, 461–557.

oldest version of this stage. The Miracle of the Virgin, which in its most typical form involves only two persecutors, was seen by Stefanovic as a later development of the Crescentia story, resulting from the cult of the Virgin. As for the versions represented by the *Gesta Romanorum* and the Florence sub-group, he regarded them as later amplifications, influenced by the Oriental versions.

If the Old English poem—the crux of Stefanovic's theory—contained the characteristic details of the first episode and the scene of reconciliation which typify the *conte de la femme chaste convoitée par son beau-frère*, it would be easier to accept its seniority. This is not, however, the case. In the Old English poem we infer that a woman, exiled by her husband upon the instigation of malevolent relatives and living alone in a cave, laments her husband and curses a vaguely indicated young man. That is all. The hypothesis that the Hildegard versions are generated from this poem is inadmissible.

The Hildegard story is the most important for Stefanovic's theory. He maintained that Birck, at the end of the fifteenth century, merely introduced into his chronicle at Kempten an old popular story, already in circulation prior to his time. If one considers the fact that there is not the least trace of an atribution to Hildegard as heroine before Birck, this theory becomes less convincing than the point of view represented by Wallensköld, who maintained that Birck simply adapted the twelfth-century Miracle of the Virgin.[48]

As to Stefanovic's suggestion about the evolution of *Crescentia*, it seems plausible, as Wallensköld argued, that by replacing St Peter for the Virgin the Latin Miracle could have generated the type represented in the *Kaiserchronik*. The reverse, however, could hardly have occurred, since the sea voyage in the Miracle during which the sailors try to abuse the heroine is clearly a fragment of the episode involving the fourth persecutor (the ship's captain). To Stefanovic the fact that both the longer European versions and the eastern stories contained the episodes of the debtor freed from the gallows and the ship's captain suggested that these incidents were added

[48] Wallensköld, 'Le Conte de la Femme Chaste', 65 ff.

to the type represented by *Crescentia*, which was then transmitted to the Orient. Stefanovic rejected, *a priori*, the possibility of a classification based on evolution by elimination of
episodes.

The last theory which has been presented in support of
European origins is that of Louis Karl.[49] He attributes the
appearance of Hungry in the European divisions of the story—
the *Gesta*, the Florence sub-group, and the Miracle—to the
influence of St Elizabeth of Hungary (d. 1231). Karl pointed
out that the basic outlines of the saint's life were similar to the
pattern of Florence's persecution, exile, saintliness, and fame
as a healer. None of the versions dating before the second
quarter of the thirteenth century mentions Hungary. Karl's
theory cannot be regarded as more than an exceedingly
interesting explanation of the appearance of a local reference
which in no way precludes the possibility of dissemination from
the east.

In an attempt to refute the theory of Germanic origins,
Adolf Mussafia,[50] in 1865, argued for the priority of the
Oriental versions of the story despite the lateness of the
manuscripts. Mussafia was convinced that the eastern stories
were introduced into the west in the form found in the
Kaiserchronik and the various redactions of the Miracle of the
Virgin. Though he agreed with the theory of eastern origins,
Wallensköld largely discredited Mussafia's view by noting that
the western versions contain an episode absent in all the
Oriental tales: 'le beau-frère, à la suite de ses premiers efforts
pour séduire l'heroine, est enfermé dans un lieu solitaire'.[51] It
is unlikely that two waves of influence could have triggered the
same innovation in the European versions. Wallensköld
maintained that the richest form of the story was found, in
logically combined episodes, among the Persian and Arabic

---

[49] 'Florence de Rome et la Vie de Deux Saints de Hongrie', *Revue
des Langues Romanes*, 52 (1909), 163–80.

[50] 'Über eine Italienische Metrische Darstellung der Crescentia Saga',
Sitzungsberichte der Phil.-Hist. Classe der Kais. Akad. der Wissenschaften,
51 (Vienna, 1865), 589–692.

[51] Wallensköld, *Florence de Rome*, II, 107–8.

versions. Although there were some differences between these, Wallensköld tried to prove by analysis and reconstruction that all the Oriental versions were traceable to a common Sanskrit source.[52] One of the eastern versions is in the *Touti-Nameh* of Nakhchabi. It is part of an earlier, lost *Touti-Nameh* (probably of the twelfth century) which is itself a somewhat altered translation of the ancient Sanskrit original, now imperfectly represented by the *Soukasaptati*. This fact alone is a strong argument in favour of an Oriental source and, to my knowledge, the relationship of the *Touti-Nameh* to the *Soukasaptati* has never been challenged.

The western development of the story is easily traced from this point. Since in all the western versions the heroine's husband is a king or emperor and they all include the imprisonment of the brother-in-law in a tower, Wallensköld concluded that the western branches have developed from a common European version which contained these two alterations of the ancient eastern story. He considered the various versions of the *Gesta Romanorum* and the Florence sub-group, all retaining the four persecutors of the ancient eastern versions, the most closely related to the Oriental versions and representatives of a literary tradition. The absence of the two persecutors (the thief rescued from the gallows and the ship's captain) in the Miracle of the Virgin, *Crescentia*, and *Hildegard* sub-groups led Wallensköld to conclude that they were products of the oral transmission of the primitive western source. The Latin Miracle of the Virgin, while omitting the debtor and ship's captain, retains possible evidence of the captain (the sea voyage). Wallensköld, therefore, advanced the notion that the oral versions of the primitive western source ended finally in a written text which was probably some version of the Latin Miracle.

Wallensköld's hypothesis that the longer western versions and the Miracle—among the shorter versions—are most closely related to the Oriental versions is, I think, correct. Besides the reasons he advanced, there is evidence of their close relationship in the very heavy stress they all place on the

[52] Wallensköld, 'Le Conte de la Femme Chaste', 9–23.

idea of justice—an emphasis which is not found in the Hildegard and Crescentia sub-group.

Not only is there the implicit justice of the concluding vindication episode in the eastern versions, together with explicit references to the justice of Allah, but there are also reinforcing details related to the idea of justice: (i) all of them contain a scene in which the brother-in-law falsely charges the heroine with adultery and brings her before a court of law; (ii) the husband in the three versions of the story contained in the *Thousand and One Nights* is actually, by profession, a judge.[53] He does not act judicially as judge or prosecutor in the story, but in 'The Jewish Cadi and His Pious Wife' the husband is characterised as a pious man. In fact, he leaves his wife in order to make a pilgrimage to Jerusalem. The three European versions which are, according to Wallensköld's theory, most closely connected to the Oriental tales seem to have been particularly influenced by these elements in the eastern versions; in the transplanting of the stories the details relating to the idea of justice were adapted for the orthodox theology.

The author of *Le Bone Florence of Rome* lays particular emphasis on the idea of God's justice, which punishes the wicked and preserves the faithful. This is particularly evident in the miracles by means of which God intervenes to save the heroine. In referring to his source, the poet says at one point:

> The boke seyþ God þat vs boght
> Many myrakyls for hur he wroght
> Many a oon and thyckfolde
> [ll. 871–3]

The story reaches a climax when all four men who have injured Florence are stricken with disease and come to the monastery to be healed. Their public confession of their attempts to assault Florence is still another manifestation of the justice of God, and the realistic description of their

---

[53] The husbands in both the 'Tale of Merhuma' (*Tuti-Nameh*) and the 'Histoire de Repsima' (*Thousand and One Days*), while not judges, are described as pious.

painful symptoms (ll. 2020 ff.) stresses the contrast between reward and punishment. The poem concludes with a reminder to the reader that God always metes out justice appropriately to the good and the wicked:

> Forþy schulde men and women als
> Them bethynke or þey be false
> 　　Hyt makyth so fowle an ende
> Be hyt neuyr so slylye caste
> 3yt hyt schamyþ þe maystyr at þe laste
> 　　In what londe þat euyr þey lende
> In meene be the iiij fekyll
> That harmed feyre Florence so mykyll
> 　　The trewest that men kende.
>
> 　　　　　　　　　　　　[ll. 2176–84]

There are similar passages in the Spanish and French versions.

The section of the *chanson* which is headed 'Piété de Florence' makes clear that Florence's *piété* consists in giving each man his due. There is a certain justice in the balance of the action in which Florence heals only after having first elicited a confession from each of her persecutors. God the Judge is evident in Florence the healer. The connection between piety and justice, as we shall see in a moment, is consistent with the medieval church's classification of piety as a part of justice.

Like the Florence sub-group, the *Gesta Romanorum* contains a justice motif. In a 'Moral' appended to the conclusion of tale 249 of the Latin *Gesta* ('De Octaviano Qui Super Omnia Uxorem Dilexit') an allegorical equation is set up—the emperor = Jesus Christ = Judge:

> The Emperor is our master Jesus Christ. The Empress is the soul which was entrusted to his brother, Mankind. But alas the Flesh so strongly enticed the soul to sin that it could not rest. What was to be done? Obviously to incarcerate the Flesh by way of penance. But Holy Church recounts to us reports that our emperor is to come out of the Holy Land on the day of Judgement. . . .[54]

---

[54] Translated from *Gesta Romanorum*, ed. Hermann Oesterley (Berlin, 1872), 652. The standard English translation by Charles Swann includes the story but omits the 'Moral'.

Evidence of the justice motif in the versions of the Miracle is slighter, perhaps because the narrative is so brief. It is particularly noteworthy that in Etienne de Bourbon's collection of exempla the story appears under the heading 'Pietas'. The Greek term for *pietas* is *eusebeia* and was used by the Greek philosophers, especially Plato, and by the Greek Fathers of the Church in the sense of respect for the gods (or God) and one's parents.[55] Among the Roman authors Vergil and Cicero stand out for the frequency of use of the noun *pietas*, or the adjective *pius*. Vergil used the noun twenty-two times in the *Aeneid*[56] where it almost invariably has the sense of the Greek *eusebeia*. Cicero formulated a definition of the word which embraced the main traditions of the term and made them comprehensive and more specific: 'This is pietas: to fulfil one's duty and conscientious service towards our own flesh and blood and those having the interests of our country at heart.'[57] In the Middle Ages Thomas Aquinas, drawing on Cicero, explained *pietas* more fully as a specific form of the virtue of justice:

> Cicero classifies piety as a part of justice. . . . What makes any virtue to be specific is that its relationship to its objective is based on some specific moral value in the objective. Since honouring a debt towards someone else is a function of justice generally, a specific kind of justice arises wherever there is a specific basis for indebtedness to any person. This is the case in regard to anyone who, in the natural course of things, is a source of our life and its development . . . piety is the response towards those sources. . . .[58]

[55] Plato, *The Republic*, trans. Paul Shorey (London, 1935), II, 497 (615c); Clement of Rome, 'The First Epistle of Clement to the Corinthians', *The Ante-Nicene Fathers*, ed. Alexander Roberts and James Donaldson (New York, 1926), I, ch. 11, p. 8; ch. 32, p. 13.

[56] A few examples: 'Aeneid' in *Vergil*, trans. R. Rushton Fairclough (London and Cambridge, Mass., 1954–6), I, l. 151; II, l. 690; VI, ll. 688, 769, 878; X, l. 824.

[57] From Cicero's *De Inventione Rhetorica* as quoted by Saint Thomas Aquinas, *Summa Theologica*, ed. and trans. Blackfriars (Virtues of Justice in the Human Community, trans. T. C. O'Brien (vol. 41)) (London and New York, 1964–), II–ii, Q. 101, Art. I.

[58] Aquinas, II–ii, Q. 101, Art. III.

In short, justice requires that one give every person what is due him. This is probably the sense in which the thirteenth-century Dominican Etienne de Bourbon understood the term as he used it in his collection of exempla. Further it is probably no accident, in the light of these findings about the justice motif, that Chaucer selected the Man of Law as narrator of the tale of Constance, one of Florence's literary cousins.

It goes without saying that the appearance of Mary, intercessor for justice from God, is a constant reminder of the idea of justice which appears in all the Miracles.

It is generally recognised that many tales popular in the west originated or received their present narrative form in the east. Three at least of the *Canterbury Tales* have been shown to have Oriental analogues: the Pardoner's account of the three rioters; the Merchant's pear-tree story; and that of the Manciple, concerning Phoebus and the speaking cow. There are several links in the chain by which Oriental fiction could have been introduced into the west. Certainly by the beginning of the twelfth century the east and west were coming into frequent contact. The pilgrimages and the crusades not only brought east and west together but they stimulated increasing travel in the west itself, whereby travellers in western Europe carried tales from one place to another by word of mouth. The growth of the mendicant orders and the roving character of the monks are additional important links in the chain uniting east and west. Also significant is the development of commerce; merchants undoubtedly could have carried tales back with them from the Orient.

It is likely that stories from the east began to reach western Europe long before the twelfth century. The Moslems, as is well known, were in Spain long before A.D. 800, so that transmission of Oriental stories to the west via Spain would have been a possibility at any time after the ninth century. If advanced developments in astrology, medicine, and chemistry of Arabic origin were introduced into Europe a century at least before the crusades, and if Sylvester II, who died in 1003, brought Arabic numerals to France, then it is not unreasonable to imagine that legendary stories might have begun to extend their influence at the same time. Wallensköld's dating of the transmission of the Oriental version of the Florence story to Europe at the eleventh century is, I think, very likely accurate.

LITERARY ASPECTS

A detailed discussion of the literary aspects of *Le Bone Florence of Rome* may be better understood after this brief summary of the action of the romance:

Garcy, the old king of Constantinople, moved by tales of Florence's beauty, decides to sue for her hand. After consulting with his barons and Florence, his daughter, King Otes of Rome rejects the offer made by Garcy's emissaries. The returning messengers are full of news about glorious Rome and beautiful Florence. Angry at his rejection, Garcy declares war on Rome and sets sail with an army. Battle begins despite Florence's last-minute offer to marry Garcy in order to save the lives of Roman knights. Mylys and Emere, sons of the King of Hungary, come to King Otes's assistance. Florence and Emere fall in love, and are betrothed. While Emere is engaged in war in Constantinople, his brother Mylys—to whose care Florence is entrusted—tries to win Florence's love after giving a false account of Emere's death. Mylys is put in prison, and then released when news of Emere's return reaches Florence. She and Mylys ride out to meet Emere. While in the woods, the wicked Mylys renews his assaults on Florence's virtue and hangs her by the hair from a tree after being rebuffed once again. Sir Tyrry rescues Florence from the woods and brings her home, where his steward, Machary, attempts to seduce Florence. He too is rejected, and takes revenge by murdering Tyrry's daughter and putting the bloody knife in the hand of sleeping Florence. Tyrry takes pity on Florence and sends her into exile in a forest. After still further adventures and attempts to compromise her virtue, Florence arrives at a convent where she is received by the nuns, one of whom she heals of a serious disease. Her fame spreads. One by one, all of her persecutors come to her for healing. Before helping them, she makes them confess their crimes against her, and is reunited in the end with Emere.

Viewed as a whole, the action of the romance leaves a dual impression. The extensive first section, irrelevant to the moral purpose of the romance, is full of typical romantic elements: the arrival of messengers from distant lands; the detailed descriptions of journeys, clothes, armour, costly gifts, palace halls, and battle scenes; and the love between a conventional chivalric knight and lady. Florence is, throughout the first half of the story, not unlike the traditionally courted ladies of romance literature. The poet is at great pains to describe her beauty, her upbringing, and her aristocratic position as daughter of the king of Rome. Wallensköld views this first part of the romance as a French poet's attempt to create a *chanson de geste* out of Oriental materials: 'C'est que le poète, tout en prenant pour sujet un conte d'origine orientale, qu'il tenait on ne sait d'où, a évidemment voulu composer une véritable chanson de geste.'[59] However near the mark this idea may be, it will hardly do to explain why the English poet retained so many of these romantic elements. It may be simply, as Dieter Mehl suggests, that the variety and swiftness of the first half was intended to 'heighten our interest'[60] in the story. With the sinful demands of Mylys, the type of the faithful, chaste, and holy wife begins to show itself. This aspect dominates the second part of the romance and gives it its exemplary character. It is with the second part that the romance begins to align itself with the legendary Crescentia–Constance material.

The poet gives no indication of some underlying significance connecting the two parts. It would have been possible to relate the suffering of the heroine in the second part to her worldliness in the first. Florence's rejection of Garcy on the very natural grounds of physical abhorrence, for instance, might have been exploited to this end, for initially Florence is selfishly ready to let knights die for her right to a younger, more appealing husband. But the poet was evidently indifferent to creating this kind of unity, and is content to develop the fabliau elements of a May–January situation and nothing more.

The first part does contain some religious elements, notably

[59] *Florence de Rome*, I, 42.
[60] Dieter Mehl, *The Middle English Romances of the Thirteenth and Fourteenth Centuries* (London, 1968), 146.

—as in the French version—long prayers to God and the saints not to disregard the petitioner. These details are, nevertheless, subsidiary to the predominant adventure-story character of the first half, and insufficient as a real link to the exemplary second half.

The poet's perceptiveness about human behaviour, his realistic vigour, and feeling for dramatic poetic effects and narrative pace are most evident in part one, where the hagiological element in his story does not interfere.

Two striking examples of the poet's perceptiveness about human behaviour occur in the presentation of the episode of Garcy's suit. There is first a splendid portrait of Garcy's shrewd ambassador (ll. 205–25). After the initial presentation of gifts, he gets right to the proposal: 'He [Garcy] byddyth, wythowt avysement, / That þy doghtur be to hym sent, / For to lygg hym by.' Almost as if to soften the impact of this demand, the speaker seems to suggest how little, in fact, would be required to satisfy what is really a harmless old man in need of comforting: 'Hys body ys bresyd, hys bones are olde / . . . she may kepe hym fro þe colde.' The rest of the speech continues the pattern of an alternating hard and soft line of attack. *Hurry and follow my instructions*!: 'Haue done now hastelye.' *Your daughter will be well taken care of. And to tell you the truth, I personally would like to see her as my queen*; *she's very pretty*: 'In comely cloþyng sche shall be cledd, / I haue grete hope he wyll hur wedd, / Sche ys a feyre lady.' *If you don't take my advice, Garcy will ravage your country*:

> And yf þou sende hur not soone,
> Hastelye, wythowten wone,
>   Then ryseth ther a stryfe,
> Ellys wyll he hygh þe nere,
> Wyth hys ryche powere,
>   And feche hur as hys wyfe.
> He wyll dystroye þy bygly landys,
> And slee all þat before hym standys,
>   And lose full many a lyfe.

You see, you have no choice. Decide as I advise: 'Haue done . . . hastelye in hye, / An answare muste we gyf Garcy.' We seem

B

to hear the chameleon voice of the diplomat as he tries to create and react to responses in his listener.

Florence's quick, even witty, answer to Garcy's proposal has the authentic sound of a court lady, made confident of her own worth by a life filled with constant attentions,

> . . . Jhesu forbede!'
> Sche seyde, 'Be God þat boght me dere,
> Me had leuyr þe warste bachylere,
>   In all my fadurs thede,
> Then for to lye be hys bresyd boones,
> When he coghyth and oldely grones,
>   I can not on hys lede.'

[ll. 243-9]

One can imagine that Chaucer's Prioress, had she stayed at court rather than entered the convent, would have reacted with equal abhorrence to such an unequal union. It is only after Florence is confronted by the bloody consequences of her natural inclination to serve her own desires that she offers to sacrifice herself to Garcy. The Florence of the first half of the romance is far from the type of the devout daughter in the *King of Tars* who rejects the Sultan because he is not a Christian.

The poet's considerable skill at realistic description, which in part two is made to serve the exemplary purpose, as in the episode where Florence and Mylys have strongly contrasting reactions to eating the hermit's bread, is used in part one primarily to entertain. For instance, Syr Garcy, a suitor at the age of 100, is presented as the comic antithesis of the chivalric knight:

> Hys flesche trembylde for grete elde,
> Hys blode colde hys body unwelde,
>   Hys lyppes blo forthy;
> He had more mystyr of a gode fyre,
> Of bryght brondys brennyng schyre,
>   To beyke hys boones by,
> A softe bath a warme bedd,
> Then any maydyn for to wedd,
>   And gode encheson why,
> For he was bresyd and all tobrokyn,
> Ferre trauelde in harnes and of warre wrokyn

[ll. 94-104]

The poet is as concrete about enumerating the physical details of the old man's repulsiveness as is Chaucer in his description of January,

> The slakke skin aboute his nekke shaketh,
> [l. 1849]

> In his night-cappe, and with his nekke lene;[61]
> [l. 1853]

or Boccaccio's Agapes on the subject of her husband's senility,

> 'le sue guance, per crespezza ruvide . . .'[62]

> 'il sottile collo ne vend ne osso nasconle.'[63]

The poet was also capable of producing dramatic effects, as in the controlled introduction which builds gradually to Florence's lament for her dead father, 'Allas,' sche seyde, 'þat Y was borne! / My fadur for me hys lyfe haþ lorne' (ll. 826–7).[64] The corpse of the dead king is brought to Rome in silence, 'Wythowten belle or procescon' (l. 797), so as not to attract the attention of the enemy or to shock the unsuspecting Florence. Once safely inside the city, the silence is broken just long enough to raise the standard and vow revenge against Garcy. The focus of the narrative shifts quickly to Florence's chamber, where the ladies-in-waiting announce that a corpse is being drawn silently into the city. Florence looks out; recognises her father's horse being led by a knight; turns pale; and goes with a maid to the receiving hall of the palace. Alone she approaches the bier, and swoons after lifting the cloth from her father's face. The lament follows. With great economy, the poet has moved through four different locations within thirty-one lines, all the time managing large numbers of characters, describing

---

[61] Both lines are from Geoffrey Chaucer's *The Merchant's Tale*, *The Works of Geoffrey Chaucer*, 2nd ed., ed. F. N. Robinson (1957), 115–27. All citations from Chaucer are to this edition.

[62] Giovanni Boccaccio's 'L'Ameto' in 'L'Ameto, Lettere, Il Corbaccio' in *Scrittori D'Italia*, No. 182, *Opere*, v., ed. Nicola Bruscoli (Bari, 1940), 94.

[63] *Ibid.*

[64] Velma B. Richmond discusses the lament in *Laments for the Dead in Medieval Narrative* (Pittsburgh, 1966), 106 ff.

a variety of actions, indicating nuances of emotion, and managing the slow, deliberate pace so that it builds to Florence's collapse and lament. Miss Richmond is put off by what she considers an unfortunate conclusion to this scene which presents the nobles, with nervous wringing of hands, selfishly wondering who will provide them with lands, horses, hawks, and hounds for the hunt now that Emperor Otes is dead. It seems to me, however, that their evident weakness gives the entire scene added point. They sound like helpless children who have lost the generous emperor on whom they depended as on a father. How, indeed, can Rome survive the loss of Otes when the city is left to such weak men?

The death of her father, followed by Mylys's false account of Emere's death, leads Florence to marry herself to God in chastity:

> Furste þen was my fadur slayne,
> And now my lorde ys fro me tane,
>   Y wyll loue no ma,
> But hym þat boght me on þe rode
>   [ll. 1102–5]

The vow sets the exemplary second half of the romance in motion. Florence's flawless beauty, which is in the first part the conventional attribute of the heroine of courtly romance, is raised to a visible symbol of Florence's virtuous nature. Left hanging from a tree by the hair, the sufferer gives off light; expelled from the court of Tyrry, Florence rides through the woods where 'all glemed there sche glode' (l. 1709). The specific virtues which she exemplifies are *castitas*, supported by *pietas* and *fortitudo*. However, the symbolic beauty of the heroine is not the most important means by which the exemplary type is demonstrated in the romance. The virtues indicated by Florence's outward appearance are manifest in her Christian behaviour. Progressively more threatening assaults by Mylys, Machary, the steward, and the sea captain put Florence's vow of chastity to a hard test. Her power to resist in each case comes from her *pietas*, the conviction that God in his justness will protect those who live in Christian virtue, and her *fortitudo*, the sure knowledge that her conduct is consistent with the commands of God. Florence's behaviour at the time of the nadir of her sorrowful history, the sea captain's coming to assert the right he believes he has purchased, is characteristic. Her *pietas* and *fortitudo* enable her to contradict his intentions, stating what she knows to be the position of God: 'Nay that schall not bee / Throw helpe of Hym in Trynyte . . .' (ll. 1846–7). Her prayer to Mary for the protection of her maidenhood indicates, further, that by this point her trust has already been ratified by her experience of heavenly aid, 'Lady Mary free, / Now thou haue mercy on me, / Thou faylyst me neuyr at nede' (ll. 1852–4). And heavenly intervention in the affairs of the deserving *is* immediate. A sudden storm leaves Florence's adversary floundering in the sea while she is washed safely to shore. This happy turn of events, like that in the other episodes, by offering concrete evidence for the heavenly reward of God-pleasing acts and for the effectiveness of prayer, calls the audience to imitate the heroine's virtues.

Without reference to the specific virtues of *castitas*, *pietas*, and *fortitudo*, Florence's conduct is frequently contrasted, in a more general way, with that of her adversaries. There is, for example, the instance of the hermit's reception of Mylys and Florence. Whereas Florence says she considers his water and barley bread a delicious meal, Mylys cannot swallow the stuff ('Hyt stekyth in my hals', l. 1472) and proceeds to beat the hermit.

Her final position as saintly healer in the sanctity of a cloister is in stark contrast to the unhappy lot of her persecutors who go to Florence with the most ghastly diseases. These are all realistically described by the poet who presents them as a strong warning to imitate the other kind of life-style. It should be noted, as Hanspeter Schelp observes, that the exemplary imperative of the 'Romance gode' (l. 2185) keeps the description from being purely realistic, as in the first half of the romance,[65]

[65] *Exemplarische Romanzen im Mittelenglischen*, Palaestra, 246 (Göttingen, 1967), 127.

> Mylys that hur aweye ledd,
> He was the fowlest mesell bredd,
>   Of pokkys and bleynes bloo.
> And Machary þat wolde hur haue slayne,
> He stode schakyng the sothe to sayne,
>   Crokyd and crachyd thertoo.

[ll. 2020-5]

This description has an obvious didactic function: to express the causal relationship between the horrible diseases and the evil actions of the persecutors.

The French *Florence de Rome*[66] contains a similar episode in which the persecutors recount the misfortunes which befell them after their attempted assaults on Florence's virtue. But the difference between the English and the French versions is instructive. It is not enough for the English poet that the diseased, maimed men recognise their sinful natures by confessing to the saintly lady. No sooner do they admit their sins and become healed than Emere, the man to whom Florence has been faithful, orders that they be burned at the stake (ll. 2116-20). Florence, it seems, manages to bring as much disaster into the lives of men that attempt to tryst with her as any Keatsian *belle dame sans merci*. The poet preserves the impression of Florence's Christian forgiveness, however, by hastening to note her reaction to Emere's orders—'Then was the lady woo' (l. 2121). Nevertheless, Emere has his way. The English poet must keep the exemplary point clear: good is rewarded and evil punished—even if the scene of confession is made to appear senseless.

By a variety of changes and additions, the English adapter

---

[66] The text of this Chanson is in vol. II of Wallensköld. It is generally said that the English poem is a translation of a lost version of the chanson which was closely related to the extant French text. If the lost version was not itself an abridgement, the English poet condensed so ruthlessly that his version would be more appropriately referred to as an 'adaptation'. The English poem contains 2,187 lines as compared with 6,410 in the French. Moreover, very few lines can be regarded as exact translation. For a close study of the relationship between the French, Spanish and English texts, see Wenzel, *Die Fassungen der Sage von Florence de Rome*.

underlines the exemplary character of the romance. He eliminates revelatory dreams and prophesies and other such fantastic elements so that the turn of events will seem to hinge on the effective virtues of the exemplary character worthy of emulation. Thus, no magic brooch protects the English heroine's virginity, only her prayers to the Virgin. The English poet does, however, retain the miraculous ringing of the bells. When Florence, washed ashore after the shipwreck, approaches Beuerfayre, the bells of the cloister begin to ring of their own accord (ll. 1892 ff.). The reason this detail was retained is obvious; bells ringing by themselves are a common sign in hagiographic literature that a saint approaches.[67] The feature is, therefore, consistent with the religious intent of the English adapter.

There are other minor changes by which the English version underlines the religious character of the romance. Pope Simon is said to have composed the tale (l. 2173) and he does, in fact, make several appearances in the poem, most notably with some cardinals in a procession which welcomes Florence back to Rome at the conclusion of the tale (ll. 2143–51). Among some rather local religious details are: the description of the seven deadly sins depicted on the wall of Emperor Otes's palace (ll. 329–33) and the reference to the doctrine of trans-substantiation (ll. 1004–5).

It is evident, as in the French version, that Florence's fate is closely connected to that of Rome. Indeed, her beauty, which inspired Garcy's love in the first part of the romance, very nearly leads to the destruction of Rome. Although the English poet retains the historical opening with the conventional Troy material of romance and announces that he comes to Rome—the second Troy—to speak of Aeneas, the Rome that really interests him is not historical Rome but Rome, the 'chefe cyte of crystendome' (l. 17). It is this Rome which provides an appropriate backdrop for the English poet's conception of the story.

This discussion of the literary aspects of the romance

[67] J. S. P. Tatlock, 'Notes on Chaucer', *MLN*, 29 (1914), 98, and P. Barry, 'Bells Rung Without Hands', *MLN*, 30 (1915), 28–9.

would not be complete without some attention to its metrics.

Le Bone Florence of Rome is a tail-rhyme romance composed in stanzas of twelve lines divided into four groups of three. Each group contains, as a rule, a couplet with four accents to the line and a concluding 'tail' with three accents. Usually the four couplets have different rhymes, while the tail-lines rhyme with one another. The danger in such a rigid stanzaic pattern is obvious. It can become monotonous, and *Florence* does have dull patches. But more frequently than not the poet shows himself capable of exploiting the inherent rhetorical possibilities of the stanzaic arrangement. While the tail-rhyme stanza has a strong tendency to fragment, it can be made, as in stanza 7 of the romance, to build to a conclusion in the twelfth line as smoothly as a well-developed paragraph:

> When Syr Garcy herde seye
> That þe emperowre of Rome had soche a may
>   To hys doghtur dere,
> He waxe hasty as the fyre,
> And gart sembyll þe lordys of hys empyre,
>   That bolde and hardy were.
> He seyde, 'Ofte haue ye blamed me,
> For Y wolde not weddyd bee,
>   Y have herde of a clere,
> Florens þat ys feyre and bryght,
> Jn all þys worlde ys not soche a wyȝt,
>   Y wyll hur haue to my fere.'
>
>   [ll. 70–81]

The poet even manages in a *tour de force* to capitalise on the natural tendency of the stanza to divide into four sections. In stanza 170 the poet uses each of the four three-line units to focus attention on the diseased appearance of one of the four persecutors of Florence:

> Mylys that hur aweye ledd,
> He was the fowlest mesell bredd,
>   Of pokkys and bleynes bloo.
> And Machary þat wolde hur haue slayne,
> He stode schakyng the sothe to sayne,
>   Crokyd and crachyd thertoo.

The marynere þat wolde haue layne hur by,
Hys yen stode owte a strote forthy,
  Hys lymmes were roton hym froo.
They put Clarebalde in a whelebarowe,
That strong thefe be stretys narowe,
  Had no fote on to goo.

[ll. 2020–31]

The tale contains the usual categories of conventional expressions—especially in the short lines—found in so many tail-rhyme romances: the summons to attention (*Hende as ye may here*, l. 1998; *As ye may vnderstande*, l. 1896); references to authorities (*In Romance as we rede*, l. 645; *And some boke seyth mare*, l. 84; *As the boke makyth mynde*, l. 2166); assertions of truth (*The certen sothe to saye*, l. 1359; *To wete wythowten wene*, l. 1086); pious expressions (*Thorow þe myght of Mary mylde*, l. 1500; *So Cryste me saue and sayne*, l. 297), etc. It is, perhaps, not so remarkable that many of these conventional phrases are alliterative, for, as Trounce suggests, it may be that 'these . . . are in a special sense the inherited material; through them the tail-rhyme poems are connected in an unbroken line with the old epic poetry'.[68]

Sometimes conventional expressions are repeated in the text with a slight alteration (e.g., *The certen sothe to saye*, l. 1359; *The certen sothe to telle*, l. 306). This kind of substitution occurs frequently in Old English formulae like *þæt wæs god cyning, þæt wæs grim cyning*. The location of the romance's dialect in the north would seem to further support the idea of influence from an alliterative tradition. Moreover, Knobbe, in a comment about literary influences, advances the opinion that the author was familiar with the alliterative *Morte Arthure*.[69] As evidence he points to the poet's making Sir Lucius Jbarnyus founder of Beuerfayre (l. 1888) instead of Julius Caesar, as in the French version; Lucius Iberius is mentioned in line 86 of the alliterative *Morte*.

What is remarkable, I think, is that alliteration is so per-

[68] A. McI. Trounce, 'The English Tail-Rhyme Romances', *MÆ*, i (1932), 171.

[69] Knobbe, 'Über die Mittelenglische Dichtung . . .', 9.

vasive in the romance. Eight hundred and forty-nine of the
2,187 lines contain alliteration, that is, more than a third.
Of the alliterating lines, 144 contain three words with alliteration on the same sound (ll. 17, 30, 38, 39, etc.), twenty contain
four such words (ll. 212, 223, 268, 287, etc.), and fifty-four
lines contain alliteration on two different sounds (ll. 12, 87,
112, 133, etc.). There are even forty instances of overflowing
alliteration of a single sound into a following line or lines (ll.
98–100, 230–1, 285–7, 352–3, etc.). From these statistics it
appears that alliteration is a vital and fundamental part of
the author's mode of thought. Basic and extended forms of the
alliterative long line occur in the poem: AA/AX (ll. 98. 640,
1345, etc.); AX/AX (ll. 95, 1343, etc.); AA/AA (l. 842, etc.).[70] A
very common variation found in the alliterative lines of
Florence is the placement of the alliteration on unstressed
syllables such as prefixes, prepositions, auxiliary verbs,
pronouns, and the second element of compounds (ll. 94, 176,
177, etc.).[71] However, in the romance as we have received it,
alliteration, while an important aspect of the metrical mach-
inery, seems to be a secondary element superimposed upon the
regular stanzaic pattern. It is tempting to wonder—if I am
correct in my assumption that we have here a copy of an
earlier English version[72]—whether there was more alliteration
in the original Middle English text.

Be that as it may, there are concrete things about the use of
alliteration which are observable and which can be commented
upon with certainty. The alliteration which we have is not
primarily structural. It appears often as an unobstrusive
undertone in conventional expressions (usually in the short
lines) or more interestingly as a stylistic device to give emphasis. The concentration of alliteration does seem to occur in
crucial passages.

[70] Marie Borroff, *Sir Gawain and the Green Knight: A Stylistic and
Metrical Study* (New Haven, 1962), 170 and her translation of *Gawain*
(New York, 1967), 56–7.

[71] See J. P. Oakden's discussion of the 'five types of license' in
Alliterative Poetry in Middle English (1930–5; rpt. New York, 1968),
178–9.

[72] See p. 41.

Often it turns up in dramatically significant dialogue, as in the speech of the ambassador who comes on Garcy's behalf to sue for Florence's hand (ll. 208–16, discussed above), the lament of the barons for their dead emperor,

> Who schall vs now geue *l*ondys or *l*ythe,
> *H*awkys, or *h*owndys, or *st*edys *st*ythe . . .?
> [ll. 841–2]

and the revelation of Mylys's wickedness addressed to Emere (ll. 1342–53). It is after this speech that Emere banishes Mylys. The speech is important also for the review it offers of the crimes committed by Mylys against Florence which might be lost sight of by this point in the tale. The technique of recapitulation is, of course, frequently used in oral composition, but it must also be said that this sort of review is likewise employed by writers of literary compositions with an awareness of their audience's need to have its recollections refreshed.

Alliteration serves a decorative function in descriptive set pieces like the portrait of old Garcy (ll. 94–104) and that of Florence and her father, Emperor Otes, in the throne room of their palace (ll. 176–82). Descriptions of battle scenes are unfailingly given emphasis with alliteration, e.g.:

> . . . . *b*odyes *b*rake owt to *b*lede
> *H*edys *h*opped vndur *h*ors fete,
> As hayle*st*ones done in þe *st*rete,
> *St*ycked was many a *st*ede.
> *F*or *F*lorence loue, þat *f*eyre maye,
> Many a *d*oghty *d*yed that *d*ay,
> [ll. 639–44]

The use of alliteration in the French chanson of which the English is probably an adaption is very slight and possibly unconscious. Even in the description of battle scenes, which can usually be depended on to contain alliteration, the French version does not employ it.

Can we assume, then, that the English poet came by his technique independently? Is the English version part of an oral tradition and the French part of a literary one? Did an oral poet who understood French hear the literary version read and develop an oral composition in English? These are tantalising questions, but even after the most exhaustive exploration of metrical evidence, clear answers are as elusive as will-o'-the-wisps. While we know that the English oral tradition is an alliterative one, and that conventional expressions and recapitulation of events characterise the oral style, a poem with all the requisite elements may still not necessarily be an oral composition. As Albert C. Baugh has demonstrated in 'Improvisation in the Middle English Romance',[73] it is difficult to make a clear distinction between oral and literary composition, since in the process of copying, translating, or adapting a scribe might feel free to draw on the conventional clichés and other devices associated with oral composition.

If *Le Bone Florence of Rome* is a copy of a more highly alliterated English version belonging to an oral tradition, the copyist was a 'poet' capable of great artistic judgement. When alliteration is no longer a *regular* element in the metrical structure, it can really become a subtle means of giving emphasis. The poet–copyist of *Le Bone Florence of Rome* seems to have discovered one way of writing a tail-rhyme stanza that avoids the metrical pitfalls Chaucer satirises in *Sir Thopas*.

RELATED TALES

It might be well to consider the treatment of the heroine as an exemplary type in three other related romances about Florence's sister-sufferers—the *King of Tars, Emaré*, and Chaucer's *Man of Law's Tale*. I have selected the *King of Tars* because it is believed to have been directly influenced by a French version of the Florence story. My reason for choosing the other tales is that they offer the opportunity to compare *Le Bone Florence of Rome* with the two best representatives of a related family of romances, the Constance cycle. Chaucer's Tale of Constance is almost always discussed as a thing apart; it will be considered here within its medieval literary context.

[73] 'Improvisation in the Middle English Romance', *PAPS*, 103 (1959), 418–54.

The *King of Tars* is a romance full of the atmosphere of the crusades and the conflict of Christianity and heathendom. The opening of the story is similar to that of *Le Bone Florence of Rome*; both romances contain a heathen ruler who, having failed to win the hand of a Christian princess, invades her country and kills many knights. It has been suggested, first by Laura Hibbard[74] and later, by Robert Geist,[75] that the French original of *Le Bone Florence of Rome* supplied the introduction to the *King of Tars*. Very likely the influence did not move in the reverse direction, since the French chanson, *Florence de Rome*, dates from the first quarter of the thirteenth century, and the *King of Tars* was composed later (*c.* 1325).

The author of the *King of Tars* is less concerned with making his heroine a type of chastity (one of Florence's dominant virtues) than he is with emphasising her *pietas* and *fortitudo* (virtues which Florence also exemplifies). The heroine's trust in God and strength of belief make her an incarnation of Christian *pietas* and *fortitudo*, enabling her to become an instrument of the Christian God's might.

To summarise the romance's action briefly, the daughter of the King of Tars reluctantly marries the heathen sultan of Damascus and gives birth to a deformed child. Each parent claims the beliefs of the other to be responsible. Whereas the prayers of the Sultan to Mahoun are futile, the child immediately becomes handsome and well-formed when it is baptised at its mother's request. The power of the Christian God is thereby verified, and the Sultan adopts the faith of his wife.

The homiletic tendency of the romance is patent in the heroine's catechising of the convert-husband in Christian dogma. Although the Sultan decides to embrace Christianity after the occurrence of the miracle, it is clear that his conversion is not complete until his wife teaches him about the

[74] Laura Hibbard, *Medieval Romance in England: A Study of the Sources and Analogues of the Non-Cyclic Romances* (New York, 1924), 15.

[75] Robert Geist, 'On the Genesis of the *King of Tars*', *JEGP*, 42 (1943), 265.

principles of Christian belief—the Trinity, the death and resurrection of Christ, and the Last Judgement. The poet's probable intention is to make the point that *pietas* and *fortitudo* are not the result of faith alone, but must be informed by knowledge. It is not enough to be moved by miracles. The beautification of the monstrous child is made possible by the prayers of a Christian whose *pietas* and *fortitudo* are grounded in knowledge. Florence's miraculous healing power does not seem to be qualified in this way.

The *King of Tars* is more consistently religious in tone than *Le Bone Florence of Rome*. Indeed, it seems to have been regarded as a devotional tale rather than a romance by the compilers of the manuscripts in which it appears. It is separated from the romances in the Auchinleck MS, where it is placed between *Adam and Eve* and the legend of Gregory; and it is included as well in the Vernon MS, which is concerned almost completely with materials which are religious in character.

The romance of the sufferings of Emaré also seems to have been regarded as a devotional tale, placed as it is among religious works in MS Cotton Caligula A. II. Emaré is another learned heroine. She is not, like the daughter of the King of Tars, an instructress of Christian dogma, but she has learned courtesy and embroidery from a lady called Abbro and, in a more limited way than Florence, practises nursing. A late work, like *Le Bone Florence of Rome*, the *Emaré* was written within ten years of the *Man of Law's Tale*, of which it is a fairly close analogue. *Emaré* and the *Man of Law's Tale* belong to the Constance cycle, a somewhat separate branch of the family of romances dealing with persecuted women who are the victims of false accusation. In *Emaré*, as well as in Chaucer's Tale of Constance, the heroine suffers persecution and exile because her mother-in-law accuses her of giving birth to a monster; in *Le Bone Florence of Rome* the sorrowful fate of Florence is the result of her brother-in-law's charge of adultery.

Although Emaré is more distantly related to Florence than she is to Constance, there are striking resemblances between them. Florence's flawless beauty and gleaming garments, for example, merely the conventional attributes of a courtly lady in the first half of the romance, become by the midpoint of the story symbolic reflections of her virtues. Emaré's celestial beauty functions in the same way from the outset of the story. Her rich robe, described at length in 109 lines, seems to be an external reflection of her inner perfection. Each time she is cast adrift on the sea like a martyr, the poet emphasises that she is wearing the beautiful garment which sets her apart, indeed, above her dreary circumstances. For both Florence and Emaré, beauty, symbolic of moral perfection, is also the basic cause of suffering. As Florence is mistaken in her magnificent dress by the wicked Machary for a 'fende of helle', so Emaré's intriguing mother-in-law takes Emaré's beauty as a sign that the heroine is an offspring of hell. In both instances, the misapprehension flows from evil which cannot recognise beauty for what it is.

The heroine's sufferings are not educative, for her virtuous nature cannot be improved. An innocent sufferer, she places her trust in God, whose providence never forsakes her. An embodiment of *pietas* and *fortitudo* like Florence and the daughter of the King of Tars, she is rewarded, after having twice been cast adrift on the sea, through the agency of God's justice,

> She was dryven toward Rome,
> Thorow the grace of God yn trone,
> That all thyng may fulfylle.[76]
>
> [ll. 679–81]

It is the unfailing justice of God's providence which Emaré's fortunes exemplify.

The poet of *Emaré* frequently rises to a high level of artistry, making his version of the Constance story one of the more humanised renderings before Chaucer's unsurpassed *Man of Law's Tale*.

Whether the Man of Law was really intended to be the narrator of Chaucer's tale is not a question that is relevant for

[76] Joseph Ritson, ed., *Emaré*, *Ancient English Metrical Romances*, 3 vols. (London, 1802), II, 232.

the present discussion; there are, however, at least two reasons which make him seem appropriate. First, as an earthly representative of justice, it is somehow fitting that he should tell a tale about the working of Divine Justice; and second, as a representative type of middle-class tastes, it is reasonable that he might be attracted to so sentimental a tale as the story of Constance and her succession of miraculous preservations. These are generally characterised by critics as 'glaring improbabilities',[77] but, in point of fact, they are not so very different from the pageant of incredible disasters which intrigue thousands of housewives on television soap operas today.

The problems in the action of the story which Chaucer inherited from his sources are mitigated somewhat by his drawing attention away from the dramatic events of the narrative to the pathos of Constance's personal situation. He is sensitive to the heroine's emotions, for instance, as she leaves her family for a strange land,

> Allas! what wonder is it though she wepte,
> That shal be sent to straunge nacioun
> Fro friendes, that so tendrely hir kepte,
> And to be bounden under subjeccioun
> Of oon, she knoweth not his condicioun?
> [ll. 267–71]

We have, too, the nice human touch of brave Constance smiling through her tears as the ship sets sail:

> She peyneth hire to make good contenance.
> [l. 322]

Aside from Chaucer's superior sensibility in managing the emotional qualities in the story, he seems to present a more comprehensive view of the central theme of God's justice than is found in any of the other of the Eustace–Constance–Florence–Griselda romances which I have read. In a sense, Chaucer's Tale of Constance is more effectively didactic because the poet's insight into the idea of God's justice is more theo-

[77] George Kane, *Middle English Literature: A Critical Study of the Romances, the Religious Lyrics, Piers Plowman* (London, 1951), 62.

logically sound. Chaucer's understanding of the propelling idea behind the legend reminds us that Chaucer's poetry cannot be detached from medieval Christianity.

Chaucer presents a rounded view of God's justice by playing on the contrast between the Man of Law's self-indulgent, misguided understanding, and the deeper view of the order of things possessed by Constance, which functions as a corrective. Keeping his eye on the 'sentence' like the dedicated Robertsonian that he is, Chauncey Wood notes quite accurately that the Man of Law wrongly makes value judgements about God's ways.[78] Whereas he only praises God when Constance escapes from a tight spot, the heroine welcomes God's 'sonde' (lines 523 and 826) whether it means good or bad Fortune. Constance's prayers to God sound the same when she is cast adrift and when she is safe on shore. Her saintly attitude apprehends that if it comes from God it must be just.

Chaucer's use of the Man of Law's attitude as a counter-weight is astute, if, perhaps, a little over-subtle. Few in Chaucer's audience, I suspect, who would have identified with the very natural reactions of the lawyer would then have realised they ought to be reacting to Fortune like the saintly Constance. Nevertheless, this tension exists, and it is important.

Professor Wood's intelligent if narrow view of the tale leads him to treat the Man of Law too harshly. Besides representing that of a Christian who has confounded personal comfort with an understanding of God's justice, the Man of Law's emotional involvement with Constance's fate is an artistic necessity. If the Man of Law were not intruding—however anti-intellec-tually—with sympathetic commentary and interpretation of the vicissitudes of the story, the audience would be much more aware of the 'glaring improbabilities' that George Kane complains of. The emotional involvement of the narrator with the plight of the heroine is also a major reason that Chaucer's narrative is a more human and moving story than *Le Bone Florence of Rome*, the *King of Tars*, and *Emaré*.

There are many romances about persecuted women in Middle English. Besides those discussed above, seven more are

[78] *Chaucer and the Country of the Stars* (Princeton, 1970), 197.

extant: *Sir Isumbras, Octavian, Sir Eglamour, Torrent of Portyngale, Sir Triamour,* Chaucer's *Clerk's Tale,* and *Lai le Freine.* Scores of similar tales are represented in the Continental literature of the Middle Ages as well. What motivated poets to write such stories? Why did they find such a ready audience?

An answer to these questions may be found in the general attitude towards women in the Middle Ages. As reflected in the literature of the period, this attitude is generally ambivalent. Among the works of individual writers like Chaucer, Lydgate, and Dunbar, misogynistic attacks on women occur as often as poems in fervent praise of women. This double vision reflects, in part, an obvious condition of human life: there are good and bad women. More significantly, it also reflects the two contradictory streams in medieval thought about women. The cult of courtly love and the chivalrous devotion inspired by the Virgin Mary tended to exalt women; on the other hand, anti-feminist clerical writing dwelt on the baneful influence of women. This negative strain in thinking about women seems to have out-weighed the positive. A reaction against courtly love (which exalted women to a level unprecedented in earlier periods) was implicit in the system. No doubt the unrequited courtly lover occasionally wondered whether he had, perhaps, over-idealised love, a reaction probably intensified by the fact that the courtly love object is an adulteress. Interestingly enough, Andreas Capallanus' manual, *The Art of Courtly Love,* includes a section entitled 'The Rejection of Love'. Despite the worship of the Virgin, clerical feeling in the Middle Ages inclined toward anti-feminism. Robert Brunne's *Handlyng Synne,* a manual of moral instruction, warns that even a chaste man alone with a woman will fall into lechery.[79] A striking example of the effect of clerical misogyny on romance writing occurs in *Gawain and the Green Knight*:

Bot hit is no ferly þaʒ a fole madde,
And þurʒ wyles of wymmen be wonen to sorʒe,
For so watz Adam in erde with one bygyled,

---

[79] Robert of Brunne, *Handlyng Synne,* ed. F. J. Furnevall, EETS, ES, 119 (London, 1901), 240.

And Salamon with fele sere, and Samson eftsonez—
Dalyda dalt hym hys wyrde—and Dauyth þerafter
Watz blended with Barsabe, þat much bale þoled.
Now þese were wrathed wyth her wyles, hit were a wynne huge
To luf hom wel, and leue hem not, a leude þat coupe.
For þes wer forne þe freest, þat folȝed alle þe sele
Exellently of alle þyse oþer, vnder heuenryche
          þat mused;
     And alle þay were biwyled
     With wymmen þat þay vsed.
     Þaȝ I be now bigyled,
     Me þink me burde be excused.[80]

[ll. 2414–28]

The Gawain poet launches this attack with the stock medieval
examples of men degraded by women.

The two streams of the ambivalent medieval attitudes
towards women seem to converge in the cycles of romances
about persecuted women. Although an allegorical reading of
the tales indicates that the heroines are types of one virtue or
another, a moment's consideration of the literal events of the
romances would lead one to suspect that their creators were
unconsciously stalking shadowy villains. In the light of the
essentially devotional nature of the Eustace–Constance–
Florence–Griselda cycle, it is likely that many of the romances
were written by clerics who believed that women, even the
best of them, were ensnaring creatures 'beautified with the
face of a noble lion, yet . . . blemished with the belly of a
reeking kid and . . . beweaponed with the virulent tail of a
viper',[81] threatening degradation of the soul. On an unconscious level, at least, there must have been something con-
genial to clerical minds in a story about the persecution of a
woman, even a woman saint.

These stories involving ambivalent attitudes toward women
did not originate in the Middle Ages. As Margaret Schlauch has

[80] *Sir Gawain and the Green Knight*, ed. J. R. R. Tolkien and E. V.
Gordon, 2nd ed., rev. Norman Davis (Oxford, 1967), 66–7.

[81] From Walter Map's 'Letter from Valerius to Ruffinus', quoted
by Katharine M. Rogers, *The Troublesome Helpmate* (Seattle, 1966),
p. ix.

demonstrated, the motifs in the families of romances involving persecuted women have folklore backgrounds.[82] Moreover, the stories emerge in eastern as well as western literature, and they do not cease to evolve in the Middle Ages. The ambivalent attitude reflected in the medieval romances must, indeed, be archetypal, perhaps stemming from a boy's initial erotic attachment to his mother and his subsequent fear of female dominance, a phenomenon amply explored by Freud. Modern permutations of the theme are numerous. The eighteenth-century novel *Clarissa Harlowe* is commonly referred to as a derivative saint's legend about a woman who 'is pure . . . and yet to be violated'.[83] Hawthorne's *The Scarlet Letter*, which bears the sub-title 'A Romance', even contains some of the motifs found in the Eustace–Constance–Florence–Griselda cycle: a distasteful proposal of marriage from an old man (here marriage is not merely threatened, it occurs); the accusation of having borne a demon child; a heroine with a flair for embroidery (like Emaré);[84] a persecuted woman turned nurse. By the twentieth century the literary theme has been provided with an explicit theoretical frame of reference by Freud, who emphasises the great influence of the mother over her son. Writers dwelling on the negative aspects of maternal influence have emphasised the woman's capacity for destruction. D. H. Lawrence, in an eccentric discussion of the *Scarlet Letter*, sounds like a direct descendent of Walter Map:

> Even when she is most sweet and a salvationist, she is her most devilish, is woman. She gives her man the sugar-plum of her submissive sweetness. And when he's taken this sugar-plum in his mouth, a scorpion comes out of it.[85]

[82] Margaret Schlauch, *Chaucer's Constance and Accused Queens* (New York, 1927).

[83] Dorothy Van Ghent, 'Clarissa Harlowe', *The English Novel* (New York, 1961), 50.

[84] In both cases there may be a trace of the medieval, indeed ancient, view that women are frivolous and only care about clothes.

[85] D. H. Lawrence, *Studies in Classic American Literature* (New York, 1953), 104.

DIALECT AND DATE

The dialect is north Midland, but its northern character must
be emphasised.

The phonology and the accidence of *Le Bone Florence of
Rome* are characterised by a combination of northern and
Midland elements such as we might expect to find in a north
Midland dialect. There are many instances of the Midland
rounded development of OE *ā* proved original by rhyme—
bloo: thertoo, ll. 2022, 2025; *foys: goys: rose: lose,* ll. 744, 747,
750, 753; *stone: tone,* ll. 340–1; *thyckfolde: colde: bolde: holde,*
ll. 873, 870, 867, 864. However, the northern preservation of
unrounded *ā* is predominant—*sa: culpa,* ll. 1360–1; *blake:
sake: wrake: take,* ll. 579, 576, 582, 585; *hale: tale,* ll. 1130,
1129; *are: fare,* ll. 1876–7; *hare: mare: sware: dare,* ll. 87, 84,
90, 93; *sare: care: mare: answare,* ll. 684, 687, 690, 693; *rase:
face,* ll. 565–6; *goost: haste,* ll. 778–9. In the last case, the *oo* is
probably a scribal error for *aa*.

The genitive singular of nouns is generally formed with the
Midland ending—*(y)s (ther gatys gayne,* l. 149), but the northern
uninflected form is also found (*Florence fadur,* l. 364).[86]

The third person feminine pronoun is characteristically the
Midland form *s(c)he*; northern *scho(o)* also appears twice and is
proved original by rhyme (ll. 1466, 1980).

The verbal inflections are similarly mixed. Northern (*-ys*) as
well as Midland (*-yth, -eth*) forms of the third person singular
present indicative appear. Also, the present participle ending
has the form *-yng* as in the Midlands as well as *-ande* which is
found in the north and north Midlands.

The manuscript contains a considerable number of ex-
clusively northern features. These are:

1. the dropping of the *-n* in the infinitive (the exceptions in
Florence tend to occur in northern texts).

2. the persistence of *-n* in the past participles of strong
verbs (*tobrokyn,* l. 103).

3. the assimilation of the vowel of the plural to that of the

[86] In nouns which end in *-s* the uninflected genitive may appear for
phonetic reasons (*a burges house,* l. 446).

singular, in the preterite of strong verbs. There are, however, exceptions among Class I and Class V verbs. In Class I verbs the preterite singular is $\bar{a}$ (*rase*, l. 565; *wrate*, l. 2173) and $\bar{\varrho}$ (*glode*, l. 1709; *rode*, l. 588) while the preterite plural is always $\bar{\varrho}$ (*abode*, l. 446; *rode*, l. 155; *schoon*, l. 156). The preterite singular of Class V verbs is $\bar{e}$ (*ete*, l. 1463) or *au* (*sawe*, l. 289), but the preterite plural is *ai* (*laye*, l. 1566).

4. the shortened stem of 'take', *ta* (l. 1107), which is proved original by rhyme.

5. the appearance of an important group of words found only in northern texts. My list of thirty-five northernisms agrees with that compiled by Dunlap[87] (*bigge, blome, busk, gayne, gere, lithe, min, nefe, raike, ser, site, thro, ware, lele, trayne, barmeteme, beld, brand, fax, helde, lende, sayne, spere, stith, strynde, swime, thikke, folde, tuggel, happe, irke, thertil, thir, brysse, strik*).[88]

On these grounds, I judge that the author of this romance lived in the northernmost part of the Midland area where both northern and Midland sounds and forms would be used, but where northern influences would be especially strong. The predominant unrounded development of OE. *a*, even before l+consonant and frequently before nasals (*lappe: happe*, ll. 113, 112; *alse: false*, ll. 752, 751; *halle: crystalle*, ll. 325–6; *walle: small*, ll. 160–1; *landys: standys*, ll. 220–1), points to an eastern part of the northern Midland area.

Professor Lillian H. Hornstein dates the manuscript between 1475 and 1500.[89] The palaeographical evidence and the relatively large number of forms not recorded with these meanings before the sixteenth century[90] in the vocabulary

[87] A. R. Dunlap, 'The Vocabulary of the Middle English Romances in Tail-Rhyme Stanzas', *Delaware Notes*, series 14 (1941), 39.

[88] *Bownes*, the southern variation of ME. *burn*, should also be noted. Since it is unique, I think it must be considered a curiosity.

[89] 'Le Bone Florence of Rome', *A Manual of the Writings in Middle English*, 131.

[90] These are *eyen*, 'young hawks' (l. 845), *forne*, 'on account of' (l. 67), *garson*, 'retainer' (l. 118), *gente*, 'courteously' (l. 2133), *hodur*, 'cuddle' (l. 112), *happe*, 'embrace' (l. 112), *hypping*, 'limping' (l. 1991), *knok*, 'attack' (l. 281), *meene*, 'intend' (l. 2182), *ryall*, 'noble' (l. 174), *rechyd*, 'launched' (l. 132), and *stekyth*, 'sticks' (l. 1472).

make 1500 seem nearer the fact than 1475. To be sure, the *terminus ad quem* would represent an unusually late date if this manuscript were the first written version of the English romance. I doubt, however, that it is the original. Very likely, it is a northern copy of a manuscript written about fifty years earlier in the north-east Midlands. It might be argued that the original could be northern and the copy from the north-east Midlands; however, by 1500, a scribe from the Midlands would be so conditioned by the London standard that he could not fail to note northern features and remove them. A northern scribe, on the other hand, less influenced by London, might still in 1500 retain and introduce into the text distinctly northern dialectal traits, especially if he were somewhat past middle age.

My assumption of a northern copy of a north-east Midland manuscript enables me to accept, in part, both Knobbe's assignment of the dialect area to the northern border of the Midlands and Wilda's[91] localisation in the southern part of the north.

[91] O. Wilda, *Ueber die örtliche Verbreitung der zwolfzeiligen Schweifreim-strophe in England* (Breslau, 1887).

SELECTIVE BIBLIOGRAPHY

MANUSCRIPT

MS Cambridge University Ff. 2.38 (More 690), ff. 239b–254a.

EDITIONS OF THE STORY OF FLORENCE

I. Middle English

Knobbe, W. Albert, *Über die Mittelenglische Dichtung Le Bone Florence of Rome*. Diss. Marburg, 1899, Marburg: N. G. Elwert'sche Verlagsbuchhandlung, 1899 (introduction).

Ritson, Joseph, ed. *Ancient English Metrical Romances*. 3 vols. London: W. Bulmer & Co., 1802. III, 1–92.

Vietor, Wilhelm, *Le Bone Florence of Rome*. Diss. Marburg, 1893, Marburg: N. G. Elwert'sche Verlagsbuchhandlung, 1893 (text).

II. Continental

Dit de Flourence de Rome, ed. Achille Jubinal, *Nouveau Recueil de Contes, Dits, Fabliaux et Autres Pièces Inédits des XIIIe, XIVe, et XVe Siècles*, VI, 88–117. Paris: E. Pannier, 1839–42.

Florence de Rome: Chanson D'Aventure du Premier Quart du 13e Siècle, ed. A. Wallensköld. *SATF*. 2 vols. 1909; rpt. New York: Johnson Reprint Corp., 1968.

Historia Critica de la Litteratura Española, ed. Amador de los Ríos, 'Cuento Muy Famoso del Enperador Ottas de Roma', V, 391–468. Madrid: J. Muñoz, 1864.

REVIEWS OF VIETOR–KNOBBE EDITION

Heuser, W., *ES*, 29 (1899), 123–5.

Holthausen, Ferdinand, *Anglia*, 10 (September 1899), 129–30.

Stengel, E., *Kritische Jahresbucher*, 7, pt. 2 (1901), 72.

Wallensköld, A., *Deutsche Litteraturzeitung* (1900), 422–4.

Weyrauch, M., *Archivum*, 110 (1900), 446.

TEXTUAL

Holthausen, Ferdinand, 'Zu Mittelenglischen Romanzen', *Anglia*, 41 (1917), 497–512.

Kolbing, E., 'Kleine Beitrage zur Erklärung und Text-Kritik Englischer Dichter', *ES*, 3 (1880), 92–105.

LANGUAGE, DIALECT

A New English Dictionary on Historical Principles, ed. James A. H. Murray. 10 vols. Oxford: Clarendon Press, 1888.

Brandl, Alois H., 'Mittelenglische Literatur', in Paul, *Grundriss der Germanischen Philologie*, II, 2, 609–718. Strassburg, 1891–3.

Curtius, F. J., 'An Investigation of the Rimes and Phonology of the Middle-Scotch Romance Clariodus', *Anglia*, 16 (1894), 387–450.

Dunlap, A. R., 'The Vocabulary of the Middle English Romances in Tail-Rhyme Stanza', *Delaware Notes*, Ser. 14 (1941), 1–42.

Kurath, Hans and S. M. Kuhn, *Middle English Dictionary*. Ann Arbor: University of Michigan Press, 1952– .

Moore, Samuel, S. B. Meech, and Harold Whitehall, 'Middle English Dialect Characteristics and Dialect Boundaries', *Essays and Studies in English and Comparative Literature*, 13. Ann Arbor: University of Michigan Press, 1935, 1–60.

Mossé, Fernand, *A Handbook of Middle English*, trans. James Walker. Baltimore: Johns Hopkins Press, 1952.

Mustanoja, Tauno, *A Middle English Syntax, Memoires de la Société Neophilologique*, XXIII. Helsinki: Société Neophilologique, 1960.

Skeat, Walter W., *Principles of English Etymology*. Oxford: Oxford University Press, 1891.

Sweet, Henry, *History of English Sounds*. Oxford: Clarendon Press, 1888.

Trounce, A. McI., 'The English Tail-Rhyme Romances', *MÆ*, 1 (1932), 87–108; 2 (1933), 34–57; 3 (1934), 30–50.

Wilda, O., *Ueber die Örtliche Verbreitung die Zweifzeiligen Schweifreimstrophe in England*. Breslau, 1887.

SOURCES AND ANALOGUES

I. General studies

Aebisher, Paul, 'Fragments de la Chanson de la Reine Sebile et du Roman de Florence de Rome', *Studi Medievali*, N.S., 16 (1943–50), 135–60.

Boyd, Beverly, *The Middle English Miracles of the Virgin*. San Marino: Huntington Library, 1964.

Chaytor, H. J., 'A Fragment of the Chanson D'Aventure, Florence de Rome', *Modern Humanities Research Bulletin*, 1 No. 2 (September 1927), 48.

Christophersen, Paul, *The Ballad of Sir Aldingar*. Oxford: Clarendon Press, 1952.

Geist, Robert, 'On the Genesis of the *King of Tars*', *JEGP*, 42 (1943), 260–8.

Gough, Alfred B., *The Constance-Saga*. Berlin: Mayer & Müller, 1902.

Hibbard, Laura, *Mediaeval Romance in England*. New York: Oxford University Press, 1924.

Hilka, Alfons, 'Zum Crescientiastoff', *Archiv*, 133 (1915), 135–41.

Hornstein, Lillian H., 'A Folklore Theme in the *King of Tars*', *PQ*, 20 (January 1941), 82-7.

——, 'The Historical Background of *The King of Tars*', *Spec.*, 16 (October 1941), 404–14.

——, 'New Analogues to the "King of Tars" ', *MLR*, 26 (October 1941), 432–42.

——, 'Trivet's Constance and the *King of Tars*', *MLN*, 55 (1940), 354–7.

Isaacs, Neal D., 'Constance in Fourteenth Century England', *Neuphilologische Mitteilungen*, 59 (1958), 260–77.

Karl, Louis, 'Florence de Rome et la Vie de Deux Saints de Hongrie', *Revue des Langues Romanes*, 52 (1909), 163–80.

Krappe, Alexander H., 'The Offa–Constance Legend', *Anglia*, 61 (1937), 361–9.

Lawrence, William W., 'The Banished Wife's Lament', *MP*, 5 (January 1908), 1–19.

Mussafia, Adolf, 'Über eine Italienische Metrische Darstellung der Crescentia Saga', *Sitzungsberichte der Phil.-Hist. Classe der Kais. Akad. der Wissenschaften*, 51 (Vienna, 1865), 589–692.

Rickert, Edith, 'The Old English Offa Saga', *MP*, 2 (January 1905), 1–56.

Schlauch, Margaret, *Chaucer's Constance and the Accused Queens*. New York: New York University Press, 1927.

Siefkin, Ortgies, *Das Geduldige Weib in der Englischen Literatur bis auf Shakspere: Der Konstanzetypus*. Diss. Leipzig, 1903. Rathenow: Buchdrucherei von Max Babenzien, 1903.

Stefanovic, S., 'Die Crescentia–Florence Sage: eine Kritische Studie ueber ihren Ursprung und ihre Entwicklung', *Romanische Forschung*, 29 (1908), 461–557.

Teubert, S., *Crescentia-Studien*. Diss. Halle, 1906.

Wallensköld, A., 'Le Conte de la Femme Chaste Convoitée par son Beau-frère', *Acta Societatis Scientiarum Fennicae*, 37 (Helsingfors, 1907), 1–172.

——, 'L'Origine et l'Evolution du Conte de la Femme Chaste', *Neophilologus Mitteilungen*, 14 (Helsingfors, 1912), 67–77.

Wenzel, Rudolph, *Die Fassungen der Sage von Florence de Rome*. Diss. Marburg, 1890. Marburg: Buchdruckerei Fr. Sommering, 1890.

Whiting, B. J., 'Proverbs in Certain Middle English Romances in Relation to Their French Sources', *Harvard Studies in Philology and Literature*, 15 (1933), 75–121.

Wickert, Maria, 'Chaucer's Konstanze und die Legende der Guten Frauen', *Anglia*, 69, pt. 1 (1950), 89–104.

II. Editions

Alfonso X el Sabio, *Cantigas de Santa Maria*, ed. Walter Mettman. 2 vols. Coimbra: Acta Universitatis Conimbrigensis, 1961.

Arabian Nights Entertainments, ed. Jonathan Scott, 'The Adventures of the Cauzee, His Wife . . .', vi, 396–408. London: Printed for Longman, Hurst, Rees, Orme and Brown, 1811.

Besançon, Etienne de, *Alphabetum Narrationum*, ed. M. M. Banks, EETS, OS, 126, 127. London: K. Paul, Trench, Trübner & Co., 1904–5.

Bonafadini, Antonio, *La Vita di Santa Guglielma*. Bologna: G. Ferrara, 1878.

The Book of the Thousand Nights and One, ed. John Payne, 'The Jewish Cadi and His Pious Wife', v, 9–13. London, 1883.

Bourbon, Etienne de, 'Liber de Septem Bonis', *Anecdotes Historiques, Legendes et Apologues Tirés du Recueil Inédit d'Etienne de Bourbon*, ed. A. Lecoy de la Marche, 115–17. Paris: Libraire Renouard, 1877.

Briccio, Giovanni, *La Historia di Flavia Imperatrice*. Venice, 1812.

Child, Francis J., ed. *The English and Scottish Popular Ballads*. 5 vols. Boston: Houghton, Mifflin & Co., 1882–98.

Coinci, Gautier de, 'De l'Emperirix qui garda sa Chastée', *Nouveau Recueil de Fabliaux et Contes Inédits*, ed. Dominique M. Méon, ii, 1–128. Paris: Chasseriau, 1823.

Contes Inédits des Mille et une Nuits, ed. G. S. Trebutien, 'La Vertuese Israelite', iii, 422–4. Paris: Dondey-Duprés, 1828.

Croix, Petis de la, trans., 'Histoire de Repsima', *Mille et un Jours*, v, 241–95. Paris: C. F. Lehoucq, 1840.

Dias, Balthasar. 'Historia da Imperatriz Porcina', *Floresta de Varios Romances*, ed. Theo. Braga, 104–49. Portugal: Typ. da Livaria Nacional, 1869.

Emaré, ed. Edith Rickert, EETS, OS, 99. London: K. Paul Trench, Trübner & Co., 1906.

Fabliaux ou Contes du XIIe et du XIIIe Siècle, ed. P. J. B. Le Grand, 'De La Bonne Imperatrice', v, 125–9. Paris: Jules Renouard, Libraire, 1829.

Garlande, Jean de, *The Stella Maris of John of Garland*, ed. Evelyn Faye Wilson. Cambridge, Mass.: published with Wellesley College by Medieval Academy of America, 1946.

Gesta Romanorum, ed. Hermann Oesterley, 'De Octavian qui Super Omnia Uxorem Dilexit', 648–53. Berlin: Weidmann, 1872.

Gesta Romanorum, trans. Charles Swan, rev. ed. E. A. Baker. London: G. Routledge & Sons, 1905.

Gobii, Johannes Junior, *Scala Celi*, copied by Luella Carter. Chicago: J. Zainer, 1928.

Grimms, Brüder, 'Hildegard', *Deutsche Sagen*, ii, 83–5. Leipzig, 1818.

Herold, Johannes, 'Discipulus Redivivus', *Promptuarium de Miraculis Beate Marie Virginis*, No. 635, ed. Bonaventura Elers. Nürnberg, 1728 [not seen].

Hoccleve, Thomas, 'Fabula de quadam Imperatrice Romana', *Hoccleve's Minor Poems*, ed. F. J. Furnivall and I. Gollancz, EETS, ES, 61, 140–73. London: K. Paul, Trench, Trübner & Co., 1892.

Die Kaiserchronik, ed. Edward Schröder, 'Crescentia', 289–314. Hannover: Hahn, 1892.

Macaire: Chanson de Geste, ed. M. Francis Guessard, *Les Anciens Poètes de la France*, ix. Paris: A. Franck, 1866.

La Manekine, ed. Hermann Suchier, *Oeuvres Poetiques de Philippe de Remi Sire de Beaumanoir*, SATF, xxvii. Paris: 1884–5.

Monmerqué, Louis and F. Michel, eds., *Théâtre Français au Moyen Age*, 'Mystère de l'Empereris de Rome', 365–416. Paris: Didot, 1840.

Nino, Antonio de, 'Favola Gentile', *Usi e Costumi Abruzzesi*, iii, 153–6. 1883: rpt. Firenze: L. S. Olschki, 1963–5.

Octavian, ed. G. Sarrazin, Altenglische Bibliothek, iii. Heilbronn: Gebr. Henniger, 1885.

Pulci, Antonio, 'Santa Guglielma', *Sacre Rappresentazione*, ed. Allesandro d'Ancona, iii, 208–34. Firenze: Successori Le Monnier, 1872.

Rosenblut, Hans, 'Ein Liepleich History Von Groszer Schone, Gedult und Kuscheiteiner Edeln Keyseryn', *Fastnachtspiele aus dem Funfzehnten Jahrhundert*, ed. Adelbert Keller, iii, 139–49. Stuttgart: Litterarischer Verein, 1853.

Tales from the Arabic, ed. John Payne, 'Story of the Pious Woman Accused of Lewdness', iii, 263–74. London: printed for the Villon Society, 1884

Timoneda, Juan, *El Patrañuelo*. Madrid: Espas-Calpe, S.A., 1958.

Tuti-Nameh, ed. Goerge Rosen, 'Geschichte der Merhuma', i, 89–108. Leipzig: F. V. Brodhaus, 1858.

RELATIONSHIP WITH FOLKTALES

Barry, P., 'Bells Rung Without Hands', MLN, 30 (1915), 28–9.

Child, Francis J., ed., *The English and Scottish Popular Ballads*. 5 vols. Boston: Houghton Mifflin & Co., 1882–98, ii, 34; iii, 235.

Dickson, Arthur, *Valentin and Orson: A Study*. New York: Columbia University Press, 1929, 72.

Fahlin, Carin, 'La Femme Innocente Exilée dans une Forêt: Motif Folklorique de la Litterature Médiévale", *Mélanges de Philologie Romane Offerts à M. K. Michaelsson*, 138–48. Göteborg, 1952.

Grundtvig, Svend., H. G. Nielsen, and A. Olrik, eds., *Gamle Folkeviser*, i, 195; iii, 782; iv, 730. Copenhagen, 1853, 1862, 1883.

Stefanovic, S., 'Ein Beitrag zur Angelsachsischer Offa Sage', *Anglia*, 35 (1908–11), 483–525.

Tatlock, J. S. P., 'Notes on Chaucer', *MLN*, 29 (1914), 98.

Thompson, Stith, *Motif Index of Folk Literature*. 6 vols. in 4. Helsinki: Suomalainen Tredeakatemia Academia Scientiarum Fennica, 1932–6.

METRE

Baugh, Albert C., 'Improvisation in the Middle English Romance', *PAPS*, 103 (1959), 418–54.

Borroff, Marie, *Sir Gawain and the Green Knight: A Stylistic and Metrical Study*. New Haven: Yale University Press, 1962.

Curschmann, Michael, 'Oral Poetry in Medieval English, French, and German Literature, Some Notes on Recent Research', *Spec.*, 42 (January 1967), 35–52.

Oakden, J. P., *Alliterative Poetry in Middle English*. 1930–5; rpt. New York: Archon, 1968.

Sir Gawain and the Green Knight, trans. Marie Borroff. New York: W. W. Norton, 1967, 55 ff.

Waldron, Ronald A., 'Oral Formulaic Technique and Middle English Alliterative Poetry', *Spec.*, 32 (October 1957), 792–802.

PALAEOGRAPHY

Dawson, G. E. and L. Kennedy-Skipton, *Elizabethan Handwriting 1500–1600*. New York: Faber, 1968.

Jenkinson, Hilary, *The Later Court Hands in England from the Fifteenth to the Seventeenth Centuries*. 1927; rpt. New York: Frederick Unger Publishing Co., 1969.

——, *Palaeography and the Practical Study of Court Hand*. Cambridge: Cambridge University Press, 1915.

Johnson, Charles and Hilary Jenkinson, *English Court Hand A.D. 1066-1500*. 2 vols. 1915; rpt. New York: Frederick Unger Publishing Co., 1967.

Parkes, Malcolm B., *English Cursive Book Hands, 1250–1500*. Oxford: Clarendon Press, 1969.

Wright, C. E., *English Vernacular Hands: From the Twelfth to the Fifteenth Centuries*. Oxford: Clarendon Press, 1960.

BIBLIOGRAPHIES

Hornstein, Lillian H., 'Le Bone Florence of Rome' and 'Eustace–Constance–Florence–Griselda Legends', *A Manual of the Writings in Middle English 1050–1400*, ed. J. Burke Severs, Fasc. 1, I, 131–2, 278–92. New Haven: Connecticut Academy of Arts and Science, 1968.

Bossuat, R., ed., *Manuel Bibliographique de la LitteratureFrançaise du Moyen Age*. Paris: Libraire d'Argences, 1951 (1st supplement, Paris, 1955; 2nd supplement, Paris, 1961).

Brown, Carleton and Rossell H. Robbins, *An Index of Middle English Verse*. New York: Columbia University Press, 1943.

A Catalogue of the Manuscripts Preserved in the Library of the University of Cambridge, ed. H. R. Luard *et al.* 5 vols. Cambridge: Cambridge University Press, 1857.

Chauvin, Victor, *Bibliographie des Oeuvrages Arabes ou Relatifs aux Arabes*. Liege: H. Vaillant-Carmanne, 1892–1907.

Renwick, W. L. and H. Orton, *The Beginnings of EnglishLiterature to Skelton, 1509*. rev. ed. London: Cresset Press, 1952.

OTHER

The Catholic Encyclopedia, ed. Charles G. Hebermann *et al.* 16 vols. New York: Robert Appleton Co., 1909.

Clement of Rome, 'The First Epistle of Clement to the Corinthians', *The Ante-Nicene Fathers*, ed. Alexander Roberts and James Donaldson, I, 5–21. New York: Scribner's, 1926.

Gibbs, A. C., *Middle English Romances*. London: Edward Arnold and Evanston, Ill.: Northwestern University Press, 1966.

Graesse, J. G. Th., Friedrich Benedict, and Helmut Plechl, *Orbis Latinus: Lexikon lateinischer geographischer Namen des Mittelalters und der Neuzeit*. 3 vols. Braunschweig: Klinkhardt & Biermann, 1972.

Hibbard, Laura, *Mediaeval Romance in England*. New York: Oxford University Press, 1924.

Hughes, Muriel J., *Women Healers in Medieval Life and Literature*. New York: Columbia University Press, 1943.

Kane, George, *Middle English Literature: A Critical Study of the Romances, the Religious Lyrics, Piers Plowman*. London: Methuen, 1951.

Mehl, Dieter, *The Middle English Romances of the Thirteenth and Fourteenth Centuries*. London: Routledge & Kegan Paul, 1968.

Plato, *The Republic*, trans. Paul Shorey. 2 vols. London: William Heinemann Ltd., 1935.

Praz, Mario, *The Romantic Agony*. London: Oxford University Press, 1933.

Richmond, Velma B., *Laments for the Dead in Medieval Narrative*. Pittsburgh: Duquesne Studies (Philological Series), 1966.

Robert of Brunne, *Handlyng Synne*, ed. F. J. Furnivall. EETS, 19. London: K. Paul, Trench, Trübner & Co., 1901.

Rogers, Katharine, *The Troublesome Helpmate*. Seattle: University of Washington Press, 1966.

Schelp, Hanspeter, *Exemplarische Romanzen in Mittelenglischen, Palaestra*, 246. Göttingen: Vandenhoech & Ruprecht, 1967.

Schofield, William H., *English Literature from the Norman Conquest to Chaucer*. New York: Macmillan Co., 1906.

Sir Gawain and the Green Knight, ed. J. R. R. Tolkien and E. V. Gordon. 2nd ed., rev. Norman Davis. Oxford: Clarendon Press, 1967.

Thomas Aquinas, St, *Summa Theologica: Latin Text and English Translation*, ed. and trans. by Blackfriars (*Virtues of Justice in the Human Community*, trans. T. C. O'Brien (vol. 41)). 60 vols.

London: Eyre & Spottiswoode and New York: McGraw-Hill, 1964–   .

Van Ghent, Dorothy, *The English Novel: Form and Structure.* New York: Harper & Row, 1953.

Vergilius Maro, Publius, *Vergil*, trans. R. Rushton Fairclough. 2 vols. London: W. Heinemann and Cambridge, Mass.: Harvard University Press, 1954–6.

Weber, Henry, ed., *Metrical Romances of the Thirteenth, Fourteenth, and Fifteenth Centuries.* 3 vols. Edinburgh: A. Constable & Co., 1810.

Wood, Chauncey, *Chaucer and the Country of the Stars.* Princeton: Princeton University Press, 1970.

The Works of Geoffrey Chaucer, ed. Fred N. Robinson. 2nd ed. Boston: Houghton Mifflin Co., 1957.

NOTE ON THE TEXT

The text of the present edition was transcribed from a micro-film copy of the MS Cambridge Ff. 2.38 and afterwards compared with the original in the University Library, Cambridge.

Instead of reproducing the appearance of the manuscript with regard to column divisions, I have separated and numbered stanzas. Capitals and punctuation are modern. Words of which the prefixes and stems are separated in the manuscript are joined together in my edition. Contractions are expanded without notice. These are common and are indicated either by a superior letter or by a vertical line above or through the affected letter. The insertion of letter a over the line usually stands for 'ra' or just the letter a itself. Other superior letters which appear are t ($w^t = wyth$, $þ^t = þat$), e ($Boþ^e = Boþe$, $þ^e = þe$), u ($þ^u = þou$) and a special form of r which is used for ur. A horizontal line through h denotes omission of m ($\hbar y = hym$) or es ($J\hbar u = Jhesu$); a curved line over on signals the dropping of y; over w, the absence of m, and over yg, the elimination of n.

Abbreviation by 'special signs' is another common method. These signs may indicate suspensions (the omission of final letters) as well as contractions. Examples of the latter are the upward curve from the end of a letter which stands for re or er, and the p with a horizontal line through its limb which stands for er. Common signs for suspensions are the broken oblique stroke curving from the end of a letter which stands for yr and the flourish turning downwards after the end of a letter which usually stands for ys. Two special signs are note-worthy for appearing nearly always without connecting strokes to other letters. One is the Tironian sign for *and* and the other is a figure, rather like a long s with the lobe of a thorn superimposed on it, which means syr. One last unique use of a superior letter remains to be mentioned with these special signs, that is, l over Roman numeral M (M^l) representing one thousand.

The text is printed as I wish it to be read. Where emenda-

O

tions have been made, the state of the manuscript is shown in footnotes. There is a minimum of emendations in the text. In general, I have emended only in order to make sense of the text or to remove certain obvious errors.

The spelling of the manuscript is reproduced. I have not attempted to regularise the appearance of *þ* and *th*, *ȝ* and *gh*, or *u* and *v*. The letter *i* is retained for vowels and *j* for consonants in order to avoid forms like *jn*.

It has been thought expedient to give in the footnotes—apart from manuscript readings for places in which I alter the text and descriptions of deletions, holes, and interlinear insertions which affect readability—the points at which Ritson (*R.*) and Vietor (*V.*) differ from my interpretation of the manuscript. Suggested emendations by Holthausen[1] which I have adopted are signalled by *H.* in the textual footnotes.

[1] Ferdinand Holthausen, 'Zu Mittelenglischen Romanzen', *Anglia*, 41 (1917), 497–512.

LE BONE FLORENCE OF ROME

1

As ferre as men ryde or gone
A more chyualrous town þen Troy was ⟨oon⟩
   In londe was neuyr seen;
Nor bettur knyӡtys þen came of hyt
In all thys worlde was neuyr ӡyt,   5
   For bothe hardy and kene.
Then came oon hyght Awdromoche,
The furste byger of Anteoche,
   And enhabyted cuntreys clene;
Antenowre was of þat barmeteme,   10
And was fownder of Jerusalem,
   That was wyght wythowtyn wene.

2

Helemytes hyght the thryd Troyon,
And was a stronge man of blode and bone,
   That fro Troye came to Awfryke;   15
Eneas be schyp gate to Rome,
The chefe cyte of crystendome,
   Then was ther none hyt lyke.
Vnto þe tyme þat þe emperowre Syr Garcy
Werryd on hyt, and herkenyth why,   20
   That many a oon sore can syke;
Of Costantyne þe nobull was he,
A doghtyar knyght þar not be
   In batell for to stryke.

3

Another emperowre reygned at Rome,   25
Syr Otes þe grawnt hyght þat gome,
   That wyght was vnder schylde;
A feyre lady he had to wyfe,

2 ⟨oon⟩, *inserted under* was *in bracket*   10 *H.* barneteme,
also possible   15 *R.* Troy   17 *R.* cytè   19 *R.* emperowr

That on a day loste hur lyfe,
 That worthy was to welde,
And dyed of a maydyn chylde,
That aftur waxe boþe meke and mylde,
 So fayre was seen but selde.

f. 239d

31

4

Whan þe emperys was dedd,
The emperowre was wylde of redd,
 He gart crysten thys chylde bryȝt,
And callyd hur Florens þys maydyn ⟨feyre⟩,
Boþe hys doȝtyr and hys heyre,
 In þys worlde was not soche a wyȝt.
Wolde ye lythe Y schoulde yow telle
Of þe wondurs þat there befelle
 Abowte in cuntreys ryght:
For þre dayes hyt reyned blode,
And bestys faght as þey were wode,
 Bothe wylde and tame wyth myght;

35

40

45

5

Fowlys in the fyrmament
Eyther odur in sondur rente,
 And felle dedd to þe grownde,
Hyt sygnyfyed þat aftur come,
Grete trybulacyons vnto Rome,
 Schulde many a man confownde;
As was for þat maydyn small,
Owtetakyn Troye and Rownsevall,
 Was neuyr in þys worlde rownde,
Syr Otes, þe nobull emperowre,
Gart norysch þe chylde wyth honowre,
 And kept hur hole and sownde.

50

55

6

He set to scole that damysell,
Tyll sche cowde of þe boke telle,

37 ⟨feyre⟩, *inserted interlinearly under* maydyn 53 *R.* Troy

And all thynge dyscrye,   60
Be þat she was xv yére olde,
Wel she cowde as men me tolde,
    Of harpe and sawtyre.
All hur bewteys for to neuyn
Myght no man vnder heuyn,   65
    For sothe nomore may I.   f. 240a
To mykyll bale was sche borne,
And many a man slayn hur forne,
    And in grete batels can dye.

7

When Syr Garcy herde seye   70
That þe emperowre of Rome had soche a may
    To hys doghtur dere,
He waxe hasty as the fyre,
And gart sembyll þe lordys of hys empyre,
    That bolde and hardy were.   75
He seyde, 'Ofte haue ye blamed me,
For Y wolde not weddyd bee,
    Y have herde of a clere,
Florens þat ys feyre and bryght,
In all þys worlde ys not soche a wyȝt   80
    Y wyll hur haue to my fere.'

8

As þe Romans trewly tolde,
He was a hundurd yerys olde,
    And some boke seyth mare.
He was arayed in ryche parell,   85
Of sylke and golde wythowtyn fayle,
    All whyte was hys hare.
He seyde 'Syrs wendyþ ouyr þe see,
And bydd þe emperowre of Rome sende me
    Hys doghtur swete and sware.   90
And yf he any gruchyng make,
Many a crowne Y schall gare crake,
    And bodyes to drowpe and dare.'

61 *R.* sche   fyftene   74 *R.* empyr

9

Hys flesche trembylde for grete elde,
Hys blode colde hys body vnwelde,   95
   Hys lyppes blo forthy;
He had more mystyr of a gode fyre,
Of bryght brondys brennyng schyre,
   To beyke hys boones by,
A softe bath a warme bedd,   100
Then any maydyn for to wedd,
   And gode encheson why,
For he was bresyd and all tobrokyn,
Ferre trauelde in harnes and of warre wrokyn.
   He tolde them redylye;   105

10

'When ye haue þe maydyn broght,
That ys so feyre and worthely wroght,
   Sche schall lygg be my syde,
And taste my flankys wyth hur honde,
That ys so feyre Y vndurstonde,   110
   Yn bedde be me to byde.
Sche schall me boþe hodur and happe,
And in hur louely armes me lappe,
   Bothe euyn and mornetyde;
Byd hur fadur sende hur to me,   115
Or Y schall dystroye hym and hys cyte,
   And þorow hys remes ryde.'

11

A prowde garson þat hyght Acwrye,
He was borne in Vtalye,
   The emperowre aftur hym sende;   120
And forty lordys wryttes wythynne,
That were comyn of nobull kynne,
   In message for to wende;
And forty stedys wyth þem he sente,

116 *R.* cytè   124 *R.* stedes

Chargyd wyth golde for a presente, 125
  'And, say hym as my frende,
That Y grete wele Syr Otes þe graunt,
And byd hym sende me hys doghtur aveaunt, *forward*
  That ys curtes and hende.'
            refined

12

He cawsyd þem to hye as þey were wode, 130
Wyth schyppes soone in to þe flode, *over*
  They rechyd ouyr the depe; *reached*
Spaynysch stedys wyth þem þey ledd,
And clopys of golde for back and hedd,
  That men myght vndur slepe. 135
Aye the wynde was in the sayle,
Ouyr fomes þey flett wythowtyn fayle,
  The wethur þem forþe can swepe.
The furste hauyn þat euyr þey hente *the first haven they found*
Was a towne þey calde Awtrement, f. 240c
  That folke þem feyre can kepe. 141
  Where people treated them well

13

       treasure
Soon ther tresowre vp they drowe, *drew*
And ther stedys strong ynowe,
  And made ther schyppys tome;
They lefte a burges feyre and wheme, 145
All ther schyppys for to зeme,
  Vnto ther gayne come. *poland   champaign*
They passed þorow Pole and Chawmpayn, *(france)*
Euyr speryng ther gatys gayne *roads near*
  Vnto the cyte of Rome. 150
       gates
They entyrde yn at þe зatys wyde,
Full ryally þorow þe cyte þey ryde,
  And dredyd no wrangdome.
       injustice

128 *R.* his avenaunt   146 *R.* yeme
148 Chawmpayn: *MS. curved mark over* w = wm
149 *R.* gane   150 *R.* cytè   152 *R.* cytè

Form

14

Thee xl[ti] messengerys as Y yow say,
Euery oon rode in feyre array,   155
   Ther sadyls schone full bryght;
Ther brydyls glyteryng all of golde,
Ther was neuyr frescher vpon molde,
   Made be day nor nyght.
A stede of Spayne, Y vnderstande,   160
Euery lorde ledd in hys hande,
   Bothe full prest and wyght;
All was couyrde wyth redd sendell,
The caryage behynde, as Y yow tell,
   Cam wyth þe tresur ryght.   165

15

Thorow þe towne þe knyghtys sange,
And euyr þer bryght brydyls range,
   Makeyng swete mynstralcy;
Lordys and ladyes of grete astate,
And odur many, well Y wate,   170
   At wyndows owt can lye.
And euyr þe formast speryd þe wayes   *first*
Vnto þe emperowrs paleys,
   Full ryall was that crye;   *the clamour was splendid*
Feyre þey were resseyuyd thore   f. 240d
Wyth hym þat was full wyse of lore,   *well recieved*   176
   Hys doghtur sate hym bye.

16

description of Florence.

In a robe ryght ryall bowne,
Of a redd syclatowne,
   Be hur fadur syde;   180
A coronell on hur hedd sett,
Hur cloþys wyth bestys and byrdys were bete,
   All abowte for pryde.
The lyghtnes of hur ryche perre, *jewelry*

154 *R.* The *V.* Thes *R.* fourti
176 *R.* hym   182 *R.* wer   184 *R.* perrè

And þe bryghtnes of hur blee, *complexion*   185
  Schone full wondur wyde.
There were kyngys in that halle,
Erlys and dewkys who rekenyth all,   *reckon*
  Full a hundurd that tyde.

17

Thes xl[ti] messengerys at ones   190
Entyrd into þes worthy wones,
  And came into the halle.
Syr Acvrye haylsyd þe emperowre,
And hys doghtyr whyte as flowre,
  That feyrest was of all.   195
He askyd of whens þat þey myght bee.
'Of Costantyne þe nobull are we.'
'Feyre, syrrys, mote yow befalle.'   *mote = must*
'A present we haue broght in hye,
Fro owre emperowre Syr Garcy,   200
  Stedys into thy stalle.

18
40

'An xl horsys chargyd ryght,
Wyth cloþys of golde, and besawntys bryght,
  Into thy tresory.
He byddyth, wythowte avysement,   205
That þy doghtur be to hym sent,
  For to lygg hym by.
Hys body ys bresyd, hys bones are olde,
That sche may kepe hym fro þe colde,
  Haue done now hastelye.   210
In comely cloþyng sche shall be cledd,
I haue grete hope he wyll hur wedd,   f. 241a
  Sche ys a feyre lady.

190 *R.* fourti   191 *R.* Entyre   193 *R.* Acwrye haylsed
194 *R.* floure
202 *R.* fourty
211 *R.* schall

19

'And yf þou sende hur not soone,
Hastelye, wythowten wone,   215
   Then ryseth ther a stryfe;
Ellys wyll he nygh þe nere,
Wyth hys ryche powere,
   And feche hur as hys wyfe.
He wyll dystroye þy bygly landys,   220
And slee all þat before hym standys,
   And lose full many a lyfe.
Haue done', he seyde, 'hastelye in hye,
An answere muste we gyf Garcy,
   At home when we can ryve.'   225

20

The emperowre seyde, as a man hende,
'Ye schall haue an answere or ye wende',
   And calde þe steward hym tylle:
'The ȝonder knyghtys to chawmbur ye lede
Of all thynge that they haue nede   230
   Serve them at ther wylle;
They are Syr Garcys messengerys,
And go we to owre councell perys,
   And leue them bydyng stylle,
To loke what beste ys for to doo,   235
Soche typyngys ys comyn vs too,
   Loke whedur we wyll fulfylle.'

21

The emperowre hys doghtur be þe hande hent,
And to a chaumbur they wente,
   Hys councell aftur hym ȝede   240
And askyd yf sche wolde sent þertylle,
For to be at Syr Garcyes wylle.
   And sche seyde, 'Jhesu forbede!'
Sche seyde, 'Be God þat boght me dere,

229 *R.* yonder
231 *V.* Serue

Me had leuyr þe warste bachylere,⁣ 245
 In all my fadurs thede,
Then for to lye be hys bresyd boones,
When he coghyth and oldely grones,   f. 241b
 I can not on hys lede.'

22

Hur fadur lykyd hur wordys wele, 250
So dud hys cowncell euery dele,
 And blessyd hur for hur fame.
They seyde, 'Yf that Garcy come,
In euyll tyme he hedur nome
 Hedurward for to drawe. 255
The garsons be not so doghtye,
But mony of þem soone schall dye,
 Yf we togedur plawe;
Go we hens owre redd ys tane,
Odur cowncell kepe we nane, 260
 Be ryght nodur be lawe.'

23

The emperowre came into þe halle,
The messengerys had etyn all,
 And stode to byde an answare.
He seyde, 'Syrs, wendyth hame 265
For here schall ye haue no game,
 God forbede hyt so ware!
Take the tresowr þat ye broght,
But my doghtur gete ye noght,
 For all yowre bostefull fare; 270
We schall stonde owre chawnce vnto,
Whedur he come or not so do,
 Full mekyll we schall not care.'

24

Then Acurye can say,
'In the begynnyng of Maye, 275
 My lorde wyll buske hym to ryde,

252 *R., V.* sawe   258 togedur: *MS.* togodur *V.* to gedur

And take the somer before hym clene,
And dystroye they londys all bedeene,
   Who ys he þat schall hym byde?'
Then answeryd Syr Egraveyne,   280
'We shall founde to knok ageyne,
   For all hys grete pryde.'
The emperowre comawndyd no man schulde do   f. 241c
Harme the messengerys vnto,
   They toke ther leue that tyde.   285

25

Then the messengerys all togedur,
Wyth þe tresowre þat þey broȝt thedur,
   Went home agayne.
Also tyte as Syr Garcy sawe,
Wyt ye well he lyste not to lawe,   290
   But mornyd in mode and mayne.
Altherfurste he toke hym tome
To spere the estyrs of Rome,
   To telle hym Acurye was fayne,
'Syr, hyt ys feyre bygged wyth halles and bowrys,   295
We tolde the vii hundurd towrys,
   So Cryste me saue and sayne;

26

'And ther lorde Syr Otes the graunt,
Wyth mekyll worschyp þey hym avaunt,
   Of curtesye he ys the welle,   300
And therto trewe as any stele,
Forþy, syr, men loue hym wele,
   Mony wyth hym do dwelle.
He ys bothe ware and wyse,
And geuyth þem gyftys of pryce,   305
   The certen sothe to telle;

286 *R.* Then
287 *R.* browght
292 *R.* come
296 *R.* Seven
303 *After H.,* do dwelle: *MS.* to dwelle *R., V.* to dwelle

And hys doghtur þe feyrest þynge,
That euyr was seen wolde or ȝynge,
　　Made of flesche and felle.

27

'Thogh a man sate on a wyght palfreye　　　310
All the longe somersday,
　　Avysyd myght he be
For to ryde Rome abowte,
And come yn whereuyr he went owt,
　　Hyt were a grete yurne.　　　315
Euery day in the yere
The feyre ys þere lyke playnere,
　　Amonge the folke so free;
Syxty dewkys are calde hys perys,　　　f. 241d
And twenty þousande bachyleres,　　　320
　　Longyth to that cyte.

28

'Of þe emperowrs pales Y wyll yow say,
Ther ys no soche in þe worlde today
　　Stondyng vndur heuyn;
The pyllers þat stonde in þe halle,　　　325
Are dentyd wyth golde and clere crystalle
　　And therto feyre and euyn.
They are fyllyd wyth syluyr as Cryste me couer,
And þere ys peyntyd wythynne and ouer,
　　The dedly synnes sueyn;　　　330
There was peyntyd wyth þyngys sere
That men myȝt mewse on many a yere,
　　Or he hyt scryed wyth steuyn.

310 *R.* palfraye
314 whereuyr: see Note to this line. *R.* wher *V.* where *R.* wente
315 *R.* yurne
321 *R.* cytè
328 Cryste: *MS.* cste
329 *R.* ther
332 *R.* yer
333 scryed: *MS.* stryed

continuing description

29

'There comyth watur in a condyte,
Thorow a lyon rennyth hyt,   *fountain in the hall*   335
    That wroght ys all of golde,
And þat standyþ in þe myddys of þe halle;
A hundurd knyȝtys and ladyes smalle
    Myght wasche there and þey wolde
All at ones on that stone;   340
Many oþer waturs come þorow þe town,   *fresh water*
    That fresche are vpon folde;
In myddys þe cyte ys oon rennande,
Tyber hyt hyght Y vnderstande,
    As men ther vs tolde,   345

30

'The effect of Rome Y haue yow tolde,
And of þe beste barons bolde,
    That lygge there wythynne;
But of þe feyrenes of þe maye
I can not telle mony a day,   350
    Ne noght Y wyll begynne, *may*
But syr,' he seyde 'Also mote Y the
Thyn eyen mon sche neuyr see   *to possess yet neither to win*
    To welde ȝyt nodur to wynne.'
Full grete othys Garcy hath sworne,   f. 242a
'Many a þousand schall dye þerforne   356
    Or Y of my brethe blynne
       cease

31

'Or þre monythys and a halfe be gone,
I schall dystroye hys landys euerychon,
    And wynne hys doghtur wyth were.'   360
Then he made to sende owt wryttys wyde,
In hys londe on euery syde,
    Messengerys can them bere;

336 wroght: g *partly obliterated by hole*   343 *R.* cyté
344 *After H.,* Tyber: *MS.* Tyger *R., V.* Tyger
347 *R.* best

And Florence fadur at hame
Ordeygned hys men on the same, *Ordered his men in the same way* 365
   Wyth armowre schylde and spere.
And þus begynneth a bale to brewe, *trouble to ferment*
Many a man therfore myght rewe, *regret*
   And wemen hyt dud grete dere. *it cost dearly.*

32

Syxty þousand sembelde þen 370
Of garsons and of odur men
   To Garcy in that stownde,
They set vp seylys and forþe þey rode,
And ay hymselfe wythowten bode, *also himself without delay*
   The formaste forthe can fownde. *find him at the head* 375
Syxty myle fro Rome ryved they,
Hyt went nere on þe thrydd day,
   Ther was not oon drowned.
They tyght þer pavylons in a stede,
The brode felde waxe all redd, 380
   So glemed golde on þe grownde.

33

The medowe was callyd Narumpy,
The water of Tyber rennyng by,
   There Garcyes pavylon stode.
All þe cloþys were of sylke, 385
The ryche ropys were ryʒt swylke, *decorative embossed*
   The boosys were redd as blode. *ornaments*
Ther was no beest þat yede on fote
But hyt was portreyed þere, Y wote,
   Nor fysches swymmyng in flode. 390
Fyftene pomels of golde þere schoon, f. 242b
An egyll and a charbokull stone,
   Wyde the lyghtnes gode.

366 *R.* With
369 wemen: *MS.* wemon
386 *R.* ryght
393 *R.* yode *V.* ʒode

34

The emperowre of Rome lay on hys walle,
And hys doghtur gente and small,   395
  Florence the feyre sche hyght;
And sye the garsons assay þer stedys,
Sterne men in stele wedys,
  The medowe all can lyght.
He seyde, 'Y haue golde ynogh plente,   400
And sowdears wyll come to me,
  Bothe be day and nyght.
Now schall Y neuyr my golde spare,
But faste vpon þys warre hyt ware,
  God helpe me in my ryght.'   405

35

The kynge of Hungary þat tyme was dedd,
And lefte hys sonnes wylde of redd,
  Syr Mylys and Syr Emere.
Ther modur was weddyd to a stedd,
Agenste all the baronage redd,   410
  As ye schall further here,
To a lorde that wonnyd thereby,
Syr Justamownde of Surry,
  That sterne was to stere.
The kynge of Naverne toke þes chyldur two,   415
And made þem knyghtys bothe tho,
  And manhode can them lere;

36

Tyll hyt felle oones on a day
They wente to a medowe to playe,
  To lerne them for to ryde;   420
Syr Emere bare in hys schylde:
A whyte dowve who so behelde,
  A blakk lyon besyde.
The whyte dowve sygnyfyed

399 *R.* medow *R.* plentè   422 dowve: *MS.* dowbe
424 dowve: *MS.* dowbe

That he was full of knyghthedd,   425
   And mekenes at that tyde;
The lyon þat he was ferse and felle,   f. 242c
Amonge hys enmyes for to dwelle,
   And durste beste in batell byde.

37

A wery palmer came þem by,   430
And seyde, 'Syrrys Y haue ferly
   That ye wyll not fare
I haue bene at grete Rome,
To seke Seynt Petur, and thens Y come,
   Straunge tythyngys harde Y thare.   435
Ther ys an emperowre þat hyght Garcy,
Is logyd in the Narumpy,
   Wyth syxty thousande and mare,
He seyth þe emperowre of Rome schall not leue
But yf he to hym hys doghtur geue,   440
   That ys so swete of sware.'

38

Than Syr Mylys and Syr Emere
Toke wyth them forty in fere,
   That were comyn of gentyll kynne,
To grete Rome euyn they rode,   445
And at a burges hows abode,
   And there they toke ther ynne
They speryd of þer oste and þer ostes,
Of þer tythyngys more and lesse,
   Or euyr they wolde blynne.   450
They fownde hyt as þe palmer tolde,
They seyde wyth Otes dwelle þey wolde,
   Whedur hyt were to lose or wynne.

39

Fyve thousande on þe morne Garcy sent
Of hys men verament,   455
   Wele arayed in ther gere.

426 8¹, *written in same hand below line*   434 *R.* seynte
455 hys men: *MS.* hys xx men

As nere as þey durste for dowte,
Fyfty of them yssewed owte,
   For to juste in werre.
That sawe Syr Mylys and Emere,   460
Wyth þer ferys bothe in fere, *military man*
   They thoght them for to feere; *fear*
They passyd owt at a posterne,   f. 242d
Os men þat schoulde of batayle lerne,
   Wyth armowre schylde and spere.   465

40

Thes fyfty had forjusted soone,
And slewe þem down wythowten mone, *Emere fights*
   All that wolde abyde;
Oon came prekyng owt of þe prees,
To Syr Emere euyn he chese,   470
   But soone was fellyd hys pryde.
Syr Emere reysyd hys spere on hyȝt, *killed the knight*
Thorow þe body he bare þe knyght,
   And downe he felle that tyde.
Than þey faght hande ouyr heuydd,   475
Many oon þere þer lyuys leuydd,
   That came on Garcyes syde.

41

repetition

The emperowre of Rome lay on hys wall,
And hys doghtur gent and small,
   Florence feyre and free;   480
Sche seyde, 'Fadur, wyth mylde steuyn, *voice*
To vs ys comyn helpe fro heuyn,
   Fro God in mageste;
Yondur ys a nobull knyght,
That styrryth hym styfly in þe fyght, *describes Emere*   485
   Beholde and ye may see.
Wyth þe whyte dowve and þe blak lyon,
The beste þat comeþ he strykeþ down, *+ prays for him*
   Helpe that he rescowde bee.'

475 *R.* hand heuydd: *MS.* hedd *V.* hedd *R.* hevydd *H.* heuidd
483 *R.* magestè

42

The emperowre calde Syr Egravayne, 490
And Syr Sampson þat was hym gayne,
   Armed well and ryght,
A hundurd men wyth þem he toke,
Vp they lepe, so seyth þe boke,
   On stedys stronge and wyght. 495
All þat were left onslayne,
Fledd vnto þer strenkyþ agayne,
   Hyt was a semely fyght.
Then swere Garcy, in full grete yre, f. 243a
That he wolde brenne all Rome wyth fyre, 500
   On the morne yf that he myght.

43

Then Syr Mylys and Syr Emere,
Wyth þer forty felows in fere,
   Come the emperowre beforne;
They salutyd hym full ⟨ryally⟩, 505
And hys doghtur þat stode hym by.
   He askyd where they were borne.
They answeryd hym full curteslye,
'We were þe kyngys sonnes of Hungary
   Owre fadur hys lyfe hath lorne, 510
And hedur are we come to the,
As sowdears, yf mystyr bee;
   We speke hyt not in skorne.'

44

'God and Seynt Petur of Rome,
Ʒylde yow yowre hedurcome,' 515
   The emperowre can sey;
'So doghtely as ye haue begonne,
Was neuer men vnder þe sonne
   So lykyng to my paye.'
Then þe maydyn þankyd þem efte, 520

498 *R.*, *V*. syght   505 ⟨ryally⟩, *written interlinearly above* hym
515 yowre, *hole in MS. above* e

He þem wythhelde wyth þem þey lefte,
    To mete then wente thay.
The emperowre set Syr Mylys hym by,
Emere cowde more of curtesye,
    And he ete wyth the maye.   525

45

Sche þoght hym a full curtes knyȝt,
Feyre, yonge, semely, and wyght,
    Hur harte to hym can ȝylde.
Syr Myles seyde þe emperowre too,
'And ye wolde at my councell doo,   530
    Ye schoulde not fyght in fylde,
But close þe ȝatys and þe bryggys vp drawe,
And kepe vs clene owt of þer awe,
    And owre wepons wyghtly welde.
And kepe þe town boþe nyght and day,   535
Tyl þey be wery and wende a way.'   f. 243b
    Syr Emere hym behelde.

46

Emere seyde Mylys vnto,
'So myght a sympull grome do,
    Kepe an holde wythynne;   540
But we wyll manly to þe felde,
And Syr Garcy batell ȝelde,
    To morne or þat we blynne.'
Then þey made crye þorow cyte
That no man schoulde so hardy bee,   545
    That waryson wolde wynne.
But folowe þe standarde whereuyr hyt goys,
And freschly fyght vpon owre foys,
    Bothe the more and the mynne.

47

Than Syr Garcy wyth mekyll pryde   550
Made to crye þe same on hys syde,
    Amonge the barons bolde;

544 *R.* cytè   547 *R.* standard whereuyr: see Note to line
314. *R.* wher *V.* where.

The kynge of Turkay he seyde than,
'Thou art a full madde man,
  And fayleste wyt for elde;   555
Syr Otes þe graunt hath noght gylte,
Let therfore no blode be spylte,
  For hym that all schall welde.'
'Nay he warnyd me hys doghtur schene,
And þat hath tymberde all my teene,   560
  Full dere hyt schall be selde.'

48

A Roman stode besyde and harde,
To þe towne full soone he farde,
  And tolde the emperowre;
The maydyn mylde vp sche rase,   565
Wyth knyghtys and ladyes feyre of face,
  And wente vnto a towre.
There sche sawe ryght in þe feldys,
Baners brode and bryght scheldys,
  Of cheualry the flowre.   570
They nowmberde þem xl M*l* men
And a hundurd moo þen hur fadur had þen,
  That were ryght styffe in stowre.

49

'Allas!' seyde that maydyn clere,   f. 243c
'Whedur all þe ȝonde folke and þere   575
  Schoulde dye for my sake,
And Y but a sympull woman.'
The terys on hur chekys ranne,
  Hur ble beganne to blake.
'Put me owt to olde Garcy,   580
Yf all þes men schulde for me dye,
  Hyt were a dolefull wrake.'
Hur fadur seyde hyt schulde not bee;
Hors and armowre askyd hee,
  And soone hys swyrde can take.   585

571 M*l*: *MS. M*l* R.* forty thousand   573 8ii, *written in same*
hand below line

50

He lepe on hys stede Bandynere,
And in hys honde he hent a spere,
　　And rode abowte all nyght.
To the lordys of the towne,
And bad þey schulde be redy bowne,　　　　　　590
　　Tymely to the fyght.
They set þer standard in a chare,
And feele folke wyth hyt can fare,
　　That hardy were and wyght,
Syxe lordys and Syr Egravayne　　　　　　595
To be all ther chefetayne,
　　And kepe hyt well and ryght,

51

The standarde was of whyte yvore,
A dragon of golde ordeygned þerfore,
　　That on the ouyrende stode;　　　　　　600
That sygnyfyed that Otes ware
In the felde as bolde as any bare,
　　And a sterne man of mode.
The vawewarde and þe myddyll soone,
And þe rerewarde owte of Rome　　　　　　605
　　The grete oost remouyd and ʒode;
Be then had Garcy takyn hys place,
And soone wythynne a lytyll space,
　　Ranne bowrnes all on blode.

52

Than Syr Otes þe graunt can calle　　　　　　610
On herawde and hys knyghtys all,
　　In myddys of the prees,
'Who so beryth hym beste today
Ageyne Syr Garcy, as Y yow say,
　　That wyrkyth me þys vnpees,　　　　　　615
I schall geue hym a feyre flowre,
Of grete Rome to be emperowre,
　　Aftur my dyssees,

598 *After R., H.*, yvore: *MS.* yvar *V.* yvar

And wedde Florens my doghtur bryȝt,
As Y am trewe crysten knyght,   620
   Certen wythowtyn lees.'

53

Syr Emere askyd hys lorde þe kynge,
Yf he myght haue þe furste rydynge,
   And he grauntyd hym tylle.
Owt of Garcyes oost came oon,   625
A prowde garson hyght Bresobon,
   A wykkyd man of wylle;
When Syr Emere wyth hym mett,
A stronge dynte on hym he sett,
   Thorow hys armowre stylle.   630
He fonde no socowre at hys schylde,
But dedd he felle downe in þe fylde,
   Hys harte blode can owte spylle.

54

Be þat þe grete oost began to sembyll,
Trumpes to blowe, and stedys to trembyll,   635
   Harde togedur they yede.
Ryche harburgens all torusched,
And stele helmes all todusched,
   And bodyes brake owt to blede;
Hedys hopped vndur hors fete,   640
As haylestones done in þe strete,
   Styckyd was many a stede.
For Florence loue, þat feyre maye,
Many a doghty dyed that day,
   In Romance as we rede.   645

55

Then Syr Garcy wyth mekyll pryde,
Made knyghtys on hys own syde,
   Syxty yonge and feyre;

626 Bresobon: *MS.* bresobon *R.* Bresebon *V.* bresebon
628 wᵗ: t *obliterated by a hole*

The warste of þer fadurs were barons,   f. 244a
And oght bothe towres and townes,   650
    And all were they ryght heyre.
When Emere and hys men wyth þem mett,
Stronge dyntys on them he sett,
    Among þem can they store;
At þe furste wynnyng of þer schone,   655
So tyte of lyuys were they done,
    That all deryd not a pere.

56

Then Garcy yede nere wode for yre,
And arayed hys batels in þat bere,
    And fared as he wolde wede;   660
He bad þer dyntys schulde be wele wared,
That no Roman on lyue be spared.
    Thowe þey wolde rawnsome bede.
Ageyne hym came Syr Otes þe graunt,
A doghty knyght and an aveaunt,   665
    On Bondenore hys stede;
When Garcy sye þat hyt was hee,
He seyde Syrrys, also mote Y the,
    We two muste do owre dede.

57

'Thou art wele strekyn in age, Y trowe,   670
But Y am ferre elder then thou,
    We two muste juste in werre;
Hyt ys sethyn Y armyd ware
Seuyn yere and somedele mare;'
    And eyther toke a spere.
So harde togedur can þey ryde,   675
Owt of þer sadyls þey felle besyde,
    And graspyd to odur gere;
Wyth scharpe swyrdys faght þey þen,
They had be two full doghty men,   680
    Gode olde fyghtyng was there.

660 wede: *MS.* wode

58

Garcy hyt Otes on the helme,
That vpon hys hedd hyt can whelme,
  Hyt sate hym wondur sare.
'Syr, wyth þys dynte Y chalenge Rome,
And þy doghtur bryght as blome,
  That brewyd hath all thys care.
When þat Y haue leyn hur by,
And done hur schame and vylenye,
  Then wyll Y of hur no mare,
But geue hur to my chaumburlayne.'
Tho wordys made Otes vnfayne,
  And tyte he gaf an answare:

f. 244b
686

690

59

'God and Seynt Petur of thys towne,
Let neuyr Rome come in thy bandome,
  And saue my doghtur sownde;
Owre fyghtyng ys not endyd ȝyt.'
On the helme Garcy he hyt,
  That he felle to the grownde.
There had Syr Garcy bene tane,
But þer came garsons many oon,
  And rescowed hym in þat stownde.
Syr Emere horsyd hys lorde agayne,
And loouyd God he was not slayne,
  And faste to fyght they fownde.

695

700

705

60

Syr Emere lokyd a lytyll hym fro,
And sawe hys brodur suffur woo,
  In a stowre fyghtande.
The Grekys had fyred hym abowte,
That he myght on no syde owte,
  But styffely can he stande.

710

695 *R.* bandoune   700 *R.* misnumbers l. 700, 710   701 *R.* ane
702 *R.* rescowd   703 lorde: de *partly obscured by a smudge*
707 *R.* suffer

He rescowde hym full knyghtly;
Many a doghty made he to dye,
  That he abowte hym fande;
Euyll quytt he hym hys mede,   715
For Mylys was þe falsyst lede
  That euyr leuyd in lande.

61

When he had rescowde hys brodur Mylon,
Of hys fomen came thretty bowne,
  Stelyng on hym stylle;   720
All þer sperys on hym þey sett,
He drewe hys swyrde wythowten let,
  And Mylys fledde to an hylle.
He seyde, 'Brodur also mote Y the,
Thou schalt not be rescowde for me';   f. 244c
  Loke whedur that he dud ylle   726
But stryked yn at anodur stowre,
And mett hys lorde þe emperowre,
  Layeng on wyth gode wylle.

62

'Mylys,' he seyde, 'where ys þy brodur?'   730
  'At the deuyll,' quod the todur,
   'I trowe beste that he bee.
He ys belefte wyth Syr Garcy,
Ageyn yow, he tolde me why,
  He myght geve more then ye.   735
Be God, he seyde, þat all may
He ys false that dar Y lay,
  Trewly trowe ye me.'
The emperowre lykyd hyt ylle,
And leyde vpon wyth gode wylle,   740
  Tyll he myght the sothe see.

718 *R*. broder   719 *R*. camen   724 8[iii], *written in
same hand below line*   735 geve, v *is written over an* r
737 *R*. dare
740 And: d *written over erasure*   leyde: le *written over erasure*

63

Forthe then lokyed þe emperowre,
And sawe Syr Emere in a stowre,
　Fyghtyng agenste hys foys;
He stroke þe stede wyth þe spurrys,　　　　745
He spared nodur rygge nor forows,
　But euyn to hym he goys;
All that he abowte hym fonde
He and hys men broght to grownde,
　That neuyr oon vp rose.　　　　750
And there was Mylys preuyd false,
Wyth hym and odur lordys alse,
　And loste all hys gode lose.

64

Then Emere toke harte hym too;
Full doghtely then can he doo.　　　　755
　Florence hym behelde,
And tolde hur maydyns bryght of ble,
'In the felde beste doyth he
　Wyth þe whyte dowve in hys schylde
And þerto the black lyon.'　　　　760
Sche cryed to hym wyth grete sowne,
　'Thou be my fadurs belde,
And þou schalt haue all thy desyre,　　　　f. 244d
Me and all þys ryche empyre,
　Aftur my fadur to welde.'　　　　765

65

When he harde þe maydyn bryght,
Hys hedd he lyfte vpon hyght,
　The wedur waxe full hate.
Hur fadur nere hande can talme,
Soche a sweme hys harte can swalme,　　　　770
　For hete he waxe nere mate.

742 *R.* lokyd　　　　758 felde: *MS.* folde　　　　759 *R.* yn
760 *R.* lyoun

When that þey had so done,
A quarell came fleyng soone,
   And thorow the hed hym smate,
They sende aftur þe pope, Symonde,   775
And he schrofe hym and hoselde on þat grounde,
   And assoyled hym well, Y wate.

66

As soone as þe emperowre ȝyldyd þe goost,
A prowde garson came in haste,
   Syr Synagote hyght hee;   780
And broght an hundurd helmes bryght
Of hardy men þat cowde well fyght,
   Of felde wolde neuyr oon flee.
Emere stroke into that stowre,
And many oon made he for to cowre,   785
   And slewe them be two and thre.
Soone thereaftur was he tane,
And knyghtys kene wolde hym haue slayne,
   But ther souereygn bad let bee.

field commander.

67

'Vnto Syr Garcy haue hym seen,   790
I trowe hys lyfe he wyll hym leen,
   He ys so feyre a knyght.'
Leve we Syr Emere in the stowre,   *narrative voice*
And speke more of the emperowre,
   How they on a bere hym dyght,   795
And how þey broght hym to þe towne,
Wythowten belle or procescyon,
   Hyt was a drery syght.
They layned hyt fro þer enmyes whyll þey myȝt,
And fro Florence þat worþy wyght,   800
   Hys own dere doghtur bryght.   f. 245a

777 *R.* wel
778 *R.* gast
797 *R.* procescoun *V.* procescon

68

Soone þe standard yn þey dud lede,
And baners bryȝt þat brode dud sprede,
   The Romans lykyd ylle,
And seyde þey schulde vpon þe morne, 805
Fyght wyth Garcy yf he had sworne,
   That hyely was on hylle.
Florence lay in a cornell,
And hur maydyns, as Y yow telle,
   That was curtes of wylle; 810
They seyde men brynge yn a bere,
And þat wyth a full mornyng chere,
   But all was hoscht and stylle.

69

Then can feyre Florence sayne,
'Ȝondur ys begonne an euyll bargayn, 815
   Y see men brynge a bere,
And a knyght in handys leede,
Bondynowre my fadurs stede';
   Then all chawngyd hur chere.
Sche and hur maystres Awdygon, 820
Went in to þe halle allone,
   Allone wythowten fere,
And caste vp þe cloþe þen was hyt so,
The lady swowned and was full woo,
   Ther myght no man hur stere. 825

70

'Allas,' sche seyde, 'þat Y was borne!
My fadur for me hys lyfe haþ lorne,
   Garcy may haue hys wylle,
All my brode landys and me,
That Y welde in crystyante,' 830
   Ther myght no man hur stylle.
Lordys and ladyes þat þere ware

816 men: *MS.* mon   817 in: n *obliterated by a hole*
830 *R.* yn

Tyll hur chaumbur can they fare,
   Lorde! That them lykyd ylle;
Knyghtys and squyers þat þere was   835
Wrange þer hondys and seyde, 'Allas!
   For drede sche schulde hur spylle.'

71

Dewkys and erles þer hondys wronge,
And lordys sorowe was full stronge,   f. 245b
   Barons myght haue no roo: 840
'Who schall vs now geue londys or lythe,
Hawkys, or howndys, or stedys stythe,
   As he was wonte to doo?'
Syr Garcy went crowlande for fayne,
As rampande eyen do in þe rayne,   845
   When tythyngys came hym too,
He bad hys men schulde make þem bowne,
And hastelye go stroye vp þe towne,
   'My byddyng that ye doo:

72

'Slo þem down where ye þem mete,   850
And fyre fasten in euery strete,
   Loke now that taste.
I schall wyrke as haue Y yoye,
As kynge Maynelay dud be Troye,
   And stroye hyt at the laste.'   855
When þey harde þat were wythynne,
To þe ȝatys can they wynne,
   And barryd them full faste,
And they wythowte yngynes bende,
And stones to þe walles þey sende,   860
   And quarels wyth arbalast.

73

They wythynne wolde haue gone owte,
her souereygn marred þem for dowte,
   And made þem to kepe ther holde,

843 *R.* wont   854 *R.* Kyng   861 arbalast: *MS.* alablaste
R., V. alablaste

They sygned to þe ʒatys *gates* of þe towne,   865
An hundurd men in armes bowne,
  That hardy were and bolde.
The pope came wythowten delyte,
And enteryd the emperowre tyte,
  They wepte bothe ʒonge and olde.   870
The boke seyþ God þat vs boght
Many myrakyls for hur he wroght, *performed*
  Many a oon and thyckfolde.

74

So longe logyd the sege there,
That þey wythynne nere famysched were,   875
  Euyll lyfe can they lede;   f. 245c
They were not ordeygned þerfore,
They had golde in warme store,
  But mete was þem full nede. *food was most required by them*
All þey cowncelde Florence to take   880
Oon of thes lordys to be hur make,
  That doghty were of dede;
For to mayntene and vpholde
Agayne Syr Garcy þat burne bolde,
  The towne leuyth all in drede.   885

75

And Awdegone hur cowncelde soo
Oon of thes lordys for to too,
  Syr Mylys or Syr Emere;
'And let hym wedde yow wyth a rynge
Ther fadur was a ryche kynge,   890
  Knowyn bothe farre and nere',
'Ye but now ys Syr Emere tane,
And Garcys men haue hym slayne,'
  Seyde that maydyn clere,
'Ye behove to haue anodur,   895

875 8^{iiii}, *written in same hand below line*
883 *After R., H.,* For to mayntene: *MS.* For mayntene *V.* For
mayntene

Take Mylys þat ys hys eldyst brodur,
    Hyt ys my cowncell wythowten were.'

76

To Syr Mylys Awdegon went,
And askyd yf he wolde assent
    To wedde that maydyn free,   900
That ys whyte as lylly flowre,
And be lorde and emperowre,
    The grettyst in crystyante.
'But God forbede and Seynt Myghell,
That þou vndurtake hyt but þou do well,   905
    And trewe man thynke to bee.'
To hyr speche answeryd he noght,
But stylle he stode and hym beþoght,
    And seyde, 'Y schall avyse me.'

77

fault in narration (p 139)

she rejects Mylys

'Avyse þe,' seyde þat maydyn feyre,   910
    'For to be my fadurs heyre?
    Lyghtly may ye thynke.   f. 245d
Be hym þat suffurde woundys fyve,
I schall neuyr be thy wyfe,
    To suffur dethys dynte.   915
Kyngys and dewkys haue me askyd,
And all þer londys wolde haue geue me ⟨at þe laste⟩,
    And many a ryall thynke.'
Forþe he yede wyth syghyng and care
That he had geuyn þat fowle answare   920
    For sorowe nere wolde he synke.

78

Thys whyle had Synagot takyn Emere,
And broȝt hym before Syr Garcy in fere,
    And seyde, 'We haue tane a knyght

903 *R.* yn   904 But God forbede: *MS.* But for god for bede
V. considers first for *crossed out*   907 hyr: *MS.* hys *R.*, *V.* hys
910 *R.* thee   912 *After H.*, ye: *MS.* y *R.*, *V.* y
917 ⟨at þe laste⟩, *inside bracket in margin*

Agenste yow fyghtyng in þe stowre,   925
We refte hym hors and armowre,
   But he ys an hardy wyght.'
'Felowe,' he seyde, 'what dyd þou there?'
'Syr, wyth my lorde on þe to were,
   That now to dedd ys dyght;   930
As sowdears my brodur and Y,
We haue noght ellys to leue by,
   Owre fadur fordyd owre ryght.

79

'Syr Phelyp of Hungary owre fadur was,
Now ys he dedd, therefore, allas!   935
   Owre modur weddyd ys newe,
Into Surry to Syr Justamownde,
That ys abowte vs to confownde,
   And owre bytter bales to brewe.
He hath dysheryted vs wythowt lees,   940
That we had leuyr warre nor pees,
   Perchawnce þat may hym rewe.'
Syr Synagot cowncelde Syr Garcy soo,
'Syr, delyuyr hym qwyte, and let hym goo,
   He semyth couenawnt and trewe.'   945

80

Than answeryd Syr Garcy,
   'When Y toke trewage of Turky   f. 246a
   Thy fadur in stede stode me;
Therfore, Y schall let the goo,
And geue hym all ye toke hym fro.'   950
   Emere knelyd on hys knee,
'Syr, when Y come into þe towne,
I and my men muste be bowne
   To greue bothe thyn and the.
Ye godys forbode, that þou me spare,   955

949 *R.* schal   954 *R.* thee   955 *After H.*, þou me
spare: *MS.* þou spare *R., V.* þou spare godys, *no longer fully legible*
because partly rubbed

D

But of þy warste wylle euyrmare.' *It would be the worst*
   Garcy, thus seyde he: *decision you ever made.*

81

'What wenyst þou wyth þy bragg and boost
For to dystroye me and myn hoost?'
   He toke hys leue and yede;   960
Syr Synagot gaue hym all togedur,
Be þe leste þonge þat he bare þedur,
   Emere lepe on hys stede.
He ledd hym þorow þe pavylons all,   *Emere*
Tyll he came nere to Romes walle,   *returns* 965
   And paste the moost drede.
Than þey wythynne were full fayne,
That þey had getyn þe gome agayne,
   Ther blysse beganne to brede.

82

And agayne Syr Emere they went,   970
And broght hym before þat lady gente,
   And askyd yf he wolde
Wedde the beste of hur elde,
And all hur londys for to welde,
   Ageyne Garcy to holde;   975
And helpe to venge hur fadurs dedd.
He dud ryght as the lady bedd, *requested*
   That hardy was and bolde.
He seyde preuely muste me do,
Tyll þe baronage be sworne vs to,   980
   Bothe the yonge and the olde.

83

Syr Sampson and Syr Egravayne,
Syr Clamadore and Syr Alayne,   f. 246b
   Wyste of that bargen newe.

957 *R.* sayde
962 þonge: on *obliterated by hole in MS.,* þonge *after V.*
975 *R.* Agayne

They went aftur Syr Geffrey of Pyse, 985
And Syr Barnarde of Mownt Devyse,
   Tho syxe were gode and trewe;
They made þem to swere þey schulde be lele,
And Syr Emers counsell heyle,
   And Florence feyre of hewe. 990
Thus he tylleþ þem be fowre and fyve,
All þey had sworne to hym be lyve,
   Then Mylys hymselfe can rewe.

84

The pope came as ye may here,
For to crowne Syr Emere, 995
   And wedd them wyth a rynge.
Sche seyde, 'Now are ye emperowre of Rome,
The grettyst lorde in crystendome,
   And hedd of euery kynge;
Ȝyt schall ye neuyr in bedde me by, 1000
Tyl ye haue broght me Syr Garcy,
   For no maner of thynge;
Or lefte hym in þe felde for dedd,
Be hym Y sawe in forme of bredd,
   When þe preest can synge.' 1005

85

Emere the emperowre can say,
'I schall do all that Y may,
   But charge me wyth no mare.'
Then þey wysche and to mete be gone,
'Of mynstralcy we kepe none, 1010
   We haue no space to spare;
Nodur harpe, fedyll, nor geest,
But ordeygn yow wyth moost and leest,
   That wyth me wyll fare;
And brynge my stede Bondynere, 1015
And feche me forþe boþe schylde and spere;'
   Full tyte þen were þey thare.

996 And wedd them: *MS.* And them, *after R.*
1007 that, a *partly rubbed*

86

Than was there no lenger bode,
But vp þey lepe and forthe þey rode,　　　　　　　　f. 246c
　　To preke aftur ther praye.　　　　　　　　　　　1020
When worde came to Syr Garcy
A sory man was he forthy,
　　That weddyd was þat may,
That was whyte as lylly flowre,
And Syr Emere crowned emperowre,　　　　　　　1025
　　'Allas!' then can he say,
'That euyr Y let þat traytur goo,
When he was in my bandome soo,
　　Me dawyd a drery day!'

87

Ther was lefte no man in þat town　　　　　　　　1030
To kepe the lady of renowne,
　　That was of temporalte,
That myght wyth ony wepon wyrke,
Owttakyn men of holy kyrke,
　　At home they let them bee.　　　　　　　　　　1035
They beganne at þe nerre syde,
And slewe down all þat wolde abyde,
　　Trewly trow ye me;
On felde þey faght as þey were wode,
Ouyr þe bentys ranne the blode,　　　　　　　　　1040
　　All tho dyed that wolde not flee.

88

Then on the felde þey freschely faght,
Many oon ther dethe there caght,
　　That came on Garcyes syde.
Syr Garcy toke hym to the fyght,　　　　　　　　1045
Wyth an hundurd in harnes bryght,
　　He durste no lenger byde;
Of all þe men he þedur broght,

1018 8ᵛ, *written in same hand below line*
1028 *R.* bandoune　　　　　1032 *R.* temporaltè

Many on lyue leuyd he noght,
 To schypp went they that tyde;   1050
They set vp sayle and forþe are gone,
To Costantyne þe nobull towne,
 Also faste as they myght glyde.

89

Also soone as Syr Emere wyste
Welnere for sorowe hys herte breste,   1055
 That he in schyppe can lende   f. 246d
He bad Syr Mylys turne agayne,
Syr Sampson and Syr Egravayne,   *3 guard Florence*
 'For Y wyll aftur wende.
Take an hundurd men of armes bryȝt,   1060
And kepe my lady day and nyght,
 That ys curtes and hende;
Say to hur Y am on the see;
Chasyng aftur myn olde enmye,
 That slewe hur derrest frende.'   1065

90

Syr Mylys seyde to þes hundurd all,
'Thys herytage to me wyll falle,
 My brodur comyþ neuyr agayne.
I wyll wedde the yonge bryde,
He slepyd neuyr be hur syde,   1070
 Nor hath hur not by layne.
All that wyll assent to me,
Grete lordys schall they bee;'
 To graunt hym þey were fayne.
Sampson seyde, 'þat wyll Y neuyr doo,   1075
Falsehedd my lorde vnto;'
 The same seyde Egravayne.

91

All þey assentyd but they two,
The todur parte was þe moo,
 And þat was þere well seen.   1080
1069 *R.* wylle

Soche wordys among þem can falle,
They presyd abowte Syr Sampson all,
    And slewe hym in that tene.
They made Syr Egraveyne to swere soon,
Or þey wolde wyth hym þe same haue done,   1085
    To wote wythowten wene; *To wit without any misery*
Sone a bere haue they ordeygned,
And the dedd corse þer on leyde,
    The sorte was false and kene;

92

And seþyn to Rome þey hym broght, *the dead body is actually Sampson's, not Emere's.* 1090
And tolde Florence worthyly wroght,
    That Emere laye there dedd;
When þat sche had swowned twyes,   f. 247a
And thereaftur syghed thryes,
    Sche wepyd in that stedd.   1095
Mylys seyde, 'My lady fre,
Thy councell wyll þat Y wedde þe,
    Hyt was my brodurs redd.'
Sche seyde, 'Y wyll weddyd bee
To a lorde that neuyr schall dye, *to a lord that will never die. Weds herself* 1100
    That preestys schewe in forme of bredd. *to God.*

93

'Furste þen was my fadur slayne,
And now my lorde ys fro me tane, *Marries herself*
    Y wyll loue no ma, *I will love no man* *to God in chastity*
But hym þat boght me on þe rode, *But him that bought me on the cross* 1105
Wyth hys swete precyus blode,
    To hym Y wyll me ta.'
Then Mylys made xii armed knyȝtys
To kepe the pales day and nyghtys, .
    Sche myght not come them fra,   1110
And also swythe Syr Egravayne,

1086 *V.* wete
1108 *R.* seven   made: a *obliterated by a hole*
1111 as *erased after* swythe, *V. considers it crossed out*

Went to þe pope, þe soþe to sayne,
  To telle he was full thra,

Egvavayne tells the Pope everything

94

How that Emere was ouyr þe see,
Chasyng Garcy to hys cuntre,   1115
  And Mylys wolde haue hys wyfe;
He had a hundurd to hys assent,
And hyght þem londys, lyþys, and rente;
  But Sampson hath loste hys lyfe,
And broght hym home vpon a bere,   1120
And tolde Florence hyt was Emere,
  All Rome he hath made ryfe;
And certys Y am sworne þem too,
'Holy Fadur, what schall Y do,
  That turned were all thys stryfe?'   1125

95

Then þe pope was not lothe,
To assoyle hym of hys othe,
  For hyt to falsehed can clyne;
'Syr, Y schall telle þe a sekyr tale, f. 247b
Hyt ys bettur brokyn then hale,   1130
  I set my sowle for thyne.'
Than he gart arme of þe spyrytualte,
And of the seculors hundurdys thre,
  Or euyr wolde he blynne; *cease*
To þe pales he made þem to brynge,   1135
For to dystroye that false weddyng,
  The matrymony was not fyne.

96

All þat they wyth false Mylys fonde
They bonde þem boþe fote and honde,
  But they wolde slee not oon,
Mylys set hys back to a pyllere,   1140

they tie up Mylys

1121 Florence, *partly smudged*   1122 hath, *partly smudged*
1133 *V.* seculers   1140 *R.* ane   1141 *R.* backe
pyllere, *partly smudged*

And seyde all schulde dye þat came hym nere;
   But smartely was he tane,
And put in an hye towre,
Be þe reuerence of þe emperowre, *Emere*   1145
   That was made of lyme and stane;
And twenty of þes odur ay in a pytt,
In stokkes and feturs for to sytt,
   Or euyr Pope Symonde blanne.

97

Than þe pope and Egravayne   1150
To telle þe lady were full fayne
   Hur lorde was on the see,
To Costantyne the nobull strekk;
All the lasse can sche recke,   *Confusion of feeling + joy*
   Tho all bryghtenyd hur blee.   *prevent Florence from comprehending the good news* 1155
They went to þe bere wythowten wone,
And caste vp þe clothe and sye Sampson,
   That semely was to see;
They dud wyth hym as wyth þe dedd,   *they buried Sampson*
They beryed hym in a ryall stedd,
   Wyth grete solempnyte.   1160

98

All thys whyle was Syr Emere
Chasyng Garcy, as ye schall here,
   As the Romans tolde;
But Garcy had getyn hys pales before,   f. 247c
And vetaylyd hyt wyth warme store,   1166
   Hys wylys were full olde.
Syr Emere set hys sege þerto,
Full doghtely þere can he doo,
   That hardy was and bolde,   1170
Wyth men of armes all abowte,
That he myght on no syde owte,
   But hamperde hym in hys holde.

1142 þat, *partly smudged*
1164 8ᵛⁱ, *written in same hand below line*

99

And þus þey segyd Garcy wyth strenkyth,
In hys pales large of lenkyth, 1175
 The Romaynce had ther wylle
Of Costantyne þe nobull cyte
In ther poscescyon for to bee,
 That many oon lykyd ylle.
Syr Emere comawndyd euery man 1180
To brooke wele þe tresur þat þey wan,
 So myght they þer cofurs fylle.
When Syr Garcy sawe all yede to schame,
He callyd to Emere be hys name,
 Downe at a wyndowe stylle: 1185

100

'Syr,' he seyde, 'also mote Y the,
Thou holdyst full wele þat þou hyghtyst me,
 When Y let the goo,
Ageyn to Rome as men may lythe,
Had Y wetyn what schulde haue be sythe, 1190
 Thou schuldyst not haue skapyd soo;
But syn Y qwyte claymed the þore,
3yt muste þou be of mercy more,
 Thou graunt þat hyt be soo.
ix thousand pownde Y schall geue þe, 1195
To wende home to thy cuntre,
 And wyrke me no more woo.'

101

'Nay, be hym þat lorde ys beste,
Tyll Y haue þys londe conqueste,
 And efte be crowned newe; 1200
And yf my men wyll so als,   f. 247d
For Y trowe þer be noon fals,
 And yf þer be þemselfe schall rewe.'
Synagot seyde, 'Be Godys wayes,

1177 *R.* cytè 1189 *R.* Ayeyn 1190 haue, *R. omits*
1195 ix: *MS.* vx *R.* Nine thowsand

He wyll holde that he says,   1205
  He ys hardy and trewe.
I rede we do vs in hys wylle,
And ȝylde þys empyre hym tylle,
  Or he vs more bale brewe.

I have to do what Otes wished.

102

'Ther ys not, Y vndurstonde,   1210
An hundurd knyghtys in þy londe
  Moo then thou haste here,
Slewe he þem not vp at Rome?
In euyll tyme we thedur come,
  Or þat thy lore can lere.   1215
Whon þat þou went Florence to wowe,
Ouyr þe stremes þou madyste vs to rowe,
  And boght thy pryde full dere;
Many a chylde lefte þou thore
Fadurles for euyrmore,   1220
  And wedows in cuntreys sere.'

You left many children fatherless + widows too.

103

There þey openyd þer ȝatys wyde,
Syr Garcy came down þat tyde,
  Wyth a drawyn swyrde in hys hande,
And wyth a keye of golde clere,   1225
And ȝyldyd vnto Syr Emere,
  Hyt sygnyfyed all the lande.
They ledd yn hys baner wyth honowre,
And sett hyt on the hyest towre,
  That þey in castell fande;   1230
And soone vpon that odur day,
They crowned hym emperowre, Y saye,
  Ther durste no man agenste hym stande.

Garcy surrendered

Crowned Emere emperor

1210 vndurstonde: o *written over* a, *after* V.
1216 *R., V.,* When
1218 *R.* pride   1219 *R.* left   1226 *R.* yeldyd
1230 *After R.,* þey in castell: *MS.* þey castell *V.* þey castell

104

Then he gave londys to knyghtys kydde,
And newe men in offyce dydd,   1235
   The lande to stabull and stere.
He seyde vnto Syr Garcye,   f. 248a
'Syr, ye muste wende home wyth me,
   Yf that yowre wylle were,
For to see Rome wythynne,   1240
That ye wende sometyme to wynne,
   And Florence þat ys to me dere;
Hyt schall turne yow to no grefe.'
Whether he were lothe or lefe,
   Forthe they wente in fere.   1245

105

Soche a nave as þere was oon
Was neuyr seen but þat allone,
   When hyt was on the see;
Then Emere þoght on Mylys hys brodur,
And on Florence feyreste of odur,   1250
   At them then wolde he bee.
He seyde vnto Syr Garcy,
And to odyr lordys þat stode hym by,
   'To Hungary soone wyll wee,
Justamownde for to forfare,   1255
And crowne Mylys my brodur þare,
   For knydyst heyre ys hee.'

106

A messengere to londe wanne,
That some tyme rode and sometyme ranne,
   Tyll he came Rome wythynne;
He tolde Florence bryght of hewe,   1260
How hys lorde was crownyd newe,
   And the empyre can wynne;

1234 *R.* gaye   1246 *After R.,* as þere: *MS.* or þere *V.* or þere
1253 lordys: y *partly obliterated by a hole*
1261 He: H *written over erasure*

And wyth hym bryngyth olde Garcy,
The lady fayne was sche forthy,   1265
    Sche was comyn of gentyll kynne.
Sche gafe hym for hys newe tythandys,
Worthe a baronry of landys,
    Or euyr wolde sche blynne.

107

Lorde that ys bothe God and man,   1270
Gyf þe emperowre had wetyn þan,
    The treson of hys brodur,
That he dud in hys absence;
To Sampson and to feyre Florence,   f. 248b
    And Egravayne the todur!   1275
The lady went vp to a towre,
Be reuerence of þe emperowre,
    And wyth hur many odur,
And toke hym downe þat cursyd thefe,
That afturward dud hur grete grefe,   1280
    Ther was neuyr no sawe sotheyr.

108

The lady preyed Syr Egravayne,
And odur lordys þat þey wolde layne
    The treson of the knyght,
And all that he hath done to me,   1285
All forgeuyn schall hyt bee,
    For Godys loue moste of myght.
Sche set hym on a gode palfray,
And bad hym wende vpon hys way,
    Agenste hys brodur ryght.   1290
When that he came to the see,
A false lesynge there made hee
    Of Florence feyre and bryght.

1268 *R.* barony
1269 Or, *partly smudged*
1270 Lorde, Lor *partly smudged*
1290 *V.* A genste

109

Syr Egravayne sadylde hys stede,
And hyed hym aftur a gode spede,   1295
   He hopyd that he wolde lye;
When Mylys sawe the emperowre,
He felle downe in a depe fowre,
   Fro hys hors so hye.
Emere seyde, 'Mylys, what eylyth the?'   1300
'Syr, thus thy wyfe hath dyght me,
   For Y seyde Y schulde hur bewrye,
When Y fonde Egravayne lygyng hur by,
In preson put sche me forthy,
   And sorowe hath made me to drye.'   1305

110

The emperowre smote down wyth hys hevydd,
All hys yoye was fro hym revydd
   Of Florence that he hadd,
All þe lykyng of hys longe trauayle
Was away wythowten fayle,   1310
   In sorowe was he stadde.   f. 248c
All the lordys that were hym by,
Recowmforde hym full kyndely,
   And bad hym not be adradd
'Tyll we the sothe haue enqueryd,   1315
Bothe of lewde and of lerydd';
   Thes wordys ʒyt made hym gladd.

111

Then came Egravayne wythowten lees,
Faste prekynge into the prees,
   The sothe he wolde haue tolde,   1320
But Mylys owte wyth a swyrde kene,
And wolde Egravayne tene,

1300 *R.* Emere, seyde Mylys
1304 *R.* yut   1306 hevydd: *MS.* hedd *V.* hedd
1310 8ᵛⁱⁱ, *written in same hand, appears an inch below* wythowten
1316 *After H.*, lerydd: *MS.* lernydd *R., V.*, lernydd

But he a mantell can folde
Ofte sythys abowte hys arme.
And kepyd hym wele fro any harme,   1325
  That hardy was and bolde.
The emperowre bad put þem insondur,
'Ane of yow schall bye þys blundur
  Whych hath the wronge in holde.'

112

Syr Egravayne seyde, 'Syr now Y schall   1330
Telle yow a full sekyr tale,
  And ye wyll here hyt wele.
Syr when ye went vnto þe see,
Ye lefte an hundurd men and vs thre,
  Armed in yron and stele,   1335
To kepe Florence tyll ye came agayne;
And þat made my brodur Sampson slayne,
  And wroght hath myn vnhele.

Egravayne tells Emere the story

Jacke concluding from of 3 lines

113

'Vnnethe were ye on the see,
When Mylys seyde, here standyth he,   1340
  That ye foreuyr were gone.
He seyde he wolde be emperowre,
And wedde yowre lady whyte as flowre,
  That worthy ys yn wone.
He had an hundurd at hys assente,   1345
And hyght þem londys and ryche rente,
  That made Syr Sampson slone.
And broght hym home on a bere tree, *wood coffin*
And tolde Florence þat hyt was ye,   f. 248d
  Then made sche full grete moone.   1350

114

'And when he wolde hur haue wedde,
Faste away fro hym sche fledde,
  And wolde haue stolyn awaye.

1328 Ane: *MS.* And *R., V.,* And   1349 *V.* that   1350 *R.* Thon

Then Mylys made to arme xii knyghtys,
To kepe þe place day and nyghtys, 1355
   And wach abowte hur lay;
And certys Y was to them sworne,
And ellys had my lyfe be lorne,
   The certen sothe to saye.
I went to þe Pope and tolde hym sa 1360
And he assoyled me a pena et culpa
   Wythowtyn any delay.

115

'Then he gart arme an hundurd clerkys,
Doghty men and wyse of werkys,
   To þe pales he can þem brynge, 1365
They bonde þe false boþe honde and fote,
And in pryson caste þem, God hyt wote,
   And þeryn cam þem thrynge;
And Florence let owt Mylys nowe,
For to wende agenste yow, 1370
   Be Jhesu heuyn kynge.
Thys wyll wytnes pope Symond,
He wolde not for a þousand pownde,
   Telle yow a lesynge.

116

'Ye schall come home, as Y yow say, 1375
Be tomorne that hyt be day,
   And thys was at the none.'
The emperowre in þys whylys
Drewe a swyrde to Syr Mylys,
   But lordys helde hym soone, 1380
He badd, 'False traytur flee!
That þou neuyr þy brodur see,
   For wykkydly haste þou done.'

1360 *a word struck out above* hym sa
1363 *R.* ame   1365 can: an *partly obliterated by a hole*
1366 *R.* hond
1368 *R.* can

Euyn to Rome ageyne he rode, *Mylys*
Hastely wythowten bode,   1385
    Or euyer he wolde awey gone.

117

To feyre Florence can he saye,
A lesyng þat hur wele can paye,   f. 249a
    'My lorde byddyth that ye schall
Come agayne hym in þe mornynge.'   1390
Blythe þer of was þat maydyn ȝynge,
    And trowed hys false tale.
Sche sente to the pope ouyr nyght,
And bad he schulde be tymely dyght,
    Wyth mony a cardynale.   1395
And sche ordeygned hur meyne als,
And went wyth hym þat was false,
    And passyd bothe downe and dale.

118

When þey came wythowte the cyte
Mylys seyde, 'My lady free,   1400
    We two muste ryde faste,
And let the pope and hys meyne
Come behynde the and me,
    For thus then ys my caste;
That þou may speke wyth my lorde þy fylle,   1405
And wyth Garcy wykkyd of wylle,
    And be nothynge agaste.
For when þe emperowre þe Pope can see,
Mekyll speche wyll ther bee,
    And þat full longe wyll laste.'   1410

119

'Mylys,' sche seyde, 'God ȝylde hyt the,
That Y soone my lorde may see,
    Thou makyste me full fayne.'

1388 A lesyng: *MS.* Alesyng
1412 That: Th *written over an erasure*   1413 *R.* makyst

The ryght wey lay euyn este,
And he lad hur sowtheweste, 1415
   And thus he made hys trayne,
Tyll þey came downe in a depe gylle;
The lady seyde, 'We ryde ylle,
   Thes gatys þey are vngayne;
I rede we lyght vnto þe grownde, 1420
And byde owre fadur þe pope a stownde,'
   He seyde, 'Nay, be Goddys payne,

120

'Thou schalt hym see neuyrmare.'
Tho þe lady syghed wondur sare,
   And felle of on hur palfray. f. 249b
He bete hur wyth hys nakyd swyrde, 1426
And sche caste vp many a rewfull rerde,
   And seyde ofte, 'Weleawaye
Schall Y neuyr my lorde see?'
'No, be God that dyed on tre,' 1430
   The false traytur can saye.
Vp he hur caste, and forþe þey rode,
Hastely wythowten any abode,
   Thys longe somersday.

121

They were nyghtyd in a wode thyck, 1435
A logge made that traytur wyck,
   Vndurnethe a tree.
There he wolde haue leyn hur by,
And sche made hur preyer specyally,
   To God and Mary feyre and free: 1440
'Let neuyr thys false fende
My body nodur schame nor schende,
   Myghtfull in mageste!'

1428 *After R.*, Weleawaye: *MS*. Wele a saye
1440 Mary feyre and free: *MS*. Mary and free *R*. Mary free *V*.
Mary and free

Hys lykyng vanysched all away.
On þe morne when hyt was day,   1445
   Ther horsys bothe dyght hee.

122

Vp he hur caste and forthe þey rode,
Thorow a foreste longe and brode,
   That was feyre and grene.
Tyll eyder odur mekyll care,   1450
The lady hungurd wondur sare,
   That was bryght and schene.
Sche had leuyr a lofe of bredd,
Then mekyll of þe golde redd,
   That sche before had seen;   1455
To hyt drewe to þe euenynge,
Then they herde a belle rynge,
   Thorow þe grace þat Godd can lene.

123

A holy Armyte fownde he there,
To greve God full loþe hym were,   1460
   For he had seruyd hym aye.
Thedur they wente to aske mete;
The Armyte seyde, 'Soche as Y ete   f. 249c
   Ye schall haue, dere damysell Y say.'
A barly lofe he broght hur too,   1465
And gode watur; full fayne was scho,
   That swete derworthe maye.
Therof the yonge lady ete,
Sche thoght neuyr noon so swete,
   Be nyght nodur be day.   1470

124

Mylys ete therof als;
He seyde, 'Hyt stekyth in my hals,
   I may not gete hyt downe.

1449 and: *MS.* n *crossed out*   1453 *R.* She
1459 *V.* mis-numbered 1460
1462 8ᵛⁱⁱⁱ, *written in same hand below line*

Chorle, God, yf þe schames dedd,
Brynge vs of thy bettur bredd, 1475
   Or Y schall crake thy crowne.'
'Be God,' he seyde, 'þat boght me dere,
I had no bettur thys vii yere.'
   The wykkyd man þo made hym bowne,
In at the dore he hym bete, 1480
And sethyn fyre vpon hym sete,
   Ferre fro euery towne.

125

The holy Armyte brente he thare,
And lefte that bygly hows full bare,
   That semely was to see. 1485
The lady beganne to crye and ȝelle,
And seyde, 'Traytur þou schalt be in helle,
   There euyr to wonne and bee.'
He made þe lady to swere an othe,
That sche schulde not telle for lefe nor loþe, 1490
   Neuyr in no cuntre,
Fro whens þou came nor what þou ys,
Nor what man broght þe fro þy blysse,
   Or here Y schall brenne the.

126

To make þat othe þe lady was fayne, 1495
And þere he wolde by hur haue layne,
   But sche preyed God to be hur schylde;
And ryght as he was at assaye.
Hys lykyng vanyscht all awaye,
   Thorow þe myght of Mary mylde. 1500
Tymely as the day can dawe,
He led hur thorow a feyre schawe,
   In wodes waste and wylde;
Euyn at vndurne lyghtyd he,
Downe vndur a chesten tre, 1505
   The feyrest in that fylde.

1502 *R.* her

127

He seyde, 'þou haste wychyd me,
I may not haue to do wyth the,
　Vndo or thou schalt abye.'
Sche answeryd hym wyth mylde mode,　　　　　　1510
'Thorow grace of Hym þat dyed on rode,
　False traytur thou schalt lye.'
He bonde hur be þe tresse of þe heere,
And hangyd hur on a tre there,
　That ylke feyre bodye;　　　　　　　　　　　1515
He bete hur wyth a ȝerde of byrke,
Hur nakyd flesche tyll he was yrke,
　Sche gaf many a rewfull crye.

128

There was a lorde þat hyght Tyrry
Wonned a lytyll thereby,　　　　　　　　　　1520
　In a forest syde,
Thedur was he comyn þat day,
Wyth hawkys and howndys hym for to play,
　In that wode so wyde.
He harde the crye of þat lady free,　　　　　1525
Thedur he went and hys meyne,
　Also faste as þey myght ryde;
When Mylys was warre of þer comyng,
He lepe on hys hors and forthe can spryng,
　And durste no lenger byde.　　　　　　　　1530

129

The feyrest palfrey lefte he there,
And hurselfe hangyd be the heere,
　And hur ryche wede;
Hur sadull and hur brydull schone,
Set wyth mony a precyus stone,　　　　　　　f. 250a
　The feyrest in that thede.　　　　　　　　1536
Sche was the feyrest creature,
And therto whyte as lylly flowre,
　In romance as we rede;

1514 hur: u *partly obliterated by a hole*

Hur feyre face hyt schone full bryght, 1540
To se hyt was a semely syght,
 Tyll hur full faste they yede.

130

Then þey lowsyd hur feyre faxe,
That was ȝelowe as the waxe,
 And schone also as golde redd. 1545
Sche myȝt not speke, þe romance seyde,
On a lyter they hur leyde,
 And to the castell hur ledd.
They bathyd hur in erbys ofte,
And made hur sore sydes softe, 1550
 For almoste was sche dedd.
They fed hur wyth full ryche fode,
And all þyng þat hur nede stode,
 They seruyd hur in that stedd.

131

The lorde comawndyd hys men euerychon 1555
That typyngys of hur þey shulde spere noon,
 Nor ones aske of whens sche were.
Vnto the stabull they ledd hur stede,
And all hur odur gere þey dud lede,
 Vnto a chaumbur dere. 1560
The lorde had a doghtur feyre
That hyght Betres, schulde be hys heyre,
 Of vysage feyre and clere;
To Florence they can hur kenne,
To lerne hur to behaue hur among men, 1565
 They lay togedur in fere,

132

In bedd togedur, wythowte lesynge.
Florence that was feyre and ȝynge,
 If any many hur besoght

1551 was: s *partly obliterated by a hole*   1556 *R.* sper

Of loue, sche gaf them soche answare   1570
That þey wolde neuyr aske hur mare,
    That was so worthely wroght.   f. 250b
Sche preyed to God þat boght hur dere
To sende hur sownde to Syr Emere,
    That hur full dere had boght;   1575
Be that he was comyn to Rome,
He thoght hyt a full carefull come,
    Where sche was he wyste noght.

133

Off Garcy Y wyll telle yow mare,
That was cawser of hur euyll fare,   1580
    And cawsyd hur fadur to be slayne,
Emere vengyd well hys dedd,
And broght hym fro hys strenkyþfull stedd, *full of strength*
    To grete Rome agayne.
There lykyd hym noght to bee,   1585
And soone thereaftur dyed he,
    The sothe ys not to layne;   *Garcy died.*
Sche sawe hym neuyr wyth hur eye,
That cawsyd hur all þat sorowe to drye,
    Of hur haue we to sayne.   1590

134

Wyth Syr Tyrry dwellyd a knyght
That hardy was, and Machary he hyght,   *Machary likes her*
    He was bolde as any bare.
To hys lemman he wolde haue had þat bryght,
And spyed hur bothe day and nyght,   1595
    Therof came mekyll care.
Tyll hyt befelle vpon a day,
In hur chaumbur stode that maye,
    To hur than can he fare;
He leyde hur downe on hur bedd,   1600
The lady wepyd sore for dredd,   *tries to bed her — rape*
    Sche had no socowre thare.

135

Before hur bedd lay a stone,
The lady toke hyt vp anon,
   And toke hyt yn a gethe, *she hit him in mouth w/a rock* **1605**
On þe mowþe sche hym hyt, *hastely*
That hys fortethe owte he spytt,
   Above and also benethe. **f. 250c**
Hys mowthe, hys nose, braste owt on blood,
Forthe at þe chaumbur dore he ȝode, **1610**
   For drede of more wrethe;

136

And to hys chaumber he hyed hym ryȝt,
And dwellyd forthe a fowrtenyght,
   And then he came agayne,
And tolde hys lorde þat he was schent, **1615**
Euyll betyn in a turnement, *he lies b/c*
   The sothe ys not to layne. *the truth is unpardonable*
'The tethe be smetyn owt of my mowþe,
Therefore my sorowe ys full cowthe,
   Me had leuyr to be slayne.' **1620**
He wolde haue be vengyd of þat dede,
Florence myght full soré hur drede, *lament*
   Had sche wetyn of hys trayne. *known + deceit*

137

A scharpe knyfe he had hym boght,
Of yron and stele well ywroght, **1625**
   That bytterly wolde byte.
And euyn to hur chaumbur he ȝode,
And vp behynde a curten he stode, *kills Tyrnys daughter Betres*
   Therof came sorowe and syte.
When he wyste they were on slope **1630**
To Betres throte can he grope,
   In sonder he schare hyt tyte.
And ȝyt the thefe or he wolde leeue,
He put the hafte in Florence neeve, *frames Florence*
   For sche schulde haue the wyte. **1635**

    1607 8ⁱˣ, *written in same hand below line*

138

Forthe at þe chaumber dore he ʒode,
And Betres lay burlyng in hur blode,
   And Florence slepyd faste.
Hur fadur thoght in a vysyon,   *Prophetic dream*
Hys doghtur schulde be strekyn downe,   1640
   Wyth a thonderblaste;
And as a þyck leyʒtenyng abowte hur ware.
Vp he starte wyth mekyll care,
   And a kyrtell on he caste;
A candyll at a lawmpe he lyght,   1645
And to hur chaumber reykyd he ryght,
   Thorowly on he thraste;   f. 250d
   thoroughly

139

And fonde Betres hys doghtur dedd,
The bedd was full of blode redd,
   And a knyfe in Florence hande.   1650
He callyd on Eglantyne hys wyfe,
Knyghtys and ladyes came belyfe,
   Wondur sore wepeande:
Gentyll wemen sore dud wepe,
And euyr can feyre Florence slepe,   1655
   That was so feyre to fande.
Sche glyste vp wyth þe hedeows store,
A sorowfull wakenyng had sche þore,
   Soche anodur was neuyr in lande.

eyes: glared stared

140

Abowte the bedd they presyd thyck,   1660
Among þem came þat traytur wyck,
   The whych had done that dede.
He seyde, 'Syr, Y schall set a stake
Wythowte þe towne a fyre to make,
   And Florence thedur lede.   1665
Ye myght see be hur feyre clothyng,
That sche was no erthely thynge,   *p 147*
   And be hur grete feyre hede.   *evil in the*
       guise of
   1664 a, *partly obliterated by a hole*   *female*
       beauty

her beauty is a sign that she is the devil

But some false fende of helle
Ys comyn þy doghtur for to qwelle,   1670
   Let me quyte hur hur mede.'

141

They dyȝt hur on þe morne in sympull atyre,
And led hur forthe vnto the fyre,
   Many a oon wyth hur ȝede;
Sche seyde, 'God of myghtys moost,   1675
Fadur and Sone and Holy Goost,
   As Y dud neuyr thys dede,
Yf Y gyltles be of thys,
Brynge me to þy bygly blys,
   For Thy grete godhede.'   1680
All that euyr on hur can see,
Wrange þer hondys for grete pyte
   And farde as they wolde wede.

142

The lorde that had þe doghtur dedd,
Hys herte turned in that stedd,   1685
   To wepe he can begynne.   f. 251a
He seyde, 'Florence, also mote Y the,
I may not on thy dethe see,
   For all the worlde to wynne.'
To hur chaumbur he can hur lede,   1690
And cled hur in hur own wede,
   And seyde, 'Y holde hyt synne.'
They set hur on hur own palfraye,
In all hur nobull ryche arraye,
   Or euyr wolde he blynne;   1695

143

And gaf hur þe brydull in hur hande,
And broght hur to þe wode þere he hur fande,
   And than he lefte hur thare.

1672 atyre, *compressed and difficult to read* R. atyr V. a tyre
1682 *R.* pytè   1692 *R.* hold   1697 *R.* ther

And betaght hur God and gode day,
And bad hur wende on hur way,   1700
   And then sche syghed sare;
'Syr,' sche seyde, 'for charyte,
Let none of þy men folowe me
   To worche me no more care.
'Nay for God,' he seyde, 'noon schulde   1705
For ix tymes thy weyght of golde';
   Home then can he fare.

144

Thorow þe foreste the lady rode,
All glemed there sche glode
   Tyll sche came in a felde.   1710
Sche sawe men vndur a galows stande,
Thedur þey ledd a thefe to hange,
   To them then sche helde;
And haylesed them full curteslye.
They askyd fro whens sche came in hye,   1715
   That worthy was to welde.
Sche seyde, 'Ye schall wete of me no mare
But as a woman dyscownfortyd sare
   Wythowten bote or belde;

145

'No leuyng lefe wyth me Y haue,   1720
Wolde ye graunt me to be my knaue,
   The thefe that ye thynke to hynge.
The more buxvm wyll he bee,
That he were borowyd fro þe galow tree,
   I hope be Heuyn Kynge.'
                              f. 251b
Then ther councell toke thay,   1726
They were lothe to seye hur nay,
   Sche was so feyre a thynge.
They gaf hym to hur of þer gyfte,
He was full lothe to leeve hys thefte;   1730
   Sche thankyd þem olde and ʒynge.

1702 *R.* charytè   1706 *R.* nyne
1713 then sche: *MS.* can *crossed out before* sche *V.* then can sche

146

Sche seyde, 'Wolde þou serue me wele,
I schulde the quyte euery dele.'
   He seyde to hur, 'ȝaa,
Ellys were Y a grete fole,   1735
And worthy to be drowned in a pole,
   The galowse þou delyuyrd me fra.'
Sche thynkyth, 'Myȝt Y come ouyr þe see,
At Jerusalem wolde Y bee,
   Thedur to ryde or ga;   1740
Then myȝt Y spyr tythandys of Rome,
And of my lordys home come;'
   But now wakenyth hur waa.

147

A burges that was the thefys reyset,
At the townes ende he þem mett,   1745
   The lady rode ouyr an hylle,
'I wende þou hadyst be hangyd hye'
And he twynkylde wyth hys eye,
   As who seyth, 'Holde the stylle.'
'Thys gentyll woman hath borowed me   1750
For Y schulde hur knaue bee,
   And serue hur at hur wylle';
And sythyn he rowned in hys eere,
'I behete the all þys ryche gere,
   Thy hows Y wyll brynge hur tylle.'   1755

148

He led hur vp into the towne,
At þys burges hows he toke hur downe,
   There was hur harburgerye.
On the hye deyse he hur sett,
And mete and drynke he hur fett,   1760
   Of the wyne redd as cherye.

1745 *R*. end   1749 Hold: *MS*. holde
1751 schulde: *MS. letters after* l *illegible because rubbed*
1758 harburgerye: *MS*. harbuergerye

The burges wyfe welcomed hur ofte,
Wyth mylde wordys and wyth softe,
　　And bad hur ofte be merye.
Tho two false wyth grete yre,　　　　　　　　f. 251c
Stode and behelde hur ryche atyre,　　　　　　　1766
　　And beganne to lagh and flyre. *mock*

149

The burges wyfe wyste ther þoght,
And seyde, 'In feythe ye do for noght
　　Yf so be that Y may.'　　　　　　　　　　1770
At nyght to chaumbur sche hur ledd, *led her to bed*
And sparryd the dore and went to bedd, *locked the door*
　　All nyght togedur they laye,
Sche calde on Clarebolde hur knaue,
'A lytyll errande for sothe Y haue　　　　　　　1775
　　At the see so graye;
Yf any schepe wende ouyr þe streme
To the cyte of Jerusalem,
　　Gode sone wytt me to saye.'

150

Clarebalde seyde the burges tylle,　　　　　　　1780
'Thys nyght had we not owre wylle,
　　We muste caste anodur wyle.' *they sold her to a marinere*
To the see they went in fere,
And solde hur to a marynere,
　　Wythynne a lytyll whyle;　　　　　　　　1785
'On covenawnt sche ys þe feyrest þynge,
That euyr ye sye olde or ȝynge,'
　　And he at them can smyle.
So mekyll golde for hur he hyght,
That hyt passyd almoost hur weyght,　　　　　　1790
　　On eyther parte was gyle.

1764 8ˣ, *written in same hand below line*　　　1767 *R.* flerye
1769 *R.* we　　　　1778 *R.* cyté　　　1779 *V. notes* w *in* wytt
written over t; t *could be a* c　saye, a *written over* l　　　1784 *R.* sold

151

'Take here the golde in a bagg,
I schall hyt hynge on a knagg,
    At the schyppborde ende.
When ye haue broght that clere,   1795
Put vp yowre hande and take hyt here;'
    Aftur hur can they wende.
They seyde a schypp ys hyred to þe,
That wyll to Jerusalem ouyr þe see,
    Sche þankyd þem as sche was hende,   1800
Sche gaf þe burges wyfe hur palfray,
Wyth sadyll and brydyll þe soþe to say,
    And kyste hur as hur frende.

152

Altherfurste to þe kyrke sche went,
To here a masse verament,   1805
    And preyed God of hys grace,
That he wolde bryng hur to þat ryke,
That euyrmore ys yoye in lyke,
    Before hys worthy face;
And or sche dyed Emere to see,   1810
That hur own lorde schulde bee,
    In Rome that ryall place.
To þe schypp þey went in fere,
And betoke hur to þe marynere,
    That louely vndur lace.   1815

153

They toke þe bagg þey went hyt had be golde,
And had hyt home in to þer holde,
    They lokyd and þen hyt was ledd;
The burges seyde to Clarebalde,
'Thou haste made a sory frawde,   1820
    God gyf þe schames dedd;
For certenly wythowten wene,

1796 here: *MS. hole obliterates letters between* h *and* e

Thou haste begyled a lady schene,
  And made hur euyll of redd.'
To the see hyed they faste,   1825
The sayle was vp vnto þe maste,
  And remeuyd was fro þat stedd.

154

All men þat to þe schypp can longe,
They went Florence to leman haue fonge,
  Ylke oon aftur odur had done;   1830
But þey faylyd of ther praye,
Thorow grace of God þat myghtys maye,
  That schope bothe sonne and moone.
Sche calde on Clarebalde hur knave,
The marynere seyde, 'Y hope ye rave,'   1835
  And tolde how he had doone.
Sche prayde God schulde hym forgeue,
A dreryar woman myȝt noon leeue,
  Vndur heuyn trone.

155

The marynere set hur on hys bedd,   1840
Sche had soone aftur a byttur spredd,   f. 252a
  The schypp sayled belyve;
He seyde, 'Damysell Y haue þe boght,
For þou art so worþely wroght,
  To wedde the to my wyve.'   1845
Sche seyde, 'Nay that schall not bee
Thorow helpe of Hym in Trynyte
  That suffurde woundys fyve;'
In hys armes he can hur folde,
Hur rybbes crakyd as þey breke wolde,   1850
  In struglynge can they stryve.

1823 *R.* hast   1825 hyed, e *partly rubbed*
  1832 Thorow, w *partly rubbed* *R.* may   1833 That: *MS. last* t
crossed out   1835 *R.* marynar   1836 *R.* hade
  1838 *R.* dreryer   1840 *R.* maryner
  1841 *R.* hadd   1847 *R.* trynytè

156

Sche seyde, 'Lady Mary free,
Now thou haue mercy on me,
   Thou faylyst me neuyr at nede.
Here my errande as þou well may,   1855
That Y take no schame today,
   Nor lose my maydynhede.'
Then beganne þe storme to ryse,
And that vpon a dolefull wyse,
   The marynere rose and yede.   1860
He hyed to the toppe of þe maste,
They stroke þe sayle þe gabuls braste,
   They hyed them a bettur spede.

157

He seyde, 'But yf þys storme blynne,
All mvn be drowned þat be hereynne,'   1865
   Then was that lady fayne.
Sche had leuyr to haue be dedd,
Then þere to haue loaste hur maydynhedd,
   Or he had hur by layne.
Then þe schypp clave insondur,   1870
All þat was yn hyt soone went vndur,
   And drowned boþe man and swayne.
The yonge lady in that tyde,
Fleytd forþe on þe schyppes syde,
   Vnto a roche vngayne.   1875

158

The marynere sate vpon an are,
But nodur wyste of odur fare,
   The todur were drowned perde,
The lady steppyd to a ston,
Sche fonde a tredd and forþe ys gon,   f. 252b
   Loudyng the Trynyte.   1880
To a noonre men calle Beuerfayre,

1874 *After H.*, schyppes: *MS*. schyp *R.*, *V.* schyp
1875 Vnto: t *written over an* o   1878 *R.* perdè
1882 Beuerfayre: *MS*. Benerfayre, *V. notes same*

That stondyþ on þe watur of Botayre,
   That rennyth in to þe grekys see,
A stepull then the lady sye,   1885
Sche þoght þe wey þedur full drye,
   And therat wolde sche bee.

159

Syr Lucyus Jbarnyus was fownder þere,
An hundurd nonnes þeryn were,
   Of ladyes wele lykeande.   1890
When that sche came nere þe place,
The bellys range þorow Godys grace,
   Wythowten helpe of hande.
Of Seynt Hyllary þe churche ys,
The twenty day of ȝowle Y wys,   1895
   As ye may vnderstande.
They lokyd and sawe no leuyng wyght,
But the lady feyre and bryght,
   Can in the cloystur stande.

160

The abbas be þe honde hur toke,   1900
And ladd hur forthe so seyth þe boke,
   Sche was redd forronne.
Sche knelyd downe before þe crosse,
And looueyd God wyth mylde voyce,
   That sche was thedur wonne.   1905
They askyd hur yf sche had ony fere;
Sche seyde, 'Nay now noon here
   Leueyng vnder the soone.'
Sche askyd an hows for charyte,
They broght an habyte to þat fre,   1910
   And þere sche was made nonne.

161

The lady þat was boþe gode and feyre,
Dwellyd as nonne in Beuerfayre,
   Loueyng God of hys loone.

1887 *R.* thereat   1901 *R.* Annd *V.* forþe   1909 *R.* charytè

And Hys modur, Mary bryght,   1915
That safe and sownde broght hur ryght
   Vnto the roche of stone.   f. 252c
A systur of þe hows was seke,
Of the gowte and odur euyls eke,
   Sche myȝt not speke nor goon;   1920
Florence vysyted hur on a day,
And helyd hur or sche went away,
   Sche wolde þer had wytten þerof none.

162

The abbas, and odur nonnes by,
Tolde hyt full openlye,   1925
   That hyt was so verraye,
Ther was noon syke nor sare,
That come þere þe lady ware,
   But they went sownde away.
The worde sprang in mony a cuntre,   1930
And into Rome the ryche cyte,
   There hur lorde in laye,
Whych had an euyll in hys hevedd,
That all hys yoye was fro hym revedd,
   Bothe be nyght and daye.   1935

163

He was so tuggelde in a toyle,
For he werryd on the kyng of Poyle,
   And he on hym agayne;
And as he schulde hys helme avente,
A quarell smote hym verament,   1940
   Thorow owt bothe bonne and brayne.
The leche had helyd hyt ouyr tyte,
And hyt was festurd wythowte delyte,
   Theryn he had grete payne;

1924 abbas: *first* b *written over an indecipherable letter*
  1927 *V.* There   1930 sprang: *MS.* sprang[a]   cuntre: *MS.* cun
crossed out R. cuntrè   1931 the ryche cyte, *partly obscured by*
brownish ink R. cytè   1933 *After R.,* hevedd: *MS.* hedd *V.* hedd

He had leuyr then all hys golde,   1945
That he had ben vndur þe molde,
    Or slyly had ben slayne.

164

He calde Egravayne hym too,
And seyde, 'What ys beste to do?
    Myn euyll encresyth ȝerne.'   1950
'Syr, at Beuerfayre dwellyþ a nonne,
The weyes thedur we ne conne,
    But we schall spyr and lerne.'
Mekyll golde wyth them they toke,
And went forthe, so seyth þe boke.   f. 252d
    Preuely and derne;   1956
And ȝyt for all þer mekyll fare,
Hyt was a grete whyle or þey came þare,
    Thogh all they hastyd ȝerne.

165

The emperowre toke hys ynne þereby,   1960
Althernext the nonnery,
    For þere then wolde he dwelle;
And Mylys hys brodur, þat graceles fole,
Dwellyd wyth oon Gyllam of Pole
    And was woxyn a fowle meselle.   1965
He harde telle of that lady lele,
And þedur was comyn to seeke hys hele,
    The certen sothe to telle;
He harberde hym far therfro
All behynde men, Y telle yow soo,   1970
    Hys sekenes was so felle.

166

And Machary was comyn alse,
Agenste the lady þat was so false,
    That slewe Betres and put hyt hur too.

1947 ben: *MS*. be *R*., *V*. be
1951 Beuerfayre: *MS*: Benerfayre *V*. Beuerfeyre

God had sende on hym a wrake,   1975
That in the palsye can he schake,
    And was crompylde and crokyd þerto.
He had getyn Syr Tyrry thedur,
And hys wyfe bothe togedur,
    Dame Eglantyne hyght schoo,   1980
The holy nonne for to praye,
For to hele hym and sche maye,
    That oght sche euyll to doo.

167

Syr Tyrrye the chastlayne
Harbarde the emperowre full gayne,   1985
    On the todur syde of þe strete;
And þe marynere þat had hur boght,
That wolde haue had hur hys leman to a ⟨wroʒt⟩,
    That on the ore can flete,
He came thedur wyth an euyll   1990
Hyppyng on two stavys lyke þe deuyll,
    Wyth woundys wanne and wete;
And Clarebalde þat was the thefe,
Came wyth an euyll þat dud hym grefe,   f. 253a
    Thes iiii there all can meete.   1995

168

The emperowre to the church went,
To here a masse in gode entent,
    Hende as ye may here;
When þat the masse was done,
The abbas came and haylesyd hym soone,   2000
    On hur beste manere,
The emperowre seyde, 'Well þou bee,
The holy nonne wolde Y see,
    That makyth þe syke thus fere;
An euyll in my hedd smetyn ys,   2005
That Y haue loste all odur blys';
    They sente aftur that clere.

1978 *R.* geten   1987 *R. omits* had
1988 ⟨wroʒt⟩, *written interlinearly under* to a *and bracketed*

169

At hur preyers þere as sche ware,
When sche sawe hur own lorde þare,
  Sche knewe hym wele ynogh.
So dud he hur he wolde not so saye,   2010
Abowte þe cloystur goon are thay,
  Spekynge of hys woghe
Then was sche warre of þe iiii þare,
That had kyndylde all hur care,   2015
  Nere to them sche droghe.
They knewe hur not be no kyns thynge,
Therof thankyd sche Heuyn Kynge,
  And lyghtly at them loghe.

170

Mylys that hur aweye ledd,   2020
He was the fowlest mesell bredd,
  Of pokkys and bleynes bloo.
And Machary þat wolde hur haue slayne,
He stode schakyng the sothe to sayne,
  Crokyd and crachyd thertoo.   2025
The marynere þat wolde haue layne hur by,
Hys yen stode owte a strote forthy,
  Hys lymmes were roton hym froo.
They put Clarebalde in a whelebarowe,
That strong thefe be stretys narowe,   2030
  Had no fote on to goo.

171

Sche seyde, 'Ye that wyll be hale,   f. 253b
And holly broght owt of yowre bale
  Of that ye are ynne,
Ye muste schryue yow openlye,   2035
And that wyth a full lowde crye,
  To all þat be here boþe more and mynne.'

2010 hym: y *partly obliterated by a hole*   2013 *R.* Spekyng
2014 *R.* four   2017 *R.* knew   2026 *R.* maryner
2032 *After V.,* th *crossed out before* Ye   2035 *R.* must

That they þoght full lothe to doo,
Mylys seyde, 'Syth hyt muste be soo,
   Soone schall Y begynne.
I lykyd neuyr wele, day nor nyght,
Syth Y ledd awey a lady bryght,
   From kythe and all hur kynne.'

2040

Mylys was sick since
confessions

172

Than he seyde to them verament,
How he þe lady wolde haue schent,
   And tolde them to the laste;
And þat he wolde haue be emperowre,
And weddyd þe lady whyte as flowre,
   And all hys false caste;
And sythe awey he can hur lede,
'For Y wolde haue refte hur maydynhede,
   That sche defendyd faste,
I had neuyr wyth hur to doo,
For Y myght not wynne hur to,
   But clene fro me sche paste.'

2045

Mylys confesses

2050

2055

173

And sythyn he tolde þem of þe barley bredd,
And how he brent þe armyte to dedd,
   And hangyd hur vp be the hare;
'Then Y sye men and howndys bathe,
And to the wode Y went for wrathe';
   There Tyrry gaf answare,
'Then came Y and toke hur downe,
And had hur wyth me vnto þe towne,
   And that rewyd me full sare;
Sche slewe Betres my doghtur schene,
That schulde my ryght heyre haue bene,
   And ȝyt let Y hur fare.

2060

2065

2051 *After H.* refte hur maydynhede: *MS.* refte fro hur hur maydyn
hede *R.* refte fro hur hur maydynhede *V.* refte fro hur maydyn
hede

174

'For sche was so bryght of blee,
And so semely on to see,
   Therfore let Y hur goo.'   *at one time*   f. 253c
Then Machary, for he muste nede,   2071
'Sche dyd me oonys an euyll dede,
   My harte was wondur throo.   *Machary*
When Y wolde haue leyn hur by,   *confesses*
My fortethe smote sche owt forþy,   2075
   That wakenyd all my woo;
I slewe Betres wyth a knyfe,
For Y wolde sche had loste hur lyfe,
   Trewly hyt was soo.'

175

Then Tyrry farde as he wolde wede,   2080
And seyde, 'False traytur dyd þou þat dede?'
   Then wepyd dame Eglantyne,
And seyde, 'Allas þat we came here,
Thys false traytur for to fere,
   That wroght vs all þys pyne.   2085
Ʒyt Y am warse for þat feyre maye,
That was so vnfrendely flemed away,
   And was gyltles therynne.   *Clarebalde*
Clarebalde seyde, "Sche came be me, *confesses*
I stode vndur a galowe tree,
   And a rope abowte hals myne;   2090

176

'Fro þe galowse sche borowed me,
For Y schulde hur knave haue bee,
   And serue hur to hur paye.
We were togedur but oon nyʒt,   2095
At the see Y solde that bryght,
   On the seconde day.'
Then spake þe marynere þat hur boʒt,   *Maryner*
'When Y wolde hur to wyfe haue wroʒt *confesses*
   Soone sche seyde me naye;   2100
   2098 *R.* maryner

Sche brake my schypp wyth a tempeste,
Sche fletyd sowþe and Y northweste,
   And syth sawe Y neuyr that maye.

177

'Vpon an ore to londe Y wanne,
And euyrsyth haue be a drery man,   2105
   And neuyr had happe to hele.
And syth Y haue be in sorowe and syte,
Me þynkyth we iii be in febull plyte,
   That cawsyd hur to wante hur wylle.'   f. 253d
Sche handylde þem wyth hur hande,   2110
Then were þey hoole, Y vnderstande,
   And odur folke full feele.
Hur own lorde, altherlaste
The venome owt of hys hedd braste,
   Thus can sche wyth them dele.   2115

178

The venome braste owt of hys ere,
He seyde, 'Y fynde yow iiii in fere,'
   Hys herte was full throo.
He made to make a grete fyre,
And caste þem yn wyth all þer tyre,   2120
   Then was the lady woo.
The emperowre toke dame Eglantyne,
Tyrrye, and Florence, feyre and fyne,
   And to the halle can goo.
They looueyd God lesse and more,   2125
That þey had fownde þe lady þore,
   That longe had be them froo.

179

Soche a feste as þere was oon,
In þat lande was neuyr noon,
   They gaf the nonnes rente,   2130

2104 Vpon: *MS.* po *illegible because blotted out in black ink*
2108 *R.* four   2114 *R.* venom   2117 *R.* fynd

And all þer golde, wythowt lesynge,
But vnnethys þat þat myȝt þem home brynge,
    And þankyd þem for that gente.

Florence seyde, 'Syr, wyth yowre leeve,
Tyrrye some þynge muste yow geue,   2135
    That me my lyfe hath lente.
He gaf hym þe cyte of Florawnce.
And bad hym holde hyt wythowt dystawnce;
    They toke ther leue and wente.

180

Tyrrye wente home to hys cuntre,   2140
And þe emperowre to Rome hys ryche cyte,
    As faste as euyr they maye.
When þe pope harde telle of þer comyng,
He went agayne þem wythowt lesynge,
    In full ryall arraye.   2145
Cardynals were somned be þer names,
And come syngyng Te deum laudamus,
    The certen sothe to saye;   f. 254a
They loouyd God boþe more and lesse,
That they had getyn þe emperes,   2150
    That longe had bene awaye.

181

Soche a brydale as þere was oon
In that lande was neuyr noon,
    To wytt wythowten wene.
There was grete myrþe of mynstrals steuyn,   2155
And nobull gyftys also geuyn,
    Bothe golde and robys schene;
Soone aftur on þe fowretenyth day,
They toke þer leue and went þer way,
    And thankyd kynge and quene.   2160
They loouyd God wyth myȝt and mayne
That þe lady was comyn agayne,
    And kept hur chaste and clene.

2137 _R._ cytè   2140 _R._ cuntrè   2141 _R._ emperowr   cytè

182

They gate a chylde the furste nyght,
A sone that Syr Otes hyght,   2165
   As the boke makyth mynde.
A nobull knyȝt and a stronge in stowre,
That aftur hym was emperowre,
   As hyt was full gode kynde.
Then the emperowre and hys wyfe,   2170
In yoye and blysse þey lad þer lyfe,
   That were comyn of gentyl strynde.
Pope Symonde thys story wrate,
In þe cronykyls of Rome ys þe date,
   Who sekyth þere he may hyt fynde.   2175

183

Forþy schulde men and women als,
Them bethynke or þey be false,
   Hyt makyth so fowle an ende.
Be hyt neuyr so slylye caste,
Ȝyt hyt schamyþ þe maystyr at þe laste,   2180
   In what londe þat euyr þey lende.
I meene be thes iiii fekyll,
That harmed feyre Florence so mykyll,
   The trewest that men kende.
And þus endyth þys romance gode   2185
Jhesu that boght vs on the rode   f. 254b
   Vnto hys blysse vs send

Amen

Explicit Le Bone Florence of Rome

2164 chylde: *y completely obliterated by a hole*
2179 *After R.*, slylye: *MS.* slylylye *V.* slylylye   2182 *R.* four
2188 *R. omits* Amen *R., V. omit* Explicit Le Bone Florence of Rome

NOTES

1 ff. The opening of the poem utilises the conventional Troy
material of chronicle and romance. It sets the story of
Florence in the framework of history. Trojans are founders
of great cities, the poet announces: Andromoche built
Antioch; Antenor, Jerusalem; Helemytes, Africa; and most
important, Aeneas founded Rome, the second Troy, which
was the capital of the Christian world. The historical background of Rome is intended to give more weight to the moral
aspects of the story of Florence, a story so closely allied to
the near destruction of Rome.

    gone. Infinitives are, for the most part, uninflected in the
manuscript. This is one of the few *-n* forms among monosyllabic verbs. Cf. also l. 1386 and *goon*, l. 1920.

2 **more chyualrous town.** There is occasional use in the poem
of the periphrastic comparison using *more*. Cf. also *more
buxom*, l. 1723. The comparative, however, is generally
formed in the text by means of *-re* or *-ar*.

10 **barmeteme.** Holthausen (*Zu Mittelenglischen Romanzen*, p.
498) suggests *barneteme*. There is no need to change the
MS reading, as both forms are used in medieval writing.
Holthausen, perhaps, prefers the spelling with *n* because
it is closer to the OE. etymon, *bearn-team*.

    Antenowre. In Greek legend, one of the wisest of the
Trojan elders. According to Dares and Dictys, he was said
to have treacherously opened the gates of Troy to the
enemy; in return for which, at the general sack of the city,
his house, distinguished by a panther's skin at the door,
was spared by the victors. Afterwards, according to various
versions of the legend, he either rebuilt a city on the site
of Troy, or settled at Cyrene, or became the founder of
Patavium (Padua). The poet's source for attributing the
founding of Jerusalem to Antenor is unclear.

    The Roman historian, Livy, born at Patavium, was
proud of the ancient connection between his native city and
Rome. Padua, like Rome, claimed a Trojan origin and
Livy is careful to place its founder Antenor side by side
with Aeneas.

16 **Eneas be schyp gate.** This syntactic pattern, subject +

object + verb, is a basic ME. sentence variation. See Mossé (*A Handbook of Middle English*, trans. J. Walker (1952), 122).

18 **none.** This form, as well as *nane* (l. 260), displaces OE. *nāwiht* which, however, remains in the form *noght* (l. 907), of similar meaning.

21 The verb *can* is frequently used in combination with an infinitive to form a simple preterite as here: *can syke* = sought. *Can* as an auxiliary verb is evidently confused with ME. *gan*, did.

22 **Costantyne þe nobull.** Almost certainly a play on *Constantinople*.

25 ff. The third stanza is incomplete; it consists of three groups of three lines instead of four. The regular stanzaic pattern is composed of twelve lines of which every third line rhymes. Cf. stanza 112, also incomplete.

28 **had.** Class II weak verbs in the first and third persons preterite indicative end in *-d(e)*. Cf. *tolde*, l. 346; *seyde*, l. 76.

40–51 The description of the horrendous phenomena surrounding the birth of Florence and the death of her mother has one source, at least, in the *Apocalypse*. Among the details of the last days of the world is a direct parallel for the poem's rain of blood: '. . . . there was a storm of hail and fire mingled with blood, that fell on earth . . .' (ch. VIII, 7–8).

40–41 *Willan* is one of the common OE. modal auxiliaries which retained its original meaning in ME. Where in MnE. *want* is preferred, the poet has used *wolde*.

41 **befelle.** The stem vowel of the past plural of OE. Class VII (Reduplicating) strong verbs has become *e*. Note also the shifts in the past singular to *ę̄* (*behelde*, l. 422) and *i* (*hyght*, l. 7).

47 **Eyther odur.** The combination stands for the indefinite pronoun *each other*.

49 The pronoun *hyt* is used as a subject referring to the preceding lines describing the strange portents.

51 **man.** The usual method of expressing the sense of 'one' is by means of *man* or *men* (l. 62). In the frequent expression *many a oon*, *oon* is an indefinite pronoun meaning 'person' (l. 873).

58–63 The extent and variety of education for noble ladies in the fifteenth century were more restricted than that for noblemen brought up in their fathers' households. Women were instructed in religion, courtesy, and letters. Florence, at fifteen, seems to be getting the equivalent of a fifteenth-century grammar-school education. She is probably learning to read and write simple Latin. Although the 'harpe' and 'sawtrye' are common medieval stringed instruments, Florence's ability to play them indicates musical training well beyond the usual in singing.

60 **all thynge.** The uninflected plural is used in this expression as well as in one which appears later in the text. *some boke seyth* (l. 84). It should be noted that the form *þyngs* (l. 331) also occurs.

68 **hur forne.** The pronoun is a subjective gen.; and the sense of the phrase is 'on account of her'.

    forne. The *MED* (*s.v. forn* prep. c) finds the earliest appearance of the sense 'on account of' in *Florence*.

78 **a clere.** The adjective meaning 'fair', 'bright', is used as a noun with reference to the fair lady herself. Cf. ll. 1795, 2007.

85 **parell.** Palatal *l* in OFr. *apareil* became *il* and then the *i* combined with the preceding vowel to form a diphthong (*parell: fayle*).

92 **Many a crowne Y schall gare crake.** The syntactic pattern of this line, object + subject + verb, is a basic ME. sentence variation. See Mossé (*A Handbook of Middle English*, trans. J. Walker (1952), 122).

93 Both *drowpe* and *dare* depend on *gare* 'to cause' (something to be done), in the preceding line.

103 **tobrokyn.** The past participle stem vowel of OE. Class IV strong verbs has become *ǭ*.

106 ff. Garcy, the eager but aged suitor, is a type of the *amans senex*, recalling January of Chaucer's *Merchant's Tale* and Agape's senile husband in Boccaccio's *Ameto*. Other examples of the general type in both European and Oriental literature are cited by L. C. Stern in *Zeitschrift für Celtische Philologie*, v, 200, 310n.

112 **hodur.** The sense of 'cuddle' makes its earliest appearance in *Florence*. See *MED s.v. hoderen*, a.

    happe. The word with the sense 'embrace' is first recorded in a manuscript dated *c.* 1450. The *MED* (*s.v. happen* v., 2, 1C) also cites its use in *Florence*.

118 **garson.** The *MED* (*s.v. garsoun*, b.) lists the sense 'retainer, follower' as having made its first appearance in *Florence*.

128 Ritson's emendation of *aveaunt* to *avenaunt* seems to be quite unjustified. The sense of *aveaunt* ('forward') suits the line as does its rhyming with *graunt*. Moreover, the metre does not require the extra syllable

132 **rechyd.** This appears to be the nautical sense of *reaching* which is illustrated in the *OED* (*s.v. reach*, v.[1], II, 15c) entirely by nineteenth-century quotations! For example, 'A rattling breeze . . . got up . . . and she reached along like a schooner' (*Hunt's Yachting Magazine*, April 1884).

138 See note to line 21.

140 **Awtrement.** Not all the place-names in the poem are easy to identify and the geography may at times seem fanciful. Garcy's emissaries seem to be taking ship to a seaport named Awtrement (or Autrement—certainly a French town) and proceeding thence (l. 148) through Poland and Champagne in northern France on to Rome. This is about the most grotesque itinerary imaginable. There is an Autremencourt (from the German, Ostremund) in the department of Aisne in northern France, and the Roman name for Chartres was Autricum, but neither of these places was a seaport or anywhere near a logical route from Constantinople to Rome. If we are to read line 148 as indicating that the party passed through Poland and Northern France, we can only attribute the route to the poet's caprice or ignorance. If, however, we are willing to credit some rather plausible corruptions in spelling, we can vindicate the poet's sound geographical sense: the party took ship from Constantinople to Awtrement (Otranto), proceeded through Pole (Apulia) and Chawmpayn (Campania) to Rome. In other words, under the leadership of Italian-born Acwrye (who would very likely be aware that Otranto was a hospitable port), they took the most direct route to Rome possible.

141 The syntax of this line is problematical. It is unlikely that the clause introduced by 'That' is a purpose clause: 'In order that the people treated them well.' The line should probably be loosely translated, 'Where people treated them well.'

145 **wheme.** The usual spelling for OE. *hw* in ME, is *wh*, but in this instance *cw* (OE. *cweme*) has shifted to *wh*.

148 See note line to 140.

155 **rode.** The past plural stem vowel of OE. Class I strong verbs has become $\bar{\varrho}$. Cf. *abode*, l. 446; *schone*, l. 156.

172 **formast.** An ordinal numeral, 'first'.

174 **Full ryall was that crye.** The sense is: 'The clamour was splendid.' *Ryall* is used colloquially to mean *splendid* or *first-rate*, a sense which *OED* (*s.v. royal*, A, I, 4) indicates first appeared in 1583.

188 There are only a few occurrences of relative **who** in the poem.

    rekenyth. The intransitive sense of 'number, amount to' is illustrated in *OED* (*s.v. reckon*, II, 15) by a single nineteenth-century quotation: 'He marched [them] into the camp before his own troop, which did not reckon nearly so many' (1877).

198 **Feyre, syrrys, mote yow befalle.** Ritson rightly observes that this interruption of the ambassador's address is a compliment on the king's part. Afterwards, the ambassador proceeds with his speech (III, 341).

    mote yow befalle. In Old English the modal auxiliary most commonly used to express permitting was *motan*. The verb does not exactly have the sense of permitting in this instance but rather that of wishing or commanding. The construction is an exact counterpart of the Latin jussive subjunctive.

212 The word 'hope' is puzzling. Everything which went before in the poem contributes to the impression that it is Garcy's intention to marry Florence once she is brought to him. Possibly the poet's inspiration was not equal to the metrical necessities of his line and he simply settled for an inaccurate phrase just to complete the line. Otherwise, 'hope' suggests an abduction of Florence with just a possibility of marrying Garcy. Stanza 19, which follows, however, makes clear Garcy's intention to wed Florence.

216 ff. The poet uses inexact rhymes of voiced and voiceless *f* (*stryfe: wyfe: lyfe: ryve*, ll. 216, 219, 222, 225).

228 **calde þe steward hym tylle.** The sense is 'called the steward to himself'.

229 The rare OE. demonstrative ȝeon 'yon' appears as ȝonder. Cf. also *Yondur* (l. 484.).

235 **what.** In strictly relative use *what* occurs without the antecedent having been expressed. Cf. ll. 1190, 1492.

244 **dere.** There is no formal distinction here between the adjective and the adverb. Cf. *all*, l. 87.

245 **Me had leuyr.** 'I would rather have.'

249 A puzzle. Loosely, perhaps something like 'I don't want to be near his direction.'

251 **euery dele.** 'In every detail,' a common phrase indicating multiplication. Cf. also *Many a þousand* (l. 356) and *Ofte sythys* (l. 1324).

252 The MS reading seems to be *fame* not *sawe*, as transcribed by Ritson and Vietor. Indeed, *f* and long *s* in which the stem descends below the line of writing are not well differentiated, and internal *w* and *m* are easily confused. Both *sawe*, in the sense of 'speech', 'discourse' and 'fame', meaning 'honour', are reasonable within the context.

254 **nome.** The past singular stem vowel of OE. Class IV strong verbs has become *ǭ*.

258 Only a slight alteration of MS *togodur* is needed for the emendation *togedur*. Vietor's original transcription of *e* rather than *o* seems in error; the lobe of the letter is so rounded as to resemble most nearly the scribe's *o*'s.

275 **begynnyng.** The present participle has the ending *-yng* and *-ande* in the manuscript. Only *-yng* forms, as here, appear as the verbal noun.

279 **he þat.** The third person singular masculine pronoun used indefinitely: 'he who', 'the one who'.

281 **knok.** The sense of 'hit' or 'strike', as here, does not appear until about 1450 (see *MED s.v. knokken*, 3b).

283 An illegible letter followed by *gc* is written over *emperowre* in the same hand, and an illegible word scrawled over *no man schulde do* in a different hand.

289 **tyte.** The sense 'alert, smart' is used figuratively to describe the messengers (l. 286). The earliest use of the adjective itself cited in the *OED* is from Shakespeare (1606): 'Thou fumblest Eros, and my Queenes a Squire More tight at this then thou' (*Antony and Cleopatra*, IV, iv. 16). See *OED s.v. tight*, a., adv., 3.

   sawe. The past singular stem vowel of OE. Class V strong verbs has become *au*.

291 There are several erased letters followed by *lenyd* beside *But* in a similar but possibly different hand.

292 **altherfurste.** Adjectives have no ending or *-e* in the manuscript except that the genitive plural *alther* remains as an intensive prefix in words such as this, meaning 'first of all'. Cf. *althernext*, l. 1961 and *altherlaste*, l. 2113.

   Ritson's transcription of *come* instead of *tome* is an understandable error. The scribe does not always take care to differentiate *c* and *t* by continuing the shaft of *t* well above the headstroke. In any event, *tome* 'opportunity' makes more sense in the context.

296 **vii hundurd towrys.** So many 'towers' might seem better to typify an eastern city like Constantinople than Rome, the centre of western civilisation. The word 'tower', however, from the twelfth century, extended to include the whole fortress or stronghold of which a tower was the original nucleus. Hence, Acurye is referring to seven hundred well-fortified buildings.

303 **do dwelle.** The emendation follows Holthausen's suggestion (*Zu Mittelenglischen Romanzen*, 500). The alteration clarifies the meaning of ll. 302–3: 'On that account, sir, men love him, / And many people live with him.' MS *to dwelle* produces incoherent lines which translate roughly: 'On that account, sir, people like to live with him', leaving the phrase *Mony wyth hym* to float superfluously.

304–5 OE. *s* between vowels remains voiced (*wyse: pryce;* cf. *rase: face,* ll. 565–6). In both examples the letter *c* is used for *s* in OFr.

314 The final curl at the end of *wher* should probably be expanded to *whereuyr* by analogy to *euyr* (in MS, *eu*).

319 In a different hand, the word *haue* is written in the margin beside *Syxty* and *helyre** above. Also above the line, *Fernde* is written twice, *Fer* once, and a series of *r*'s and *e*'s appear.

321 In a similar but possibly different hand, the word *Fen* and four *n*'s in a series are written in the centre margin.

324 The word *Full* is written in the centre margin in a similar hand.

325 **The pyllers þat stonde in þe halle** suggest detached columns, a motif derived from Roman triumphal arches. Old Somerset House in the Strand (1546–9), influenced by the Italian style, contains such columns in its centre triple entrance.

The letters *gc* are written in the centre margin in a similar hand; also at 327.

328 **Cryste.** MS *cste* must signify *Cryste* even though there is no special sign to indicate the omission of *ry.*

329 ff. The painting of the seven deadly sins and 'þyngys sere' are most likely on the palace walls and not pillar decorations. As Gothic architecture is characterised by the almost total disappearance of wall-space and the introduction of stained glass, the wall painting would indicate that the palace is

built in the Romanesque style with its vast surfaces of walls and vaulting. There are almost no Romanesque buildings in England but numerous examples in provincial France—Tavant, Old Pouzauges, St Chef in Dauphiné, etc.

330 **The dedly synnes seuyn** are the seven capital sins: pride, envy, wrath, sloth, avarice, gluttony, and lust. They are distinguished from other sins because they are focal points of sins—sins which stand at the root of other sins. The conception of the seven deadly sins permeated medieval and Renaissance literature as well as art. A few examples of the idea in English literature occur in Chaucer's *Parson's Tale*, Gower's *Confessio Amantis*, and Spenser's *Fairie Queene* (Book I, Canto iv).

333 **scryed.** The sense of the line leaves no doubt that the poet intended *scryed*; however, the scribe wrote *stryed*. Comparison of the questionable letter with other *c*'s and *t*'s in the manuscript indicates that the shaft protrudes well above the headstroke which is quite broad, the case with most *t*'s.

334–41 The description of the fountain suggests that the poet had in mind the celebrated Fountain of Lions in the Alhambra, the oldest well-preserved Islamic palace in the world. It was built in Granada between 1248 and 1354. The Court of the Lions itself dates from the fourteenth century and is formed by the buildings of the Palacio del Harem, which was the private residence of the Nazarite kings. The fountain is fed by a remarkable conduit five miles long, and the water does run through the mouths of the supporting lions. Although the fountain's large alabaster basin could not support a 'hundurd kny3tys and ladyes', many people could wash in it. The poet's reference to the 'oþer waturs' recalls the four streams and innumerable springs which flow to the central fountain. Indeed, it is impossible to escape the sound of water anywhere in the Alhambra.

344 The emendation of ms *Tyger* to *Tyber* yields the name of the familiar Roman river. Note that the manuscript does read *Tyber* at l. 383.

354 In a similar hand, *full grete othys* is written inside a box in the bottom margin. The word *Full* is also written over the box.

355 In a hand different from that which wrote the text as well

as the other marginalia, four illegible words are written vertically in the centre top margin.

363 bere. The infinitive indicates that were the present tense form of the OE. Class IV strong verb used in the text, it would have become *ẹ̄*.

364 Florence fadur. The uninflected genitive is occasionally used as in this instance. However, the genitive singular and plural of nouns is generally formed with the ending -(*y*)*s* (*ther gatys gayne*, l. 149; *þe emperowrs paleys*, l. 173).

365 'Ordered his men in the same way.'

Same, preceded by the definite article, is used as a demonstrative which indicates identity. Cf. l. 551.

369 wemen. MS *wemon* is an unlikely plural and is easily altered to the more familiar form. Although letter *e* in which the stem and lobe of the letter is formed in a single circular movement resembles *o*, the *o* in question is too rounded to have been intended as *e*.

374 hymselfe. The intensive pronoun is used as the subject of the sentence. It refers to *Garcy*.

382 Narumpy. The city of Narnia (present-day Narni) is, as l. 376 indicates, just about sixty miles north of Rome. The water of the Tiber is more or less 'running by' (l. 383), Narni being about seven miles up the river Nera (the Roman Nar) from the confluence of the Nera and the Tiber. The form of the name, Narumpy, is rather unusual; it is not clear whether there was a meadow near Narnia so named or whether the poet took the name from the name of the city.

The movement of the forces from Constantinople is not hard to follow, but one must assume that the troops were put ashore at some place like modern Civitavecchia. To arrive at 'Narumpy' they would have had to move some fifty miles inland.

385–90 The red 'boosys' appear to be round decorative embossed ornaments affixed to the rich ropes described which apparently control the silk cloths, holding them back, perhaps, when desired. These cloths are very likely tapestries with representations of fishes and a variety of animals. Thus, *þere* (l. 389) is taken to refer not to *boosys* but to *cloþys* (l. 385).

393 gode. The lobe of *g* is rounded and completely closed in the manuscript; the letter cannot be read as *y* (Ritson) or *ʒ* (Vietor). *Wyde the lytghnes gode* (roughly, 'as wide as the beautiful brightness') modifies *charbokull stone*. This stone evidently spans the length of the 'brightness' created by the fifteen 'pomels of golde'.

394 lay on hys walle 'watches from the ramparts'.

403-4 The sense of the lines is 'Now I shall not refrain from spending my gold, provided that it be spent on this war.' This translation, however, does not retain *hyt* as an indefinite subject in an impersonal construction.

408 Mylys and Emere are related to the many contrasted and quarrelling brothers, whether twins or no, in folklore and literature, who seem to reflect a sense of what we know as sibling rivalry. Cain and Abel, Jacob and Esau, Amphion and Zethus (in Euripides) are ancient instances; *Valentine and Orson* is an example from medieval romance.

422, 424 Ritson's transcription of the word *dowve*, without any indication of his alteration of the manuscript is in error. Even Vietor, whose text is strenuously diplomatic, notes his correction of MS *dowbe*. The pronounced hooks on the ascenders of the letter *b* preclude confusion with *v*.

443 in fere. Probably 'in company', i.e. with a company of fighting men. At ll. 922-3, there is what seems at first to be an unusual application of the phrase to a single knight: *Thys whyle had Synagot takyn Emere, / And broȝt hym before Syr Garcy in fere.* Such a use would not be unique; the phrase is applied to a lone knight fighting in *Rauf Coilȝear* (l. 702). However, Synagot's subsequent words, '*We haue tane a knyght . . .*', indicate that *in fere* applies not to Emere alone but to Synagot's martial company with which Emere has very likely fallen in.

446 a burges hows. In nouns which end in *-s*, the uninflected genitive may appear for phonetic reasons.

447 they toke ther ynne 'they took up their quarters'.

449 more and lesse 'all without exception'. Cf. l. 2149 where the phrase refers to persons of all ranks, high and low.

455 hys men is also recorded by Ritson and Vietor. The MS reading is *hys xx men*. The *x*'s do not appear to be crossouts, and the roman numeral, 'twenty', makes no sense as 'Fyve thousande' men cannot be taken from twenty.

461-2 Play on *fere* (military men in a company) and *feere* (verb, fear).

475 heuydd. See note to line 1306.

480 feyre and free is a commonly used alliterative pair.

498   Unless a very sloping short leg on the letter *y* is deceptive, the preceding letter appears to have a quite clear headstroke. Therefore, a *fyght* not a *syght* was *semely*.

522   **thay.** A common spelling for the personal pronoun from the fourteenth to the seventeenth century. The form appears three times in *Florence* (cf. also ll. 1726, 2012).

539   **grome.** In late Middle English the word became confused with *gome* 'man', which it eventually replaced. Cf. modern *bridegroom*, OE. *brȳdguma*. Here *grome* means 'man'.

547   Cf. note to line 314.

549   **the more and the mynne.** 'Those of high rank and those of low.' Adjectives are sometimes used in the text with the definite article as nouns signifying a person or persons.

559   **nay.** Used as an introductory word, without any direct negation. This usage first appears *c.* 1460 (see *OED s.v. nay*, A. adv.,1 d).

560   **teene.** This word for 'rage' contains a certain coloration of 'vexation' proper to Garcy's situation. Cf. the Pardon Scene of *Piers Plowman*. After a priest translates the pardon and declares, in effect, 'This is no pardon!', Piers tears it up for 'pure tene' (B. VII, 116).

571   **They nowmberde þem.** The reflexive relation is expressed by means of the simple personal pronoun, *þem*.

     nomberde. This sense, 'amounted to', is cited by the *OED* (*s.v. number*, v.,2 b) as appearing first in a fifteenth-century MS of uncertain date. The pronoun 'þem' is a redundant filler which re-emphasises the subject 'They', referring to the knights in the field. Vietor's diplomatic text neglects to note the bar running through the superscript *l*.

598   The emendation of *yvar* to *yvore* involves very little alteration of the manuscript reading and provides an improved rhyme word for *perfore*.

599   **A dragon of golde.** According to folklore, dragons can be both benevolent and malevolent. In the east, where snakes are large and deadly, the serpent was symbolic of the principle of evil. In Greece and Rome, on the other hand, while the Oriental idea of the serpent as an evil power gave birth to a plentiful brood of terrors, dragons were also conceived as beneficent powers.

     The qualities of dragons being protective and terror-inspiring, and their effigies highly decorative, they were early used as warlike emblems. From the conquered Dacians

the Romans in Trajan's time borrowed the dragon ensign.
Under the late east Roman emperors the dragon ensign
became the ceremonial standard of the emperors. The
imperial fashion spread. In England before the conquest
the dragon was chief among royal ensigns of war.

603 **mode.** An appropriate word for 'temperament' or 'disposition' in this military context, as the Old English senses of *mōd* are felt as overtones: 'courage', 'arrogance', 'pride', 'power', 'violence'.

604–5 The consonants *m* and *n* are rhymed together: *soone* with *Rome*.

611 **herawde.** The sense 'king's messenger' does not appear in manuscripts until *c.* 1440. See *MED s.v. heraud*, 2.

613 **Who so.** Simple interrogative pronouns are used as generalising relatives in the manuscript, as here, usually reinforced by *so*.

618 **dyssees.** Although OFr. *s* in loanwords tended to retain the French quality, the *ss* in this word represents voiceless *s* (: *prees: vnpees: lees*, ll. 612, 615, 621).

628 **mett.** In the first and third persons preterite indicative, Class III weak verbs end in *t(e)*. Cf. also *lefte*, l. 1219; *boght*, l. 244).

637–8 **torusched** and **todusched.** The prefix *to* is a particle expressing separation, 'asunder, in pieces'. In OE. as well as ME. there are well over a hundred compound verbs formed with *to-*. Only a few such verbs are found after 1500. See *OED s.v. to, prefix*[2].

645 **In Romance as we rede.** The romance referred to is probably the original French text (see also ll. 1164, 1539), sometimes called the 'boke' (ll. 84, 494). At one point, the poet suggests that he has consulted more than one version of the story (l. 84).

649 **The warste** 'most inferior' (in terms of rank).

651 'And all of them were rightful heirs' (i.e., to the aforementioned properties).

654 'They [i.e., Emere and his men] all furnished [them].' The reader must supply the object 'them' which refers back to 'dyntys'.

655–7 A difficult group of lines: 'At the first winning of their shoes, they [i.e., Garcy's new knights] killed so many straightway that they lost nothing.'

655 **wynnyng of þer schone.** Ritson notes (III, 341) a similar phrase in *The Squyre of Low Degre:*

> For, and ye my love should wynne,
> With chyvalry ye must begynne,
> And other dedes of armes to done,
> Through which ye may *wynne your shone.*

When a knight accomplished some noble deed, he was said 'to win his spurs'. 'To win his shoes' is a similar but less elegant expression.

schone. An -*en* plural. Most nouns form the plural by adding *s*, *es*, or *ys*.

657 **deryd not a pere** 'risked not a thing', 'lost nothing'.

660 **wede.** There is no doubt that the poet intended the verb *wede*, 'to become mad'. Note, in fact, that a form of the expression, *fared as he wolde wede* ('behaved as if he would become mad'), is used at l. 1683. Nevertheless, the scribe wrote *wode*. Each letter of the word is shaped exactly like that in the adjective *wode*, written two lines above. Evidently, the similarity of the spelling, as well as the meaning of the words, together with their proximity, caused the scribe to write *wode* twice.

668 **mote Y the.** In Old English the modal auxiliary most often used to express permitting was *motan*. The verb continues to be used for permission in this instance. *So moot I thee* ('So may I prosper') is a frequent adjuration in Chaucer.

670 **strekyn in age.** The past participle in this phrase, meaning *advanced in years*, is a special use of the verb *stryke* in the intransitive sense 'to go'. See *OED s.v. stricken*, pa. pple. and ppl. a., A.

671 **elder.** Several adjectives retain the Old English mutated comparatives and superlatives. Cf. also *nerre*, l. 1036; *eldyst*, l. 896; *grettyst*, l. 903.

695 It is not necessary to follow Ritson in emending MS *bandome* to *bandoune*. *Bandome* sounds close enough to *towne* to constitute a tolerable off-rhyme. *Bandoune*, however, is a phonologically possible derivative of OFr. *bandon*.

701 Ritson's emendation of MS *oon* to *ane* improves the rhyme scheme and is phonologically possible as a derivative of OE. *ān*. However, it is unjustifiable for two reasons: (i) *oon* always, in this MS, follows the adjective *many* in the ex-

pression (abbreviated here), *many a oon*; (ii) the usual MS form of the pronoun 'one' used to refer to a person is *oon*.

702 **rescowed**. Ritson transcribes *rescowd*; usually when he drops *e*, it is in the final position.

707 Why Ritson should have changed MS *suffur* to *suffer* is unclear. Certainly the letter *u* is too distinct to misread, but Ritson seems to prefer the *er* ending to *ur*. For example, he invariably prints *er* for the abbreviation indicating *ur* whenever it appears, even though unabbreviated words, like MS *suffur*, with analogous suffixes are consistently written *ur* in the manuscript. Ritson's practice is not consistent. At l. 915, he does print MS *suffur* as *suffur*.

745 **spurrys**. Knobbe considers *spurrys*: *forows* a rhyme (see p. 30). It is an off-rhyme between *ŭ*: *ū*.

758 It is probably best to emend *folde* to *felde*. This emendation involves very little alteration of the manuscript reading and gives a word which is more appropriate in the context since *folde* refers to an enclosure for domestic animals and Florence is speaking of a plain which is the scene of military operations, i.e., a field of battle.

762 Proper understanding of this line may call for a reading like: 'Thou be of my father's courage.' If the line is read in the most literal way, it is difficult to tell what Florence means.

770 **sweme . . . swalme**. The emphasis given these words by the *sw* alliteration tends to underscore the sense of dizziness conveyed by the meaning of both words.

775 **þe pope, Symonde**. 'Pope Symonde' might have occurred to the poet as being the original name of St Peter, the first Pope.

778 Ritson evidently emends MS *goost* to *gast* because *goost* does not rhyme with *haste*. The emendation, nevertheless, alters the clear *oo* manuscript reading too much. An alteration to *aa* might be more justifiable, particularly since the evidence in the manuscript is that OE. ā tends to waver between *ā* and long open *ǭ*.

787 **tane**. The stem vowel of the pp. of OE. Class VI strong verbs has become *ā*. Note also *slayne*, l. 788 and the shifts to *ai* (*onslayne*, l. 496) and *o* (*sworne*, l. 355).

789 Who the 'souereygn' is seems unclear. In the broadest sense, this must be Garcy; however, as the sovereign tells the knights to send Emere to Garcy (ll. 790 ff.) he must be something like a field commander.

797 **procescyon.** Vietor prints *procescon* as if it were not an abbreviation. However, the curved line in the MS over *on* signals the dropping of *y*.

814 **sayne.** Infinitives in the text are mostly uninflected. This is one of the few *-n* forms among monosyllabic verbs.

820 **maystres Awdygon.** As a title of courtesy prefixed to the surname (in early use also to the Christian name), 'mistress' first appears in the *Paston Letters*, 1471. See *OED s.v. mistress*, sb., III 14.

834 Unless *Lorde* is regarded as an exclamation, this line is puzzling.

835 **þat þere was.** The singular verb, *was*, is used after the plural subject, 'Knyghtys and squyers'.

841–2 The lament of the barons gains particular emotional effect by the addition of alliteration. Note a similar use of alliteration in a passage from *Emaré* describing the heroine's plight, cast adrift on the open sea:

> She was so dryven fro wawe to wawe,
> She byd her hede and lay full lawe,
> For watyr she was full woo.
>
> [ll. 322–4]

845–6 The comparison seems to have a proverbial quality. Although Whiting (*Proverbs in Certain Middle English Romances*, 120) considers the comparison original to the English version, he does not feel it is inspired by a proverb —native or otherwise.

845 **eyen.** An *-en* plural form, here meaning 'young hawks'. The form appears again at l. 353 where the word, however, has the meaning 'eyes'. Cf. Glossary.

According to the *MED* (see *s.v. eie* n. 3b), the sense of 'young hawks' appears first in *Florence*, of which the MS is dated by the *MED* about 1500.

851 **fasten.** Best understood in the sense of 'land, cast' (*MED s.v. fasten*, v. (1), 3b). This meaning first appears in a manuscript dated about 1400.

861 **quarels wyth arbalast.** The manuscript reading, 'alablaste', is probably a mis-spelling for 'arbalast', a cross-bow furnished with a special mechanism for discharging arrows, bolts or stones. The *OED* cites a contemporary reference

from Caxton: *A quarel . . . shotte out of Arbalaste* (1483).

875 **famysched.** The meaning 'starved' first appears in a manuscript dated *c.* 1450. See *MED s.v. famishen.*

878 **store.** This sense of 'abundant supply' does not appear until 1471. See *OED s.v. store,* sb., 4.

879 **þem.** A usage paralleling the Latin dative of reference, as may be seen by the literal translation: 'Food was most required by them'.

883 The addition of *to* to MS *For mayntene* provides an extra syllable which improves the rhythm of the line. Moreover, parallel infinitives seem likely since the preposition *for* is so often paired with infinitives (cf. l. 24, *for to stryke;* l. 64, *for to newyn*).

903 **grettyst.** An adjective with umlaut in the superlative. In the comparative, when the Old English ending *-ra* is added after final *-e,* a long stem-vowel is lost and a parasitic vowel develops from syllabic *r.* The short vowel is transferred to the superlative, hence ME. *grettyst.*

907 **hyr.** Mylys hesitates to reply to the preceding statement made by Awdegon (Florence's maid). Clearly the pronoun before *speche* should be *hyr.*

910 There seems to be a shift here that could be explained by part of the action being omitted or being assumed by the reader. In the preceding stanza we have the visit of Awdegon and Mylys and their conversation about a possible wedding with Florence. But there is a shift from line 909 to line 910; in the latter it is Florence herself who seems to be speaking. This would imply that Awdegon had returned to Florence with Mylys's message and that we are now hearing Florence's reaction. There is a problem with this assumption. It seems that Mylys and Florence are face to face when she says '*Avyse þe. . . .*' She is not just uttering an exclamation but is actually addressing Mylys.

The author must have forgotten that in stanza 76 he had Awdegon and Mylys talking. In any event, there is a fault in the narration here.

912 The emendation of MS *y* to *ye* improves our understanding of the situation. *y* means that Florence is the one who is thinking 'lyghtly', but there is no reason to think that if Mylys expects to inherit her father's wealth he should feel cheerful or foolish. Quite the reverse. No, she must be

warning him that if such is his expectation, *he* is thinking foolishly. Hence *ye*.

913 **woundys fyve.** An allusion to the five wounds of Christ's crucifixion.

916 **askyd.** Knobbe considers the rhyme *askyd*: *laste* an illustration of long *ā* (see p. 37). More likely, the sound is *ă*.

922–3 See note to line 443.

930 'That' seems to refer back to Emere himself, but the reference is an implicit one as Emere does not mention himself. The line means 'I who am now prepared to die.'

933 **Owre fadur owre ryght.** 'Our father refused us our inheritance.'

940–1 The sense is roughly, 'Since he has left us without protection, we don't care if there is war or peace.'

948 **in stede stode me.** 'was of service to me.'

955–6 In the preceding lines Emere explains that if he were left free and came into town, he would be obliged to do grief to Garcy and his people. He goes on here to say, in effect, that there would be no sound reason for Garcy's letting him go: 'The gods forbid that you spare me; it would be the worst decision you ever made.'

955 The addition of *me* introduces an unstressed syllable which avoids the awkwardness of two successive heavy stresses, *thăt p̄ou spāre*.

Also, *me* reminds us of what is being spared. Note another example of the object of *spare* appearing immediately before the verb: *my golde spare*, l. 403.

959 **myn.** The first person singular adjectival possessive pronoun used to qualify the following noun, *hoost*. Cf. 1064, 1338.

991–2 Final *f* is sometimes voiced and sometimes not (*fyve: lyve*, but cf. *fyve: wyfe*, ll. 913–14).

992 **be lyve.** Ritson lists *be lyve* as an error which should be corrected to *belyve* (III, 440). The words should, however, remain separate as the noun *lyve* is often used in the phrase *sworne . . . be lyve*, meaning 'sworn . . . with one's life'.

993 **Mylys himselfe.** The pronoun 'hymselfe' is an intensifier. As Mylys is the subject rather than the object of 'rewe', he is not ruing himself but rather he himself is ruing.

1000 It is difficult to assess Florence's motivation here. She says she will not sleep with her husband Emere until he has brought her Garcy or left him in the field for dead. Then she affirms this with the strongest oath she can summon. Saintly heroine or not, she strikes one as somewhat vindictive.

1022 The instrumental of the simple demonstrative, OE. *þy*, remains in *forthy*, 'on that account'.

1028 Probably by analogy to his emendation of MS *bandome* to *bandoune* at the end of l. 695, Ritson again emends the word used within the line at 1028. The second, internal MS *bandome* ratifies the contention that a shift of OFr. *bandon* to ME. *bandoune* is not a feature of the spelling in this manuscript.

1036 **nerre.** The sense 'nearest' appears in a manuscript dated *c.* 1470. (See *OED s.v. nar*, a., 1 b.)

1049 The sense is that Garcy didn't leave many of them alive.

1050 Probably *tyde* here has the sense of time or occasion, but it could also refer to a literal tide. That is, they went to the ship when the tide was there.

1084 **Egraveyne.** The insertion of letter *a* over the line stands for *ra*. Cf. *trauelde*, l. 104; *prayde*, l. 1837; *grace*, ll. 1511, 1832).

1086 **To wote** appears to have the sense of present-day 'To wit'. The line means that they would do the same thing with Egraveyne: 'To wit without any misery', if he did not swear. It is not until ll. 1126 ff. that it is clear that Egraveyne did, indeed, swear.

1090 ff. The dead body which is presented to Florence as Emere's is Sampson's. Cf. l. 1157.

1093–4 **swowned twyes . . . syghed thryes.** It is common for medieval writers to be specific about numbers as there was a great deal of interest in numerology. Dante, for example, in the *Inferno*, Canto XXVI, ll. 130 ff., has Ulysses note that he had seen the moon wax and wane *five* times before a storm blew up, causing his ship to be whirled about *three* times and at the beginning of the *fourth* revolution, to be cast into the sea. Keats imitates this medieval penchant for specific numbers in *La Belle Dame sans Merci*: 'And there I shut her wild, wild eyes / With kisses four.'

1101 **forme of bredd.** The Eucharistic bread which, in the Mass, becomes the body of Christ. The priest does 'schewe' the Host when he raises it after the consecration for the congregation to see.

1107 **ta.** The voiceless velar stop, spelt *c* in OE. and *k* in ME., is entirely dropped at times when in final position (Note *ma: fra: thra*, ll. 1104, 1110, 1113). Sometimes it is silent (*askyd: laste*, ll. 916–17).

1140 Ritson's emendation of MS *oon* to *ane* improves the rhyme
scheme and is phonologically possible as a derivative of
OE. *ān*. Nevertheless, it is an unjustifiable alteration, as
the usual manuscript form of the pronoun *one* used to
refer to a person is *oon* (Cf. ll. 7, 343, 378, etc.).

1145 Who the emperor is is unclear, as the old emperor was
slain and the poet has not indicated that someone else took
his place. Later, lines 1297–1300 indicate that the emperor
is Emere.

1148 **stokkes.** Both Ritson and Vietor read the manuscript at
this point as *strokkes*, and then finding it in error, correct
to *stokkes*. Examination of the original manuscript reveals
not the slightest trace of a letter *r*.

1154 **All the lasse can sche recke.** Confusion of feeling and joy
prevent Florence from comprehending the good news.

1174–5 The voiceless stop appears instead of the voiced finally
before voiceless consonants in the group *ng*, as in the rhyme
strenkyth : *lenkyth*.

1179 **many oon lykyd ylle.** That is, many a resident of Constantinople 'lykyd ylle'.

1203 **þemselfe schall rewe.** The personal pronoun with the
adjective *self* is used alone as the subject of a sentence.

1246–7 The emendation of MS *or þere* improves the sense of the
line which is roughly: 'A ship such as was there / Was
never seen.' The preposition *or* creates a pointlessly obvious
statement: 'Such a ship before there was one / Was never
seen.'

1281 **sotheyr.** The *th* in this noun is written for OFr. *d* in *soudier*
and thus is rhymed with *odur* (l. 1278).

1300 The punctuation indicating that Mylys is asking the
question of Emere is in error. It must be Emere who has
asked the question of Mylys, he who has just fallen off a
horse and 'eylyth'. The question allows Mylys to lie at
length about Florence's honour. Vietor's diplomatic text is
entirely unpunctuated and therefore offers no guidance.

1306 The rhyme with *revydd* makes *hevydd* preferable to MS *hedd*.
Also *hevydd* is phonologically probable as it can be derived
from OE. *hēafod*. Cf. the emendation at ll. 475, 1933.

1316 Only a slight alteration of MS *lernydd* is required to give
lerydd, a word which improves the rhyme with *enqueryd* and
which has the same meaning as *lernydd*, though derived
from a different Old English verb: *lǣran*.

1328 MS *And* must be emended to *Ane* in order to provide a subject for the clause.

1329 **Whych** is used in the manuscript with reference to persons as well as things. Cf. l. 1933.

1330 ff. Stanza 112 lacks a concluding group of three lines. Cf. stanza 3.

1348 **bere tree** 'wooden coffin'. The word *tree* in ME. often refers to something made of wood rather than the tree itself. In this MS note also l. 1430 where **tre** is a reference to Christ's cross.

1361 **a pena et culpa** 'From punishment and guilt'. Cf. B. VII, l. 3 of *Piers Plowman*. There a mere Pardon, which normally remits the *punishment* due to sins and does not forgive their guilt, absolves the Plowman. Properly only the sacrament of Penance offered total absolution, while pardons and indulgences remitted only the temporal punishment.

Here Egravayne receives absolution *a pena et culpa* in the true sense as his confession involves him in the judicial process by which the penitent is at once the accuser and the person accused, while the priest pronounces judgement and sentence. The grace conferred is deliverance from the guilt of sin and in the case of mortal sin from its eternal punishment (cf. *Catholic Encyclopedia*, XI, 619 ff., *s.v. Penance*).

But what is Egravayne guilty of and why does he make his confession to the Pope, Bishop of Rome?

Technically, he is an accomplice in the sin of *Raptus Violentiæ* (abduction by violence). This sin is committed when a reluctant woman is forcibly transferred with a matrimonial intent from a secure and free place to a morally different one and there held by threats, great fear, or fraud equivalent to force (cf. *Catholic Encyclopedia*, I, 32 ff. *s.v. Abduction*). It is not necessary that actual change of locality occur. Some jurists claim 'virtual change' from a state of freedom to that of subjection to be sufficient to constitute 'abduction'.

Christian law in the time of Innocent III with respect to abduction was the ecclesiastical discipline up to the six-teenth century, and it was vague. Not only does it not specify what the punishment of an accomplice should be, but Innocent III's decree let the abductor himself off easily. His decree practically made abduction worth trying, since marriage could occur as long as the woman's prior reluctance changed to willingness—even while in the power of the captor. It may have been the laxity of this decree which led Mylys, the clear-cut abductor, to commit an even more audacious abduction of Florence later in the poem.

As for Egravayne's confession to the Pope, it seems to anticipate the entirely new discipline introduced by the Council of Trent (1545–63), for according to the Council, whether the abduction ended with marriage or not, 'the abductor with all of his advisers, accomplices, and abettors' was to be 'excommunicated and declared forever infamous, incapable of acquiring dignities'.

The right to absolve in a case of excommunication belongs to him who can excommunicate and who has imposed the law. In Egravayne's case, the power would be the Pope's, as he is Bishop of Rome and the crime was committed in his jurisdiction. Hence the confession to Pope Symond.

1363 The misreading of *ame* for *arme* is an understandable error. Long-tailed *r* has lost its shoulder stroke and so is not easily distinguished from the minim strokes which make up the letter *m*. Nevertheless, the prominent descender and connecting stroke make the *r* sufficiently distinctive.

1377 **at the none** 'the hour of nones', a daily office said at the ninth hour of the day (about 3 p.m.) but in late Middle English use sometimes earlier; hence MnE. *noon*.

1384 The 'he' referred to is evidently Mylys.

1401 ff. Knobbe, having concluded that the *a* in *laste* (l. 1410) is long, incorrectly considers the Old Norse *a* in the closed syllable lengthened on the basis of rhyme (*caste* (ON. *kast*): *faste: agaste: laste*).

1428 **Weleawaye** is an emendation of MS *wele a saye* to the common interjection.

1430 **dyed on tre** 'died on the cross'. See note to line 1348.

1435 **were nyghtyd** 'were overtaken by night.' The *OED* cites this appearance in *Florence* as the earliest occurrence of this special use of the verb *nyghte* (see *s.v. night*, v.). A similar verb in OHG. is *nahten* (G. *nachten*).

1438–44 The chastity of the heroine is saved by her prayer to the Virgin Mary who makes the persecutor forget his passion. This miracle and others which occur under the influence of the Virgin Mary's power (cf. ll. 1499–500, 1852 ff.) underscore the ties that *Florence* has to Tales of the Virgin. The pattern in nearly all these tales is the same: some mortal, either saint or sinner, is in difficulty and prays to the Virgin, who grants him deliverance as a reward for either his sanctity or his repentance, as the case may be.

1440 The emendation of ms *Mary and free* to *Mary free* suggests that the scribe, having just written *and* before the word *Mary*, carelessly wrote it again. More likely, the scribe's eyes moved faster than his hand when he came to the common alliterative pair 'feyre and free' (cf. l. 480), and he dropped the word *feyre*.

1466 **scho.** This form of the feminine nominative pronoun is found typically in the north and is first seen in literary records towards the end of the thirteenth century. Cf. l. 1980.

1472 **stekyth in.** When the verb *sticks* is used intransitively and paired with *on*, *to*, *unto*, or *in*, it may have this sense of 'cleaves, adheres'. The *OED* (*s.v. stick*, v¹., II, 8) indicates the earliest appearance of the usage in a manuscript dated 1558.

1478 **yere.** An uninflected noun expressing measurement. Cf. *pownde*, l. 1373 and *myle*, l. 376. It should be observed that the *-ys* form of *yere* occurs along with the uninflected form (*yerys*, l. 83).

1489 The narrator passes from indirect discourse (*He made þe lady* ...) to the direct discourse of ll. 1492–4. When we read *From whens þou came* ..., we are aware of an inconsistency in the recounting of these remarks. The absence of a clear transition in the narrative testifies to the poet's lack of perfect craft.

1498 The scribe practised writing *w* in the centre margin.

1516–17 OE. voiceless palatal stop *c* is represented by *k* rather than the usual *ch* in the rhyme *byrke: yrke*, probably as a result of Scandinavian influence. Cf. *swylke: sylke*, ll. 386, 385; *lyke: ryke*, ll. 1808, 1807.

1532 **hurselfe.** For metrical reasons the reflexive form is (illogically) used here rather than the simple object *hur*.

1534–47 The beauty of Florence, like that of Emaré, has something celestial about it. Florence's beauty, which in the first part of the romance is the conventional attribute of the courtly tale, is here raised to a visible symbol of her virtue. Florence, as Emaré, is surrounded by an aura of

light and brightness. Cf. ll. 1708–9; when she rides through
the forest it begins to shine.

1566 **lay.** The past plural stem vowel of OE. Class V strong
verbs has become *ai*.

1567 **wythowte lesynge.** Why should Florence and Betres lie?
The phrase makes somewhat more sense if taken as an
implicit reference to the narrator's storytelling. The phrase
may be an assurance that the poet is telling us the truth.

1569 **any many.** This unusual expression seems to be a plural
form of *anyone*.

1583 **strenkþfull stedd.** Ritson's transcription reads *strenkth full
stedd*. The manuscript indicates, however, a clear connecting
stroke between þ and *f* which creates the adjective meaning
'full of strength'.

1592 **Machary.** This name occurs as Macaire in the Sibilla group
of stories about the persecuted queen who is Charlemagne's
wife. Macaire, the king's steward, is a villain who tries to
make love to Sibilla and, having been thwarted, accuses
her of adultery. He furnishes proof by smuggling someone
into the queen's bed. In the respect that Macaire is the
only persecutor, the Sibilla group is distinct from Florence.
Also in contrast with Florence, Sibilla bears a son in exile,
who plays a part in bringing about the reunion of his
parents. Several notable resemblances to the story of
Florence are that the queen is sent out into a wood for
punishment and lives in exile for many years before her
honour is vindicated. The story of Sibilla was the subject
of an early French *chanson de geste*, but that poem is now
preserved only in an Italianised version in which the
queen's name is Blanchefleur. F. Guessard (ed., *Macaire*)
has tried to restore the poem to its original French form.
A second version of the story occurs in *La Reine Sibille*.

1605 **yn a gethe.** The word *gethe* is used only in this expression
meaning 'spiritedly, hastily'. Cp. OI. *geð* 'mind, spirit'; OE.
ge(h)þu.

1617 The line is best understood as the narrator's explanation of
Machary's lie about the tournament. He lies because 'The
truth is unpardonable'.

1618–20 As at line 1489, the narrator passes from indirect discourse to direct discourse without clear transition.

1624 ff. The motif of the bloody knife is also introduced into
Gower's legend of Constance and Chaucer's *Man of Law's*

Tale. It does not, however, occur in *Emaré*, another related tale.

1639 ff. A masterly, dramatic description of Sir Tyrry's prophetic dream and his anxious candlelit walk to his murdered daughter's chamber.

1647 thorowly. The sense 'fully' does not appear in manuscripts until 1473. See *OED s.v. thoroughly*, 2.

1657 glyste. Referring to eyes: 'glared', 'stared'. The first appearance of this usage is in a manuscript dated *c.* 1450 (MED. *s.v. glisnen*, 2 b).

1662 The whych. The combination is used as a relative pronoun. Mustanoja (*A Middle English Syntax, Mémoires De la Société Neophilologique*, XXIII (1960), p. 198) suggests that the combination may be an imitation of OFr. *liquels*.

1666–9 The villainous Machary takes Florence's beautiful clothing and appearance as a sign that she is a devil. The implication is that evil cannot comprehend beauty. His view of evil in the guise of female beauty is also a common motif of medieval anti-feminist literature.

1692 It is unclear what Syr Tyrry holds to be sin. The pronoun *hyt* may refer either to Florence's presumed murder of Betres or to the act of putting Florence to death.

1708–9 See note to lines 1534–47.

1730 A strange idea. From what the thief says later in the following stanza, it is evident that he would not prefer hanging to giving up his life of thievery.

1756 ff. Although there seem to be no proverbs in the romance, B. J. Whiting feels that one incident, occurring in other stories belonging to the Florence–Constance cycle, 'was almost certainly inspired by a proverb' (*Proverbs in Certain Middle English Romances*, 119). That is the betrayal of Florence by the thief whom she had saved from the gallows. Whiting, however, neglects to supply the proverb he was thinking of.

1758 Vietor, not distinguishing the overlapping curls from *b* and *h* of *he*, l. 1759, concludes that the second *r* in *harburgerye* is written over a letter *g*.

1767 flyre. The sense is 'to mock', and according to the *MED* (see *s.v. flerien*) this meaning first appears in a manuscript dated *c.* 1440. The line from *Florence* is also cited. The sense of the word accords well with the situation described in which the thief and burgess flash knowing glances at one another as they hatch an evil scheme.

F

The emendation of MS *flyre* to *flerye* is not needed. The workmanlike poet who wrote *Florence* may have been content enough with the slight alteration of his usual tail rhyme scheme: *yre: atyre: flyre*.

1769 The misreading *we* for MS *ye* is puzzling, as the letter *y* is quite distinct.

1828–30 The lines mean 'all the men who departed for the ship tried to make love to Florence'.

1875 **roche.** In the twelfth-century Latin Miracle version of the tale the empress is exposed on a rock in the middle of a river (Bibliothèque Nationale, MS 14463).

1882 **Beuerfayre.** The MS reading *Benerfayre* must be in error. The English poet evidently means to Anglicise the French name for the convent, Beau-Repaire. Hence he needs the vowel *u*, not a consonant.

1888 **Lucyus Jbarnyus.** The reference to him as the founder of 'Beuerfayre'—in the French versions Beau-Repaire, a convent said to have been founded by Julius Caesar—has been taken as an indication that the poet had in mind the Lucius Iberius of the alliterative *Morte Arthure*, l. 86 (Knobbe, 9).

1892–3 Bells ringing of their own accord are common in hagiographic literature. The bells of Madrid are said to have rung spontaneously when the body of St Isidore was removed from the churchyard into the church. Bells also were supposed to have rung out miraculously to announce the murder of St Landry, *curé* of Lanslevillard. In the romance *Cheuelere Assigne* there is an unequal duel in which a twelve-year-old defeats a practised warrior. The religious, almost ritual character of the duel is underlined by the miraculous ringing of all the bells (ll. 272–4). Other examples are cited by Tatlock, *MLN*, 29 (1914), 98 and Barry, *MLN*, 30 (1915), 28–9.

1894 **Seynt Hyllary.** Bishop of Poitiers, one of the greatest religious luminaries of France in the fourth century. His feast day is in January, but it is celebrated on the 14th not the *twenty day of zowle*.

1910 **þat fre.** An adjective meaning 'noble or gracious in character', preceded by the demonstrative pronoun, takes on the force of a noun. Hence the sense, 'that noble lady'.

1927 ff. Nuns occasionally play the role of healer in medieval romances. The writings of Hildegarde, in fact, demonstrate the knowledge of herbs and medicine which an abbess might actually acquire (see M. Hughes, *Women Healers in Medieval Life and Literature*, 4).

1930 The superscript *a* above the *g* in MS *sprang* is puzzling, as no *a* has been omitted.

1933 **hevedd.** Cf. note to line 1306.

1947 MS *be* is emended to *ben* as the sentence structure, paralleling l. 1946, is improved by the repetition of the past participle *ben* rather than the infinitive form *be*. In other parts of the manuscript as well, the past participle appears either as *ben* or *bene*.

1976 **schake.** This infinitive of the OE. Class VI strong verb indicates that, were the present form used in the text, the present tense stem vowel would be *ā*. Cf. also *fare*, l. 593. Other infinitives of Class VI verbs indicate shifts to *a* (*stande*, l. 711), and *au* (*drawe*, l. 255).

1991 **hyppyng.** The word with this meaning, 'limping', is first recorded in a manuscript dated *c.* 1450 (see *MED s.v. hippen*, 2). Its appearance in *Florence* is also cited. Ritson claims *deuyll* as a 'corrected' reading for MS *deyll*. While the handwriting in the manuscript is somewhat compressed, *deuyll* is clearly discernible as the original reading.

   Hyppyng on two stavys lyke þe deuyll. The phrase is a curious one, the earliest instance of which appears here in *Florence* (see B. J. Whiting, *Proverbs in Certain Middle English Romances*, 121).

2027 Although *standen . . . astrote* ('to bulge') is a common phrase (see *MED s.v. astrote*), it is not necessary to follow Ritson in 'correcting' MS *a strote* (III, 441). The poet may not have intended the adverb *astrote* but rather the noun *strote* ('projection, bulge') which stands in apposition to *yen*.

2037 **the more and mynne.** See note to line 549.

2051 Omitting *fro hur* improves the rhythm of the line. A stronger, more clear four-stress line emerges by reducing the number of unstressed syllables, and no damage is done to the meaning. In fact, redundancy is eliminated.

2072 **oonys.** 'At one time'. There are some common adverbs consisting of inflected forms of nouns and adjectives used independently, such as the genitives *oonys* and analogically *twyes* (l. 1093) and *thryes* (l. 1094).

2091 **myne.** The first person singular adjectival possessive pronoun used to qualify the preceding noun, *hals*.

2107–8 Knobbe theorises that the guttural spirant, spelt *gh*, ȝ, remains in Middle English, in the consonant group *ht* (p. 45). It is impossible to conclude anything with certainty from a study of the rhymes; however, the loss of [χ] is possibly indicated by the spellings *syte* (for *syght* or *syȝt*) and *plyte* (for *plyght* or *plyȝt*).

2133 **gente.** The word seems to be used as an adv. meaning 'courteously' and is cited by the *MED.* (see *s.v. gent* adj., 2) as having made its first appearance in *Florence*.

2147 **Te deum laudamus.** The famous hymn of thanksgiving whose composition is sometimes ascribed to St Ambrose.

2149 **more and lesse.** See note to line 449.

2175 **Who** is employed as an indefinite pronoun. The principal use made of *who* in the text, however, is as the interrogative pronoun (l. 279).

2176 ff. In the didactic closing stanza, the poet draws a universal moral from the events in the spirit of the exemplary tale. Attention is called to the unhappy fates of the four evildoers and to the vengeful decree of God against them. The poet calls his work 'þys Romance gode', that is, a meaningful romance for those who hear the call to follow the model of the saintly Florence.

2179 MS *slylylye* obviously needs to be corrected by dropping one *ly.*

2182 **meene be.** The sense here is 'to intend to refer to'. The *OED* (*s.v. mean*, v¹, 1 e) lists the first appearance of this construction as occurring in Mores, *Edward V* (1513): 'That ment he by the lordes of the quenes kindred. . . .'

Explicit **Le Bone Florence** . . . The poet seems to have been careless about gender. *La Bonne Florence* would be more correct unless it was to be understood that there was an ellipsis of 'Le Livre de la Bon[n]e Florence . . .'

GLOSSARY

This glossary is designed to record every form of every word which occurs in the manuscript except for words in Latin. References are limited to the first three consecutive appearances of a word. Idiomatic phrases, especially those constructed on a few fundamentally important verbs such as *do, make, take,* are fully recorded as well. Words subject to variation in form because of inflexion are set out according to a fixed order. Verbs, for example, are listed under the infinitive if it appears, followed by the imperative (which has the same form as the infinitive), the present tense (in order of person in the singular, then the plural), the past tense (singular, representing first or third person, second person singular, then plural), the subjunctive, present preceding past (singular, then plural), and the present and past participles. Less affected are nouns and adjectives. Plural and genitive forms (in that order) of the noun are given under the singular when it is recorded, and, likewise, the comparative and superlative forms of the adjective are entered under the uninflected form when it also appears. Where a single word occurs in several parts of speech, the arrangement of entries is noun, adjective, adverb, verb, etc. Cross-references are as full as possible. Parentheses enclose letters which may appear as alternative spellings.

In the etymologies, each etymon cited is given in the dialectal form that best accounts for the form in the manuscript. Therefore, the native Old English forms are Anglian, the Old French forms Anglo-French. The marking of long vowels has not been attempted in Old French. In Old English stable long vowels are marked with a macron as in *ān*; those which were shortened or of uncertain quantity are marked as in *ofdrĕdd*, except that æ when long is printed as *ǣ* and when shortened or of uncertain quality as *œ*, vowels lengthened in Old English (e.g. before *ld*) are marked as in *báld*. Long vowels in Old Norse are shown as in *ár*. Cross-references in bold type refer to entries in this glossary.

Entries are arranged so that ʒ has a separate place after *g*, and þ, *th*, a separate place after *t*. *i* and *y* (except as a consonant) are treated as the same letter and take the order of *i*. *u* and *v* are alternative forms of the same letter; when representing a vowel they come in the position of modern *u*, when a consonant in that of *v*. The same principles are observed for medial *u*.

ABBREVIATIONS

a.	adoption of	ad.	adaption of
abbrev.	abbreviation	adj.	adjective
absol.	absolute	adv.	adverb
acc.	accusative	aphet.	aphetic

app.	apparently	nom.	nominative
art.	article	num.	numeral
assoc.	association	obj.	object, objective
attrib.	attributive	*OED*	*The Oxford English*
auxil.	auxiliary		*Dictionary*
card.	cardinal	ord.	ordinal
coll.	collective	orig.	originally
comb.	combinations	pass.	passive
comp.	comparative	phr.	(in) phrase(s)
cond.	conditional	pl.	plural
conj.	conjunction	poss.	possessive
const.	construed with	pp.	past participle
cont.	contraction	pr.	present
cp.	compare	prec.	preceding (word)
dat.	dative	prep.	preposition
demons.	demonstrative	prob.	probably
dial.	dialect, dialectal	pron.	pronoun
dim.	diminutive	pr. p.	present participle
esp.	especially	pt.	past
f.	formed on	refl.	reflexive
fem.	feminine	rel.	relative
fig.	figurative	sg.	singular
gen.	genitive	subj.	subjunctive
imper.	imperative	suff.	suffix
impers.	impersonal	sup.	superlative
indef.	indefinite	temp.	temporal
infin.	infinitive	tr.	transitive
infl.	influenced	v.	verb
interj.	interjection	var.	variant
intr.	intransitive	vbl. n.	verbal noun
masc.	masculine	=	corresponding to
MED	*Middle English Dic-*	+	combined with
	tionary (Michigan)	*	theoretically recon-
n.	noun		structed
neut.	neuter		

LANGUAGES AND DIALECTS

A.	Anglian dialects of Old	L.	Latin
	English	LG.	Low German
AF.	Anglo-French	Merc.	Mercian
CF.	Central (Old) French	MDu.	Middle Dutch
Dan.	Danish	ME.	Middle English
E.Fris.	East Frisian	ML.	Medieval Latin
Fr.	French	MLG.	Middle Low German
G.	German	MnE.	Modern English
Icel.	Icelandic	Norw.	Norwegian

Nth.	Northumbrian	ON.	Old Norse
ODan.	Old Danish	ONth.	Old Northumbrian
OE.	Old English	ONFr.	Northern dialects of Old French
OFr.	Old French		
OHG.	Old High German	OS.	Old Saxon
OI.	Old Icelandic	OSw.	Old Swedish
OIr.	Old Irish	SW.	Swedish

A

a *indef. art.* a 2, 14, 23, etc.; (*with num.*) 189, 338, 356, etc.; **an** (*before vowels*) 224, 227, 264, etc.; **an** *adj.* one 781, 866; **ane** *as subject:* one 1328; *many a oon,* many a one 873, 1674; *weleawaye,* weleawaye 1428. [OE. *ān.*]

abbas *n.* abbess 1900, 1924, 2000. [OFr. *ab(e)esse.*]

abyde *pr. subj. sg.* remain 468, 1037; **abode** *pt. pl.* remained, stayed 446. [OE. *abīdan.*]

abye *v.* pay for, atone for 1509. [OE. *abycgan.*]

abode *n.* stop, stay 1433. [rel. to *abide.*]

aboute *adv.* about, on all sides, here and there 42, 183, 588, etc.; round about 313, 708, 714, etc.; ready to 938. [OE. *abūtan.*]

absence *n.* absence 1273. [OFr. *absence.*]

adradd *pp.* afraid 1314. [OE. *ofdrĕdd.*]

aftur *prep.* in pursuit of 120, 1020, 1064, etc.; behind 240, 985, 1797; after, for 618, 775; according to 1295; *temp.* after 32, 49, 1059, etc.; *oon aftur odur,* one after another; *adv.* afterwards 765. [OE. *æfter.*]

afturward *adv.* afterwards 1280. [OE. *æfterweard.*]

agayne, ageyn(e) *adv.* again, back 281, 288, 497, etc. [ON. *i gegn,* OE. *ongegn.*]

agaste *pp.* astonished 1407. [*a* + OE. *gæsted,* afflicted.]

age *n.* age, time of life 670. [OFr. *age.*]

agenste, *prep.* against 410, 1233; in pursuit of 1233, 1290. [Extended from OE. *ongegn* + adv. *-es.*]

ay(e) *adv.* always, ever 136, 374, 1147, etc. [ON. *ei.*]

all *adj.* all 5, 64, 80, etc.; a whole 588; *pron.* all, everything 60, 163, 221, etc.; all (the people), everyone 195, 468, 496, etc.; *all thyng,* everything 1553. (OE. *al(l).*]

all *adv.* all, entirely, altogether 87, 103, 157, etc.; everywhere 183; *all on blode,* entirely with blood 609; *all in myddys,* amidst 611; *all tyll,* until 964; *all away,* completely (away) 1444. [OE. *al(l).*]

allas *interj.* alas! 574, 826, 836, etc. [OFr. *alas.*]

allone *adj.* alone, only 821, 822, 1247. [Orig. *all adv.* + *one.* Aphet. in northern dial. to *lone.*]

almoost, almoste *adv.* almost, nearly 1551, 1790. [OE. *eall e mæst,* nearly all.]

als *adv.* also, as well 1201, 1396, 1471, etc. [Reduced form of *also.*]

also, alse *adv.* as 289; also, as well 352, 668, 724, etc.; *also swithe,* as quickly (as possible), straightway; *also . . . as,* as . . . as 289, 1053, 1054, etc. [OE. *al-swā.*]

alther *intensive prefix in* **altherfurste,** first of all 292, 1804; **althernext,** next of all 1961; **altherlaste,** last of all 2113. [OE. *alra gen. pl.*]

altherfurste, altherlaste, althernext. See **alther.**

am *1 sg. pr.* am 620, 671, 1063, etc. [OE. *eam, am.*]

among(e) *prep.* among 428, 654, 552, etc.; in the midst of 318. [OE. *on mong.*]

an. See **a.**

and *conj.* and 6, 9, 11, etc. [OE. *and.*]

ane. See **a.**

any *adj.* any, some 91, 101, 301, etc.; *any many*, pl. of anyone 1876. [OE. *ǽnig.*]

anodur *adj.* another 25, 727, 1659. [OE. *ān* + *ōþer.*]

anon *adv.* at once, straightway 1604. [OE. *on ān.*]

answare, answere *n.* reply 224, 264, 693, etc. [OE. *andswaru.*]

answeryd *pt. sg.* answered 280, 907, 946, etc.; *pt. pl.* 508. [OE. *an(d)swarian.*]

arayed *pp.* dressed 85, 456; *pt. sg.* prepared 659. [OFr. *areier.*]

arbalast *n.* cross-bow 861. [OFr. *arbaleste.*]

are *n.* oar 1876. [OE. *ār.*]

are *pr. pl.* are 197, 208, 232, etc. [OE. (Nth.) *aron.*] See **art, be(e).**

arme *n.* arm 1324; **armes** *n. pl.* arms 113, 1849. [OE. *earm.*]

arme *v.* arm 1132, 1354, 1363; **armyd, -ed** *pp.* 492, 673, 1108, etc. [OFr. *armer.*]

armes *n. pl.* arms, weapons 866; *men of armes*, fighting men 1060, 1171. [OFr. *armes.*]

armyte *n.* hermit 1459, 1463, 1483, etc. [OFr. *(h)ermite.*]

armowre *n.* armour 366, 465, 584, etc. [OFr. *armeüre.*]

arraye *n.* array, dress 155, 1694, 2145. [OFr. *arei.*]

art *2 pr. sg.* art 554, 670, 1844. OE. *eart.*]

as *adv.* (just) as 52, 62, 73, etc. [As prec.]

as *conj.* (even) as, like 82, 126, 154, etc.; as if, as though 44, 130, 660, etc.; as (one who) 219; *with oaths*, so 328, 620; *(as)* . . . *as, also* . . . *as (followed by acc.)* 1, 194, 289, etc.; **ays**, while, when 136. [Reduced from *als.*]

aske *v.* inquire 1557, 1571; re-quest 1462; **askyd** *pt. sg.* asked, inquired 507, 584, 622, etc.; *pt. pl.* 916, 1715, 1906; *pp.* 196, 241. [OE. *ăxian.*]

assay(e) *v.* make trial of, put to the proof 397, 1498. [OFr. *essayer.*]

assent(e) *n.* service, disposal 1117, 1345. [OFr. *asente.*]

assent *v.* agree 899; support 1072; **assentyd** *pt. pl.* agreed 1078. [OFr. *asentir.*]

assoyle *v.* absolve 1127; **assoyled** *pt. sg.* 777, 1361. [OFr. *assoillir.*]

astate *n.* estate, rank 169. [OFr. *estat.*]

at *prep.* at 25, 190, 225, etc.; from 171, 364, 631; according to 231, 530, 1752, etc.; to 433; with 731, 1251; by 1185; *at the (þe) last*, finally 855, 917. [OE. *æt.*]

avaunt *v.* praise 299. [OFr. *avanter.*]

aveaunt *adj.* of a person, worthy, honourable 665 [OFr. *avena-(u)nt.*]

aveuant *adv.* forward 128. [OFr. *avant.*]

avente *v.* remove (one's helmet) 1939. [OFr. *esventer.*]

avyse *v.* deliberate 909, 910; **avysyd** *pp.* advised. [OFr. *aviser.*]

avysement *n.* the process of advising 205. [OFr. *a(d)visement.*]

away(e), awey *adv.* away 536, 1298, 1352, etc. [OE. *on-weg.*]

awe *n.* dread, fierceness, rage. [ON. *agi;* OE. *eӡe.*]

B

bachylere *n.* young knight 245

bachylers *n. pl.* 320. [OFr. *bacheler.*]

back *n.* back 134, 1141. [OE. *bæc.*]

bad(d) *pt. sg.* bade, asked, requested 590, 661, 789, etc.; ordered 1381; *pt. pl.* 1314. [OE. *biddan.*] See **bedd**.

bagg *n.* bag (money-bag) 1792, 1816. [ON. *baggi.*]

bale *n.* trouble, misery, sorrow 67, 367, 1209, etc.; **bales** *n. pl.* 939. [OE. *balu.*]

bandome *n.* power, rule 1028. [OFr. *bandon.*]

baner *n.* banner 1228; **baners** *n. pl.* 569, 803. [OFr. *ban(i)ere.*]

bare *n.* boar 602, 1593. [OE. *bār.*]

bare *adj.* only 421, empty 1484. [OE. *bær.*]

bare *pt. sg.* laid open, bore open 473; carried 962. [OE. *beran;* cf. OE. *beran ūp.*]

bargayn, bargen *n.* bad or unfortunate business 815, 984. [OFr. *bargaine.*]

bargen. See **bargayn**.

barley, barly *n.* barely 1465, 2056. [OE. *bærlīc.*]

barmeteme *n.* people, tribe 10. [OE *bearn-team; barm-* by assoc. with OE. *barm,* lap.]

baronage *n.* barons collectively, nobles, lords 410, 980. [OFr. *barnage.*]

baronry *n.* the domain of a baron 1268. [OFr. *baronie.*]

barons *n. pl.* barons 347, 552, 649, etc. [OFr. *barun.*]

barryd *pt. pl.* fastened with bars 858. [OFr. *barrer.*]

batayle, batell *n.* battle, fight 24, 429, 464; **batels** *n. pl.* 69, 659. [OFr. *bataille.*]

batell. See **batayle**.

bath *n.* bath 100. [OE. *baþ.*]

bathe. See **both, boþe**.

bathyd *pt. pl.* bathed 1549. [OE. *baðian.*]

be *prep.* by, beside 108, 111, 159, etc.; by means of 16; according to 261, 2146; *(in oaths)* 244, 736, 913; etc.; *be that adv.* by the time 61, 634; *conj.* since, because 1576. [OE. *be.*] See **by(e)**.

be(e) *v.* be 77, 206, 211, etc.; *3 pr. sg.* 23, 278, 732, etc.; *pl.* 358, 1618; *pr. subj. sg.* 196, 312; *jussive subj.* 557, 789; *finite verb with pp. forms pass.* 122, 163, 211, etc.; **ben(e)** *pp.* 433, 700, 1947. [OE. *bēon.*]

bedd, *pt. sg.* requested 977. [OE. *biddan.*] See **bad(d)**.

bedd(e) *n.* bed 100, 111, 1000, etc. [OE. *bedd.*]

bede *pt. pl.* offered 663. [OE. *bēodan,* already confused with *biddan.*]

bedeene *adv.* forthwith, withal 278. [See *MED.*]

befalle *v.* happen, chance 198; **befelle** *pt. sg.* 41. [OE. *be-fallen.*]

beest *n.* animal, creature 388; **bestys** *n. pl.* 44, 182. [OFr. *beste.*]

before, beforne *prep.* in front of, ahead of 221, 277, 971, etc.; *adv.* earlier 1165, 1455. [OE. *beforan.*]

began, beganne. See **begynne**.

begynne *v.* begin 351; *3 pr. sg.* 367; **began, beganne** *pt. sg.* 579, 639, 815; *pt. pl.* 1036; *pp.* 517, 815, 1009. [OE. *beginnan.*]

begynnyng *vbl. n.* beginning 275. [f. prec. v. + *yng.*]

begonne. See **begynne**.

behelde, *pt. sg.* beheld, looked 422, 537, 756, etc. [OE. *be-háldan.*]

behete *1 pr. sg.* promise 1754. [OE. *be + hátah.*]

beholde *imper.* behold 486. [OE. *be-háldan.*]

behynde *prep.* behind, 164; *adv.* 1403. [OE. *behíndan.*]

beholde. See **behelde.**

behove v. *impers.* must needs, ought 895. [OE. *be-hōfian.*]

beyke v. bake 99. [OE. *bacan.*]

belde n. courage 762, 1719. [OE. *béldo.*]

belyfe, -lyve *adv.* eagerly 1652; rapidly 1842. [From ME. phr. *bi live.*]

belyve. See **belyfe, -lyve.**

belle n. bell 797, 1457; **bellys** n. pl. 1892. [OE. *belle.*]

bende pr. pl. bend 859. [OE. *béndan.*]

ben(e). See **be(e).**

bentys n. pl. grassy grounds, fields 1040. [A special use of ME. *bent*, grass; OE. *beonet.*]

bere n. clamour, outcry 659. [OE. *ge-bēre.*]

bere n. bier 795, 811, 816, etc. [OE. *bēr.*]

bere v. bear, carry 363; **beryth** 3 pr. sg. behaves, comports himself (with arms); **borne** pp. born 67, 119, 507, etc. [OE. *beran.*]

beryed pt. pl. buried 1160. [OE. *byrgan.*]

beryth. See **bere.**

besawntys n. pl. gold coins 203. [OFr. *besan*, pl. *besanz.*]

besyde prep. beside 423, 562, 677. [OE. *be-sīdan*, at the side.]

beste n. the best (men) 488; best (thing) 1949; *adj. sup.* best 347, 973, 2001; *adv.* 235, 429, 613, etc. [OE. *betst.*]

bete pt. sg. beat 1426, 1480, 1516; pp. embroidered 182. [OE. *bēatan.*]

bettur *adj. comp.* better 1475, 1478, 1863; more valiant 4; *adv.* 1130. [OE. *betera, bet(t)ra, adj.*]

bewteys n. pl. beautiful features 64. [OFr. *beauté.*]

bethoght pt. sg. reflected, thought 908. [OE. *biþencan.*]

bewrye v. distort 1302. [OE *bewrēon.*]

byd(d) *imper.* ask 89, 115, 128. [OE. *biddan.*]

byddyng n. bidding, commands 849. [f. *byd(d).*]

byddyth 3 pr. sg. ordered 205, 1389. [OE. *biddan.*]

byde v. tr. withstand 279; stand (and face) 429; *intr.* stay, await 111, 264, 1047; pr. pl. 1421; **bydyng** pr. p. 234. [OE. *bīdan.*]

by(e) prep. beside, by, along 99, 177, 207, etc.; by means of 932; near 412. [OE. *bĭ.*]. See **be.**

byger n. builder 8. [From *ME. biggen.*]

bygged pt. sg. built 295. [*ON. byggva.*]

bygly *adj.* strong, mighty 220, 1484, 1679. [Obscure.]

byrdys n. pl. birds 182. [OE. *bridd*, young bird (late Nth. pl. *birdas*).]

byrke n. birch 1516. [Northern. OE. *bierce, byrce.*]

byte v. pierce 1626. [OE. *bītan.*]

bytter, -ur *adj.* bitter, hard 939, 1841; **bytterly** *adv.* 1626. [OE. *bitter.*]

black, blak(k) *adj.* black 423, 487, 760. [OE. *blæc.*]

blake v. to become pale 579. [Prob. OE. *blāc*, pale.]

blamed pt. pl. blamed, rebuked 76. [OFr. *bla(s)mer.*]

blanne. See **blynne.**

blaste n. blast (thunder) 1641. [OE. *blæst.*]

ble(e) n. hue, complexion 185, 579, 757, etc. [OE. *blēo.*]

blede v. bleed 639. [OE. *blēdan.*]

bleynes n. pl. sores 2022. [OE. *blegen.*]

blessyd *pp.* blessed 252. [OE.
  blĕtsian.]
blynne *v.* cease 357, 450, 543;
  pr. subj. sg. 1864; blanne *pt. sg.*
  put an end to 1149. [OE.
  blinnan.]
blys, blysse *n.* happiness, joy 969,
  1679, 2006, etc. [OE. *bliss.*]
blo *adj.* blue 96. [OFr. *bleu.*]
blode *n.* blood 14, 43, 95, etc.
  [OE. *blōd.*]
blome *n.* flower 686. [ON. *blóm,*
  blómi.]
bloo *adj.* black and blue 2022.
  [ON. *blá-r.*]
blowe *v.* blow 635. [OE. *blāwan.*]
blundur *n.* trouble, confusion 1328,
  [Obscure.]
blythe *adj.* happy, glad 1391.
  [OE. *blīþe.*]
bode *n.* delay 374, 1018, 1385.
  [Aphet. f. *abode.*]
body(e) *n.* body 95, 208, 473, etc.;
  bodyes *n. pl.* 93, 639. [OE.
  bodig.]
boght, boȝt *pt. sg.* bought, ransomed 244, 871, 1105, etc.;
  pp. 1575, 1843, 1987. [OE.
  bycgan.]
boke *n.* book 59, 84, 494, etc. [OE.
  bōc.]
bolde *adj.* bold, valiant 75, 347,
  552, etc. [OE. *báld.*]
bonde *pt. sg.* bound 1139, 1366,
  1513. [OE. *bindan.*]
bone, bonne *n.* bone 14, 1941;
  bones, boones *n. pl.* 99, 208,
  247. [OE. *bān.*]
bonne. See bone.
Boones. See bone.
boosys *n. pl.* bosses (raised ornaments) 387. [OFr. *boce.*]
boost *n.* boast 958. [Obscure].
borne. See bere.
borowed, -yd *pt. sg.* rescued
  2092; *pp.* 1724, 1750. [OE.
  borgian.]

bostefull *adj.* proud 270. [Obscure.]
bote *n.* cure, redress, salvation
  1719. [OE. *bōt.*]
bothe, boþe *adj.* both 114, 402,
  461, etc.; each 416; *adv.* 6, 32, 45,
  etc.; as well 162. [ON. *baðir.*]
bowne *adj.* prepared, dressed 178,
  866; ready 719, 847, 953, etc.;
  bound, setting out for 590.
  [ON. *búinn.*]
bowrys *n. pl.* bowers, chambers
  295. [OE. *búr.*]
bowrnes *n. pl.* A small stream,
  brook 609. [Southern variation
  of ME. *burn,* OE. *búrne.*]
bragg *n.* arrogant or boastful
  language 958. [Obscure.]
brayne *n.* brain 1941. [OE. *brægn.*]
brake. See breke.
braste. See breste.
bredd *n.* bread 1004, 1101, 1453,
  etc. [OE. *brēad.*]
brede *v. intr.* spread, grow 969.
  [OE. *brēdan.*]
breke *v.* break 1850; brake *pt. sg.*
  2101; *pt. pl.* 639; brokyn *pp.*
  1130. [OE. *brecan.*]
brenne *v.* burn 500, 1494; brent(e)
  pt. sg. 2057, 1483; brennyng *pr.*
  p. 98. [ON. *brenna.*]
brennyng. See brenne.
brent(e). See brenne.
bresyd *adj.* bristling 103, 208, 247.
  [Obscure.]
breste *v.* burst 1055; braste *pt. sg.*
  1609, 1862, 2114, etc. [OE.
  berstan; ON. *bresta.*]
brethe *n.* breath 357. [OE *brép.*]
brewe *v.* ferment 367, 939, 1209;
  brewyd *pt. sg.* 687. [OE. *breow-*
  an.]
brydale *n.* wedding feast 2152.
  [OE. *bryd-eale.*]
bryde *n.* bride 1069. [OE. *brȳd.*]
brydull, brydyll *n.* bridle 1534,
  1696, 1802; brydyls *n. pl.* 157,
  167. [OE. *brídel.*]

bryggys *n. pl.* (draw-)bridges 532. [OE. *brycg*.]

bryght, bryȝt *n.* fair one 1594, 2096; *adj.* bright, splendid, fair 79, 98, 156, etc. [OE. *berht*.]

bryghtenyd *pp.* brightened 1155. [OE. *berhtnian*.]

bryghtnes *n.* splendour, 185. [OE. *berht-nes*.]

brynge *v.* bring 811, 816, 1135, etc.; *imp.* 1015, 1475; *pt. subj. pl.* 2132; **bryngyth** *3 pers. sg.* 1264; **broght, broȝt** *pt. sg.* 781, 923, 1048, etc.; *pt. pl.* 268, 287, 749, etc.; *pp.* 106, 199, 1001, etc. [OE. *bringan*.]

bryngyth. See **bryng(e).**

brode *adj.* broad, wide 380, 569, 803, etc. [OE. *brād*.]

brodur *n.* brother 707, 718, 724, etc.; **brodurs** *n. gen.* 1098. [OE. *brōþor*.]

broght, broȝt. See **bryng(e).**

brokyn. See **breke.**

brondys *n. pl.* pieces of burnt wood 98. [OE. *bránd, brónd*.]

brooke *v.* enjoy, use. 1181. [OE. *brūcan*.]

burges *n.* townsman 1744, 1780, 1819; *gen.* 446, 1757, 1762, etc.; *n. pl.* 145. [OFr. *burgeis*.]

burlyng *pr. p.* wallowing (in blood) 1637. [OFr. *bourler* (beside *bouler*), roll.]

burne *n.* warrior, knight, man 884. [OE. *béorn*.]

buske *v.* to prepare oneself, make haste 276. [ON. *búask*, refl.]

but *adj.* except 1078, 1105. [OE. *būtan*.]

but *adv.* only 33, 577, 1192. [OE. *būtan*.]

but *conj.* but 257, 291, 352, etc.; however 269, 349, 789; unless 389, 956; *but yf* unless 440. [OE. *būtan*.]

buxvm *adj.* obedient, willing 1723. [OE. stem of *būgan* + *-sum*.]

C

caght *pt. pl.* received, got 1043. (ONFr. *cach(i)er*, infl. by ME. *lach(che)*.]

calde. See **calle.**

calle *v.* call (summon, name) 610; *pr. pl.* 1882; **calde, callyd** *pt. sg.* 228, 490, 1184, etc.; *pp.* (*pass.*) 319. [ON. *kalla;* OE. (late) *ceallien*.]

callyd. See **calle.**

cam(e). See **come.**

can *v.* know, know how to, can *1 pr. sg.* 249, 350, 375; *3 pr. sg.* 169, 215, 598, etc.; *pr. pl.* 399, 417, 654; **conne** *pr. pl.* 1952; **cowde, cowthe** *pt. sg.* 59, 62, 524, etc.; *pt. pl.* 782. [OE. *can, con, cūþe*.]

can *v. auxil. used with infin. as equivalent of simple pt.* (*can dye* = died, 69) 21, 69, 138, etc. [Confused with ME. *gan*, did.]

candyll *n.* candle 1645. [OE. *cāndel, cōndel*.]

cardynale *n.* cardinal 1395; **cardynals** *n. pl.* 2146. [OFr. *cardinal*.]

care *n.* woe, misery 687, 1450, 1596, etc.; anxiety 919, 2015. [OE. *caru*.]

care *v.* be concerned for 273. [OE. *carian*.]

carefull *adj.* full of grief, anxious 1577. [OE, *carful, cearful*, f. *caru*, care.]

caryage *n.* carriage 164. [ONFr. *cariage*.]

caste *n.* stroke, trick 1404, 2049. [ON. *kast*.]

caste *v.* cast, put 823. *3 pr. sg.* 1427, 1432, 1447, etc.; *pr. pl.*

1157, 1367; *pr. pl.* scheme 1782. [ON. *kasta*.]

castell *n.* castle 1230, 1548. [ONFr. *castel*.]

cawser *n.* originator, author 1580. [f. ME. *causen*.]

cawsyd *pt. sg.* 130, 1581, 1589; *pt. pl.* 2109. [ML. *causare*.]

certen *adj.* certain, sure, definite 306, 621, 1359, etc. [OFr. *certain*.]

certenly *adv.* certainly 1822. [OFr. *certain*.]

certys *adv.* certainly, truly 1123, 1357. [OFr. *certes*.]

chalenge *1 pr. sg.* defy, dare 685. [OFr. *ca-*, *chalonger*, *-langer*, *-lenger*.]

charbokull *n.* red-coloured precious stone 392. [OFr. *charbuncle*.]

chare *n.* chariot, car 592. [OFr. *char*.]

charge *imper.* burden 1008. [OFr. *charger*.]

chargyd *pt. pl.* burdened 125, 202. [OFr. *charger*.]

charyte *n.* charity, Christian love 1702; *for charyte* (formula used in prayers or requests) 1909. [OFr. *charité*.]

chasyng *pr. p.* chasing 1115, 1163. [OFr. *chac(i)er*.]

chaste *adj.* chaste, pure 2163. [ad. L. *costus*, *casta*.]

chastlayne *n.* governor of a castle 1984. [AF. *castelain*.]

chaumber, -ur, chawbur *n.* room (usually a small private room or bedroom) 229, 239, 833, etc. [OFr. *chambre*.]

chaumburlayne *n.* chamberlain, groom of the chamber 691. [OFr. *chamberlain*.]

chawnce *n.* chance, fortune 271; *per chawnce* perhaps 942. [OFr. *ch(e)ance*.]

chawngyd *pt. sg.* changed 819. [OFr. *cha(u)ng(i)er*.]

chefe *n.* leader, head 596. [OFr. *chef*, *chief*.]

chefe *adj.* chief, principal 17. [OFr. *ch(i)ef*.]

chekys *n. pl.* cheeks 578. [OE. *cē(a)c*.)

chere *n.* (expression of) face 812, 819. [OFr. *ch(i)ere*.]

cherye *n.* cherry 1761. [AF. *cherise*, taken as *pl.* form, but with the vowel of OE. *cirse*, *ciris-beam*.]

chese *pt. sg.* made his way 470. [OE. *céosan*.]

chesten *v.* to put in a chest 1474. [f. ME. *chest(e)*.]

cheualry *n.* knighthood, knightly conduct 570. [OFr. *chevalerie*.]

chylde *n.* child 31, 36, 56, etc.; **chyldur** *n. pl.* 415. [OE. *cild*, pl. *cildru*.]

chyualrous *adj.* chivalrous 2. [OFr. *chevalerie*.]

chorle *n.* man (of low birth) 1474. [OE. *ceorl*.]

church(e) *n.* church 1894, 1996. [OE. *cirice*, *circe*.]

cyte *n.* city 17, 116, 150, etc. [OFr. *cité*.]

claymed *pt. sg.* claimed 1192. [OFr. *clamer*.]

clave *pt. sg.* cleaned 1870. [OE. *clifan*.]

cled(d) *pt. sg.* clad 1691; *pp.* (*pass.*) 211. [OE. *clǣþan; pt. clǣdde*.]

clene *adv.* entirely 9, 277, 533, etc. [OE. *clǣne*.]

clere *n.* fair lady 78, 1797, 2007. [OFr. *cler*.]

clere *adj.* fair 574, 894, etc.; bright 326, 1225. [OFr. *cler*.]

clerkys, *n. pl.* priests 1363. [OFr. *clerc*.]

clyne *v.* incline or tend 1128. [OFr. *cliner*.]

cloystur *n.* monastery 1899, 2012. [OFr. *cloistre*.]

close *imper.* close, fasten 532. [OFr. *clos*, n.]

clothe *n.* cloth 823, 1157; *n. pl.* **cloþys, clothys** clothes 134, 182, 385; cloths 203. [OE. *claþ*.]

cloþyng, clothyng *n.* clothing 211, 1666. [f. ME. *clothe* v. + *yng*.]

cofurs *n. pl.* strong boxes 1182. [OFr. *cofre, coffre*.]

coghyth *3 pr. sg.* coughs 248. [Akin to MDu. *cuchen* and LG. *kuchen*, of echoic origins.]

colde *n.* cold 209. [OE. *cáld*.]

colde *adj.* cold 95. [OE. *cáld*.]

comawndyd *pt. sg.* commanded 283, 1180, 1555. [OFr. *commander*.]

come *v.* come 314, 1373, 1403, etc.; *1 pr. sg.* 434, 952, 1738; *3 pr. sg.* 1928; *pr. pl.* 147, 341, 504, etc.; *pr. subj. sg.* 253, 272; *pt. subj. sg.* 1110; *jussive subj.* 695; **cometh, comyth** *3 pr. sg.* 334, 488, 1068; **cam** *pt. sg.* 1368; **came** *pt. sg.* 7, 15, 165, etc.; *pt. pl.* 4, 192, 469, etc.; **comyn** *pp.* (*pass.*) 122, 236, 444, etc. [OE. *cuman, cóm, comon, cumen*.]

come *n.* arrival, coming 1577. [OE. *cyme*.]

comely *adj.* fair, beautiful. [OE. *cým̃lic*, infl. by assoc. with ME. *becomen*.]

cometh. See **come**.

comyn. See **come**.

comyng *vbl. n.* coming, advent 1528. See **come**.

comyth. See **come**.

condyte *n.* conduit 334. [OFr. *conduit*.]

confownde *v.* throw into con-

fusion or disorder 51, 938. [OFr. *confondre, confundre*.]

conne. See **can**.

conqueste *pp.* conquered 1199. [OFr. *conquerre*.]

cornell *n.* circlet worn on head 808. [AF. *coronal* (in sense of head of spear) and L. *coronăl, -is* adj.]

corse *n.* body 1088. [OFr. *cors*.]

covenawnt *n.* agreement 1786. [OFr. *covenant*.]

couenawnt *adj.* agreed, agreeable, trustworthy 945. [OFr. *covenant, convenant*.]

couer *v.* shield, protect (*fig.*) 328; **couyrde** *pp.* (*pass.*) covered 163. [OFr. *cuvrir, courir*, later *couvrir*.]

cowde. See **can** *v.*

cowncelde *pt. sg.* advised, counselled 886, 943; *pt. pl.* 880. [OFr. *co(u)nseill(i)er*.]

cowncell, counsell *n.* counsel, advise 240, 260, 899, etc. [OFr. *co(u)nseil*.]

cowncell *n.* council 233, 251, 1097. [OFr. *cuncile*. In English confused with ME. *conseil*, later *counsel* until the sixteenth century.]

cowre *v.* cower 785. [Perhaps f. Norse; cf. Sw. *kura*, to squat.]

cowthe. See **can** *v.*

crachyd. See **crake**.

crake *v.* crack 92, 1476; **crakyd** *pt. pl.* 1850; **crachyd** *pp.* 2025. [OE. *cracian*, to crack (sound).]

creature *n.* creature 1537. [OFr. *creature*.]

crye *n.* shouting, clamour, proclamation 174, 544, 1518, etc. [OFr. *cri*.]

crye *v.* proclaim; *made to crye*, had proclaimed 551; **cryed** *pt. sg.* shouted 761. [OFr. *crier*.]

cryed. See **crye**.

crystalle *n.* crystal 326. [OFr. *cristal.*]

crysten *adj.* Christian 620. [OE. *cristen.*]

crysten *v.* to administer baptism 36. [OE. *cristnian.*]

crystendome *n.* Christian lands 17, 998. [OE. *cristen, -dōm,* Christianity.]

crystyante *n.* Christianity 830, 903. [OFr. *crestienté.*]

crokyd *adj.* crooked 1977, 2025. [ON. *krókr, n.*]

crompylde *pp.* crimpled 1977. [Echoic, dim. of ME. *crump.*]

cronykyle *n.* chronicle 2174. [a. AF. *chronicle* = OFr. *cronique.*]

crosse *n.* cross 1903. [ON. *kross,* from OFr. *cros.*]

crowlande *pr. p.* trembling, quivering 844. [OFr. *croler, croller, crouler.*]

crowne *n.* crown of the head 92. [OFr. *coroune;* cf. ON. *krúna.*]

crowne *v.* crown 995, 1256; **crowned, -yd;** *pt. pl.* 1232; *pp.* (*pass.*) 1025, 1200, 1262. [AFr. *coruner, corouner.*]

crowned, -yd. See **crowne.**

cuntre *n.* land 115, 1196, 1491, etc.; **cuntreys** *n. pl.* 1221. [OFr. *cuntrié, contrée.*]

cursyd *pp.* cursed 1279. [OE. (late) *cŭrsian,* from OIr. *cúrsagim.*]

curten *n.* curtain 1628. [a. OFr.; L. *cortina.*]

curtes *adj.* gracious 129, 526, 810, etc. [OFr. *corteis, curteis.*]

curtesye *n.* courtesy, grace 300, 524. [OFr. *corteisie, curteisie.*]

curteslye *adv.* courteously 508, 1714. See **curtes.**

D

day(e) *n.* day 159, 311, 316, etc.; *on a day,* one day 29, 1925; *mony a day,* many days, a long time 350; *oones on a day,* once upon a time 418; **dayes** *n. pl.* 43. [OE. *dæg.*]

dayes. See **day.**

dale *n.* (bottom of) valley 1398. [OE. *dæl.*]

dame *n.* dame, lady 1980, 2082, 2122. [OFr. *dame.*]

damysell *n.* damsel 58, 1464, 1843. [OFr. *damisele.*]

dar *1 pr. sg.* dare 737. [OE. *dearr, dorste.*] See **durste.**

dare *v.* cower 93. [OE. *darian.*]

date *n.* date 2174. [OFr. *date.*]

dawyd *pt. sg.* dawned 1029. [OE. *daȝian.*]

dedd *n.* death 976, 1582, 1821, etc. [A variant, usually northern, of ME. *deþ.*]

dedd *adj.* dead 34, 48, 406, etc. [OE. *dēad.*]

dede *n.* deed 882, 1621, etc.; *as obj. of do* 669. [OE. *dēd.*]

dedly *adj.* deadly 330. [OE. *dēadlic.*]

defendyd *pt. sg.* defended 2052. [OFr. *defendre.*]

deyse *n.* high table 1759. [AF. *deis* and CF. *dois.*]

delay *n.* delay 1362. [ad. Fr. *délai,* f. OFr. *delaier, delayer.*]

dele *n.* part, detail 251; *euery dele,* in every detail 251, 1733. [OE. *dæl.*] See **somedele.**

dele *v.* deal; *wyth them dele,* have to do with them 2115. [OE. *dǣlan.*]

delyte *n.* delight 868, 1943. [OFr. *delit.*]

delyuyr *imper.* set free, liberate 944. [OFr. *de(s)livrer.*]

delyurd *pt. sg.* delivered, set free 1737. [OFr. *de(s)livrer.*]

dentyd *pp.* inlaid 326. [OFr. *denté* and L. *dentātus.*]

depe *adj.* deep (sea) 132, 1298, 1417. [OE. *dēop.*]

dere *n.* harm 369. [OE. *daru,* infl. by *derian.*]

dere *adj.* dear, prized 72, 801, 1298, etc.; **derrest** *sup.* 1065. [OE. *deore.*]

dere *adv.* dearly, at great cost 244, 561, 1477, etc. [OE. *dēore.*]

deryd *pt. pl.* afflicted, hurt 657. [OE. *derian.*]

derne *adv.* stealthily 1956. [OE. *derne.*]

derrest. See **dere** *adj.*

derworthe *adj.* sumptuous 1956. [OE. *dēorwurþe.*]

desyre *n.* desire 763. [OFr. *desir.*]

dethe *n.* death 1043, 1688; **dethys** *n. gen.* 915. [OE. *deaþ.*]

dethys. See **dethe.**

deuyll *n.* devil 731, 1991. [OE. *dēofol.*]

dewkys *n. pl.* dukes 188, 319, 838, etc. [OFr. *duc.*]

dyd. See **do.**

dye *v.* die 69, 257, 356, etc.; **dyed** *pt. sg.* 31, 1430, 1511, etc.; *pt. pl.* 644, 1041. [ON. *deyja.*]

dyed. See **dye.**

dyght, dyȝt *pt. pl.* arranged, prepared 795; dressed 1672; *pp.* 1301, 1394, 1446; *to dedd ys dyght,* put to death 930. [OE. *dihtan.*]

dyntys *n. pl.* strokes, blows 653, 661. [OE. *dynt.*]

dyscownfortyd *pp.* distressed, grieved 1718. [OFr. *desconforter.*]

dyscrye *v.* write 60. [OFr. *descrire,* var. of *descrivre.*]

dysheryted *pp.* disinherited 940. [OFr. *desheriter.*]

dyssees *n.* death 618. [L. *decessus,* f. *decedere.*]

dystawnce *n.* quarrelling; *wythowt distawnce,* indisputably 2138. [OFr. *destance.*]

dystroye *v.* destroy 116, 220, 278, etc. [OFr. *destruire.*]

do(o) *v.* 235, 283, 641, etc.; *3 pr. sg.* 272; *pr. pl.* 845, 905, 1769, etc.; **dyd, dud** *pt. sg.* 251, 726, 854, etc.; *pt. pl.* 369, 802, 803, etc.; **done, doone** *pp.* 656, 689, 772, etc.; *haue done . . .,* get it done, be quick 210, 223. [OE. *dōn.*]

doghtely *adv.* mightily, valiantly 1169. [f. *doghty(e).*]

doghty(e) *adj.* doughty, brave 256, 665, 680, etc.; as *n.* hero 644, 713; **doghtyar** *sup.* 23. [OE. *dohtig.*]

doghtyar. See **doghtye.**

doghtur, -yr *n.* daughter 23, 72, 90, etc. [OE. *dohtor.*]

dolefull *adj.* doleful 582, 1859. [OFr. *dol, doel, deol, diol* + *-ful.*]

dome *n.* judgement, doom 153. [OE. *dōm.*]

done. See **do(o).**

doone. See **do.**

dore *n.* door 1480, 1610, 1636, etc. [OE. *duru, dor.*]

down(e) *adv.* down 467, 474, 488, etc. [OE. *of dūne, adūne.*]

dowte *n.* fear 457, 863. [OFr. *doute.*]

dowve *n.* dove 422, 424, 487, etc. [OE. **dūfe; ON. dúfa.*]

dragon *n.* dragon 599. [OFr. *dragon.*]

drawe *v. intr.* approach 225; **drewe** *pt. sg. drew to,* became 1456; **droghe** *pt. sg.* drew, approached 2016. [OE. *dragan.*]

drawe *v. tr.* pull 532; **drewe** *pt. sg.* 722; **drowe** *pt. pl.* 142; **drawyn** *pp.* 1224. [OE. *dragan.*]

drawyn. See **drawe.**

dredd, drede *n.* fear 885; *for drede* for fear 837, 1601, 1611. [From OE. *drǣdan.*]

drede *adj.* fearful 966. [f. prec.]

drede *pr. subj. sg.* (might) dread 1622. [OE. *drǽdan.*]

dredyd *pt. pl.* feared 153. [OE. *drǽdan.*]

drery *adj.* sad, melancholy 798, 1029, 2105; **dreryar** *comp.* 1838. [OE. *dreoriʒ.*]

dreryar. See **drery.**

drewe. See **drawe.**

drye *adj.* dry 1305, 1886. [OE. *drȳge.*]

drynke *n.* drink 1760; *esp. in mete and drink.* [f. OE. *drincan.*] See **mete.**

droghe. See **drawe.**

drowe. See **drawe.**

drowned *pt. sg.* drowned 378; *3 pt. pl.* 1872; *pp.* (*pass.*) 1736, 1865, 1878. [See *MED.*]

drowpe *v.* drop 93. [OE. *dropian.*]

dud. See **do(o).**

durste *pt. sg.* dared 429, 1047, 1233, etc.; *3 pt. pl.* 457. [OE. *dearr, durron; dorste.*] See **dar.**

dwelle *v.* live, dwell 303, 428, 452, etc.; **dwellyth** *3 pr. sg.* 1951; **dwellyd** *pt. sg.* 1591, 1613, 1913, etc. [OE. *dwellan.*]

dwellyd. See **dwelle.**

dwellyth. See **dwelle.**

E

eere, ere *n.* ear 1753, 2116. [OE. *ēare, ēaran* (pl.).]

effect *n.* essential content, sum and substance 346. [L. *effectus,* OFr. *effect.*]

efte *adv.* a second time, once more 520; afterwards, then 1200. [OE. *eft.*]

egyll *n.* eagle 392. [OFr. *egle, aigle,* f. L. *aquila.*]

eyder. See **eyther.**

eye *n.* eye 1588, 1748; **eyen, yen** *n. pl.* eyes 353, 2027. [OE. *ēage,* pl. *egan.*]

eyen. See **eye.**

eyen *n. pl.* young hawks 845. [Var. of *nyesse* (ODan. *nyas*) and *eyes* (ODan. *eyas*), a nestling hawk; OFr. *niais* nestling.]

eylyth *3 pr. sg.* troubles, afflicts 1300. [OE. *eglian.*]

eyther *pron.* either 1791; each one 675; *eyther odur, eyder odur* each the other, one another 47, 1450. [OE. *ǽghwǽþer, ǽgþer.*]

eke *adv.* also 1919. [OE. *ēc.*]

elde *n.* age 94, 555, 973. [OE. *éldo.*]

elder *comp. adj.* older 671. [f. *elde.*]

eldyst *sup. adj.* oldest 896. [f. *elde.*]

ellys *adj.* following a limiting noun, *noght ellys* 932 nothing else. [f. adv.]

ellys *adv.* otherwise 1358, 1735. [f. OE. *elles.*]

ellys *conj.* unless 217. [f. adv.]

emperes, -ys *n.* consort of the emperor 34, 2150. [OFr. *emper-(e)ris, emperesse.*]

emperowre *n.* emperor 19, 25, 35, etc.; **emperowrs** *gen. n.* 173, 322. [OFr. *empereor.*]

emperowrs. See **emperowre.**

empyre *n.* realm 74, 764, 1208, etc. [OFr. *empire, empere.*]

encheson *n.* reason or grounds (for a given opinion, decision, or act); *encheson why* 102. [OFr. *enchaison.*]

encresyth *3 pr. sg.* grows, prospers 1950. [AF. *encreisser, encresser.*]

ende *n.* end, concluding part 600, 1745, 1794; conclusion 2178. [OE. *ende.*]

endyd *pp.* ended, ceased 697. [OE. *ge-endian, endian.*]

endyth *3 pr. sg.* ends 2185. [OE. *ge-endian, endian.*]

enhabyted *pt. sg.* inhabited, dwelled 9. [OFr. *enhabiter*.]

enmye *n.* enemy 1064; **enmyes** *n. pl.* 428, 799. [OFr. *enemi, anemi*.]

enqueryd *pp.* asked 1315. [OFr. *enquerre*.]

entent *n.* mind, heart, spirit 1997. [OFr. *entente*.]

enteryd *pt. sg.* buried 869. [OFr. *enter(r)er*.]

entyrd(e) *pt. pl.* entered 151, 191. [OFr. *entrer*.]

erbys *n. pl.* herbs 1549. [OFr. *erbe*.]

erles, -ys *n. pl.* nobles 188, 838. [OE. *eorl*.]

errande *n.* errand 1775; petition, prayer 1855. [OE. *ærende;* ON. *erendi*.]

erthely *adj.* wordly 1667. [OE. *eorþlic;* ME. *ĕrthe*.]

este *n.* east 1414. [OE. *ēast*.]

estyrs *n. pl.* dwellings, buildings 293. [OFr. *estre;* ? also OFr. *estree*, road.]

ete 1 *pr. sg.* eat 1463; *pt. sg.* ate 525, 1468, 1471. [OE. *etan*.]

etyn *pp.* eaten 263. [OE. *etan*.]

euenynge *n.* evening 1456. [OE. *ēfnung*.] See **euyn**.

euery *pron. euery oon*, everyone 155. [OE. *æfre*.]

euery *adj.* every 161, 316, 362, etc. [OE. *æfre*.]

euerychon *pron.* one and all 359, 1555. [*euery* + ME. *on*.]

euerydele *adv.* completely, thoroughly 251, 1733. [*euery* + *dele*.]

euyll *n.* misfortune 1616, 1950; disease 1933, 1990, 1994; sin 1983; *n. pl.* diseases 1919. [OE. *yfel*.]

euyll *adj.* bad 254, 815, 876, etc.; defective 1824. [OE. *yfel*.]

euyll *adv.* badly 715. [OE. *yfele*.]

euyn *n.* evening 114. [OE. *ēfen*.]

euyn *adj.* smooth 327. [OE. *efen, efn*.]

euyn *adv.* straight, directly 445, 470, 747, etc. [OE. *efen, efne*.]

euyr *adv. with particularising force:* at any time at all 139, 308, 717, etc.; always, at all times 149, 167, 172, etc.; forever 1386; *comb. and phr.* **euyr:** *euyrmore*, for ever afterward 1220, 1808; *foreuyr*, for all time 1341; *euyrsyth*, ever since 2105; in a comparison: at any time, in any way or manner *as . . . as euyr* 2142; at any time at all 2181. [OE. *æfre*.]

euyrmore. See **euyr**.

F

face *n.* face 566, 1540, 1809. [OFr. *face*.]

fadur *n.* father 115, 180, 250, etc.; applied to God 1124, 1676; applied to the Pope 1421; **fadurs** *n. pl.* 649; *gen. n.* 246, 762, 818, etc. [OE. *fæder*.]

fadurles *adj.* without a father 1220. [OE. *fæderlēas*.]

faght. See **fyght**.

fayle *n.* failure 137, 1310. [OFr. *faille*.]

fayleste, faylyst *pr. pl.* lack, want 555; disappoint 1854. [OFr. *faillir, falir*.]

faylyd *pt. pl.* failed 1831. [OFr. *faillir, falir*.]

fayne *adj.* joyful, happy 294, 967, 1074, etc.; *for fayne*, for joy 967. [OE. *fægen*.]

fayre *adj.* beautiful, attractive 33. [OE. *fæger*.]

falle *v.* fall 1067, 1081; **felle** *pt. sg.* 474, 632, 699, etc.; happened 418; *pt. pl.* 48, 677. [OE. *fallan (fēol, fēollon, feallen)*.]

fals, false *adj.* disloyal, treacherous

737, 751, 1089, etc.; **falsyst** *sup.* 716. [OFr. *fals.*]

falsehed(d) *n.* deceitfulness 1076, 1128. [From *fals.*]

fame *n.* good reputation 252. [OFr. *fame.*]

famysched *pp.* (*pass.*) starved 875. [Prob. from AF; cp. OFr. *afamer.*]

fande. See **fynde.**

farde. See **fare.**

fare *n.* behaviour, conduct 270, 1957; fortune 1580, 1877. [OE. *faru.*]

fare *v.* advance 593; go 833, 1599, 1707, etc.; journey, travel 432, 1014; **farde** *pt. sg.* 563, 2080; *pt. pl.* 1683; **fared** *pt. sg.* behaved 660. [OE. (i) *faran* (*fōr, faren*); (ii) *fēran* (*ferde*).]

fared. See **fare.**

farre *adj.* distant 891. [OE. *feor(r).*]

faste *adv.* quick 705, 1053, 1319, etc.; tight, firm 858, 1638, 2052. [OE. *fæste.*]

faste *pp.* (*pass.*) bestowed 404. [OE. (*ge-*)*fæstan.*]

fasten *imper.* set 851. [OE. (*ge-*) *fæstan.*]

faxe *n.* hair of the head 1543. [OE. *feax.*]

febull *adj.* unhappy, sorry 2108. [OFr. *feble.*]

feche *v.* go after, get 219; *imper.* 1016. [OE. *fetian, feccan.*]

fed *pt. pl.* supplied with food 1552. [OE. *fēdan.*]

fedyll *n.* a bowed stringed instrument, viol, violin 1012. [OE. *fipele.*]

feele *adj.* bold, audacious 593; treacherous 2112. [OFr. *fel.*]

feyre *n.* good fortune 317. [Partly f. OE. *fæger* n., partly f. *fæger* adj.]

feyre *adj.* beautiful, fair 28, 37,

79, etc.; **feyrest(e)** *sup.* 195, 307, 1250, etc. [OE. *fæger.*]

feyre *adv.* splendidly 141, 175, 295. [OE. *fægre.*]

feyrenes *n.* beauty 349. [OE. *fægernes.*]

feyrest. See **feyre.**

feythe *n.* in oaths: *in feythe*, truly 1769. [OFr. *feid* (early), later *fei.*]

fekyll *adj.* of human beings: inconstant, changeable. [OE. *ficol.*]

felde, fylde *n.* plain 380, 531, 632, etc.; **feldys** *n. pl.* 568. [OE. *feld.*]

felle *n.* the skin as one of the parts of the body, *fleshe and felle* 309 [OE. *fel(l).*]

felle *adj.* fierce in combat 427; grievous, virulent 1971. [OFr. *fel.*]

felle. See **falle.**

felowe *n.* man, chap 928; **felows** *n. pl.* comrades 503. [ON.; cp. OI. *felagi* share-holder.]

fende *n.* mortal foe 1669. [OE. *fēond.*]

fende *jussive subj.* defend 1441. [Aphet. **defend.**]

fere *n.* of persons: in a group, in company, together *in fere* 443, 461, 503, etc.; **ferys** *n. pl.* forces 461. [OE. *gefēr*, company.]

fere *n.* spouse, mate 81. [OE. *gefēra.*]

fere *n.* fear 822, 923, 1906. [OE. *fēr.*]

fe(e)re *v.* fear 462, 2004, 2084. [OE. (*ge-*)*færen.*]

ferly *n.* astonishment, *have ferly* be astonished 431. [From ME. adj. *fĕrlĭ*, OE. **feorlic*, strange.]

ferre *adj.* much 671. [OE. *feor(r).*]

ferre *adv.* far, afar 1, 104, 1482. [O.E (i) *feorh;* (ii) *feorran.*]

ferse *adj.* ferocious, wild 427. [OFr. *fers.*]

feste *n.* feast, banquet 2128. [OFr. *feste*.]

festurd *pp.* ulcered 1943. [From ME. *festre* n.; OFr. *festrir*.]

fete *n. pl.* feet 640. [OE. *fōt*; pl. *fēt*.]

fett *pt. sg.* fed 1760. [OE. *fēdan*.]

feturs *n. pl.* shackles, fetters 1148. [OE. *feotor*.]

fyftene *card. num.* fifteen 391. [OE. *fiftēnē*.]

fyfty *card. num.* fifty 458; a set of fifty persons 466. [OE. *fiftig*.]

fyght *n.* fight 485, 498, 591, etc. [OE. *fe(o)hte*.]

fyght *v.* fight 531, 548, 705, etc.; **faght** *pt. sg.* 44; *pt. pl.* 475, 679, 1039, etc.; **fyghtande, fyghtyng** *pr. p.* 708, 744, 925; *used as n.* 681, 697. [OE. *fe(o)htan (fæht, fuhton, fohten)*.]

fylde. See **felde.**

fylle *n.* one's heart's desire 1405. [OE. *fyll*.]

fylle *pt. subj. pl.* (might) fill 1182. [OE. *fyllan*.]

fyllyd *pp.* (*pass.*) filled 328. [OE. *fyllan*.]

fynde *v.* find, encounter; *1 pr. sg.* 2117; **fande** *pt. sg.* 714, 1697; *pt. pl.* 1230; *used as infin., That was so feyre to fande* 1656. [OE. *findan (fand, fundon, funden)*.]

fyne *adj.* consummate in virtue 2123. [OFr. *fin*.]

fyne *adv.* in the end, at last 1137. [Aphet. form of ME. *afin*.]

fyre *n.* fire 73, 97, 500, etc. [OE. *fȳr*.]

fyred *pp.* kindled (a fire) 709. [From **fyre** n.]

fyrmament *n.* sky 46. [OFr. *firmament*.]

fysches *n. pl.* fishes 390. [OE. *fisc*; pl. *fiscas, fixas*.]

fyve *card. num.* five 991; *before*

'thousand' 454; *with a common noun* 913, 1848. [OE. *fīf(e)*.]

flankys *n. pl.* sides of the abdomen 109. [CF. *flanc*.]

fledd(e). See **flee.**

flee *v.* run away, flee 783, 1041, 1381; **fledd(e)** *pt. sg.* 723, 1352; *pt. pl.* 497. [OE. *flēon*.]

flemed *pp.* (*pass.*) banished, exiled 2087. [OE. (*ge-)flēman*.]

flesche *n.* flesh 94, 309, 1517. [OE. *flǣsc*.]

flete *v.* float, drift 1989; **flett** *pt. pl.* drifted, sailed 137; **fletyd** *pp.* floated 1874, 2102. [OE. *flēotan (flēat)*.]

fletyd. see **flete.**

flett. See **flete.**

flyre *v.* mock, sneer, 1767. [Cp. Norw. *flire*, giggle, grin.]

flode *n.* river 131, 390. [OE. *flōd*.]

flowre *n.* flower 194, 616, 901, etc.; the most excellent 570. [OFr. *flour, flor, flur*.]

fode *n.* food 1552. [OE. *fōda*.]

folde *n.* earth, world 342, 758, 873. [OE. *fólde*.]

folde *v.* fold 1323; embrace 1849. [OE. *fáldan*.]

folke *n.* (*coll. or pl.*) people, persons 141, 318, 575, etc. [OE. *folc*.]

folowe *v.* follow 547; *jussive subj.* 1703. [OE. *folgian*.]

fomen *n. pl.* enemies 719. [OE. *fáhmon*.]

fomes *n. pl.* seas 137. [OE. *fām*.]

fonde *pt. sg.* found 631, 748, 1138, etc. [OE. *findan*.]

fonge *pp.* seized 1829. [OE. *fōn*.]

for *prep.* as regards 6; *with infin.* 24, 64, 101, etc.; for the space of 43; for the sake of 52, 183, 558, etc.; on account of 94, 96, 252, etc.; as 125, 302; suitable for 134; in spite of 270, 282. [OE. *for*.]

for *conj.* because 716, 1059, 1128, etc. [From prep.]

for. See **fowre.**

ſorbede *imper.* prohibit, stop; in exclamations; *Jhesu forbede* 243; *God forbede hyt* 267, *God forbede* 904. [OE. *forbēodan.*]

forbode *3 pt. pl.* prohibited 955. [OE. *forbēodan.*]

foreste *n.* wilderness 1448, 1521, 1708. [OFr. *forest.*]

forgeue *v.* forgive 1837; *pp.* 1286. [OE. *forgefan.*] See **geue.**

forjusted *pt. pl.* defeated in battle 466. [Cp. **juste.**]

formast(e) *adj.* first 172, 375. [From **forme**; L. *forma,* OFr. *fourme.*]

forme *n.* shape 1004, 1101. [L. *forma,* OFr. *fourme.*]

forne *prep.* on behalf of, on account of 67. [From adv. *fǒrn*; OE. *foran, forne.*]

forows *n. pl.* ditches, trenches 746. [OE. *furh.*]

forronne *pp.* overcome with walking 1902. [OE. *for* + *runnen.*]

forty *num.* forty; *cardinal as adj.* 121, 124, 443, etc. [OE. *fēowertig.*]

forþy, forthy *adv.* on that account 96, 302, 1022, etc. [OE. *forþȳ, forþī.*]

fote *n.* foot 388, 1139, 1366, etc. [OE. *fōt*; pl. *fēt.*]

forthe *adv.* forward, ahead, onward 138, 373, 375, etc. [OE. *forþ.*]

fowle *a.;j.* ugly 920, 2178; **fowlest** *sup.* 2021. [OE. *fūl.*]

fowlys *n. pl.* birds 46. [OE. *fugol, fuglas.*]

fownde *v.* proceed, set out 281, 371. [OE. *fundian.*]

fownde *pt. sg.* found 1459; *pt. pl.* 451, 705; *pp.* 2126. [OE. *findan.*]

fownder *n.* the founder (of a country) 11, 1888. [From L. *fundator.*]

fowre *num.* four 991. [OE. *fēower.*]

fowrtenyght *n.* two weeks 1735, 2158. [From the early ME. phrase.]

fra. See **from.**

frawde *n.* dishonest act 1820. [OFr. *fraude.*]

fre. See **free.**

fre(e) *adj. of a people:* politically independent 318; noble in character, gracious 480, 900, 1096, etc.; *as n.;* person of noble character 1910. [OE. *frēo.*]

frende *n.* friend 126, 1065, 1803. [OE. *frēond.*]

fresche *adj. of water:* not salt 342; **frescher** *comp. of colours:* brighter 158. [OFr. *freis*; fem. *fresche*; cp. OE. *fersc.*]

freschly *adv.* boldly 548, 1042. [From **fresche.**]

fro(o). See **from.**

from *prep.* from 2043; **fra** 1110, 1737; **fro(o)** 15, 200, 209, etc. [OE. *fram* and ON. *frá.*]

fulfylle *v.* comply with, execute 237. [OE. *fulfyllan.*]

full *intensive with adv.* very 152, 273, 505, etc.; *intensive with adj.* very, most 156, 162, 174, etc.; *adv. with num.* fully 189; *adj.* filled 425. [OE. *ful(l).*]

furste *ord. num. as adj.* first 8, 139, 623, etc.; *ord. num.* 1102; *altherfurste* first of all 292, 1804. [OE. *fyrst.*] See **alther.**

further *adv.* to a greater degree 411. [OE. *furþor, forþor.*]

G

ga. See **go.**

gabuls *n. pl.* heavy ropes used

on ships 1862. [Var. of ML *cabulus*.]

gaf(e). See **geue.**

gayne *n.* advantage, help 147, 149. [ON. (cp. OI. *gegn* adj.) and OFr. *gäin*.]

gayne *adj.* of persons: ready, well-disposed 491. [ON. *gegn*.]

gayne *adv.* close by, near 1985. [From *adj.*]

galow(e)tree *n.* gallows, place of execution 1724, 2090. [OE. *galga*.]

galows(e) *n.* gallows, place of execution 1711, 1737, 2092. [OE. *galga*.]

game *n.* revelry, amusement, 266. [OE. *gamen, gomen*.]

gare *v. auxil. with infin.:* to cause (something to be done) 92; **gart** *pp.* 36, 56, 74; prepared (oneself) 1132, 1363. [ON.; cp. OI. *göra, görva, gera, gerva.* Cp. also OE. *gearwian,* ME. *yaren*.]

garson *n.* retainer, follower 118, 626, 779; **garsons** *n. pl.* 256, 371, 397, etc. [OFr. *garçon*.]

gate. See **gete.**

gates *gen. n.* journey's, expedition's. 149 [ON.; cp. OI. *gata*.]

gatys *n. pl.* roads 1419. [ON.; cp. OI. *gata*.]

gaue. See **geue.**

geest *n.* an invited guest 1012. [ON.; cp. OI. *gestr*.]

gente *adj.* graceful, attractive 395, 479, 971; *adv.* courteously 2133. [OFr. *gente*.]

gentyl(l) *adj.* of noble rank or birth 444, 1266, 1654, etc. [OFr. *gentil*.]

gere *n.* fighting equipment, armour 456; the equipment of a riding horse 678; wearing apparel 1559, 1754. [ON.; cp. OI. *görvi, gervi.* Also cp. OE. *gearive.*]

gete *v.* bring 1473; *3 pr. sg.* obtain 269; **gate** *pt. sg.* went 16; *pt. pl.* obtained, got 2164; **getyn** *pp.* got 968, 1165, 1978, etc. [ON.; cp. OI. *geta*; pt. *gat,* pl. *gatum*; pp. *getenn*.]

getyn. See **gete.**

gethe *n. only in phr.: yn a gethe,* spiritedly, hastily [ON.; cp. OI. *geð,* mind, spirit; OE. *ge(h)þu*.]

geue, geve *v.* give, bestow gratuitously 224, 616, 691, etc.; *3 pr. sg.* 440; **geuyth** *3 pr. sg.* 305; **gaf(e), gaue** *pt. sg.* 693, 961, 1234, etc.; *pt. pl.* 1729, 2130; **yf** *pr. subj.* 1474; **geuyn** *pp.* 917. [ON. *gefa*; OSw. *gifa.* See *OED*.]

geuyn. See **geue.**

geuyth. See **geue.**

gyf *conj.* if 1271. [Northern var. of ME *ʒif*.]

gyftys *n. pl.* gifts 305, 1729, 2156. [ON. *gift*.]

gyle *n.* crafty trick 1791. [OFr. *guile*.]

gylle *n.* gully 1417. [ON. *gil*.]

gylte *n.* transgression, misdeed 556. [OE. *gylt*.]

gyltles *adv.* guiltless 1678, 2088. [From **gylte**(OE. *gylt*).]

gladd *adj.* joyful 1317. [OE. *glæd,* Merc. **gled*.]

glemed *pt. sg.* radiated, shone 381, 1709. [From ME. *glem* n., a beam.]

glyde *v.* pass through (the sea, etc.) 1053; **glode** *pt. sg.* 1709. [OE. *glidan (glād, glidon, gliden*).]

glyste *pt. sg.* glared, stared 1657. [OE. *glisnian*.]

glyteryng *pr. p.* glittering 157. [Blend of ON. (cp. OI. *glitra* to glitter) and OE. (cp. *gliddrian* to slip, be unstable.).]

glode. See **glyde.**

go(o) *v.* go 848, 944, 949, etc.; *pr. pl.* 233, 259; **goys** *3 pr. sg.*

547, 747; **gon(e), goon** v. walk 1386, 1920 *ryde or gone*, ride on horseback or walk 1; *pp.* 862; (*pass.*) 358, 1009. [OE. *gān.*] See **ȝede, ȝode.**

god(d) n. God, 244 267, 405; **god(d)ys** n. *pl.* 955; *gen. n.* 1422, 1892. [OE. *god.*]

gode adj. good 97, 102, 393, etc. [OE. *gōd*, adj.]

godhede n. divinity 1680. [From *God*; also cp. OE. *godhād.*]

goys. See go.

golde n. the metal gold 86, 125, 134, etc. [OE. *góld.*]

gome n. man 26, 968. [OE. *guma.*]

gon(e). See go.

goon. See go.

goost n. soul of a dead person 778; *holy goost*, the Holy Ghost 1676. [OE. *gāst.*]

gowte n. gout 1919. [OFr. *gote, goute,* and ML. *gutta.*]

grace n. God's favour 1458, 1511, 1806, etc. [OFr. *grace.*]

graceles adj. worthless, contemptible 1963. [From *grace.*]

graye adj. grey 1776. [OE. *grēg* and ON. (cp. OI. *grār*).]

graspyd pt. pl. reached for 678. [? OE. *grǣpsan*; cp. Norw. *krafse.*]

graunt, grawnt adj. *used as noun,* great one, king 26, 127, 298, etc. [OE. *grēat.*] See **grete.**

graunt v. concede (something to someone) 1074, 1721; *pr. pl.* permit 1194; **grauntyd** pt. *sg.* permitted 624. [OFr. *granter,* var. of *crĕanter.*]

grauntyd. See graunt.

grefe n. hardship, distress 1243, 1280, 1994. [CF. *gref* and CF. *grief, grieve.*]

grekys n. *pl.* Greeks 709; *gen. n.* 1884. [OE. *Grēc.* pl. *Grēcas.*]

grene adj. green 1449. [OE. *grēne.*]

grete adj. great, large 50, 69, 94, etc.; **grettyst** *sup.* 903, 998. [OE. *grēat.*] See **graunt, grawnt.**

grete 1 *pr. sg.* greet 127. [OE. *grētan,* weak.]

grettyst. See grete.

greue v. injure 954, 1460. [OFr. *grever.*]

grome n. a youth, young man. [Prob. OE. **grŏm, *grōma*) Akin to OE. *grōwan.* Infl. by OE. *guma.*]

grones 3 *pr. sg.* groans 248. [OE. *grānian.*]

grope v. feel 1631. [OE. *grāpian.*]

grownde, grounde n. ground 48, 381, 699, etc. [OE. *grúnd.*]

gruchyng *vbl.* n. grumbling 91. [OFr. *gr(o)ucher.*]

ȝ

ȝaa adv. yea, yes 1734. [OE. *gǣ, gē(a).*]

ȝatys n. *pl.* gates 151, 532, 857, etc. [OE. *gæt* (pl. *gatu*).]

ȝede pt. *sg.* went 240; *pt. pl.* 1674. [OE. *ēode.*]

ȝelde v. take vengeance on 542. [OE. *geldan.*]

ȝelle v. utter a loud cry 1486. [OE. *ȝellan.*]

ȝelowe adj. yellow 1544. [OE. *ȝeolu.*]

ȝeme v. govern, control. [OE. *ȝieman.*]

ȝerde n. branch of a tree 1516. [OE. **ȝiérd, ȝyrd, ȝird.*]

ȝerne adv. quickly 1950, 1959. [OE. *ȝéorne.*]

ȝylde v. yield 528; 1 *pr. pl.* 1208; **ȝyldyd** pt. *sg.* handed over 1226; *pr. subj. sg.* 1411; *pr. subj. pl.* 515; *ȝyldyd þe goost,* died 778. [OE. *geldan.*]

ȝynge adj. young 1391, 1568, 1731, etc. [OE. *ȝiong.*]

ȝyt *adv.* yet, still 5, 354, 697, etc. [OE. *gēt, gȳt.*]

ȝode *pt. sg.* went 606, 1610, 1627, etc. [Prob. altered form of OE.] See **ȝede.**

ȝonder *adj.* over there, away there 229. [ME *ȝonder, ȝender,* corresp. to OS. *gendra,* adj., on this side.]

ȝondur *adv.* there 815. [OS *gendra,* adj., on this side.]

ȝowle *n.* December or January 1895. [OE. *ȝeól.*]

H

habyte *n.* monastic habit 1910. [OFr. *(h)abit.*]

had. See **haue, have.**

hadyst. See **haue, have.**

hafte *n.* hilt of a knife 1634. [Merc. **heft* and ON. (cp. OI. *hepti*).]

hale. See **hole.**

halfe *n.* a half part of an object 358. [OE. *half.*]

halle *n.* royal residence 187, 337; large public room in a palace 192, 262, 325, etc.; **halles** *n. pl.* 295. [OE. *hal(l).* Also cp. OFr. *hale.*]

hals *n.* neck 1472, 2091. [OE. *hals.*]

hame, home *n.* a plot of enclosed ground, home 225, 265, 364, etc. [OE. *hām.*]

hamperde *pt. pl.* enclosed 1173. [? From ME. *hamper* n., a receptacle.]

hande, honde *n.* human hand 109, 161, 238, etc.; **handys, hondys** *n. pl.* 817, 836, 838, etc. [OE. *hónd, hánd* and ON. (cp. OI. *hönd*).]

handylde *pt. sg.* touched 2110. [OE. *handlian.*]

hange, hynge *v.* hang 1628, 1712,

1970; **hangyd** *pt. sg.* 1514, 1532, 2058; *pp.* 1747. [OE. *hangian* and ON. (cp. OI, *hengja*).]

happe *n.* luck, fortune 2106. [ON. (cp. OI. *happ*); also cp. OE. *gehæp* adj.]

happe *v.* embrace 112. [? Blend of ME. *lappen* and OFr. *happer,* to seize.]

harbarde, harberde *pt. sg.* sheltered 1969, 1985. [From ME. *herberwe* n. temporary dwelling. Also cp. OE. *herebeorgian,* to lodge.]

harburgens *n. pl.* coats or jackets of mail 637. [OFr. *hauberjon.*]

harburgerye *n.* temporary lodging-place 1758. [OFr. *herbergerie, herberge.* Cf. ME. *herberwe.*]

harde *adj.* difficult to bear, full of hardship 435; near, close by 562, 636, 676. [OE. *hearde.*]

harde. See **here.**

hardy *adj.* strong in battle, stout-hearted 6, 75, 545, etc. [OFr. *hardi.*]

hare *n.* hair of the head 87, 2058. [OE. *hēr* and ON. (cp. OI. *hár*).]

harme *n.* injury, damage 284, 1325. [OE. *hearm.*]

harnes *n.* body armour 104, 1046. [OFr. *harneis.*]

harpe *n.* harp 63, 1012. [OE. *hearpe* and OFr. *harpe.*]

harte *n.* heart of a human being or an animal 528, 754, 770, etc. [OE. *heorte.*]

harteblode *n.* lifeblood 633. [From *harte* and ME. *blod.*]

haste *n.* speed in phr., *in haste* 779, speedily 779. [Cp. OFr. *en haste.*]

haste. See **haue, have** .

hastely *adv.* quickly, in a hurry 210, 215, 223, etc. [From *haste.*]

hasty *adj.* swift, quick 73. [From *haste*.]

hastyd *pt pl.* hurried 1959. [OFr. *haster*.]

hate *adj.* high in temperature, hot 768. [OE. *hāt*.]

hath. See haue, have.

haue, have *v.* possess, own 81, 227, 266, etc.; *1 pr. sg.* have (an abstraction) 212, 400, 431; *pr. pl.* 932; *haue need*, to be under compulsion 230; *haue done*, to finish 210, 223; *finite v. as auxil. before pp.* 78, 106, 199, etc.; **haste** *2 pr. sg.* 1212, 1383, 1507, etc.; **hath** *3 pr. sg.* 355, 510, 556, etc.; **had(d)** *pt. sg.* 28, 71, 97, etc.; *pt. pl.* 263, 466, 680, etc.; **hadyst** *2 pt. sg.* 1747. [OE. *habban, haf-.*]

hauyn *n.* refuge 139. [OE. *hæfen*, port and ON. (cp. OI. *höfn*).]

hawkys *n. pl.* hawks 842, 1523. [Merc. *heafuc*.]

haylestones *n. pl.* hailstones 641. [OE. *hagol-stān*.]

haylsyd, haylese(y)d *pt. sg.* greeted (with respect) 193, 1714, 2000. [ON.; cp. OI. *heilsa*.]

he *pron.* he 22, 28, 36, etc.; *used indefinitely*: he that, he who, the one who 279, 1340; **hym** *acc. and dat.* him: *as object of a v. or prep.* 116, 120, 126, etc.; *dative of interest* 228; **hymselfe** himself: *emphatic pron. having same referent as subject* 374, 993; **hys** *adj.* his: *modifying a n. which denotes something owned or in one's charge* 74, 116, 117, etc.; *modifying a n. denoting a relation* 38, 72, 90; *modifying a n. denoting a part* 94, 95, 96. [OE. *hē*; *him*, dat.; *his*, gen.]

hed(d), hede *n.* human head 134, 181, 744, etc.; leader, chief 999,

1668; **hedys** *n. pl.* 640. [OE. *hēafod*.]

hede. See hed(d), hede.

hedeows *adj.* horrible 1657. [OFr. *hidous, hideus*.]

hedur *adv.* hither, here 254, 511. [OE. *hider*.]

hedurcome *n.* coming to this place 515. [From *hedur* adv. and *come* n.]

hedurward *adv.* in this direction 255. [OE. *hiderw(e)ard*.]

heere. See heyre.

heyle *v.* salute, hail 989. [From ME. *heil* adj., interj.]

heyre, heere *n.* heir 38, 651, 911, etc. [AF. *heir, aire*.]

helde *v.* move, go, 1713. [OE. *héldan*.]

helde *pt. pl.* contained 1380. [OE.; cp. A. *haldan* (*heold, halden*).]

hele *n.* health 1967. [OE. *hǣlu, hǣl*.]

hele *v.* cure, heal 1982, 2106; **helyd** *pt. sg.* 1922, 1942. [OE. *hǣlan*; ? also cp. OI. *heila*, to make whole.]

helyd. See hele.

helle *n.* hell 1487, 1669. [OE. *hel, helle*.]

helme *n.* helmet 1939. [OE. *helm* and ON. (cp. OI. *hjalmr*).]

helpe *n.* assistance 482, 489, 1847, etc. [OE. *help*.]

helpe *v.* to rescue, preserve 976; *God helpe . . .* 405. [OE. *helpan* and ON. (cp. OI. *hjālpa*).]

hende *adj.* courtly, refined 129, 226; near, close by 1800, 1998. [OE. *gehende*.]

hens *adv.* from this place, away 259. [From *henne* adv.]

hent(e) *pt. sg.* took hold of 238; *pt. pl.* arrived at (a place) 139, 587. [OE. *hentan*.]

herawde *n.* king's messenger 611. [AF. *heraud, herald*.]

here *adv.* in this place, here 1212, 1340, 1494, etc. [OE. *hēr.*]

here *v.* hear 411, 994, 1163, etc.; *imper.* 1855; **herde, harde** *pt. sg.* 70, 766, 1527, etc.; *pt. pl.* 856, 1457. [OE. *hēran.*]

hereynne *adv.* herein 1865. [OE. *hēr* + OE. *inn.*]

herytage *n.* inheritable property 1067. [OFr. *iretage, iritage, (h)eritage.*]

herkenyth *imper.* pay attention 20. [OE. *hercnian.*]

herte *n.* heart 1055, 1685. [OE. *heorte.*]

hete *n.* high body temperature 771. [OE. *hētu, hētē.*]

heuydd *n.* head 475, 1306. [OE. *hēafod.*]

heuyn *n.* heaven 65, 324, 482; **heuyn-trone** *n.* heaven's throne 1839, 2018. [OE. *heofon, heofen.*]

heuynkynge *n.* king of heaven 1371, 1725. [OE. *heofon-cyning.*]

hewe *n.* colour 990, 1261. [OE.; cp. Merc. *hēow, hīow, hīo*; Nth. *hīw.*]

hye *adj.* high, lofty 1144, 1299, 1747, etc.; *in hye* in haste 199, 1715; **hyest** *sup.* 1229. [OE. *hēh.*]

hye *v.* go quickly, travel rapidly 130, 199; **hyed** *pt. sg.* 1295, 1612, 1861; *pt. pl.* 1825, 1863. [OE. *hīgian.*]

hyely *adv.* high up 807. [From ME. *heigh* adj. and OE. *hēalīce.*]

hyght *pt. sg.* named 7, 626, 1519, etc.; promised 1118, 1346; *refl.* be named 13, 26, 118, etc.; **hyghtyst** *2 pt. sg.* called 1187. [OE. *hātan.*]

hyȝt, hyght *n.* height; *on hyȝt, vpon hyght adv. phr.* up high, aloft 472, 767. [OE. *hēhþo.*]

hylle *n.* hill 723, 807, 1746. [OE. *hyll.*]

hym. See he.

hymselfe. See he.

hynge. See hange.

hyppyng *pr. p.* limping, hobbling 1991. [OE. **hyppan.*]

hyred *pp.* (*pass.*) rented 1798. [OE. *hȳrian.*]

hys. See he.

hyt *pron.* it: *as sybject of v.* 295, 315, 335, etc.; *as object of v.* 333; *as a grammatical subject emphasising a clause which precedes hyt* 49; *pleonistic uses accompanying a subject emphasising a clause which precedes hyt* 4, 18, 20, etc.; *indefinite subject in impersonal constructions having to do with weather* 43, *with time* 377, 418, *with the actions of an indefinite agency* 404. [OE. *hit.*]

hodur *v.* cuddle, hug 112. [Cp. MnE. dial. *howder*, to huddle and LC. *hudern*, to shelter, cover.]

holde *n.* restraint 540, 864, 1173, etc.; *hath . . . in holde*, possesses 1329. [OE. *gehāld.*]

holde *v.* have in one's possession 975; keep 1205; *1 pr. sg.* consider 1692; *holde the stylle*, keep still, be silent 1749; **holdyst** *2 pr. sg.* 1187. [OE. *hāldan.*]

ho(o)le, hale, holy *adj.* healthy 57, 1130, 2032; cured 2033, 2111. [OE. *hāl.*]

holy *adj.* holy, divine 1034, 1124, 1459, etc. [OE. *hālig.*]

holy goost *n.* the third person of the Trinity 1676. [OE. *hālig gāst, sē hālga gāst.*]

home. See hame.

homecome *n.* homecoming, return 1742. [OE. *hōm-cŏme.*]

honde. See hande.

honowre *n.* honourable use 56; splendour 1228. [OFr. *hono(u)r.*]

hoole. See hale.

hoost *n.* army 959. [OFr.]

hope *n.* trust, confidence 212. [OE. *hopa.*]

hope *1 pr. sg.* hope 1725, 1835. [OE. *hopian.*]

hopyd *pt. sg.* hoped 1296. [OE. *hopian.*]

hopped *pt. pl.* bounced 640. [OE. *hoppian.*]

hors *n.* horse 584, 640, 926, etc.; horsys *n. pl.* 202, 1446. [OE. *hors.*]

horsyd *pt. sg.* helped (somebody) to mount a horse 703. [OE. *horsian.*]

hoscht *adj.* silent, quiet; *hoscht and stylle* 813. [Prob. imitative; cp. ME. *hissen* v.]

hoselde *pt. sg.* administered Holy Communion 776. [OE. *hūslian.*]

how *adv.* in which manner or way 795, 796, 1114, etc. [OE. *hū.*]

howndys *n. pl.* dogs used in hunting 842, 1523, 2059. [OE. *hund.*]

hows *n.* house, dwelling 446, 1484, 1755, etc. [OE. *hūs.*]

hundred, hu(o)ndurd *adj. card. num. as adj.* 83, 296, 338, etc.; *as noun* 189, 1046, 1066, etc.; hundurdys *n. pl.* 1133. [OE. *hundred* and ON. (cp. OI. *hundrað*).]

hungurd *pt sg.* suffered from hunger 1451. [OE. *hyngrian.*]

hur. See sche, she.

hurselfe. See sche, she.

I

i *n.* The Roman numeral for one, used alone and to form other numerals 2014, 2108, 1995, etc.

I *pron.* I 66, 212, 359, etc.; me *acc. and dat.* me: *direct obj.* 62, 76, 89, etc.; *governed by prep.* 111, 115, 401, etc.; *for the nom.* 113, 979; my *adj.* my 81, 108, 109, etc.; *as obj. of prep.* 2075; myn(e) *pron.* mine: *qualifying a following n.* 959, 1064, 1338, etc.; *qualifying a preceding n.* 2091 [OE. *ic, mē, mīn.*] See Y.

Y *pron.* I 40, 77, 78, etc. [OE. *ic.*] See I.

yen. See eye.

yf. See geue, geve.

yf *conj. (usually with subj.)* if 91, 214, 241, etc. [OE. *gef, gi(e)f.*]

ylle *adv.* cruelly 726; ill 739, 804, 834, etc.; badly 1418. [ON. *illr*; *illa* adv.]

in *adv.* within 3, 334, 337, etc.; surrounded by 1443; *fig. context:* in state of 499, 513, 885, etc.; clad in 104, 155, 178, etc.; during the period 254, 275, 459, etc. [OE. *inn.*]

yn *adv.* in 151, 314, 727, etc. [OE. *innan,* prep., adv.; *inne* adv.]

in *prep.* within 42, 46, 54, etc.; enclosed in 161, 187, 323, etc.; clothed in 398, 866, 1046. [OE. *in* and L. *in* and ON. (cp. OI. ī).]

yn *prep.* in 91, 1344. [OE. *in.*]

yngynes *n. pl.* engines of war 859. [a. OFr. *engin.*]

ynne *n.* lodging, *they toke ther ynne* they took up their quarters 447. [OE. *inn.* n.]

ynogh *adj.* enough 400, 2010. [OE. *ʒenōh.*] See ynowe.

ynowe *adj. pl.* of 'enough' 143. [OE. *ʒenōh.*]

insondur *adv.* separately 47, 1327, 1632, etc. [From ME. phr. *in sonder.*]

into *prep.* into (a liquid) 131; into (an enclosed space) 191, 192, 199, etc. [OE. *inn to.*]

yre *n.* anger 499, 658. [OFr. *ire.*]

yron *n.* iron 1335. [OE. *īren.*]

js *3 pr. sg.* as copula or auxiliary with *pp.* 437. [OE. *is.*]

ys *3 pr. sg.* is 79, 80, 107, etc. [OE. *is.*]

yssewed *pt. pl.* came out (of persons), *yssewed out* 458. [From OFr. *issu*, pp. of *issir.*]

yvore *n.* ivory 598. [OFr. *ivoire.*]

ywroght *pp.* formed 1625. [OE. ȝe-*worht*, pp. of ȝe*wyrcan.*]

J

juste *v.* fight with spear or lance on horseback with another knight 459, 672. [OFr. *jo(u)ster, juster.*]

K

keye *n.* key 1225. [OE. *cæg.*]

kene *adj.* bold 6, 788, 1089; sharp-pointed 1321. [OE. *cēne.*]

kenne *v.* give instruction to (n.) 1564; kende *pt. pl.* knew 2184. [OE. *cennan*; senses influenced by ON. (cp. OI. *kenna*).]

kepe *v.* contain (persons), hold 141, 540, 597, etc.; *fig.* preserve 209, 1031, 1061, etc.; *imper.* 533, 535; kepyd, kept *pt. sg.* kept (n. in a certain state) 57; *pt. pl.* 2163; *pt. sg.* preserved 1325. [OE. *cēpan.*]

kydde, kythe *n.* offspring 1234; homeland 2043. [OE. *cȳþ, cȳþþu.*]

kynde *n.* natural disposition, temperament 2169. [OE. (ge)*cȳnd.*]

kyndely *adv.* courteously, pleasantly 1313. [Cp. OE. (ge)*cȳnd elīce.*]

kyndylde *pp. fig.* caused, produced 2015. [From ME. *kindel* v.]

kyndyst *sup. adj.* (heir) having most rights by birth, most

lawful (heir) 1257. [Cp. OE. (ge)*cȳnde.*]

kynge *n.* king 406, 415, 553, etc.; kynges, kyngys *n. pl.* 187, 509, 916. [OE. *cyning.*]

kynne *n.* race, clan, family 122, 444, 1266, etc. [OE. *cyn.*]

kyns *suff.* combining with no (*no-kyns*, 2017) *to form adj. denoting* no certain . . ., no specific . . . [OE. *nanes cynnes.*]

kyrke *n.* entire community of Christians; also, church of Rome 1804; *holy kyrke* 1034. [OE. *cir(i)ce* and ON. *kirkja.*]

kyrtell *n.* cloak or coat for men 1644. [OE. *cyrtel.*]

kyste *pt. sg.* kissed 1803. [OE. *cyssan.*]

kythe. See kydde.

knagg *n.* peg, fastener 1793. [Cp. E.Fris. *knagge*, Sw. *knagg*, Dan. *knage.*]

knaue, knave *n.* servant 1721, 1751, 1774, etc. [OE. *cnafa* (? Merc. **cneafa*), infl. *cnafan.*]

knee *n.* knee 951. [OE. *cnēo(w).*]

knelyd *pt. sg.* knelt 951, 1903. [OE. *cneowlian.*]

knewe *pt. sg.* knew 2010; *pt. pl.* 2017. [OE. *cnāwan.*]

knyfe *n.* knife 1624, 1650, 2077. [Late OE. (from ON.) *cnif* and ON. (cp. OI. *knīfr*).]

knyght *n.* a noble warrior 23, 473, 484, etc.; knyghtys, knyȝtys *p. pl.* 4, 166, 229, etc. [OE. *cniht*; pl. *cnihtas.*]

knighthedd *n.* skill in fighting 425. [From ME. *knight* and -*hēd(e)* suff.; cp. OE. *cnihthād.*]

knyghtly *adv.* in a warlike manner 712. [From *knyght n.*]

knok *v.* attack or injure (n.), fight 281. [OE. *cnucian* and *cnocian* and ON. (cp. OI. *knoka*).]

knowyn *pp.* known about 891. [OE. *cnāwan.*]

L

lace *n.* noose, snare 1815. [OFr. *laz, las.*]

lad(d). See **lede.**

lady *n.* consort of a ruler 28, female head of a household 213, 824, 971, etc.; **ladyes** *n. pl.* 566, 832. [OE. *hlǣfdige.*]

lagh, lawe *v.* laugh 290, 1767; **loghe** *pt. sg.* 2019. [OE. *hlæhhan.*]

lande, londe *n.* earth 3, 717, 1258; *fig.* domain 362, 1199, 1211; property 1227, 1236; **landys, londys** *n. pl.* properties 220, 359, 829, etc. [OE. *land, lond.*]

lappe *1 pr. sg., refl.* me *lappe,* I wrap myself 113. [From ME. *lappe* n., loose sleeve.]

large *adj.* spacious 1175. [L. *larga.*]

lasse. See **lesse.**

laste *adj. sup.* latest; *in phr. at the* (*þe*) *laste* finally at last 855, 917, 2180; *to the laste* every bit, to the last detail 2046. [Prob. from adv. Also cp. OE. *læt* adj. and *lætest.*]

laste *v.* endure 1410. [OE. *lǣstan.*]

lawe *n.* law 261. [OE. *lagu*; cp. OI. *lög* pl., from **lagu.*]

lawe *v.* See **lagh, lawe.**

lawmpe *n.* lamp 1645. [L. *lampas.*]

lay *v.* set watch, *wach . . . lay* 1358; *1 pr. sg.* wager, bet 737, 808; *3 pr. sg.* exposes (himself) to view 394, 478; **leyde** *pt. sg.* set watch 740, placed 1547; *pt. pl.* 1600; *pp.* laid out (corpse) 1088; **layned** *pt. pl.* put (something) upon the ground 799; **layeng** *pr. p.* overthrowing 729. [OE. *lecgan.*]

layne *v.* grant the loan of, forgive 1283, 1587, 1617. [f. ME. *loan* n.]

leche *n.* physician 1942. [OE. *lǣce.*]

led(d). See **lede.**

lede *n.* man 716. [OE. *lēod.*]

lede *n.* direction, guidance 249. [From **lede** v.]

lede *v.* conduct, guide 802, 1559, 1665, etc.; pass (one's life) 876; **le(e)de** *3 pr. sg.* 817; *pr. pl.* 229; **lad(d), led(d)** *pt. sg.* 161, 764, 1415, etc.; *pt. pl.* 133, 1228, 2171. [OE. *lǣdan.*]

le(e)de. See **lede.**

leen *v.* grant temporary possession of a thing 791. [OE. *lǣnan.*]

lees *n.* property, protection 940. [a. AF. *les.*]

lees *n.* leash 1318. [OE. *leas.*]

leest *n.* lowest in power or position 1013. [OE. *lǣst.*]

leeve *n.* permission 2134. [OE. *lēaf.*]

lefe *adv.* willing 1244; *adj. absol., esp. in for lief or loath* 1490; *quasi-n.* friend 1720. [OE. *lēof, līof.*]

lefte. See **le(e)ue.**

leyȝtenyng *n.* lightning 1642. [Special use of ME. *lightening.*]

lele *adj.* loyal 988, 1966. [OFr. *leal,* AF. *leël.*]

leman, lemman *n.* sweetheart 1829, 1988, 1594. [Early ME. *leofmon.*]

lende *v.* go, depart 1056. [OE. *lendan.*]

lene *v.* grant the temporary possession of (a thing) 1458; **lente** *pp.* 2136. [OE. *lǣnan.*]

lenger *adv.* longer 1018, 1047, 1530. [OE. *lengra, lengre.*]

lenkyth *n.* length 1175. [OE. *lengþu.*]

lente. See **lene.**

lepe *pr. pl.* rise up; *pt. sg.* 586, 963; sprang upon (a horse's saddle) 1529; *pt. pl.* rose up 1019. [OE. *hlēapan (hlēop, hlupon)*.]

lere *v.* teach 417, 1215; **lerydd** *pp.* 1316. [OE. *lǣran*.]

lerne *v.* teach 420, 464, 1565, etc. [OE. *leornian*.]

lesynge *n.* lie 1292. 1374, 1567, etc. [OE. *lēasing*.]

lesse, lasse *adj.* comp. of little, not so much 449, 2125, 2149; **leste** *sup.* slightest 962. [OE. *lǣs* adv., *lǣssa* adj.]

leste *adj.* slightest 962. [OE. *lǣssa, lǽs(es)t*.]

let *n.* stoppage 722. [From **let** v.]

let *v.* allow 949, 1402; *pt. sg.* 2067, 207; *let awt,* allowed to go 1369; *pt. pl.* let . . . *be,* left undisturbed 1188; *imper.* 557, 695, 889, etc. *let be,* leave undisturbed 789. [OE. *lǣtan, lētan*.]

leve *n.* permission asked for or granted 960; *toke ther leue,* departed (with expression of farewell) 285, 2139, 2159. [OE. *lēaf*.]

le(e)ue *v.* subsist 932, live 1838; **leuyd** *pt. sg.* 717; *pt. pl.* 941; **leu(e)yng** *pr. p. adj.* living 1720, 1897, 1908. [OE. *libban*.]

le(e)ve *v.* depart 439, 1633; leave alone, depart from 1730; *pr. pl.* 234, 793; **leuyth** *3 pr. sg.* 885; **lefte** *2 pt. sg.* 1219; *pt. pl.* 1334; *pt. sg.* abandoned 1484, 1531, 1098; *pt. pl.* 521; *pp.* abandoned 1003; remained 1030; (*pass.*) 496; **leuyd** *pt. sg.* left, caused to remain 1049. [OE. *lǣfan*.]

leuyr *adv. in construction with* '*have*': *had leuyr,* would rather have 245, 941, 1453, etc. [OE. *lēof, līof*.]

lewde *adj.* unlettered 1316. [OE. *lǣwede*.]

lye, lygg *v.* lean 171, to lie (in bed) 247, 108, 207, etc.; **lygge** *pr. pl.* dwell?; **lay(e)** *pt. sg.* was situated 1414, 1603, 1932; lay (dead) 1092; slept 1637, 1773; *pt. pl.* 1566; **layne, leyn** *pp.* slept (with) 688; slept (by) 1071, 1438, 1496, etc.; **lygyng** *pr. p.* 1303. [OE. *licgan*.]

lyfe *n.* life 29, 222, 510, etc. **lyuys** *n. pl.* 476, 656. [OE. *līf*.]

lyfte *pt. sg.* raised 767. [ON. *lypta*.]

lyght *v.* descend (from a horse) 399; *1 pr. pl.* 1420; *pt. sg.* set burning 1645; **lyghtyd** *pt. sg.* 1504. [OE. *līhtan*.]

lyghtly *adv.* cheerfully 2019, foolishly 912. [OE. *lě(o)htlice,* f. *lěoht*.]

lyghtnes *n.* brightness 184, 393. [OE. *līhtnes*.]

lyke *adj.* having the same characteristics, like 18, 1808, 1991. [Early ME. *lich, līk* (? late OE. **līc*).]

lykeande *pr. p. adj.* agreeable 1890. [f. ME. *lyke* v.] See **lykyng.**

lykyd *pt. sg.* was pleased 739, 834, 2041, etc.; *pt. pl.* 804, 1179. [OE. *lician*.]

lykyng *n.* pleasure (sensual) 1309, 1444, 1499. [OE. *licung*.]

lykyng *pr. p. adj.* agreeable 519. [f. ME. *lyke* v. + *ing*.] See **lykeande.**

lylly *n.* lily 901, 1024, 1538. [OE. *lilie*.]

lyme *n.* cement used in building; usually coupled with stone; *lyme and stane* 1146. [OE. *līm*.]

lymmes *n. pl.* limbs 2028. [OE. *lim*.]

lyon *n.* lion 335, 423, 427, etc. [L. *leo, leōnem*.]

lyppes *n. pl.* lips 96. [OE. *lippa*.]

lyste *pt. sg.* paid attention 290. [OE. *hlystan*.]

lyter *n.* a framework supporting a bed 1547. [AF. *litere*, OFr. *litiere*.]

lytyll *adv.* little 608, 706, 1520, etc. [OE. *lȳtel*.]

lythe *adj.* supple 841. [OE. *lȳðe*.]

lythe *v.* listen 40, 1189. [ON. *hlýða*.]

lyþys *n. pl.* warm shelters 1118. [? var. of ME. *lewth*.]

lyve *n.* life; *used in phrase*: *sworne . . . be lyve*, sworn . . . with one's life 992. [OE. *līf*.]

lyue *adj.* alive, living 1049; *attrib. use in on lyue*, alive 662. [OE. *on life*.]

lofe *n.* loaf 1453, 1465. [OE. *hlāf*.]

logge *n.* temporary dwelling 1436. [OFr. *loge*, *loige*, arbour, hut.]

logyd *pt. sg.* dwelt 874; *pp. (pass.)* has his abode 437. [OFr. *logier*.]

loke *v. fig.* to turn or fix one's regard 235, 237; *imper.* see, find out 726; behold 852; **loky(e)d** *pt. sg.* looked 706, 742; *pt. pl.* 1818, 1897. [OE. *lōcian*.]

longe *adj.* long, with reference to duration 311, 874, 1309, etc. [OE. *lang, long*.]

longe *v.* depart 1828. [OE. *langian*.]

longyth *pr. pl.* belong 321. (Aphet. f. OE. *ȝelang*, at hand.]

loone *n.* gift 1914. [a. ON. *lán*.]

loouyd. See **loue**.

lorde *n.* lord, one who has dominion 161, 276, 298, etc.; **lordys** *n. pl.* 74, 121, 169, etc. [OE. *hlāford*.]

lore *n.* learning, scholarship 176, 1215. [OE. *lār*.]

lorne *pp.* lost 510, 827, 1358. [ME. *leese* v.]

lose *n.* fame, reputation 753. [OFr. *los*.]

lose *v. intr.* perish 453. [OE. *losian*.]

lose *v. tr.* destroy, be the ruin of 222; be deprived of 1857; **loste** *pt. sg.* 29, 753; *pp.* 1119, 1868, 2006, etc. [OE. *losian*.]

lothe *n.* harm, injury 1490. [OE. *lāð*, orig. neut. of adj. *lāð*, loath.]

lothe *adj.* reluctant, unwilling 1126, 1244, 1460, etc. [OE. *lāð*.]

loudyng *pr. p.* praising 1881. [L. *laudare*.]

loue *n.* a beloved person 643; *in religious sense, applied to paternal affection of God: For godys love* 1287, 1570. [OE. *lufu*.]

loue *v.* hold dear 1104. *3 p. sg.* 302; **loou(e)yd** *pt. sg.* praised 704, 1904; *pt. pl.* 2149, 2161; **loueyng** *pr. p.* 1914. [OE. *lufian*.]

louely *n.* beautiful person 1815. [See **louely** adj.]

louely *adj.* beautiful 113. [OE. *luflic*, f. *lufu*, love n. + *lic*, *-ly*.]

lowde *adj.* loud 2036. [OE. *hlūd*.]

lowsyd *pt. pl.* set free 1543. [f. *loose* adj.]

M

M¹ *abbrev.* Roman numeral symbol for a thousand 571.

ma. See **moo**.

madde *adj.* mad, insane 554. [Aphet. OE. *gemǣd(e)d*.]

made. See **make**.

madyste. See **make**.

mageste *n.* greatness and glory of God 483, 1443. [a. OFr. *majestét*.]

may(e) *n.* maiden 71, 349, 525, etc. [OE. *mǣȝden*.]

may *1 pr. sg.* can, may: *auxil. of predication with a following simple infin.* 66, 828, 912, etc.; *2 pr. sg.* 1405, 1855; *3 pr. sg.*

209, 828; *pr. pl.* 486, 1189, 1896; *pr. subj. sg.* 942; *with ellipsis of 'do'*, 680; *God . . . all may* 736. [OE. *mæʒ (maʒon, meahte)*.]

maydyn *n.* maiden 520, 565, 574, etc.; **maydyns** *n. pl.* 757, 809, 1391. [OE. *mæʒden*.]

maydynhedd, -hede *n.* virginity 1857, 1868, 2051. [f. **maydyn** + ME. *hedd*.]

maye *n.* May. [OFr. *Mai* and L. *Maium*.]

mayne *n.* power; *wyth myʒt and mayne* 2161. [OE. *mæʒen*.]

mayntene *v.* defend, protect 883. [ME. *maintene, -teine*, f. OFr. *maintenir*.]

maystr *n.* master 2180. [OE. *mæʒester, maʒister*.]

maystres *n.* mistress, as a title of courtesy prefixed to the Christian name 820. [OFr. *maistresse*.]

make *n.* mate 881. [OE. *ʒemaca*.]

make *v.* cause to become 847; bring into existence 1495, 1664, 2119; *pr. subj. sg.* 91; **makyste** *2 pr. sg.* cause to become 1413; **makyth** *3 pr. sg.* causes to become 2004; *the boke makyth mynde*, the book records 2166; **madyste** *2 pt. sg. const. infin. with 'to'* 1217; **made** *pt. sg.* made 416; caused (something to happen) 416; brought into existence 647, 1292, 1416, etc.; *const. inf. with 'to'* 988, 1084, 1108, etc.; caused to become 1122, 1317, 1479, etc.; produced (a sound) 1350; composed of 1146; *pt. pl.* made 144; caused to become 692; *const. inf. with 'to': made to crye* had announced 551, *made . . . to dye* caused to die 713 (also 785, 864); produced (a

sound) 554; *pp. (pass.)* made 159, 309; caused to become 1824, 1911; *pp.* brought into existence 1824; **makeyng** *pr. p.* bringing into existence 168. [OE. *macian*.]

makeynge. See **make**.

makyste. See **make**.

makyth. See **make**.

man, mon *n.* human being (irrespective of sex or age) 51, 65, 68, etc.; adult male person 14, 353, 554, etc.; *n. pl.* 816; **men** *n. pl.* human beings (irrespective of sex or age) 1, 62, 135, etc.; adult males 365, 371, 398, etc. [OE. *man(n), mon(n)*.]

maner(e) *n.* species, kind, sort. Often with ellipsis of *of* 1002; customary mode of acting 2001. [a. AF. *manere*.]

manhode *n.* qualities becoming a man; manliness, courage, valour 417. [OE. *man(n), mon(n)* + *hood*.]

many, mony *adj.* many, *used distributively with a sg.: many a oon*, many a person 21, 51, 68, etc.; *with 'an' or 'a' prefixed to the n.:* 92, 222, 332, etc.; many, a great number of 872, 1049, 1278, etc.; *placed after the n.: odur many* 170; *any many* 1569; *n.* 303. [OE. *maniʒ, moniʒ*.]

manly *adv.* courageously 541. [f. *man* n. + *ly*; OE. *mannlice*.]

mantell *n.* sleeveless cloak 1323. [OE. *mentel* and OFr. *mantel*.]

mare, more *adj.* more, greater in number or amount 84, 438, 674; *absol. and quasi-n. in the sense 'greater': more and lesse* 449, *the more and the mynne* 549, 2037 = persons of all ranks; all without exception; something that is more 1008. [OE. *māra*.]

G

mare, more *adv.* again 1571; more 1579; chiefly with prefixed word *no more (mare)* 690, 1717, *euyrmore* 956, *neuyrmare* 1423. [OE. *māra*.]

marynere *n.* sailor 1784, 1814, 1835, etc. [a AF. *mariner*.]

marred *pt. sg.* hindered, interfered with 863. [OE. *merran*.]

masse *n.* Eucharistic service 1805, 1997, 1999. [OE. *mæsse*.]

maste *n.* mast 1826, 1861. [OE. *mæst*.]

mate *adj.* overcome 771. [OE. a. OFr. *mat* (at chess).]

matrymony *n.* action of marrying 1137. [a. OFr. *matremoine*.]

me. See **I.**

mede *n.* duty; *Euyll quytt he . . . hys mede*, He did his duty poorly 715; reward 1671. [OE. *mēd*.]

medowe *n.* any tract of grass land 382, 399, 419. [OE. *mǣdive*.]

meene *1 pr. sg.* intend 2182. [OE. *mǣnan*.]

meete *v.* meet, encounter 1995; **mete** *pr. pl.* come upon 850; **mett** *pt. sg.* met 628, 728; *pt. pl.* 652. [OE. *mētan*.]

meyne *n.* body of retainers 1396, 1402, 1526. [a. OFr. *meyné*, *mesne*.]

meke *adj.* gentle, courteous 32. [Early ME. *meoc*, a. ON. *miuk-r*.]

mekenes *n.* gentleness of spirit 426. [From *meke* + *nes*.]

mekyll *adj.* great, *in various applications* 67, 273, 299, etc. [OE. *micel*.]

men. See **man.**

mercy *n.* compassion 1193, 1853. [a. OFr. *merci*.]

merye *adj.* joyous 1764. [OE. *myr(i)ȝe*.]

mesell(e) *n. fig.* foul person 2021, 1965. [a. OF. *mesel*, leprous, leper.]

message *n.* the carrying of a communication; a mission 123. [a. OFr. *message*.]

messengere *n.* messenger 1258; **messengerys** *n. pl.* 154, 190, 232, etc. [ME. *messager*, *-ier* (OFr. also *messagier*).]

mete *n.* dinner 522; food 879, 1009, 1462, etc. [OE. *mete*.]

mete *v.* See **meete.**

mett. See **meete.**

mewse *v.* ponder 332. [a. *Fr. muser*.]

my. See **I.**

myddyl *n.* the middle point 604. [OE. *middel*, *midl* adj., also n. masc. by ellipsis of *dǣl*, part.]

myddys *prep.* midst 337, 343, 612. [Evolved from ME. *in-middes*, *on-middas*.]

myght *n.* bodily strength 45, 1287; power 1500; **mytghys** *n. pl.* (Of God): with reference to commanding influence 1675, 1832. [OE. *miht*.]

myght *pt. sg.* could: expressing ability or power 65, 368, 501, etc.; *pt. pl.* 135, 332, 339, etc.; *pt. subj. sg. expressing subjective possibility (with infin.)* 539, 623, 735; *pt. subj. pl.* 196, 1053; *pt. subj. sg. statement of future contingency deemed improbable: myȝt Y come*, If I might 1738; *used with infin. to convey a suggestion* 312. [OE. *mæȝ (maȝon meahte)*.] See **may.**

myghtfull *adj.* mighty 1443. [From *myght* n. + *-full*.]

mykyll. See **mekyll.**

mylde *adj.* Of a person's disposition: kind 32, 565, 1500: low 481; quiet, kind (general application) 1510, 1763, 1904. [OE. *milde.*]

myle *n.* miles (*sg. form used with a pl. number: Syxty myle* 376). [OE. *mīl.*]

myn(e). See **I.**

mynne *adj.* less. Always coupled with *more, mare* 549, 2037. [a. ON. *minne.*] See **more, mare.**

mynstralcy *n.* practice of playing and singing 1010; *Makeyng sweete mynstraley,* making sweet music 168. [ad. OFr. *menestralsie -trancie.*]

mynstrals *gen. n. pl.* minstrelss', singerss' 2155. [a. OFr. *menestral.*]

myrakyls *n. pl.* miracles 872. [a. OFr. *miracle.*]

myrthe *n.* musical entertainment 2155. [OE. *myrgþ.*]

mystyr *n.* need 97, 512. [a. OFr. *mestier, mester.*]

mode *n.* fierce courage 603; humour, disposition 1510. [OE. *mōd.*]

modur *n.* feeling, *in phr.*: *mode and mayne* 291. [OE. *mōd.*]

modur *n.* mother 409, 936, 1915. [OE. *mōdor.*]

molde *n.* earth, ground 1946; *vpon molde,* in the world 158. [OE. *molde.*]

mo(o)ne *n.* complaint, lamentation 467, 1350. [OE. **mān, rel.* to *mǣnan* v.]

monythys *n. pl.* months 358. [OE. *mōnað.*]

moo *adj.* more 572, 1212; *n.* the greater 1079; **ma** *adv.* more, to a greater extent 1104. [OE. *mā.*] Cp. **mare, more.**

moone *n.* moon 1833. [OE. *mōna.*]

moost, moste *absol.* (*quasi-n.*) greatest persons. *Usually in association with leest: moost and leest* 1013; *adj.* greatest, with

reference to power 1287, 1675. [OE. *mǣst.*]

more. See **mare.**

morne *n.* morning 454, 501, 805, etc. [OE. *morȝen* (inflected also *morȝn-, morn-*).]

morne *v.* grieve 543; **mornyd** *pt. sg.* grieved 291. [OE. *murnan.*]

mornetyde *n.* the morning. [OE. *morȝen* (inflected also *morȝn-, morn-*) + *tyde.*]

mornyng *pr. p. adj.* sorrowing, lamenting 812. [f. ME *morne* v. + *yng.*]

mornynge *n.* morning 1390. [ME. *morivening, morning,* f. *morwen, morne* + *yng.*]

moste. See **moost.**

mote *pr. subj. sg.* In *wishes forming a periphrastic subj.:* **may:** *mote Y the . . .* 668, 724, 1186, etc.; *pr. subj. pl.* **mote** *yow befalle . . .* 198. [OE. *mōt.*]

mownt *n.* mountain. *Used in proper names of mountains: Mownt Devyse* 986. [OE. *munt.*]

mowthe *n.* mouth 1606, 1609, 1618. [OE. *mūþ.*]

muste *1 pr. sg.* must: *used to express a certain futurity* 979; *3 pr. sg.* 2039, 2071; *pr. pl.* 224, 669, 672; *imper.* 1193, 1238. [OE. *mōste,* pl. *mōston,* pt. of *mōt.*]

N

nay *adv.* nay, no: *introductory word, without direct negation* 559, 1198, 1705; *used to express negation* 1422, 2100; *to seye hur nay* to make denial to her 1727, *sche seyde nay* she made denial 1846, 1907. [a. ON. *nei.*]

nakyd *adj.* unsheathed (sword) 1426; unclothed 1517. [OE. *nacod.*]

name *n.* name 1184; *n. pl.* 2146. [OE. *nama, noma.*]

nane. See **none.**

narowe *adj.* narrow 2030. [OE. *nearu, nearo.*]

nave *n.* fleet 1246. [a. OFr. *navie.*]

ne *conj.* nor: *following a negative clause* 351; *adv.* not: simple negative 1952. [OE. *ne, ni.*]

nede *n.* need; *in phr.* haue nede, require 230; necessity 1854. [OE. *nēd.*]

nede *adv.* (*with 'must'*) necessarily, of necessity 2071. [OE. *nēde, nēdes.*]

nede *pt. sg.* stood in need of, required 1553, 879. [OE. *nēdian*, f. *nēd* n.]

neeve *n.* fist 1634. [ad. ON. *hnefi, nefi.*]

nere *adv.* close 217, 377, 457, etc.; almost 658, 875, 921, etc.; *in phr.* far and neer 891. [a. ON. *nær.*]

nerre *adj. comp.* nearest 1036. [OE. *nērra*, comp. of *nēh.*]

neuer. See **neuyr.**

neuyn *v.* mention 64. [a. ON. *nefna.*]

neuyr, neuer *adv.* never, at no time 3, 5, 54, etc. [OE. *nǣfre*, f. *ne + ǣfre.*]

newe *adj.* new 984, 1200, 1235, etc. [OE. *nēowe.*]

newe *adv.* newly, recently 936. [OE. *nēowe.*]

nygh *adv.* near: *in predicative use with the v. 'to be'* 217. [OE. *nēh.*]

nyght *n.* night 159, 402, 535, etc.; **nyghtys** *n. pl.* 1109, 1355. [OE. *niht, næht.*]

nyghtyd *pp.* (*pass.*) overtaken by night 1435. [From the n.]

no *adj.* not any 65, 153, 266, etc. [OE. *nān.*]

no *adv.* no: *used to express a negative reply to a question* 1430.

[Southern and midland form of OE. *nā.*]

nobull, nubull *adj.* illustrious 55, 122, 197, etc.; splendid, impressive 1694. [a. OFr. *noble.*]

nodur *conj.* neither 746, 1012, 1442; *pron.* neither (of two persons) 1877. [OE. *nowðer.*]

noght *adv.* not at all 269; not 351, 556, 1049, etc.; *n.* nothing 907, 932, 1769. [OE. *nōwiht*, f. *ne + awiht.*]

nome *v. intr.* go, pass 254. [Var. of ME. *nyme* v. by assimilation to the pt. forms.]

nomore *n.* nothing more 66. [From OE. *nā + more* n.]

none *n.* midday 1377. [OE. *nōn* neut.]

none, nane, noon *pron.* not any 18, 260, 1010, etc.; no one 1923, 1469, 1705, etc. [OE. *nān*, f. *ne + ān.*]

nonne *n.* nun 1911, 1913, 1951, etc.; **nonnes** *n. pl.* 1889, 1924, 2130. [OE. *nunne.*]

nonnery *n.* a place of residence for nuns 1961. [Prob. ad. AF. **nonnerie*, f. *nonne*, nun n.]

nonnes. See **nonne.**

noon. See **none.**

noonre *n.* nunnery 1882. [prob. ad. AF. **nonnerie.*]

nor *conj.* nor 4, 159, 390. etc. [Prob. a cont. of ME. *nother.*]

norysch *v.* nurture 56. [ad. OFr. *noris(s), nuris(s).*]

northweste *adv.* north-west 2102. [f. OE. *norð, norþ + OE. west.*]

nose *n.* nose 1609. [OE. *nosu.*]

not *adv.* not: *following the v.* 39, 80, 249, etc.; *following an auxil.* 77, 273, 432, etc.; *preceding infin.* 23, 1314; *with adverbs* 214; *after 'or'* 272; *with terms of number: not oon* 1140. [Abbrev. of ME. *nought* adv.]

nothynge *adv.* not at all 1407. [From *no* adj. + *thynge*.]

now(e) *adv.* now, at the present time, 210, 403, 841, etc. [OE. *nū*.]

nowmberde *pt. pl.* amounted to 571. [ad. OFr. *nombrer*.]

nubull. See **nobull.**

O

odur, odyr, oþer *adj.* other 260, 341, 371, etc.; *pron. eyther odur, eyder odur* one another 47, 1450; *odur many*, many other 170, other persons 1147; *odur day* another day 1231; *feyreste of odur* fairest of any 1250; *oon aftur odur* one after another 1830. [OE. *oþer, oðer*.]

of *prep.* of: *indicating origin or source* 4, 8, 10, etc.; *indicating the cause of an action, feeling, etc.* 31; *introducing the agent after a pass. v.* 104; *indicating the material or substance of which anything consists* 14, 86, 98, etc.; *after intr. verbs especially those of learning, knowing, hearing* 41, 59, 63, etc.; *indicating a distinguishing mark by which a person or thing is characterised* 184, 185, 349, etc.; *in partitive expression* 195, 347; *in the sense of 'belonging to' or 'pertaining to'* 169, 176, 257, etc. [OE. *of.*]

offyce *n.* public service 1235. [a. AF. and OFr. *office*.]

ofte *adv.* many times 76, 1324, 1428, etc. [OE. *oft*.]

oght *pt. sg.* owed 1983; *pt. pl.* owned 650. [OE. *āhte*.]

olde *adj.* old 208, 580, 1064, etc.; of any specified age 61, 83; great, grand (after *gode*) 681; *n.* 870, 981, 1731, etc. [OE. *ald*.]

oldely *adv.* in the manner of one who is old 248. [*olde* + *ly*.]

on *adv. used idiomatically:* ... *mewse on* 332; movement into a position above 472. [OE. *on*].

on *prep.* upon 181, 310, 381, etc.; *expressing contact with any surface* 249, 478; *expressing position with reference to a place* 362, 477, 551, etc.; *indicating the day of an occurrence* 29, 377, 418, etc.; *of state or condition on blode* 609, *on lyue* 662, 1049. [OE. *on.*]

ones, oones, -ys *adv.* at one time 2072; *preceded by a prep.: at ones* 190, 340; under any circumstances 1557; *oones on a day* one day 418. [OE. *ānes.*]

ony *adj.* any 1033, 1906. [OE. *ǣnig.*] See **any.**

onslayne *pp.* made assault 496. [*on slay.*]

oon *num. adj.* one 2, 881, 887, etc.; *pron.* a person 7, 343, 378, etc.; *after pronominal adj. without a contextual reference: many a oon* 21, 873, 1674; *many oon* 476, 701, 785; *oon aftur odur*, one after another 1830; *everyoon* 155; a single person 1140; a single thing 1246, 2128, 2152. [OE. *ān.*]

oones, -ys. See **ones.**

oost, oste *n.* host 448, 606, 625, etc. [OFr. *host.*] See **host.**

openyd *pt. pl.* opened 1222. [OE. *openian.*]

openlye *adv.* without concealment, so that all may hear 1925, 2035. [*open* adj. + *lye*.]

or *prep.* before 272, 357, 358, etc. [OE. *ār* adv. The sense is that of the comparative, OE. *ǣr.*]

or *conj.* or 1, 116, 227, etc. [Phonetically reduced form of ME. *odur* conj.]

ordeygn *v.* furnish 1013; **ordeygned**

pt. sg. ordered 365, 1396; *pt. pl.* prepared 877; *pp.* prepared 1087. [a. OFr. *ordener.*]

ore *n.* oar 1989, 2104. [OE. *ār.*]

os *conj.* as 464. [contr. OE. *ealswā.*] See **as.**

oste. See **oost.**

ostes *n.* hostess 448. [OFr. *hôtesse.*] See **hostess.**

othe *n.* promise 1127, 1489, 1495; **othys** *n. pl.* acts of swearing 355. [OE. *āþ.*]

oþer. See **odur.**

ouer, -yr *adv.* on the other side 329, over 1040; across 1114; surpassing 1942. [OE. *ofer* adv. and prep.]

ouyr *prep.* across 88, 132, 137, etc.; over 475, 1746. [OE. *ofer.*]

ouyrend *n.* top 600. [**ouyr** + ME. *end* n.]

ouyrmore *adv.* moreover, furthermore 956. [*ouyr* adv. + *more* adv.]

ouyrnyght *adv.* night before 1393. [*ouyr* prep. + *nyght* n.]

own *adj.* own: *used after possessive case or adj. to emphasise possessive meaning* 647, 801, 1691, etc. [OE. *āȝen.*]

owre. See **we.**

owt(e) *adv.* out 53, 171, 314, etc.; through 463; from 625; *with ellipsis of intr. v., functioning as a v. without inflexion: Mylys owte wyth a swyrde,* Mylys drew out a sword 1321; *from a contained condition into one of accessibility hys nose braste owt on blood* 1609, *The tethe be smetyn owt of my mowþe* 1618, *broght owt of . . . bale* 2033, etc. [OE. *ūte.*]

owt *v. intr.* to go out 710, 1172. [OE. *ūtan.*]

owttakyn *pp.* excepted 1034. [*owte* adv. + *take* v.]

P

paye *n.* satisfaction 615, 941, 2094. [a. OFr. *paie.*]

paye *v.* pacify, content 1388. [a. Fr. *payer.*]

payne *n.* suffering 1422, 1944. [a. OFr. *peine.*]

pales, paleys *n.* palace 322, 173, 1109, etc. [a. OFr. *palais, paleis.*]

palfray(e), palfrey *n.* a saddlehorse for ordinary riding 310, 1288, 1425, etc. [a. OFr. *palfrei.*]

palmer *n.* pilgrim 430, 451. [a. AF. *palmer, paumer.*]

palsye *n.* palsy, disease of the nervous system 1976. [OFr. *paralisie, -lysie.*]

parell *n.* preparation, equipment 85. [Aphet. form of ME. *apareil,* apparel.]

parte *n.* faction 1079, 1791. [OE. ad. L. *pars;* thirteenth-century a. Fr. *part.*]

passed, -yd, paste *pt. sg.* went through 463, 966; *pt. pl.* 463; *pt. sg.* travelled 1398; *pt. pl.* 148; *pt. sg.* surpassed 1790; *pt. sg.* escaped 2055. [a. OFr.*passer.*]

pavylon *n.* stately tent 384; **pavylons** *n. pl.* 379, 964. [a. Fr. *pavillon.*]

pees *n.* peace 941. [Early ME. *pais,* a. OFr. *pais.*]

peyntyd *pp.* (*pass.*) painted 329, 331. [ad. OFr. *peindre.*]

perchawnce *adv.* as is possible 942. [a. AF. *par chance.*]

perde *adv.* By God!, assuredly 1878. [a. OFr. *par dé.*]

pere *n.* pear; a type of something small: *deryd not a pere,* risked not a thing 657. [OE. *pere, peru.*]

perys *n. pl.* peers 233, 319. [a. OFr. *per, peer.*]

perre *n.* jewellery 184. [a. OFr. *pierrie, pierie*.]

pyllere *n.* pillar 1141; *n. pl.* 325. [a. OFr. *piler*.]

pyne *n.* suffering 2085. [OE. *pin, a. L. *poena*.]

pyte *n.* tenderness 1682. [a. OFr. *pit(i)é*.]

pytt *n.* hole of captivity 1147. [OE. *pytt*.]

place *n. short for* 'place of battle' 607; quarters 1355; general designation for city 1812; convent 1891. [a. Fr. *place*.]

play(e), plawe *v.* practise sport 419, 1523; *pr. pl.* move energetically 258. [OE. *plез(i)an*.]

playnere *n.* assembly 317. [a. AF. *plener*.]

plawe. See **playe**.

plente *adj.* abounding 400. [a. OFr. *plentet*.]

plyte *n.* guilt 2108. [OE. *pliht*.]

pokkys *n. pl.* pustules 2022. [OE. *poc, pocc*.]

pole *n.* small body of still water 1736. [OE. *pōl*.]

pomels *n. pl.* balls 391. [a. OFr. *pomel*.]

pope *n.* Pope, head of Roman Catholic Church 775, 868, 994, etc. [OE. *pápa*.]

pore *n.* needy. [a. OFr. *povre*.]

portreyed *pp.* (*pass.*) represented 389. [a. OFr. *portrai-, pourtray-*.]

poscescon *n.* control 1178. [a. OFr. *possession, -un*.]

posterne *n.* side way 463. [a. OFr. *posterne*.]

powere *n.* body of armed men 218. [a. AF. *pouair*.]

pownde *n. pl.* English money of account 1195, 1373. [OE. *pund* (pl. *pund*).]

praye *n.* troop 1020; victim 1831. [OFr. *proie* and ML. *praeda*.]

praye *v.* beseech 1981; *pt. sg.*

1837; **preyed** *pt. sg.* 1282, 1497, 1573, etc. [a. OFr. *preier*.]

precyus *adj.* of great price 1106, 1535. [a. OFr. *precios*.]

prees *n.* multitude 469, 612, 1319. [a. OFr. *presse*.]

preest *n.* priest 1005; **preestys** *n. pl.* 1101. [OE. *prēost*.]

preyed. See **praye**.

preyer *n.* prayer 1439; **preyers** *n. pl.* 2008. [a. OFr. *preiere*.]

preke *v.* ride fast 1020. [Late OE. *prician*.]

prekyng *vbl. n.* galloping 469; 1319. [ME. *preke* v. + *yng*.]

present(e) *n.* gift 199, 125. [a. OFr. *present*.]

presyd *pt. pl. Of an attacking force:* bore heavily on 1082; crowded 1660. [a. OFr. *presser*.]

preson, pryson *n.* prison 1304, 1367. [a. OFr. *prisun, prison*.]

prest *adj.* ready for action 162. [a. OFr. *prest*.]

preuely *adv.* stealthily 1956. [ME. *prive, privy* adj. + *ly*.]

preuely *adv.* bravely 979. [ME. *preue* + *ly*.]

preuyd *pp.* proved, shown to be 751. [a. OFr. *prover*.]

pryce *n.* value; in adj. phr. *of pryce*, of great worth 305. [a. OFr. *pris*.]

pryde *n.* splendid ornamentation 183; arrogance 282, 550, 646; inordinate self-esteem, 471, 1218. [OE. *prӯdo*.]

pryson. See **preson**.

procescyon *n.* festive marching 797. [Early ME. a. Fr. *procesion*.]

prowde *adj.* lordly 118, 626, 779. [Late OE. *prūt, prūd*.]

put *v.* push 1327; *pt. sg.* placed 1304, 1634, 1974; *pt. pl.* 2029; *pp.* 1144; *imper.* send by force 580, thrust 1796. [Late OE. *putian*.]

Q

quarell *n.* a short, square-headed arrow 773, 1940; **quarels** *n. pl.* 861. [a. OFr. *quarel, quarrel,* etc.]

quene *n.* king's wife 2160. [OE. *cwēn.*]

quyte *v.* hand over 1671; reward 1733; **quytt** *pt. sg.* acquitted himself (of a task) 715. [a. OFr. *quiter.*]

quod *3 pt. sg.* said 731. [pt. of ME. *quethe.*]

qwelle *v.* kill 1670. [OE. *cwellan.*]

qwyte *adv.* completely 944, 1192. [ME. *quyt* adj.]

R

rayne *n.* rain 845. [OE. *reʒn.*]

rampande *adj.* rearing 845. [a. Fr. *rampant, pr. p.* of *ramper.*]

range *pt. pl.* rang 167, 1892. [OE. *hringan.*]

ranne *pt. sg.* of liquids: flowed 1040; went on foot 1259; *pt. pl.* flowed 578, 609. [OE. rinnan (*ran, *runnon, ʒerunnen*).]

rase *pt. sg.* got up 565. [OE. *rīsan.*]

rave *v.* show signs of madness 1835. [? a. OFr. *raver.*]

rawnsome *n.* ransom 663. [a. OFr. *rancon.*]

rechyd, rekyd *pt. sg.* aimed 1646; *pt. pl.* launched 132. [OE. *reacan.*]

recke *v.* heed 1154. [OE. *reccan* (? *rēcan*).]

recomforde *pt. pl.* consoled 1313. [ad. F. *renconforter.*]

redd *n.* reason, faculty of deliberation 35, 407; counsel 259; advise 1098. [OE. *rǣd, rēd.*]

redd *adj.* red 163, 179, 380, etc. [OE. *rēad.*]

rede *1 pr. sg.* advise 1207, 1420. [OE. *rǣdan, rēdan.*]

rede *pr. pl.* read 645, 1539. [OE. *rǣdan, rēdan.*]

redy *adv.* already 590. [Early ME. *readi.*]

redylye *adv.* with willingness 105. [f. *redy* + *lye.*]

refte *pt. pl.* deprived (by force) 926; pp. 2051. [OE. *rēafian.*]

reygned *3 pt. sg.* ruled 25. [a. OFr. *regner.*]

rekyd. See **rechyd, reykyd.**

reyned *pt. sg.* descended like rain 43. [OE. *reʒnian.*]

reyset *n.* refuge 1744. [a. OFr. *recet.*]

reysyd *3 pt. sg.* lifted 472. [a. ON. *reisa* = OE. *rēran.*]

rekenyth *3 pr. sg.* amount to, number 188. [OE. *(ge)recenian.*]

remes *n. pl.* kingdoms 117. [a. OFr. *reaume.*]

remouyd, remeuyd *pt. sg.* moved 606; taken away 1827. [a. OFr. *remouvoir.*]

rennyng *pr. p.* flowing 343, 383. [OE. *rinnan.*] See **rennande.**

rennyth *3 pr. sg.* flows 335, 1884. [OE. *rinnan.*]

renowne *n.* fame 1031. [a. AF. *renoun, renun.*]

rente *n.* source of income 1118, 1346, 2130. [a. OFr. *rente, rende.*]

rente *pt. sg.* tore 47. [OE. *rendan.*]

rerde *n.* cry 1427. [OE. *rēord.*]

rerewarde *n.* third division in the line of battle 605. [a. AF. *rerewarde.*]

rescowde, -ed *pt. sg.* saved 712; *pt. pl.* 702; *pp.* 718, 725; *pp. (pass.)* 489. [a. OFr. *rescoure.*]

resseyuyd *pp. (pass.)* welcomed 175. [ad. ONFr. *receivre, receyvre;* OFr. *recoivre.*]

revedd, revydd *pp.* robbed 1934, 1307. [OE. *rēafian.*]

reuerence *n.* power 1145, 1277. [a. OFr. *rēverence.*]

rewe *v.* regret 368, 942, 993, etc.; **rewyd** *pt. sg.* 2064. [OE. *hrēowan.*]

rewfull *adj.* pitiable 1427, 1518. [f. ME. *rew + ful.*]

ryall *adj.* noble 174; grand 178, 918, 1160, etc. [a. OFr. *roial.*]

ryally *adv.* with pomp 152, 505. [f. *ryall.*]

rybbes *n. pl.* ribs 1850. [OE. *rib, ribb.*]

ryche *adj.* valuable 85, 184, 386, etc.; mighty 218, 890, 1931, etc. [OE. *rīce.*]

ryde *v.* ride (a horse, a ship) 1, 117, 152, etc.; *pr. pl.* 1418; *pt. sg.* 588, 1259, 1384, etc.; *pt. pl.* 155, 373, 445, etc. [OE. *rīdan.*]

rydynge *vbl. n.* a mounted combat 623. [f. *ryde + ynge.*]

ryfe *adj.* abundant 1122. [Late OE. *ryfe.*]

rygge *n.* back (animal's) 746. [Northern form of ME. *rydge.*]

ryght *n.* that which is consonant with equity 261; duty 405; justifiable claim 933. [OE. *riht.*]

ryght *adj.* just 42, 1498; legitimate 651, 2066; correct 1414. [OE. *riht.*]

ryght, ryʒt *adv.* in due order 165; straight 202, 568, 597, etc.; with intensive force: *before adj.* 178, 386, 573; to the full 492; exactly 977; without delay 1290, 1612, 1646. [OE. *rihte.*]

ryke *n.* kingdom 1807. [OE. *rīce.*]

rynge *n.* circlet of precious metal (token of marriage) 889, 996. [OE. *hring.*]

rynge *v.* ring 1457. [OE. *hringan.*]

ryse *v.* rise 1858; **ryseth** *3 pr. sg.* mounts up 216; **rose** *pt. sg.* got up 750, 1860. [OE. *rīsan.*]

ryseth. See **ryse.**

ryve *v.* arrive 225; **ryved** *pt. pl.*

376. [ad. OFr. *river*, aphet. form of *arriver.*]

robe *n.* long outer garment 178; **robys** *n. pl.* 2157. [a. OFr. *robe.*]

roche *n.* rock 1875, 1917. [a. OFr. *roche, rocche.*]

rode *n.* cross 1105, 1511, 2186. [OE. *rōd.*]

romans, romance *n.* romance, tale in verse 82, 1539, 1546, etc.; used without article (with plural sense) 645. [a. OFr. *romanz, romans.*]

roo *n.* rest 840. [a. ON. and Icel. *ró = OE. rōw.*]

rope *n.* rope 2091; **ropys** *n. pl.* 386. [OE. *rāp.*]

rose. See **ryse.**

roton *pp.* rotted 2028. [OE. *rotian.*]

rowe *v.* row 1217. [OE. *rōwan.*]

rownde *adj.* spherical 54. [a. OFr. *ro(u)nd-.*]

rowned *pt. sg.* cried out 1753. [ad. OFr. *roungier.*]

S

sa. See **so.**

sadylde *pt. sg.* saddled 1294. [OE. *sadolian.*]

sadull, sadyll *n.* saddle 1534, 1802; **sadyls** *n. pl.* saddles 156, 677. [OE. *sadol.*]

safe *adj.* free from hurt 1916. [OFr. *sa(u)f.*]

say *imper.* try 126. [Aphet. form of ME. *assay.*]

say(e), sey(e) *v.* speak, say, tell 70, 274, 516, etc.; *1 pr. sg.* 154, 322, 614, etc.; *3 pr. sg.* 1026, 1387; *imper.* 1063; **sayne** *v.* 814, 1112, 1590, etc.; *pr. subj. sg.* 297; **seyth** *3 pr. sg.* 84, 439, 494, etc.; **says** *3 pr. sg.* 1205; **seyde** *pt. sg.* 76, 88, 223, etc.; *pt. pl.* 253, 452, 805, etc. [OE. *secgan.*]

sayle *n.* sail 136, 1051, 1826,

etc.; **seylys** *n. pl.* 373. [OE.
seʒ(e)l.]

sayled *pt. sg.* sailed 1842. [OE.
siʒlan.]

sayne. See say(e), sey(e).

says. See say(e), sey(e).

sake *n.*; for my sake, on my
account 576. [OE. *sacu.*]

salutyd *pt. pl.* addressed with
respect 505. [ad. L. *salūtāre.*]

same *n.* the same, the aforesaid
person or thing 365, 551, 1077,
etc. [a. ON. *same.*]

sange. See synge.

sare *adj.* in pain 1927. [OE. *sār.*]

sare *adv.* Of suffering: severely
684, 1424, 1451, etc. [OE. *sāre.*]

sate. See set, sytt.

sate. See sytt.

saue *pr. subj. sg.* protect 297, 696.
[a. OFr. *sauver.*]

sawe *n.* story 1281. [OE. *saʒu.*]

sawe. See see.

sawtrye *n.* stringed musical instrument 63. [OE. *(p)saltere.*]

schall, shall *auxil. forming (with
pr. infin.) the future: 1 pr. sg.*
92, 116, 359, etc.; *3 pr. sg.* 108,
112, 279, etc.; *pr. pl.* 227, 257,
266, etc.; **schalt** *2 pr. sg.* 725,
763, 1423; **sch(o)ulde,** *auxil.
forming (with pr. infin.) the
conditional pt. sg.* 40, 51, 283,
etc.; *pt. pl.* 464, 531, 576, etc.;
schulyst *2 pt. sg.* 1191. [OE.
sceal, scūlon, scōlde.]

schake *v.* tremble 1976. [OE.
scacan.]

schakyng *pr. p. (adv.)* trembling
2024. [OE. *scacun.*]

schalt. See schall, shall.

schame *n.* infliction of disgrace
689; disgrace 1183, 1856; *god
gyf þe schames dedd,* God give
thee a shameful death 1474,
1821. [OE. *schamu, scamu.*]

schame *v.* shame 1442; **schamyth**
3 pr. sg. 2180. [OE. *scamian.*]

schare *pt. sg.* cut through 1632.
[OE. *sceran (*scer, scēron,
scoren).*]

scharpe *adj.* keen-edged 679, 1624.
[OE. *scearp.*]

schawe *n.* thicket 1502. [OE.
sceʒa.]

sche, she *pron.* she 59, 67, 108,
etc.; **scho(o)** 1466, 1980; **hur**
acc. and dat. her 37, 57, 81,
etc.; *adj.* her 29, 64, 109, etc.;
subjective gen. 68; **hurselfe** *refl.
as indir. obj.* herself 1532. [OE.
prob. fem. demons. pron. *sēo*
and *hēo; hire.*]

scheldys. See schylde.

schende *v.* disgrace 1442; **schent**
pp. (pass.) 1615, 2045. [OE.
scéndan.]

schene *adj.* beautiful 559, 1452,
1823, etc. [OE. *scēne.*]

schepe. See schyp.

schewe *pr. pl.* exhibit to view
1101. [OE. *scēawian, sceāivian.*]

schylde *n.* shield 27, 366, 421, etc.;
protection 1497; **scheldys** *n. pl.*
shields 569. [OE. *scild.*]

schyp(p)e, schepe *n.* ship 16, 1050,
1056, etc.; **schyppes, -ys** *n. pl.*
131, 144, 146; *n. gen.* 1874.
[OE. *scīp.*]

schyre *adj.* bright 98. [OE. *scīr.*]

scho. See sche.

schone *n. pl.* shoes 655. [OE.
scoh.]

schone, schoon *pt. sg.* radiated
186; gleamed 655, 1540, 1545;
pt. pl. gleamed 156, 391, 1534.
[OE. *scīnan (scán, scinon).*]

schope *pt. sg.* created 1833. [OE.
sceppan (scōp, scapen).]

schoulde, sculde. See schall, shall.

schryue *v.* hear confession of 2035;
schrofe *pt. sg.* 776. [OE. *scrīfan
(scrāf, scrifon, (ʒe)scrifen).*]

schyppborde *n.* side of a ship 1794. [*schypp* + ME. *borde* n.]

scole *n.* school 58. [OE. *scōl.*]

scryed *pt. sg.* described 333. [Aphet. form of ME. *descry.*]

se. See **see.**

seconde *adj.* second 2097. [a. Fr. *second.*]

seculors *n. pl.* non-ecclesiastical men 1133. [a. OFr. *seculer.*]

see *n.* sea 88, 1063, 1114, etc. [OE. *sǣ.*]

see *v.* perceive 353, 486, 741, etc.; 2 *pr. sg.* 1382; **sawe** *pt. sg.* 289, 1004, 2103; *pt. pl.* 1897; **sye** *pt. sg.* 667, 1157, 1885, etc.; *pt. pl.* 397, 1787; **seen** *pp.* 790, 1455; *pp. (pass.)* 3, 1080, 1247. [OE. *seon,* (*seah, sāwon, sēgon, ȝesewen.*)]

sege *n.* a beleaguering 874, 1168. [a. OFr. *sege.*]

segyd *pt. sg.* laid siege to 1174. [f. *sege.*]

seyde. See **say(e), sey(e).**

seylys. See **sayle.**

seynt *adj.* saint (prefixed to name of canonised persons) 434, 514, 694, etc. [a. OFr. *sainte, seint.*]

seyth. See **say(e), sey(e).**

seke. See **se(e)ke, syke.**

se(e)ke, syke *v.* find 1967; go in search of 21, 434, 2004; **sekyth** 3 *pr. sg.* 2175. [OE. *sēcan.*]

se(y)ke *adj.* sick 1918, 1927. [OE. *sēoc.*]

sekenes *n.* disease 1971. [*seke* adj. + *nes.*]

sekyr *adj.* certain, sure 1129, 1331. [OE. *sicor.*]

selde *adv.* seldom 33. [OE. *seldan.*]

selde *pp.* paid for, avenged 561. [OE. *sellan.*]

sembyll *v.* assemble 74, 634; **sembelde** *pt. pl.* 370. [Aphet. variation of ME. *assemble.*]

sembelde. See **sembyll.**

semely *adj.* of a pleasing appearance 527, 1485, 1541, etc.; of great proportions 498. [a. ON. *sœmiligr.*]

semely *adv.* handsome 1158. [a. ON. *sœmiliga.*]

semyth 3 *pr. sg.* appears to be 945. [ME. *seme,* a. ON. *sœma.*]

sende *v.* commission to go to a place or person 89, 115, 128, etc.; 2 *pr. sg.* 214; *pr. pl.* 860; *pt. sg.* 120; *pt. pl.* 775; *pp.* 1975; **sent(e)** *pt. sg.* 124, 454; dispatched (a message) 1393; *pt. pl.* 2007; *pp.* 206. [OE. *sendan.*]

sendell *n.* thin silken material 163. [a. OFr. *cendal.*]

sent(e). See **sende.**

sent *v.* assent 241. [a. OFr. *a(s)sēnter.*]

sere *adj.* various 331, 1221. [ON. *sēr.*]

serue *v.* render service (to) 1732, 1752, 2094; *imper.* 231; **seruyd** *pt. pl.* 1554; *pp.* 1461. [a. OFr. *servir.*]

set(t) *v.* place; 1 *pr. sg. set my soule,* bet my soul for 1131; 3 *pr. sg.* 1840; *pr. pl.* 1693; *pt. sg.* 523, 629, 653, etc.; put in the way of following a course 58; caused to be in a certain condition 684; *pt. pl.* 373, 592, 721; set up, raised to an elevated position 1051; *pp.* 1535; **sete** 3 *pr. sg.* 1481; **sate** *pt. sg.* caused to be in a certain condition 684. [OE. *settan.*]

set. See **sytt.**

sete. See **set.**

sethyn *adv.* next in order 1090, 1481. [OE. *siþþan.*]

seuyn *adj.* seven 330, 674. [OE. *seofon.*]

syclatowne *n.* cloth of gold or other rich material 179. [a. OFr. *ciclaton, -un.*]

syde *n.* side 108, 180, 362, etc.; **sydes** *n. pl.* 1550. [OE. *sīde*.]

syghed *pt. sg.* sighed 1094, 1424, 1701. [ME. *sihen*, *siʒen*, etc.]

syghyng *vbl. n.* sorrow 919. [f. ME. *sihen v.*]

sygned *pt. pl.* assigned 865. [Aphet. f. ME. *assygned*.]

syght *n.* sight 798, 1541. [OE. *sihð*.]

sygnyfyed *pt. sg.* foreshadowed 49; betokened 424, 601, 1227. [ad. F. *signifier*.]

syke *v.* See se(e)ke, syke.

syke *adj.* See se(e)ke.

sylke *n.* silk 86, 385. [OE. *seoloc*.]

syluyr *n.* silver 328. [OE. *siolfor*, *seolfor*.]

sympull *adj.* simple 539, 577, 1672. [a. OFr. *simple*.]

syn *adv.* subsequently 1192. [Contracted from ME. *sithyn*.]

synge *v.* say mass 1005; **sange** *pt. pl.* sang 166; **syngyng** *pr. p.* singing 2147. [OE. *singan*.]

syngyng. See synge.

synke *v.* fall, degenerate 921. [OE. *sincan* (*sanc*, *suncon*, *suncen*).]

synne *n.* a sin (without article) 1692; **synnes** *n. pl.*; *dedly synnes seuyn*, seven deadly sins 330. [OE. *syn(n)*.]

syr *n.* title of honour of a knight, placed before the Christian name 19, 26, 55, etc.; *n. pl.* 88; **syrrys** *n. pl.* 265, 198, 431, etc. [Reduced form of ME. *syre*.]

systur *n.* nun 1918. [OE. *sweoster*.]

syte *n.* care, *in phr.*: *sorowe and syte* 1629, 2107. [a. ON. *sȳt*.]

sytt *v.* sit 1148; **sate** *pt. sg.* 177, 310, 1876; **set** *pt. sg. of things:* was situated 181. [OE. *sittan* (*sæt*, *sæton*, *ʒeseten*).]

sythe *adv.* afterwards 1190, 2050. [Reduced form of OE. *siððan*.]

sythyn, sethyn *conj.* then 1753, 2056; since 673. [OE. *siþþon*.]

sythys *n. pl.* times 1324. [OE. *sīþ*, *sīð*.]

syxe *adj.* card. num. six, *used with a noun* 595, 987. [OE. *sex*, *six*, etc.]

syxty *adj.* card. num. sixty, *used with a noun* 319, 370, 376, 438, etc. [OE. *syx-*, *sextiʒ*.]

skapyd *pp.* escaped 1191. [Aphet. var. of ME. *eskape*.]

skorne *n.* derision 513. [OFr. *escorne*.]

slayn(e). See slee.

slee *v.* kill, 221 1140; **slewe** *pt. sg.* 786, 1065, 1213, etc.; *pt. pl.* 467, 1037, 1083; **slayn(e)** *pp.* 68, 788, 893; (*pass.*) 704, 1102, 1337; **slone** *pp.* (*pass.*) 1347; **slo** *imper.* 850. [OE. *slēan* (*sloʒ*, *slōh*, *slōʒon*, *slæʒen*).]

slepe *v.* sleep 135, 1655; **slepyd** *pt. sg.* 1070, 1638. [OE. *slēpan* (*slēp*, *slēpon*, *-slāpen*).]

slewe. See slee.

slyly(lye) *adv.* stealthily 1947; cleverly? [f. ME. *slyh* adj. + *ly*.]

slo. See slee.

slone. See slee.

slope *n.* sleep 1630. [OE. *slāp*.]

small(e) *adj.* small 52, 338, 395, etc. [OE. *smæl*.]

smartely *adv.* promptly 1143. [f. ME. *smart* adj.]

smetyn *pp.* infected 2005; *pp.* (*pass.*) struck 1618. [OE. *smītan* (*smāt*, *smiton*, *smiten*).]

smyle *v.* smile 1788. [OE. **smīlan*.]

smote *pt. sg.* struck 1940, 2075; lowered (down) 1306. [OE. *smītan* (*smāt*, *smiton*, *smiten*).]

so(o), sa *adv.* in the manner described 267, 381, 517 etc.; *with the v. 'do', passing into the sense of 'that'* 272; *at the be-*

*ginning of a clause with con-
tinuative force* 251, 874; to that
extent 33, 107, 1110, etc.; *in
oaths* 297; so (that), *in limiting
sense* 422; thus 494, 539, 772,
etc.; *conj.* so that 1182. [OE.
swā.]

soche *demons. adj.* of the character
described 39, 71, 80, etc.; *pron.*
persons or things before mentioned 323, 1463. [OE. *swelc,
swilc.*]

socowre *n.* protection 631, 1602.
[a. OFr. *sucurs, soc(c)ours.*]

softe *adj.* producing agreeable
sensations 100; smooth 1550;
pleasing 1763. [OE. *sŏfte.*]

solde *pt. sg.* sold 2096; *pt. pl.* 1784.
[OE. *sellan.*]

solempnyte *n.* observance of cere-
mony 1161. [a. OFr. *solempneté.*]

some *adj.* certain (*with pl. nouns*)
100; a certain (*with sg. nouns*)
1669; *some tyme,* at one time
or another 1241, 1259. [OE.
sum.]

somedele *adj.* a little 674. [f. OE.
sum adj. + *dēl,* n.]

somedele *adv.* somewhat 674. [OE.
sume dēle.]

somer *n.* pack-horse 277. [a. OFr.
somer.]

somersday *n.* a day in summer
311, 1434. [Cf. OFris. *sumersdey*
Midsummer day.]

somned *pp.* (*pass.*) summoned
2146. [a. OFr. *somondre.*]

sone. See **soon.**

son(n)e *n.* son; God the Son 1676,
1779; **sonnes** *n. pl.* sons 407,
509. [OE. *sunu.*]

sonne *n.* sun 518, 1833, 1908. [OE.
sunne.]

soon(e), sone *adv.* within a short
time 142, 131, 214, etc.; *Also
soon as,* as soon as 1054. [OE.
sōna.]

sore *adj.* painful 1550. [OE. *sār.*]

sore *adv.* with great exertion,
laboriously 21; with verbs of
lamenting and denoting fear
1601, 1622, 1653, etc. [OE.
sāre.]

sory *adj.* distressed 1022; unfortunate 1820. [OE. *sāriʒ.*]

sorowe *n.* grief 839, 921, 1055,
etc. [OE. *sorʒ.*]

sorowfull *adj.* unhappy 1658. [OE.
sorʒful.]

sorte *n.* fate 1089. [a. OFr. *sort.*]

sothe *n.* truth 306, 741, 1112, etc.
[OE. *sōð.*]

sotheyr *n.* soldier 1281; **sowdears**
n. pl. 401, 512, 931. [a. OFr.
soud(i)er.]

souereygn *n.* king 789, 863. [a.
OFr. *soverain.*]

sowdears. See **sotheyr.**

sowle *n.* soul 1131. [OE. *sāwol,
sāwel.*]

sownde *adv.* in safety 57, 696,
1574, etc. [f. ME. *sownde* adj.]

sowne *n.* sound (produced by the
voice) 761. [a. AF. *soun;* OFr.
son.]

sowþe *adv.* towards the south
2012. [OE. *suð.*]

sowtheweste *adv.* towards the
south-west 1415. [OE. *suðwest.*]

space *n.* without article: lapse of
time 608, 1011. [ad. OFr.
espace.]

spaynysch *adj.* Spanish 133. [f.
ME. *Spayne* + *ysh.*]

spake. See **speke.**

spare, spere *v.* save 293; refrain
from using 403, 1556; leave
unused 1011; **spared** *pt. sg.*
refrained from using 746; *pp.*
left unused 662; **speryd** *pt. pl.*
refrained from using 448. [OE.
sparian.]

sparryd *pt. sg.* bolted 1772. [var.
of ME. *sparre* v.]

speche *n.* words 907, 1409. [OE. *sp(r)ĕc.*]

specyally *adv.* expressly 1439. [OFr. *(e)speciaument.*]

spede *n.* pace 1295, 1863. [OE. *spēd.*]

speke *v.* talk 1546, 1920; *speke wyth*, talk to 1405; *pr. pl.* utter 513; discourse 794; **spake** *pt. sg.* 2098; **spekynge** *pr. p.* 2013. [OE. *sp(r)ecan, (sp(r)eac, sp(r)econ, ꝫesp(r)ecen).*]

spere. See **spare.**

spere *n.* spear 366, 465, 472, etc.; **sperys** *n. pl.* 721. [OE. *spere.*]

speryd *pt. sg.* shut up 172. [a. MLG. *speren.*]

spering *pr. p.* closing 149. [a. MLG. *speren.*]

spyed *pt. sg.* watched 1595. [ad. OFr. *espier.*]

spylle *v.* destroy 837; run out 633; **spylte** *pp. (pass.)* wasted 557. [OE. *spillan.*]

spyr *v.* publish 2013. [Special sense of ME. *spir, speir* v.]

spyrytualte *n.* body of ecclesiastical persons 1132. [ad. OFr. *spiritualté.*]

spytt *3 pr. sg.* spit out 1607. [Northern OE. *spittan.*]

sprang *pt. sg.* spread (of fame, rumour) 1930. [OE. *springan.*]

sprede *v.* unfurl 803. [OE. *sprēdan.*]

spurrys *n. pl.* spurs 745. [OE. *spura, spora.*]

squyers *n. pl.* squires 835. [ad. OFr. *esquier.*]

stabull *n.* stable 1558. [a. OFr. *estable.*]

stabull *v.* make stable 1236. [a. OFr. *establer.*]

stadde *pp. (pass.)* burdened 1311. [Early ME. *stude, stede.*]

stake *n.* post 1663. [OE. *staca.*]

stalle *n.* stable 201. [OE. *steall.*]

standard(e) *n.* flag 547, 592, 598, etc. [Aphet. a. OFr. *estandard.*]

stande, stonde *v.* stand 711, 1899; wait for 271; *agenste hym stande*, oppose 1233; *pr. pl.* 325; **standys** *3 pr. sg.* 221; **standyth, stondyth, standyþ** *3 pr. sg.* 337, 1340, 1883; **stode** *pt. sg.* 384, 506, 562, etc.; *in stede stode me* was of service to me 948; *. . . nede stode,* required 1553; *pt. pl.* stood in position *(with infin. expressing accompanying action)* 264; *stode owte* 2027; **stondyng** *pr. p.* 324. [OE. *standan (stōd, stōdon, ꝫestanden).*]

standys. See **stande, stonde.**

standyth, stondyth, standyþ. See **stande, stonde.**

stane *n.* rock 1146. [OE. *stān.*]

starte *pt. sg.* jumped 1643. [OE. **stertan;* cp. *styrtan.*]

stavys *n. pl.* walking sticks 1991. [OE. *stæf.*]

stedd, stede *n.* another 409; place 1095, 1160, 1554, etc.; an enclosure 379. [OE. *stede.*]

stede *n.* stallion 160, 586, 642, etc.; **stedys** *n. pl.* 124, 133, 143, etc. [OE. *steda.*]

stekyth *pr. sg.* sticks 1472. [OE. *stician.*]

stele *n.* steel 638, 1335, 1625; *trewe as any stele,* thoroughly trustworthy 398. [OE. *stēle.*]

stelyng *pr. p.* coming stealthily 720. [OE. *stelan.*]

steppyd *pt. sg.* stepped 1879. [OE. *steppan (stōp, (be)stapen).*]

stepull *n.* tall tower 1885. [OE. *stēpel.*]

stere *v.* govern, rule 414; guide 825, 1236. [OE. *stȳran.*]

sterne *adj.* resolute in battle 398; *adv.* harshly 414. [OE. *styrne.*]

steuyn *n.* voice 333, 481, 2155. [OE. *stefn.*]

steward *n.* a major-domo 228. [OE. *stiweard.*]

styckyd *pp.* (*pass.*) pierced 642. [OE. *stician.*]

styffe *adj.* resolute, steadfast 573. [OE. *stif.*]

styf(fe)ly *adv.* firmly 711; hard 485. [f. *styffe* + *ly.*]

stylle *adj.* calm, quiet 630, 813. [OE. *stille.*]

stylle *adv.* silently 234; motionless 908, 1185, 1749. [OE. *stille.*]

stylle *v.* quiet 831. [OE. *stillan.*]

styrryth *3 pr. sg. refl.* acts energetically 485. [OE. *styrian.*]

stythe *adj.* strong 842. [OE. *stið.*]

stode. See stande, stonde.

stokkes *n. pl.* stocks (instrument of punishment) 1148. [OE. *stoc(c).*]

stolyn *pp.* (*with 'away'*) gone unobserved 1353. [*stelan* (*stæl, stælon, stolen*).]

stondyng. See stande, stonde.

ston(e) *n.* stone 340, 392, 1879, etc.; stones *n. pl.* 641, 860. [OE. *stān.*]

store *n.* accumulated goods, supply 878, 1166; *fig.* 1657. [aphet. f. *astore* n., a. OFr. *estor.*]

store *v.* furnish 654. [Aphet. var. of *astore* v., a. OFr. *estorer.*]

story *n.* tale 2173. [a. AF. *estorie.*]

storme *n.* storm 1858, 1864. [OE. *storm.*]

stownde *n.* moment 372, 702, 1421. [OE. *stund.*]

stowre *n.* armed conflict 708, 727, 743, etc.; *in phr.* styffe *in stowre,* brave in battle 573. [a. AF. *estur*; OFr. *estour.*]

straunge *adj.* unusual 435. [a. OFr. *estrange.*]

strekyn *pp.* (*pass.*) *in phr.: strekyn in age,* driven inwards with age 670. [OE. *strīcan* (*strāc, stricon, stricen*).]

strekk *adv.* straightway 1153. [f. ME. *streke adj.*]

streme *n.* stream 1777; *n. pl.* 1217. [OE. *strēam.*]

strenkyþ, -th *n.* fortress 497, 1174. [OE. *strengðu.*]

strenkyþfull *adj.* full of strength 1583. [f. *strenkyþ* + *full.*]

strete *n.* road 641, 851; stretys *n. pl.* 2030. [OE. *strēt.*]

stryfe *n.* discord 216, 1125. [a. OFr. *estrif.*]

stryke *v.* to deal a blow 24; strykeþ *3 pr. sg.* 488; stryked *pt. sg.* made (his) way into 127; stroke *pt. sg.* 745 *pt. pl.* 1862; *stroke in,* made his way into 784. [OE. *strīcan.*]

strynde *n.* lineage 2172. [OE. *strȳnd.*]

stryve *pr. pl.* wrangle 1851. [ME. *strīven,* a. OFr. *estriver.*]

stroye *v.* destroy 848, 855. [Aphet. f. ME. *destroye.*]

stroke. See stryke.

strong(e) *adj.* physically powerful 14, 143, 495, etc.; *of suffering:* hard to bear 839. [OE. *stráng, stróng.*]

strote *n.* projection 2027. [OE. **strūt.*]

struglynge *vbl. n.* the action of struggle 185. [ME. *strugle* v. + *ynge.*]

suffur *v.* endure 707, 915; suffurde *pt. sg.* 913, 1848. [a. AF. *suffrir, soeffrir.*]

swayne *n.* servant 1872. [a. ON. *sveinn.*]

swalme *v.* faint 770. [f. ME. *swalm* n.]

sware *n.* speech. [Partly OE. **swaru,* partly ON. *svar.*]

sware *adj.* loth 90. [OE. *swer, swēre.*]

sweme *n.* swoon, dizziness 770. [OE. *swīma.*]

swepe *v.* drive along 138. [ME. *swepe.*]

swere *v.* swear, take an oath 988, 1084, 1489; *pt. sg.* 499; **sworne** *pp.* 355, 806, 992; *pp.* (*pass.*) 980, 1123, 1357. [OE. *swerian* (*swŏr, sworen*).]

swete *adj.* dearly loved 1106, 1467, 1469; lovely 90; pleasing to the ear 168, 441. [OE. *swēte.*]

swylke *adj.* such 386. [Northern form corresponding to OE. *swilc.*]

swymmyng *pr. p.* swimming 390. [OE. *swimman* (*swamm, swummon, swummen*).]

swyrde *n.* sword 585, 722, 1224, etc.; **swyrdys** *n. pl.* 679. [OE. *sweord.*]

swythe *adv.* without delay 1111. [OE. *swiðe.*]

sworne. See **swere.**

swowned *pt. sg.* swooned 824; *pp.* 1093. [ME. *swoꝛene, swoꝛeny, swowene.*]

T

ta. See **take, ta, too.**

take, ta, too *v.* seize 277, 585, 887, etc.; accept 880; *1 pr. sg.* bring 1856; *imper.* seize 268, 1792, 1796; accept 896; *weakened sense of* seize 1060; **toke** *pt. sg.* seized 2122; accepted 415; brought 493, 675, 1079; *toke . . . leue,* departed 960; *pt. pl.* captured 950; brought 443; ate and drank 447; *toke . . . leue* departed 285, 2139, 2159 (see **leue**); *toke downe,* cut down 1279; *toke hym tome,* took the opportunity 292; **takyn** *pp.* captured *pp.* (*pass.*) 53; seized 1034; *weakened sense of* seized 607; **tane** *pp.* captured 787, 892, 924 (*pass.*) 1103, 1143; con-

veyed 700; (*pass.*) accepted (advice) 259. [Late OE. *tacan* (*toc, tacen*).]

tale *n.* story 1129, 1331, 1392. [OE. *talu.*]

talme *v.* become exhausted, faint 769 [Akin to ON. *talma.*]

tame *adj.* domesticated 45. [OE. *tam.*]

tane. See **take, ta, too.**

taste *n.* trial, attempt 852. [a. OFr. *tast.*]

taste *v.* explore by touch 109. [a. OFr. *taster.*]

telle *v.* recount 40, 306, 350, etc.; make known 294; *þe boke telle,* read the book 59; *1 pr. sg.* recount 164, 1970; **tolde** *pt. sg.* made known 346, 564, 757, etc.; recounted 105, 451, 734, etc.; reckoned 1320; *pt. pl.* discerned 296; recounted 62, 82, 345, etc.; made known 1091. [OE. *tellan.*]

tempeste *n.* storm 2101. [a. OFr. *tempeste.*]

temporalte *n.* laity [app. a. AF. **temporelté.*]

te(e)ne *n.* rage, wrath, 560, 1083. [OE. *tēona.*]

tene *v.* injure 1322. [a. OE. *tēonian.*]

terys *n. pl.* tears 578. [OE. *tēar.*]

tethe *n. pl.* teeth 1618, *fortethe* front teeth 1607, 2075. [OE. *tōþ, tōð.*]

th-. See **þ, th.**

tyde *n.* any definite time in the course of the day, *mornetyde* morning 114; time 189, 285, 426, etc. [OE. *tīd.*]

tyght *pt. pl.* set firmly 379. [Obscure.]

tyl(l), tyll(e) *prep.* of time: until 59, 418; *adv.* unto 228, 833, 624, etc.; until 741, 965, 980, etc. [ONth. *til.*] See **þertylle.**

tylleth *3 pr. sg.* persuades, wins over 991. [OE. **tyllan.*]

tyme *n.* a particular period 19, 1214; general state of affairs at a particular period 254; *þat tyme*, a particular period characterised in some way 406; *some tyme* occasionally 1241, 1259; **tymes** *n. pl.* used to express the multiplication of a number: *ix tymes* 1705. [OE. *tīma.*]

tymely *adv.* soon, quickly 591, 1394, 1501. [Late OE. *tīmlice.*]

tymberde *pp. fig.* caused, brought about 560. [OE. *timbran.*]

tyre *n.* apparel 2120. [Aphet. f. ME. *atyre.*]

tyte *adv.* smart, alert 289, 656, 693, etc. [ad. ME. *thyght.*]

tyþyngys, tythandys, tythadys *n. pl.* events 236; news 435, 449, 846, etc. [Late OE. *tidung.*]

to(o) *prep.* to *expressing motion towards* 15, 16, 48, etc.; *expressing purpose, condition, or status* 28, 72, 81, etc.; *before an infin. in adverbial relation* 111, 130, 235, etc.; *before infin.* 551, 617, 635, etc.; *indication obj.* 529, 754, 846, etc.; *adv.* according to, in order to 881, 938. [OE. *tō.*]

tobrokyn *pp.* broken down 103. [OE. *tobrecan.*]

today, todey *adv.* today 613, 1856. [OE. *to dæg.*]

todusched *pt. pl.* dashed to pieces 638. [ME. *todaschen.*]

togedur, togodur *adv.* together 258, 636, 676, etc. [OE. *to gædere.*]

togodur. See **togedur, togodur.**

toyle *n.* strife 1936. [a. AF. *toil, toyl.*]

toke. See **take.**

tolde. See **telle.**

tome *n.* opportunity 292. [a. ON. *tóm.*]

tome *adj.* empty 144. [OE. *tōm.*]

tomorne *n.* tomorrow 1376. [f. *to* + OE. *morȝenne.*]

too. See **to.**

too. See **take, ta, too.**

toppe *n.* highest part 1861. [OE. *top(p).*]

torusched *pt. sg.* dashed in pieces 637. [ME. *to-ruschen*, f. *to* + *ruschen.*]

town(e) *n.* city 2, 341, 535, etc.; village 140, 166; **townes** *n. pl.* 650; *gen. n.* 1745. [OE. *tūn.*]

towre *n.* tower 567, 1144, 1229, etc.; **towres, -ys** *n. pl.* 296, 650. [OE. *torr.*]

trayne *n.* deceit 1416, 1623. [a. OFr. *traine.*]

traytur *n.* betrayer 1027, 1381, 1431, etc. [a. OFr. *traitre.*]

trauayle *n.* labour 1309. [a. OFr. *travail.*]

trauelde *pp. (pass.)* tormented 104. [a. OFr. *travaillier.*]

tre(e) *n.* tree 1437, 1505, 1514; the cross on which Christ was crucified 1430; pieces of wood 1348. [OE. *trēo.*] See **galow(e).**

tredd *n.* path 1880. [Early ME. *trede.*]

tree. See **tre.**

trembyll *v.* quiver 635; **trembylde** *pt. sg.* 94. [a. Fr. *trembler.*]

treson *n.* treachery 1272, 1284. [a. AF. *treysoun, tresun, treson.*]

tresory *n.* a place for valuables 204. [a. OFr. *tresorie.*]

tresowr(e), tresur *n.* a store of anything valuable 142, 165, 268, etc. [a. OFr. *tresor.*]

tresse *n.* braid of the hair 1513. [a. OFr. *tresse.*]

trewage *n.* tribute 947. [a. OFr. *treuage.*]

trewe *adj.* of persons: steadfast 301, 987, 1206; honest 620, 906,

945; **trewest** *sup.* most honest 2184. [OE. *trēowe.*]

trewly *adv.* honestly 82; used to emphasise statement: indeed 738, 1038, 2079. [OE. *trēowlīce.*]

trybulacyons *n. pl.* miseries 50. [a. OFr. *tribulacion.*]

trynyte *n.* in phr.: *Hym in trynyte* 'Him in threeness' 1847; trinity 1881. [a. OFr. *trinite.*]

troyan *n.* inhabitant of Troy 13. [ad. L. *Trōiānus.*]

trone *n.* seat of God 1839. [a. OFr. *trone.*] See **heuyn.**

trowe *pr. sg.* believe, trust 670, 732, 791, etc.; *imper.* 738, 1038. [OE. *trēowan, trēowian.*]

trowed *pt. sg.* believed 1392. [OE. *trēawan, trēowian.*]

trumpes *n. pl.* trumpets 635. [a. F. *trompe.*]

tuggelde *pt. sg.* dragged about 1936. [app. rel. to ME. *tugge.*]

turne *v.* change 1243; *turne again* return 1037; **turned** *pt. sg.* changed 1685; *pp.* (*pass.*) returned 1125. [OE. *turnian.*]

turnement *n.* a meeting for knightly sports 1616. [OFr. *turnement.*]

twenty *adj.*: *as multiplier before a num.* 320; *in conjunction with a n.* 1147; *used for the ordinal* twentieth 1895. [OE. *twenti3.*]

twyes *adv.* two times 1093. [Late OE. *twi3es.*]

twynkylde *pt. sg.* blinked 1748. [OE. *twinclian.*]

two *adj. card. num.* two, *with n.* 415, 1078, 1401, etc. [OE. *twā.*]

Þ, Th

thay. See **þey, they.**

than. See **then.**

þankyd, -ed, thankyd *pt sg.* gave thanks 520, 1731, 1806; *pt. pl.* 2133, 2160. [OE. *þancian.*]

þar(e), thare, þer(e), ther(e), thore *adv.* in (or at) that place 216, 317, 339, etc.; *with v.* 'to be' 18, 158, etc.; *used unemphatically to introduce a clause: with intr. verbs* 41, 334. [OE. *þǣr, þēr.*]

þar *3 pr. sg.* need 23. [OE. *þearf.*]

þat, that *dem. adj.* that: *indicates a thing or person pointed out* 10, 26, 52, etc. [OE. *þæt.*]

þat, that *rel. pron. introducing a clause defining or restricting the antecedent* 12, 15, 19, etc. [Unstressed form of the dem. pron.]

þat, that *conj. introducing a dependent clause* 21, 49, 61, etc. [OE. *þǣt.*]

þe, the. See **þou, thou.**

þe, the(e) *def. art* the 8, 13, 17, etc.; *generally or universally* 19, 22, 26, etc. [OE. *se* (late *þe*).]

thede *n.* nation 246, 1536. [OE. *þēod.*]

þedur, thedur *adv.* to that place 287, 962, 1048, etc. [OE. *þider.*]

thee. See **þe, the(e).**

thefe *n.* thief 1279, 1633, 1712, etc.; **thefys** *n. pl.* 1744. [OE. *þēof.*]

thefte *n.* larceny 1730. [OE. *þēofð.*]

þey, they, thay *pron. pl.* they 44, 130, 132, etc.; **þem, them** them: *as dir. obj.* 105, 130, 138, etc.; *indir. obj.* 305, 653; *obj. of prep.* 124, 133, 257, etc.; *refl.* 462, 571; **þer, ther** *poss. adj.* their: 142, 143, 144, etc.; **þemselfe** themselves: *as emphatic nom.* 1203. [OE. *þā*; ? ON. *þeim,* ?OE. *þæm*; OE. *þēra*; See *OED.*]

þemselfe. See **þey, they, thay.**

þen, then, than *dem. adv.* at that time 7, 18, 216, etc. [OE. *þanne, þænne, þon.*]

þen, then *conj.* than: *used after comp. adv.* 2, 4, 101, etc.; *with ellipsis of preceding comp.* 247; *conj. adv. of time:* then 499, 502, 520, etc. [OE. *þanne, þænne, þon.*]

thens *adv.* from there 434. [ME. *þannes.*]

þer, ther. See þey, they, thay.

þer(e), ther(e). See þar(e), thare, þer(e), ther(e), thore.

thereaftur *adv.* after that time 787, 1094, 1586. [OE. *þǣr æfter.*]

þereby, thereby *adv.* near that, adjacent to 412, 1520, 1960. [OE. *þǣrbi.*]

þerfore, ther- *adv.* for that reason 368, 557, 599, etc. [Early ME. *þerfore.*]

therforne *adv.* therefore 356. [Alteration of ME. *therfore,* from OE. *-foran.*]

therfro *adv.* from that place 1969. [ME. *ther + fro.*]

þeryn, theryn(ne) *adv.* in that place 447, 1368, 1944; in that particular 2088. [OE. *þǣrin.*]

therof, therof *adv.* of it 1468, 1471, 1629. [OE. *þærof.*]

thertylle *adv.* thereto 241. [ME. *þar till.*]

þerto, therto(o) *adv.* besides 301, 327, 760, etc. [OE. *þēr tō, þærtō.*]

þes, thes *dem. adj. sg.* this 191; *pl.* these 190, 466, 581, etc. [See *OED.*]

thetodur *n. pron.* the other 731, 1079, 1275, etc. [ME. *þe toþer.*]

þy, thy. See þou, thou.

þyck, thyck *adj.* dense 1435, 1642, 1660. [OE. *þicce.*]

thyckfolde *adv.* in quick succession 873. [OE. *þicce + fōld* suff.]

thyn(e). See þou, thou.

thynge, þonge *n.* thing 962;

applied to a person 307, 1667, 1728, etc.; *all thynge,* everything, all things 60, 230; *no maner of thynge* 1003; **þyngys** *n. pl.* 331. [OE. *þing.*]

thynke *pr. sg.* consider 913; *pr. pl.* intend 1722; *pr. subj. sg.* intend 906. [OE. *þyncan (þǎhte, ʒepǎht).*]

thynke *n.* possession 918. [OE. *þing.*]

þynkyth, thynkyth *pr. sg.* imagines 1738, 2108. [OE. *þyncan (þǎhte, ʒepǎhte).*]

þys, thys *dem. adj.* this: *used in accord with n.* 5, 36, 37, etc. [See *OED.*]

tho *dem. pron.* those 416, 692, 987, etc. [OE. *þā.*]

thogh, thowe, tho *conj.* howbeit: *introducing a subordinate clause* 310, 663, 1155, etc.; *introducing a restricting statement:* however 1479. [OE. *þēh.*]

þoght *n.* idea 1768. [OE. *þoht.*]

þoght, thoght *pt. sg.* considered 526, 1469, 1577, etc.; *pt. pl.* 2038; *pt. sg. with on:* remembered 1249; *pt. sg.* contemplated 1639; *pt. pl.* planned 462. [OE. *þync(e)an, (þūhte, ʒepūht).*]

thonderblaste *n.* clap of thunder 1641. [OE. *þunor + blæst.*]

þonge. See thynge, þonge.

thore. See þar(e), thare, þer(e), ther(e), thore.

þorow, thorow *adv.* through 117, 148, 152, etc. [OE. *ðurh, þurh.*]

thorowly *adv.* fully, completely 1647. [OE. *þurh + ly.*]

þou, thou *pron.* thou 214, 554, 670, etc.; **þe, the** *acc.* thee 668, 724, 929, etc.; *refl.* thyself 910; **þy, thy(n)(e)** *adj.* 201, 204, 206, etc. [OE. *þu, þē, þin.*]

þousand(e), thousand(e) *n.* card. num., thousand: *after another*

num. sg. used as coll. pl. 356,
370, 438, etc.; adj. followed by
pl. n. 320, 1373. [OE. þusend.]
thowe. See **thogh.**
thra adj. persistent 1113. [ME. a.
ON. þra-r.]
thraste pt. sg. pressed 1647. [OE.
þræstan.]
þre, three adj. card. num. three
in accord with n. 43, 358, 1133,
etc.; in phr.: be two and three,
by twos and threes 786. [OE.
þrī.]
thretty adj. card. num. thirty 119.
[OE. þritiȝ.]
thryd(d) adj. third, ord. num.:
with n. expressed 13, 377. [OE.
þridda.]
thryes adv. three times 1094. [ME.
þriȝes.]
thrynge v. press hard, use oppression 1368. [OE. þringan,
(þrang, þrungon, þrungen).]
throo adj. angry, violent 2118.
[ME. a ON. þrár; þráliga.]
throte n. throat 1631. [OE. þrote.]
þus, thus adv. in this way 367, 957,
991, etc. [OS. thus.]

V (vowel)

vndo imper. undress 1509. [OE.
on-, undon.]
vndur prep. below 65, 324, 518,
etc.; with reference to something
which covers; clothes, etc. 27, 135.
[OE. under.]
vndurne n. third hour of the day;
about 9 a.m. 1504. [OE. undern.]
vndurnethe prep. beneath 1437.
[OE. underneoðan..]
vndurstande, vndurstonde v. to
have knowledge 1896; 1 pr. sg.
110, 160, 344, etc. [OE. under-
stonden, -standen.]
vndurtake 2 pr. sg. take in hand
905. [OE. underniman with substitution of take.]

vnfayne adj. displeased 692. [OE.
unfæȝen.]
vnfrendely adv. in an unfriendly
manner 2087. [vn + ME.
frendely.]
vngayne adj. of ways: not plain or
direct 1421; difficult of access
1875. [vn + ME. gayne; cp.
ON. úgegn, unreasonable.]
vnhele n. misfortune 1338. [OE.
unhēlu.]
vnnethe adv. scarcely 1339. [OE.
uneaðe, f. un + eaðe.]
vnnethys adv. scarcely 2132. [f.
prec. + s.]
vnpees n. strife 615. [vn ME. +
pees, prob. after unfrith.]
vnto prep. until 19, 2063; directed
towards 50, 147, towards 150,
173, 497, etc.; with a view to
271; indicating the persons towards whom action is directed
284, 538, 790, etc.; to 1333; as
high ME. 1826. [f. on the analogy
of ME. vntill. Cp. OS. untō.]
vnwelde adj. weak, feeble 95. [vn
ME. + welde adj.]
vp adv. up 142, 373, 494, etc.;
with verbs denoting consuming
or destroying, stroye up 848.
[OE. up(p).]
vpholde v. support, stay 883. [Cf.
OFris. op-, uphalaa.]
vpon prep. on 158, 342, 683, etc.;
indicating the cause espoused by
the agent 404; against 548;
on top of 1120, 1876, 2104;
up towards 767; indicating day
of an occurrence 1597. [OE. upp-
on.]
vs. See **we(e).**

V (consonant)

v The Roman numeral symbol for
five: vij, 296; vx 1195.
vanysched, -t pt. sg. disappeared

1444, 1499. [Aphet. ad. OFr. *evanissir*.]

vawewarde *n.* vanguard 604. [Reduced form of *vamward*.]

venge *v.* avenge 976; **vengyd** *pt. sg.* 1582; *pp.* 1621. [ad. OFr. *vengier, venger*.]

venome *n.* poisonous fluid 2114, 2116. [a. AF. and OFr. *venim* (*venym*).]

verament *adv.* really, truly 455, 1805, 1940, etc. [ad. AF. *veirement*.]

verraye *adv.* in truth 1926. [From OFr. *verai*.]

vetaylyd *pt. sg.* supplied with victuals 1166. [ad. AF. and OFr. *vitailler*.]

vylenye *n.* wrongdoing of a shameful nature 689. [a. AF. *vile(i)nie, vilanie*.]

vysage *n.* face 1563. [a. AF. and OFr. *visage*.]

vysyon *n.* dream 1639. [a. AF. *visiun, visioun*; OFr. *vision*.]

vysyted *pt. sg.* went (in order to assist the sick) 1921. [ad. OFr. *visiter*.]

voyce *n.* without article: singing 1904. [a. AF. *voiz, voice*; OFr. *vois*.]

W

waa *n.* distress 1743. [OE. *wā*.]

wach *v.* attend diligently 1356. [OE. *wæcc-*, a doublet of *wacian*.]

way, wey *n.* course of travel 1289, 1414, 1700, etc.; **wayes, weyes** *n. pl.* 1952; roads 172; *be Godys wayes*, by God's providence 1204. [OE. *weʒ*.]

wakenyd *pt. sg.* stirred up 2076. [OE. *wæcnan*.]

wakenyng *vbl. n.* rousing 1658. [OE. *wæcnan*.]

wakenyth *3 pr. sg.* awakens 1743. [OE. *wæcnan*.]

wall(e) *n.* wall, rampart of stone 394, 478, 965; **walles** *n. pl.* 860. [OE. *wall*.]

wan(ne). See **wynne.**

wanne *adj.* deadly 1992. [OE. *wann*.]

wante *v. tr.* to be destitute of 2109. [Prob. a ON. *vanta*.]

ware *adj.* watchful, vigilant 304. [OR. *ʒewær*.]

wared *pp.* guarded 661. [OE. *warian*.]

waryson *n.* reward 546. [a. OFr. *warison*.]

warme *adj.* warm 100; rich 878, 1166. [OE. *wearm*.]

warnyd *pt. sg.* denied 559. [OE. *wiernan; wearnian*.]

warre *n.* war, 104, 404, 941. [Late OE. *wyrre, werre*, a. northeastern OFr. *werre*.]

warre *adj., predicative use:* aware, conscious 1528, 2014. [OE. *wær*.]

warse *adj.* worse 2086. [OE. *wyrsa, wiersa*.]

warste *adj. used as the sup. of the adjs.* bad, evil *or* ill 956; most inferior 649. [OE. *wyrresta, wyrsta*.]

warste. See **was.**

was *pt. sg.* was 2, 3, 5, etc.; **were** *pt. sg.* came from 1557; *pt. pl.* were 44, 75, 122, etc.; *pt. subj. sg.* might (would) be 315, 404, 453, etc.; **ware** *pr. subj. sg.* 267, 601, 673, etc.; **warste** *pt. subj. sg.* 245. [OE. *wæs* (*wes*); *wǣron*, etc.; ON. pl. *várum*, etc.]

wasche *v.* wash 339. [OE. *wascan*.]

waste *adj.* uninhabited 1503. [a. OFr. *wast(e)*.]

wate. See **wytt.**

water, watur *n.* water 383, 334, 1466, etc.; *n. pl.* rivers 341. [OE. *wæter*.]

waxe *n.* wax 1544. [OE. *weax.*]

waxe *pt. sg.* became 32, 73, 380, etc. [OE. *weaxan.*]

we(e) *pron.* we 197, 224, etc.; **owre** *adj.* our 200, 233, 259, etc.; **vs** *acc.* us 236, 345, 533, etc.; *obj. of a prep.* 482, 980; *refl.* ourselves 1207. [OE. *wē, ūre, ūs.*]

wed(d)(e) *v.* marry 101, 212, 619, etc.; *1 pr. sg.* 1097; *pt. sg.* 2048; *pp.* 77, 409, 1351; *pp. (pass.)* 936, 1023, 1099. [OE. *weddian.*]

weddyng *n.* marriage 1136. [f. *wedd(e)* + *yng.*]

wede *n.* garment 1533, 1691; **wedys** *n. pl.* 398. [OE. *wǣd; wǣde.*]

wede *v.* become mad 1683, 2080. [OE. *wēdan.*]

wedows *n. pl.* widows 1221. [OE. *widwe, widuwe.*]

wedur *n.* weather 768. [OE. *weder.*]

wey. See **way.**

weyght *n.* weight 1706, 1790. [OE. *wiht.*]

wel(l), **wele** *adv.* skillfully 62, 1181, 1732; *with v. of greeting:* with friendly words 127; satisfactorily 250, 456, 661, etc.; *used as intensive to strengthen v., with verbs of pleasing* 302, 170, 290, etc. [OE. *wel(l).*]

welcomed *3 pt. sg.* greeted 1762. [OE. *wilcumian.*]

welde *v.* possess 30, 354, 558, etc.; handle with skill 534; *1 pr. sg.* 830. [OE. *(ge)weldan.*]

wele. See **wel(l).**

weleawaye *interj.* wellaway 1428. [OE. *weʒ lá weʒ.*]

welle *n.* source 300. [OE. *well(a).*]

welnere *adv.* wellnigh 1055. [Early ME. f. *wel* + *nere.*]

wemon, woman *n.* woman 369, 577; **wemen, women** *n. pl.* 1654, 2176. [OE. *wīfmon, wīfman.*]

wende *v.* return 123, 1059, 1196; travel 1238, 1700, 1797; depart 1289; go forward 1370; *pr. pl.* go forward 1777; go 227; depart 536; **went(e)** *pt. sg.* travelled 1276, 1360, 1397, etc.; returned 314, 898; departed 1772, 1922; *impers.* with *hyt* happened 377; *pt. pl.* travelled 985, 1112, 1245, etc.; returned 288; departed 239, 419, 821; thought 1816; turned 970; *went crowlande* (see **crowlande**), [OE. *wendan.*]

wene *n.* misery 12, 1086, 1822, etc. [OE. *wēa.*]

wenyst *pr. pl.* expect, think 958. [OE. *wenian.*]

went(e). See **wende.**

wepe *v.* shed tears 1654, 1686; **wepyd** *pt. sg.* 1095; **wepte** *pt. pl.* 870. [OE. *wēpan.*]

wepon *n.* weapon; **wepons** *n. pl.* 534. [OE. *wǣpen.*]

were. See **was.**

wery *adj.* weary 430, 536. [OE. *wēriʒ.*]

werkys *n. pl.* moral actions 1364. [OE. *we(o)rc.*]

werre *n.* war 459, 672. [Late OE. *wyrre, werre,* a. ONFr. *werre.*]

werryd *pt. sg.* made war upon 20, 1937. [f. *werre.*]

wete *v.* know 1717; **wetyn** *pp.* 1623. [ME. *wēte(n)* var. f. *wite(n).*]

wete *adj.* bloody 1992. [OE. *wēt.*]

wetyn. See **wytt.**

wethur *n.* violent wind 138. [OE. *weder.*]

whan, when, whon *adv.* at what time; on what occasion 34, 70, 106, etc. [OE. *hwanne, hwonne, hwenne.*]

what *pron. elliptical for what the thing* 235, 1190, 1492, etc.; *interrogative pron. of neut. gender*

928, 958, 1124, etc.; *adj.* whatever 2181. [OE. *hwæt.*]

whedur *conj.* whether 237, 272, 453, etc. [OE. *hivæþer, hweþer.*]

whelebarowe *n.* wheelbarrow 2029. [ME. *whele* + *barowe.*]

whelme *v.* swell 683. [f. *whalme* n., possibly represents unrecorded OE. derivative **wælman.*]

wheme *adj.* pleasing 145. [ME. *cweme, queme.*]

when *rel.* when *in reference to an occurrence in the past* 628, 652, 667, etc.; *in reference to future time* 688, 952, 1188. [OE. *hwanne, hwænne.*]

whens *n.* from which place 196, 1492, 1557, etc. [thirteenth-century ME. *whannes, whennes,* f. *whanne.*]

where *adv.* at what place 507, 730, 1578; *rel.* 850. [OE. *hwær.*]

whereuyr *conj.* wherever, at any place which 314; *adv.* wherever 547. [f. *where* + *euyr.*]

whether *conj. introducing an alternative statement* 1244. [OE. *hwæþer.*]

why *rel. pron.* an account of which 20, 102, 734. [OE. *hwī.*]

whych *pron. rel.* which 1329; who 1662, 1933. [OE. *hwilc.*]

whyle *n.* time 922, 1162, 1785, etc. [OE. *hwīl.*]

whylys *adv. preceded by a demonstrative adj.: þys whylys,* this time 1378. [orig. OE. *sumehwiles, oðerhwiles,* etc.]

whyll *conj.* during the time that 799. [abbrev. of OE. *þā hwīle þe.*]

whyte *adj.* white 87, 194, 422, etc. [OE. *hwīt.*]

who *pron. rel.* who (of person or persons) 188, 279, 613, etc.; (of an animal) 422; *in dependent clause without correlative,* whoever 2175. [OE. *hwā.*]

whon. See **whan, when, whon.**

wychyd *pp.* affected (a person) with witchcraft 1507. [OE. *wiccian.*]

wyck *adj.* wicked 1436, 1661. [adj. use of OE. *wicca.*]

wyde *adj.* having a great extent 151, 393, 1524. [OE. *wīd.*]

wyde *adv.* over a large region 186, 361, 1222. [OE. *wīd.*]

wyfe, wyve *n.* wife 28, 219, 914, etc. [OE. *wīf.*]

wyght, wyʒt *n.* a living being in general 12, 39, 80, etc. [OE. *wiht.*]

wyght *adj.* courageous 27, 495, 527, etc. [a. ON. *vigt.*]

wyght *adj.* white 162, 310. [OE. *hwīt.*]

wyghtly *adv.* bravely 534. [f. *wyght* adj. + *ly.*]

wykkyd *adj.* bad in moral character 627, 1406, 1479. [app. f. ME. *wick* adj.]

wykkydly *adv.* immorally [f. as prec. + *ly.*]

wylde *adj.* untamed 45, 1503; unruly, uncontrolled 35, 407. [OE. *wilde.*]

wylys *n. pl.* ruses 1167. [Obscure.]

wyll *auxil.* of the future (*with infin.*) will: *1 pr. sg.* 32, 81, 351, etc.; *3 pr. sg.* 212, 217, 220, etc.; *pr. pl.* 237, 401, 432, etc.; **wolde** *auxil. of cond.* would: *pt. sg.* 77, 241, 500, etc.; *pt. pl.* 40, 450, 452, etc.; *pt. subj. sg.* 546, 899; *pt. subj. pl.* 339. [OE. *willan, wyllan; wōlde, walde.*]

wylle *n.* pleasure 231, 242, 828, etc.; disposition 627, 810, 1406; intention 729, 740, 956. [OE. *willa.*]

wynde *n.* wind 136. [OE. *wind.*]

wyndowe *n.* window 1185; **wyndow.** *n. pl.* 171. [a. ON. *vindauga.*]

wyne *n.* wine 1761. [OE. *wīn.*]

wynne *v.* obtain 546, 1241, 1263, etc.; obtain as a wife 354, 360; be victorious 453; go 857; tempt 2054; **wan(ne)** *pt. sg.* gained (land) 2104; *pt. sg.* arrived at 1258; *pt. pl.* acquired 1181. [OE. *winnan* (*wann*, *wunnen*).]

wynnyng *vbl. n.* taking, conquest 655. [f. ME. *wynne* + *yng.*]

wyrke *v.* cause, bring to pass 853, 1197; wield (a weapon) 1033; **wyrkyth** *3 pr. sg.* 615. [OE. *wyrcan.*]

wys. See **wytt.**

wyse *adj.* informed 176, 304, 1364. [OE. *wīs.*]

wyse *n.* manner 1859. [OE *wīse.*]

wyt *n.* wisdom 555. [OE. *wit.*]

wyt *v.* See **wytt.**

wyte *n.* punishment 1635. [OE. *wīte.*]

wytnes *v.* bear witness 1372. [f. ME. *wytnes* n.]

wyth *prep.* with 56, 125, 131, etc.; together with 45, 133. [OE. *wiþ* blended with *mid* (*miþ*).]

wythhelde *pt. sg.* engaged in (his) service 522. [*wyth* + *holde.*]

wythynne *adv.* inside 121, 329, 348, etc. [OE. *wiþ-innan.*]

wythowt(e) *prep.* without 205, 859, 940, etc. [Late OE. *wiþūtan.*]

wythowten, -yn *adv.* lacking 12, 86, 215, etc.; exclusive of 137.

wytt *v.* know 2154; *pr. subj.* God *sone wytt me . . .*, God's son help me 1779; **wote** *v.* 1086 (*var. of wytt*); *1 pr. sg.* 389; *3 pr. sg.* 1367; **wate** *1 pr. sg.* 170, 777; **wys** *1 pr. sg.*; *I wys* I know (*erroneous present form of wytt*); **wyste** *pt. sg.* 1054, 1578, 1630, etc.; *pt. pl.* 984; **wetyn** *pp.*

1190, 1271; **wyt** *imper.* mark, note 29. [OE. *witan.*]

wytten *v.* blame 1923. [f. ME. *wytte* + *en.*]

wode *n.* woods 1435, 1524, 1697, etc.; **wodes** *n. pl.* 1503. [OE. *wudu.*]

wode *adj.* mad 44, 130, 658, etc. [OE. *wōd.*]

woghe *n.* woe 2013. [OE. *wā.*]

wolde *adj.* old 308. [OE. *ald.*]

woman. See **wemon.**

wondur *adv.* wondrously 186, 684, 1424, etc. [Partly OE. *wundor*; partly OE. *wundrum.*]

wondurs *n. pl.* extraordinary natural occurrences 41. [OE. *wundor.*]

wone *n.* conduct 1344; action of staying, *in phr.*: *wythowten wone*, without delay 215, 1156. [Aphet. f. ME. *i-wune*, *i-wone*, OE. *ʒewuna.*]

wones *n., sg.* and *pl.* palace 191. [a. ON. *ván.*]

wonte *pp.* accustomed 843. [OE. *ʒewunod*, pp. of *ʒewunian.*]

woo *n.* affliction 707, 1197, 2076; *adv.* distressed 824. [OE. *wā.*]

worche *v.* cause 1704. [OE. *wyrcan* (*worhte*, *geworht*).]

worde *n.* word 1021; news 1930; **wordys** *n. pl.* 250, 692, 1081, etc. [OE. *word.*]

worlde *n.* chiefly *this world* 5, 39, 54, etc. [OE. *woruld.*]

worschyp *n.* respect, honour 299. [OE. *weorðscipe.*]

worthe *adj.* equivalent to (something) in value 1268. [OE. *weorþ(e)*, *wyrþe.*]

worthely, -yly *adv.* with elegance 107, 1091, 1572, etc. [f. ME. *worthy* + *ly.*]

worthy, -þy *adj. of persons:* estimable 30; *of things:* good 191, 800, 1344, etc. [OE. *wyrþig,* merited, infl. by *wyrþe*, worth(y).]

worthyly. See **worthely, -yly**.

wote. See **wytt**.

woundys *n. pl.* wounds 913, 1848, 1992. [OE. *wund*.]

wowe *v.* woo 1216. [Late OE. *wōȝian*.]

woxyn *pp.* become 1975. [OE. *weaxan* (Nth. *wōx, weaxen*).]

wrake *n.* occasion of suffering 582, 1975. [OE. *wræc*.]

wrangdome *n.* injustice 153. [ME. *wrang + dome*.]

wrange, wronge *pt. pl.* twisted 836, 838. [OE. *wringan* (*wrang, wrungon, wrungen*).]

wrate *pt. sg.* wrote 2173. [OE. *wrītan*.]

wrathe, wrethe *n.* anger 1611, 2060. [OE. *wræððu*.]

wryttes, -ys *n. pl.* documents 121; formal orders 361. [OE. *writ*.]

wroght, wroȝt *pt. sg.* performed 872; caused 2085; *pp.* formed 336, 1091, 1338, etc.; taken (to wife) 2099. [OE. *wyrcan*.]

wronge. See **wrange**.

wronge *n.* that which is morally unjust. [f. ME. *wrange* adj.]

X

x the Roman numeral symbol for ten 154, 190, 202, etc.

Y

ye *pron. pl.* ye 40, 76, 106, etc.; **yow** *acc. and dat.* 40, 154, 164, etc.; **yowre** *poss. pron. and adj.* your 515, 1239, 1343, etc. [OE. *gē, ēow, ēower*.]

yede *pt. sg.* went 388, 658, 919, etc.; *pt. pl.* 636. See **ȝede**.

yere *n.* year 316, 332; *pl. with num. expressing a person's age* 61; *with numeral expressing duration* 674; **yerys** *n. pl.* 83. [OE. *ȝēr*.]

yoye *n.* joy 853, 1307, 2171. [OFr. *joie*.]

yondur *adj.* over there, away there 484. [ME. *ȝonder, ȝender*, corresp. to OS. *gendra* adj., on this side.]

yonge *adj.* young 527, 648, 981, etc. [OE. *ȝeoung, ȝung, inng*, Nth. *ȝing*.]

yow. See **ye**.

yowre. See **ye**.

yurne *n.* day 315. [a. OFr. *jornee, journee*.]

INDEX OF PROPER NAMES